CRISIS IN BYZANTIUM

CRISIS IN BYZANTIUM

The *Filioque* Controversy in the
Patriarchate of Gregory II of Cyprus
(1283-1289)

by
Aristeides Papadakis

ST VLADIMIR'S SEMINARY PRESS
CRESTWOOD, NY
1997

Library of Congress Cataloging-in-Publication Data
Papadakis, Aristeides.
    Crisis in Byzantium: the Filioque controversy in the patriarchate of Gregory II of Cyprus (1283-1289) / by Aristeides Papadakis. —Rev. ed.
    p.   cm.
    Includes bibliographical references and index.
    ISBN 0-88141-176-0
    1. Council of Blachernae (1285)   2. Gregory II of Cyprus, Patriarch of Constantinople, 1241-1290.   3. Holy Spirit—Procession—History of doctrines—Middle Ages, 600-1500.   4. Trinity—History of doctrines—Middle Ages, 600-1500. 5. Orthodox Eastern Church—Doctrines—History.   6. Constantinople (Ecumenical patriarchate)—Doctrines—History.   7. Orthodox Eastern Church—Relations—Catholic Church.   8. Catholic Church—Relations—Orthodox Eastern Church.   I. Title.
BX220.P36   1997
231'.3—dc21   97-33514
                                                                                                              CIP

ISBN 0-88141-176-0

Revised edition

First published by
Fordham University Press, 1983

PRINTED IN THE UNITED STATES OF AMERICA

CONTENTS

Abbreviations

BS — *Byzantinoslavica.* Prague, 1929—.

BZ — *Byzantinische Zeitschrift.* Leipzig/Munich, 1892—.

Dossier de Lyon — V. Laurent and J. Darrouzès, *Dossier Grec de l'Union de Lyon 1273-1277*, Paris, 1976.

DTC — *Dictionnaire de Théologie Catholique.* Paris, 1903-1950.

EO — *Échos d'Orient.* Istanbul/Paris, 1897-1942.

Gregoras — Nicephorus Gregoras, *Byzantina Historia*, edd. L. Schopen and I. Bekker. 3 vols. Bonn, 1829-1855.

Laurent, *Regestes* — V. Laurent, *Les Regestes des actes du Patriarcat de Constantinople*, I, *Les Actes des Patriarches*, fasc. 4: *Les Regestes de 1208 à 1309*, Paris, 1971.

Mansi — J. D. Mansi, *Sacrorum conciliorum nova et amplissima collectio.* 31 vols. Florence/Venice, 1759-1798.

Metochites — George Metochites, *Historia dogmatica*, ed. A. Mai, *Patrum novae bibliothecae* VIII, pt. 2 (Books I-II), Rome, 1871; X, pt. 1 (Book III), Rome, 1905.

OCP — *Orientalia Christiana Periodica.* Rome, 1935—.

Pachymeres — George Pachymeres, *De Michaele et Andronico Palaeologis libri tredecim*, ed. I. Bekker. 2 vols. Bonn, 1835.

PG — J.-P. Migne, *Patrologiae cursus completus, Series graeca.* Paris, 1857-1866.

PL — J.-P. Migne, *Patrologiae cursus completus, Series latina.* Paris, 1844-1855.

REB — *Revue des Études Byzantines.* Bucharest/Paris, 1946—.

Rubeis, *Vita* — B. M. de Rubeis, *Gregorii Cyprii patriarchae Constantinopolitani Vita*, PG 142.17-220.

Troitskij, *Arsenij* — I. E. Troitskij, *Arsenij i Arsenity*, ed. J. Meyendorff. London, 1973.

Chronology

7 May - 17 July 1274	Council of Lyons
6 July 1274	Union of Lyons
Autumn 1274	Publication of *Cum sacrosancta*
16 Jan. 1275	Union liturgy at Blachernae: feast of St. Peter in Chains
28 Dec. 1266-9 Jan. 1275	First patriarchate of Joseph I
26 May 1275	Election of John XI Beccus to the patriarchate
2 June 1275	Elevation of Beccus to the patriarchate
18 Oct. 128	Excommunication of Michael VIII by Pope Martin IV
11 Dec. 1282	Death of Michael VIII
26 Dec. 1282	Arrest of John XI Beccus
30 Dec. 1282	Deposition of John XI Beccus
31 Dec. 1282-23 March 1283	Second patriarchate of Joseph I
8 Jan. 1283	Exile of John XI Beccus
28 March 1283	Election of Gregory II of Cyprus to the patriarchate
11 April 1283	Elevation of Gregory II to the patriarchate: Palm Sunday
19 April 1283	Anti-unionist council: Easter Monday
Lent 1284	Adramyttium meeting with Arsenites
5 Feb. 1285-Aug. 1285	Council of Blachernae
ca. 1286-1287	Deposition of Gerasimus of Heracleia
ca. 1286	Defection of George Moschabar
Aug. 1285-1286	Publication of Gregory II's *Apology*
1288	Publication of Mark's commentary
late 1288	Gregory II's refutation of Mark: *The Confession*
late 1288-early 1289	Mark's *Report* to the Synod
late 1288-early 1289	Gregory's πιττάκιον to the emperor
June 1289	Resignation of Gregory II of Cyprus
1290	Death of Gregory II of Cyprus

FOREWORD TO THE ST. VLADIMIR'S PRESS EDITION

The exclusive endorsement by all Christians of the common Creed without the *Filioque* has long been recognized as a practical necessity in ecumenical circles. This was in point of fact the remarkable conclusion of a Memorandum submitted by two faith and Order Commission consultations to all member churches of the World Council of Churches nearly two decades ago. Invariably and indeed routinely such statements regarding the "normative"character of the original non-interpolated version of the Creed have long had the support of Orthodox theologians. On purely historical grounds, certainly, dropping the addition would be a genuine ecumenical event. As the present study of the patriarchate of Gregory II illustrates, the dogmatization of the *Filioque* at the Council of Lyons (1274) was in all essential respects a *local* western development in which the Christian East was never formally or creatively involved. To borrow the words of Father Boris Bobrinskoy, "the Nicene-Constantinopolitan confession of faith is a fundamental given, shared by East and West, and it should become once again the point of departure for our fraternal dialogue" (*St. Vladimir's Theological Quarterly*, 34 [1995], 125). This is to say that the far more important aspects of the question could be given center stage if the alteration of the Creed were first deleted. As the late John Meyendorff often emphasized, no one would question today the fact that there is a real difference between Cappadocian and Augustinian models of trinitarian theology.

A basic theme of the present work dealing with the Byzantine reaction to Lyons is that the problem of the *Filioque* is ultimately a trinitarian and, therefore, a theological question in the full patristic sense of the word. At the council of 1285 the discussion focused chiefly on the fundamentals of the faith in the Holy Trinity, rather than on the technicalities of the words. To describe it as a quarrel over words or as a polemic would not do. Contrary to the classroom cliché, in brief, East-West medieval debates on the procession were not all one extended dialogue of the deaf. To be sure, as the only official Orthodox conciliar response to the *Filioque*, the contribution of the see of Constantinople in 1285 is historically and theologically important. The Church in effect remained *ecumenical* in its theology, even as it qualified St Photius' formulas. In the search for Christian unity and ecclesiological rapprochement this has relevance today as well. For all these reasons, the decision of St. Vladimir's Seminary Press to again reissue this study, first published in 1983, is commendable. The author is no less greatful to the Graduate School of the University of Maryland for its generous financial assistance in support of this publication.

Aristeides Papadakis
University of Maryland Baltimore County

PREFACE

Of the early attempts to heal the schism between the Byzantine and Western Churches, none is as famous as the Council of Lyons. After nearly two decades of intensive preparation—primarily between the pope and the emperor, Michael VII—union was solemnly declared at the Council's fourth session, 6 July 1274. Older historians, it is true, still speak of Lyons as a "union council"—a label for which (we now know) it can never qualify, in terms of proceedings, purpose, or results. Less familiar, perhaps, is the Byzantine reaction that followed. Although it had been gathering strength for several years, it erupted with elemental violence only at the conclusion of the council and the accession of the unionist patriarch, John XI Beccus (1275-1282).

For all that, its more significant second phase—the principal focus of this study—occurred in the patriarchate of Gregory II of Cyprus (1283-1289). for it is then that the settlement of 1274 was formally discussed and repudiated by the Byzantine Church. As we should expect, the heart of this theological debate was the *Filioque*, which had just received its final dogmatic formulation at Lyons. In Byzantium, it is true, the issue of the *Filioque* had been a permanent center of interest for most of the thirteenth century. Even so, the decisions that were officially endorsed in 1285 by the Byzantine Church were, in the main, the result of Gregory's doctrinal meditations on the matter. It was only in his patriarchate that the issue was, at last, dogmatically adjudicated.

The medieval debate over the *Filioque* has almost always been seen simply as a verbal dispute. From the *terminological* issues of the late thirteenth century, the reader may, indeed, get the impression that the discussion was *only* about words. All the same, my study and investigation of several years into the details of this controversy lead me to the conclusion that the question was not concerned with a theological technicality at all. On the contrary, what was at stake was the Trinity of persons subsisting in the divine essence. In short, it dealt with the focal point of Christian revelation itself. As such, the issue is fundamentally *theological*. The active hostility with which the Byzantine viewed the Western doctrine did have its theological justification. In point of fact, the discussion during Gregory's patriarchate constitutes one of the most substantive expressions of that justification as well as one of the more thorough Trinitarian debates inside the Byzantine world.

And yet, no full-length narrative of this important debate exists. The present modest study is an attempt to fill this gap and to introduce the subject to the reader. The broader reasons for writing the book, its background, scope and central theme, will be considered in the Introduction. Here, I wish to note that only those questions which bear on the main theme were considered. I do not pretend to offer a complete history of Gregory's patriarchate, theology or personality. For example, his humanist background and training, which is discussed in Chapter 2, is explored only insofar as it helps to introduce the man who became patriarch in 1283. Likewise, Chapter 5 serves to introduce, in a slightly more exhaustive manner, Gregory's theology. I have also imposed limits on Chapter 1, my discussion of the first phase of the reaction under Beccus. I saw no need to repeat previous scholarship, or to expand the work to include a detailed discussion of unionist theology. This itself would have entailed a second volume.

In writing this study, I have relied on the foundations laid by numerous scholars. A look at the footnotes will be sufficient to show how much I owe to the work of others. I must, however, acknowledge the help of those on whom I have often relied for advice and encouragement. The Reverend Dr. John Meyendorff's endlessly generous support and valuable criticism have meant much to me. For Sir Steven Runciman's encouragement, kindness, and wise counsel—always so gracefully displayed—I am most grateful. My thanks are also due to Professor Ihor Ševčenko of Harvard, for his impeccable criticism and advice regarding Mark's *Report*. It is my pleasant duty to express my appreciation to all of them. I need hardly add that I alone am responsible for all errors of fact, interpretation, or omission.

For help in understanding some difficult and obscure Greek passages, I am indebted first and foremost to my friends Dr. Angela Hero and Dr. Alice-Mary Maffrey Talbot. Likewise, I wish to thank , for generous help of another kind, Mr. John Azarias, Mr. Miguel Creus, Mr. Constantine Georgiou, and Mr. Bruce Grimes. I also extend my appreciation to Professors J. Paramelle and J. Darrouzès, of the Institut de Recherche et d'Histoire des Textes and of the Institut Français d'Études Byzantines, respectively, for their generous help with matters dealing with the manuscripts of the *Tomus* of 1285. Further, I wish to express my gratitude to the University of Maryland for two Summer

Faculty Fellowships, which provided me with the needed leisure to finish my work. Finally, I owe a very special debt to the librarian, Mrs. Irene Vaslef, and the staff of Harvard university's Dumbarton Oaks Library and Collection in Washington, D.C. Without this unrivaled library and its superb facilities, research in the Byzantine field, as all American Byzantinists know, would often be impossible.

Aristeides Papadakis
University of Maryland
Baltimore County

INTRODUCTION

The history of Byzantine theological thought after A.D. 843 has never had a good press. The suppression of the last major heresy of iconoclasm, according to many historians, brought to a close the age of the councils and the Christological conflicts. Equally, it marked the end of the great period of theological creativity in Byzantium, which, in turn, gave way to an age of repetition and conservatism in matters theological. It was enough to preserve the hallowed past of the seven ecumenical councils with their irrevocably fixed formulations, and the equally authoritative synthesis of the Church Fathers. The past, in fact, was a deposit of doctrine. In the words of the charter of Orthodoxy—the *Synodicon* of 843— the Church was already in possession of "the faith of the apostles, the faith of the Fathers, the faith of the Orthodox, the faith that has sustained the universe."[1] Armed with this calm conviction, the Byzantine, for the most part, was content to repeat, coordinate, and systematize what the Fathers had written. The profusion of χρήσεις in councils, in polemical tracts, and in apologetic and dogmatic *panopliae* all attest to this essentially Byzantine phenomenon.[2]

The Byzantine remained instinctively conservative, a fact borne out by the absence of any major theological movement within Byzantium after the ninth century. Thus, the first theological judgment added to the *Synodicon,* the one concerning the philosophical investigations of John Italus, came some two hundred years later, in 1076. Characteristically, even with the Crusades, when God, to use Fulcher of Chartres' phrase, "transferred the West into the East,"[3] and when conditions for mutual observation and interaction between the two worlds improved, theological discussion was minimal. As one historian put it recently, the two remained substantially uninquisitive of each other, unless threatened.[4] The disruptive and tenacious nature of such movements as iconoclasm or monophysitism during the early Byzantine period was not characteristic of the centuries following the settlement of 843.

For much historiography, then, what occured after the liquidation of iconoclasm was more like an inferior sequel than an organic continuation of the early patristic age. To speak of "development" or "revival" in the history of Byzantine theology after the ninth century would be unacceptable. To be

sure, Professor Ihor Ševcenko's perceptive judgment that "sudden and fundamental changes occurred in the empire's doctrinal, intellectual and artistic
life"[5] is indisputable; that 843 forms a watershed in the history of Christian
Byzantium is undeniable. To say with Harnack, however, that from the seventh century "the history of dogma in the Greek Church came to an end [so
that] any revival of that history is difficult to imagine"[6] is questionable at best.
On the contrary, the earlier interest in theology and revival never really van-
ished, as events in the thirteenth and fourteenth centuries show. The present
study of Gregory II's patriarchate is an example of such a revival. And, although Gregory's thought is not a revolutionary innovation, it is also not a
mere formal repetition of the past. In the final analysis, it is a genuine reevaluation as well as an organic development of patristic tradition.

With the thirteenth century, the age of theological debate returned, re-
calling, *mutatis mutandis,* the earlier age of Christology. This begins in the
reign of Michael VIII Palaeologus (1261-1282) and his patriarch, John XI
Beccus (1275-1282), the sustaining spirit of his pro-Western religious policy.
Indeed, Michael VIII "made headlines" by launching one of the stormiest pe-
riods in Byzantine ecclesiastical history and theology. Doctrinally, the period
was one of the more significant and most lively; theological issues once again
became a matter of passionate concern. The great controversy over the union
of the Churches during this period, the substantive debate over the procession
of the Holy Spirit "from the Son" or "through the Son," the disruptive quarrel
of Arsenius, and the equally crucial crisis of hesychasm that followed in the
early fourteenth century were, in the main, fought out on the field of dogma.

In the internal life of the Byzantine Church, no patriarchate in the second
half of the thirteenth century is of greater historical and theological significance than that of Gregory II of Cyprus (1283-1289). In scope and importance, it compares favorably with the patriarchates of Photius and Cerularius.
Like them, Gregory acquired both fame and notoriety; and, although he was
never as renowned a figure as his more celebrated predecessors, he was certainly controversial. At the same time, he was a figure of pivotal importance in
a period when the Church was confronted by mayor events and problems re-
quiring both immediate and permanent solutions. The years during which he
occupied the throne of the patriarchs of Constantinople—six years and more
of troubled Church history—mark, on the one hand, the restoration of Orthodoxy, and, on the other, the end of the Union of Lyons, with which the

Church had been saddled for eight years. Suffice it to say that his name is inseparable from the history of the two Churches in the thirteenth century.

Additionally, the patriarch was confronted by an uninterrupted succession of internal problems—the schism of Arsenius and Joseph (already in its eighteenth year), the unionist movement which had polarized the Byzantine Church (and was still vigorously promoted by his exiled predecessor, John Beccus), and, finally, the confusion and controversy generated by the publication in 1285 of his own *Tomus.* This last episode resulted in a general crisis of confidence in the patriarch. Increasingly, some of his own synod came to believe that he had failed to fulfill the high hopes placed on him at his election. As one observer put it at the time, you were either Arsenius' man, or you were for Joseph, or for Beccus, or you followed Gregory.[7] Probably few patriarchs had found the empire and the Church more hopelessly torn and divided as did Gregory II in 1283. The religious turmoil created by Michael VIII was as much a legacy to the new patriarch as to his son and heir, Andronicus II.

Although Gregory was unable to solve the dispute with the Arsenite *petite église* (it was reconciled to the official Church and the Palaeologan dynasty in September 1310), he was more successful in his handling of the unionist movement and the peace of Lyons. This was finally and formally repudiated by imperial decree and the solemn decision of the Church at the Council of Blachernae in 1285. This council, which was an exhaustive debate on the *Filioque,* or more precisely, on the procession of the Holy Spirit "from the Son" or "through the Son," was convened by Gregory, who was both its chairman and the moving force of its dogmatic decisions. One thread in this development, it is true, was the crisis in which Gregory became the center of controversy. Still, unionism (and Beccus for that matter) ceased to be a source of disturbance and division; the last evidence of Michael's religious policy was finally dismantled. As the same observer, quoted above, notes, the very large council that Gregory convened did much to heal the Church's ills,[8] for these had jeopardized its internal life since 1274.

Of greater significance is the fact that the Council of 1285, with its synodal *Tomus* penned by Gregory himself, was a solid theological achievement. The discussion that forms the backdrop of his patriarchate must rank among the most important on the *Filioque,* that long-standing issue that had its origins with the Carolingians. Overall, the tone of the discussion had been set as early as 1234 at the Council of Nymphaeum, when six of this assembly's seven colloquia dealt exclusively with this controversial question. (The synodal definition of this assembly, published unilaterally by the Byzantine Church, is concerned entirely with the procession of the Holy Spirit.) Nevertheless, it is under Gregory that the *Filioque* became a subject of unrestricted and sustained controversy, making it, perhaps, the only thorough trinitarian debate inside the precincts of the Byzantine Church. As the only detailed *conciliar* reaction of medieval Byzantium to the *Filioque*, the *Tomus'* significance can scarcely be exaggerated.

It is sometimes stated that the attempts at union between Greeks and Latins never went to the heart of the matter, since too many theologians were content to throw at each other the ready-made arguments, or proof-texts, of the patristic reservoir. A quotation from the Fathers, however misused or misinterpreted, was thought sufficiently conclusive to justify any point in theology without further demonstration. Time and again, it is assumed that Byzantium said little, if anything, on the *Filioque*; its proverbial conservatism and fidelity to the Photian tradition did not allow it. Photius' refutation of the *Filioque* in the *Mystagogy*, it is argued, remained where it had been left in the ninth century. This became, in the words of V. Laurent, a "national dogma,"[9] the sole basis of discussion. The controversial literature of the eleventh and twelfth centuries as a result lacks any substantive development of the question. Alternatively, it is often alleged that the dispute was about whether any addition could be made to the creedal formula. That is to say, the issue was over a "mere liturgical variation,"[10] over a question of procedure, rather than a question of substance.[11] What concerned the Byzantines most was the integrity of the text of the ancient creed, rather than the addition of the clause itself.

However true such a conclusion may be for certain other councils and debates, it is demonstrably false for the Council of Blachernae and Gregory of Cyprus. The Synod of 1285 with its *Tomus*—the major patriarchal council and key doctrinal document of the century—did get down to fundamentals, and said, in fact, a great deal about the doctrine of the procession. It was the only synodal reaction of the Byzantine Church to the *Filioque*. Though anchored in the Byzantine past, it was then that the doctrine was finally discussed and dogmatically settled. For the Synod of 1285 went well beyond the unionist council of 879, where the unauthorized *Filioque* was first raised, and its addition to the creed explicitly condemned.[12] As such, it was a significant reassessment and reevaluation of a long-drawn-out question. Considering the absence of any conciliar formulation on the subject until then, the Synod of 1285 was no small achievement.

A contention of this study is that 1285 is a date of fundamental importance in the history of the *Filioque* and of late-Byzantine theology. An Orthodox theologian of the first rank (and the Church which approved his theology) found Photius' arguments wanting and by going creatively beyond them, enriched, deepened, but also stretched the Photian formulations. During the long summer of Byzantine civilization, the creative mainstream of Byzantine theology was neither languishing nor inarticulate. Gregory's short, but notable, patriarchate forms a milestone in late-Byzantine theology and is central to the period.

This pronounced theological revival in the patriarchate of Gregory II has never been a subject of serious study, except sporadically. Its importance and significance have certainly not been surveyed in the same systematic and extensive way as the early period of Michael VIII. On the contrary, knowledge of the religious contours of Andronicus' reign is modest and disappointing. This is on the whole surprising since the *Histories* of Pachymeres, George Metochites, and Gregoras (the first two are major witnesses and participants in these events) contain a wealth of descriptive detail on the theological currents of the age, and the liquidation of Lyons under Gregory and the emperor, Andronicus II. Ecclesiastical affairs were patently no less important to them than the whole tide of political events sweeping over Anatolia at the time. Besides, there is the abundant theological speculation of these years, which makes Lyons one of the most documented episodes of the thirteenth century. Unlike his father, Andronicus did not place any limits on literary activity or theological discussion.

This neglect is more than casually reflected in practically all the secondary literature. Both D. M. Nicol and H. Evert-Kapessowa, for example, have treated the violent opposition to Michael's policy almost as the only material for their studies; both pass rather briefly over the *Tomus* and Gregory himself, as if they were of little importance.[13] Similarly, S. Runciman and D. J. Geanakoplos confine themselves to the period before 1282, and examine, both fully and factually, the history of the union negotiations and the diplomacy involved.[14] Equally, the basic volume on the Council of Lyons by B. Roberg is notable for its comprehensive use of sources, and the reediting of a number of important texts. But it, too, stops at 1282, as if the Byzantine reaction had ended then.[15]

W. Norden's earlier work on Byzantine-papal relations, *Das Papsttum und Byzanz*,[16] which canvasses the period 1054-1453, is hardly different. Only a few pages of this classic and thorough study, which has since been complemented by Roberg's volume, is concerned with 1282-1300. For all that, no mention is made of Gregory II or the Council of 1285! In all fairness, it should be noted that Norden's focus was the diplomatic negotiations under the Lascarids and the first Palaeologus, Michael VIII. A more recent example is the study of Andronicus II by A. Laiou; the work is a substantial assessment of this emperor's policy and conduct toward the Latin West. This policy was undeniably dictated by the restoration of Orthodoxy, which took place under Gregory II. Unaccountably, however, this fact, not to mention the religious roots of much of the emperor's behavior, is given short shrift. Andronicus' religious policy is perused in some five pages, while Blachernae and Patriarch Gregory's *Tomus* is summarily treated in a single paragraph.[17] For the most part, this exhausts the author's interest in the religious setting of Andronicus' early years.

There are, however, exceptions. The labors of the Russian scholar I. E. Troitskij, (1834-1901) on the thirteenth-century Byzantine Church are among the more important.[18] His recent editor points out that his monograph on the Arsenites, of which nearly one-fifth is devoted to Gregory's patriarchate and a discussion of Blachernae, "is the most complete and perceptive study on the internal life of Byzantine society published in the nineteenth century."[19] In light of this, it is surprising that both the book and the journal—the study first appeared in *Khristianskoe Chtenie*, the journal of the St Petersburg Theological Academy—were, until recently, inaccessible and, therefore, largely unknown.[20] Of equal interest is Troitskij's separate treatment of the theological controversy in which Gregory II was involved. It is the most detailed study on the subject. Further, it incorporates Russian translations of a number of vital documents from the debate, including Gregory's two principal works, the *Tomus* and *On the Procession of the Holy Spirit*.[21] His work is, in the main, based on Pachymeres and Gregoras, whose narrative *Histories* the author quotes frequently and extensively.

Another nineteenth-century scholar was the archimandrite Andronicus Demetracopoulos (1826-1872). His useful and oft-quoted *History of the*

Schism and his later *Orthodox Greece* contain some matter on Lyons and the restoration under Gregory.[22] His selective incorporation of a great deal of unpublished manuscript material, coupled with a liberal use of the Byzantine historians, are outstanding features of his work. Despite a polemical flair (his *Orthodox Greece* is a reply to Leo Allatius' *De ecclesiae occidentalis atque orientalis perpetua consensione libri tres*),[23] his information is, for the most part, reliable. However, he too depends on Pachymeres and Gregoras, and, like Troitskij, includes far too little scholarly analysis and interpretation. Yet both of these contributions continue to be significant and useful, despite the advances made since they were written, especially in the area of unpublished material.[24]

The short study on Beccus by another Greek scholar, A. D. Zotos, has remained virtually unknown, largely because of its inaccessibility and the hostile review of V. Grumel.[25] The study ignores such primary and secondary literature as George Metochites' *Dogmatic History*, and Bernard M. de Rubeis' valuable "historical notes" and introductory analysis of Gregory's patriarchate; O. Raynaldi's *Ecclesiastical Annals* is also not mentioned. Yet, this ill-informed work is not wholly without merit. Even if its interpretation is off the mark on several points, the work has the virtue of presenting a factual picture, based almost solely on Pachymeres. Also, the author's presentation of Beccus' theology is a reliable summary statement. It is not true that he strips Beccus' work of all authority and significance.[26] This consideration brings us to the fact that Zotos' study likewise focused on events before 1283. His ignorance of what followed is glaring; he mentions Gregory's *Tomus* several times, yet he is completely unsuspecting of both its significance and originality.

Such, then, is the content and approach of the extant secondary literature dealing with the late-thirteenth century. Apart from one or two older studies, it is largely concerned with events before the patriarchate of Gregory II and the reign of Andronicus II. Typically, the internal situation in Byzantium after Michael VIII's death in 1282, the reaction of Byzantium to the Union of Lyons (outside its political context as it affected the Church's life and theology), and Gregory's doctrinal contribution are only fitfully examined, if at all. As one scholar put it, neither the dogmatic questions nor the "justice of a religious doctrine" has any place in her work.[27]

But even when the patriarchate has been explored, the results have seldom been positive. This is undeniably the case with the pioneer work of the late Père V. Laurent. This scholar's familiarity with and mastery of the registers of the acts of the patriarchate (grounded on a remarkable knowledge of the sources), his publication of valuable texts, and his life-long concern for prosopography, sigillography, and chronology are well known. Characteristically, his lengthy study of the Arsenites and his numerous articles on Blachernae, Beccus, and other major ecclesiastics, scattered in *Echos d'Orient* and in the *Revue des Études Byzantines,* are the indispensable scholarly foundations for anyone working in the thirteenth century.[28]

Regrettably, however, Laurent's work, leaving aside the wide learning and depth that it reflects, was often the result of *parti pris.* It was increasingly influenced more by confessional polemics than by purely objective considerations. Dedicated he was; detached he was not. The practice of Western scholars to seek out Byzantine ecclesiastics, theologians, or events, which would lend support and authority to Roman teaching, was a temptation he could not resist.[29] This is reflected both in his view of the events of 1283-1285, which he frequently described as a schismatic restoration,[30] and in his admiration for and preoccupation with that permanent Byzantine minority, the unionists—"les catholiques byzantins." Understandably, he was especially fond of Gregory's implacable adversary, Beccus—the one man allegedly capable of mending the schism, were it not for Michael's brutality and Andronicus apostasy. Beccus was a man of true ecumenical vision, the true prototype of all who sought to restore—at any cost—the Church's lost unity. Indeed, this "prélat catholique"[31] was the finest patriarch of the Byzantine Church during the Palaeologan age.[32] Beccus has attracted a disproportionate amount of scholarly attention that is all but hagiographic in its affection for the unionist patriarch. And, although Laurent's promised monograph on the patriarch never appeared, he worked hard to promote this approach. Today, it is *de rigueur* to admire Beccus for his "tolerance," his "theological competence," his "exceptional personality," and his "martyrdom."[33] He has become in most of the literature a figure of heroic mold.

On the other hand, Laurent's view of Beccus' opponents is uniformly hostile. They are all seen as adversaries. His treatment of Patriarch Joseph I, a gentle but insistent voice of moderation, and the members of his entourage, such as Job Iasites (who is described as the soul of schism itself), is a good illustration. Even the historian and deacon, George Pachymeres, a former classmate of Patriarch Gregory and a signatory of the *Tomus,* is a "notorious schismatic."[34] Patriarch Gregory, of course, has a central place in all this. Not only was he a "perjurer" and a paradigm of the "crafty and ambitious cleric," but he helped perpetuate the schism in Christendom that the unionists were trying to mend.[35] Clearly, Beccus alone could claim a monopoly on virtue.

This essentially negative attitude is even reflected in the work of those specialists for whom Gregory's physiognomy is not unknown. Characteristically a recent massive and impressive study of the development of Byzantine doctrine in which Beccus is frequently quoted, does not contain a single reference to Gregory of Cyprus.[36] And yet, the alternative may be just as unfortunate. For when he is discussed, it is only in the shadow of Beccus. In short, few specialists want to put much premium on his theology on the procession, or on his valiant effort to enter into dialogue with the Latins. His exegesis is either viewed as second-string, if not peripheral, holding no more than a tenuous position in the history of doctrine, or as outright "heresy" or "error."[37]

This prevailing image of the patriarch is, obviously, not the image projected earlier in this Introduction. More to the point, the contemporary evidence itself, viewed collectively, suggests a very different picture. Apart from such hostile critics as Beccus and George Metochites, the overwhelming number of Gregory's contemporaries praise, rather than condemn him. Among the most eloquent is his early detractor John Chilas, metropolitan of Ephesus; he took a prominent role both in the attack on Gregory and in the maneuvers to revise the *Tomus.* Even so, Chilas eventually found his position untenable.[38] Typical, too, is the view of another Byzantine, Gennadius Scholarius, for whom both the *Tomus* of 1285 and the Council of Blachernae were "ecumenical." (Characteristically, Laurent would have both labeled as "schismatic acts."[39]) Equally, the synod's *Declaration,* a brief rebuttal to the "uninitiated" and a confirmation of Gregory's Orthodoxy, is no less explicit in its praise.[40] We shall have occasion to examine this and other evidence in the pages that follow.

In light of all the above, then, a fresh view of the field is in order. A more equitable, believable, and non-partisan verdict on Patriarch Gregory II of Cyprus is highly desirable. Certainly, his thought should be evaluated in its own living context, within his own spiritual and theological tradition, and apart from Western scholastic categories by which it is often viewed. Beyond this it is necessary to penetrate deeper into the causes and the reasons for the opposition to the *Tomus,* and the resulting resignation of Gregory. Indeed, these twin poles in Gregory's stormy career (around which the present study revolves) have been neglected far too long, and need to be set in a more accurate and meaningful perspective.

Our first concern, then—the central point of this study in historical theology—is Gregory's doctrinal contribution as reflected and expressed at the Council of Blachernae. For Blachernae may well be the most important contribution of the Byzantine Church to the *Filioque* controversy. It has been persuasively argued, for example, that, in the late Byzantine period, the Eastern position on many issues was not always clear or settled. Often, it was during the theological tussles with the west, "in response to a Western attack or a Western formulation, that the East first achieved some conceptual clarity on a doctrine."[41] That this was the case in Byzantium in the aftermath of Lyons, when an official and textually determined statement was urgently needed, is undeniable. It was then that the Byzantine Church, by endorsing Gregory's formula of the eternal manifestation of the Spirit by the Son, supplied the doctrine of the procession with that "conceptual clarity" which it had hitherto lacked.

Our second task will be to sketch the circumstances, issues, and debates of which Gregory was the center, especially from the time of the publication of the *Tomus* in 1285 to his resignation in 1289. We will retrace the attacks leading to the dramatic conflict and campaign that eventually cost the patriarch his throne. More specifically, we will focus on the negative reactions of some individuals against the alleged theological infelicities of the Orthodox patriarch, and will show that, by and large, these reactions were not theologically motivated. In short, we hope to show that the entrenched view, which maintains that Gregory's Orthodoxy provoked his fall and that the *Tomus* is a "schismatic document,"[42] is more a misreading of the evidence than anything else.

A final observation: Gregory was naturally wounded when he was driven by his adversaries to make his first concession, and to withdraw to the monastery of the Hodegetria. He actually said as much—with deep personal poignancy—to a friend, the monk Methodius. And yet, he neither "deemed himself unhappy nor did he lament bitterly." He would not despair, he said, even if he were obliged to abandon his leadership. The future would see the vindictiveness and moral cowardice of his adversary. Indeed, it would be he (in truth, he was the leading humanist and theologian of the day) who would be the recipient of posterity's "attention," rather than the ones who were now abusing him.[43] The pages that follow are, in part, an attempt to fulfill a patriarch's hope in posterity's obligation.[44]

NOTES

1. J. Gouillard, "Le Synodikon de l'Orthodoxie: Edition et commentaire," *Travaux et mémoires*, 2 (1967), 51.

2. For a discussion of the consequences and shortcomings of this method of justifying a point of theology, see G. Joussard, "De quelques conséquences et particularités qu'a entrainées en patristique grecque l'adoption du genre florilège pour traiter l'argument de tradition," *Analecta Gregoriana*, 68 (1954),17-25. V. Grumel, "Les aspects généraux de la théologie byzantine," *EO*, 30 (1931), 395-96; idem, Le patriarcat byzantin: De Michel Cérulaire à la conquête latine. Aspects généraux," *REB*, 4 (1946),357-63. M. Jugie, *Le Schisme Byzantin. Aperçu historique et doctrinal* (Paris, 1941), p.328. See also A. Schmemann, "St. Mark of Ephesus and the Theological Conflicts in Byzantium," *St. Vladimir's Seminary Quarterly*, N. S. 1 (1957), 19.

3. *Historia Hierosolymitana*, ed. H. Hagenmeyer (Heidelberg, 1913), III, 37, 748.

4. A. Bryer, "Cultural Relations Between East and West in the Twelfth Century," *Relations Between East and West in the Middle Ages*, ed. D. Baker (Edinburgh, 1973), pp. 77-94.

5. "The Anti-iconoclastic Poem of the Pantocrator Psalter," *Cahiers archéologiques*, 15 (1965), 40.

6. A. von Harnack, *Lehrbuch der Dogmengeschichte*, II (Tübingen, 1931), 511; quoted in J. Pelikan, *The Christian Tradition: A History of the Development of Doctrine*. II: *The Spirit of Eastern Christendom 600-1700* (Chicago, 1974), 1.

7. Joseph Calothetus, *Vita Athanasii*, ed. A. Pantocratorinus, *Thrakika*, 13 (1940), 87.

8. Ibid., 87.

9. "Les signataires du second synode des Blakhernes (été 1285)," *EO*, 26 (1927),129.

10. R. G. Heath, "The Western Schism of the Franks and the '*Filioque*',"*Journal of Ecclesiastical History*, 23, No. 2 (1972), 97. See also J. Pelikan, "The Doctrine of *Filioque* in Thomas Aquinas and its Patristic Antecedents," in *St Thomas Aquinas Commemorative Studies*, I (Toronto, 1974), 327: "The original collision over the *Filioque* had come not in a theological disputation about ἀρχή in the Godhead, but in a eucharistic celebration, where the divergent texts of the Nicene Creed had disturbed the peace of the liturgy."

11. Cf. A. Palmieri, "*Filioque*,"*DTC*, 5, pt. 2 (Paris, 1913), col. 2322; S. Runciman, *The Great Church in Captivity* (Cambridge, 1968), pp. 85, 96; J. Meyendorff, *Byzantine Theology* (NewYork, 1979), p.92.

12. Mansi, XVII, 520, 516; Photius, *Mystagogy*, *PG* 102.380-81, F. Dvornik, *The Photian Schism: History and Legend* (Cambridge, Mass., 1948), pp. 194ff.

13. D. M. Nicol, "The Greeks and the Union of the Churches: The Preliminaries to the Second Council of Lyons, 1261-1274," *Medieval Studies Presented to A. Gwynn, S.J.*, edd. J. A. Watt et al. (Dublin, 1961), pp.454-80; idem, "The Greeks and the Union of the Churches: The Report of Ogerius, Protonotarius of Michael VIII Palaeologos, in 1280," *Proceedings of the Royal Irish Academy*, 63, sect. C, I (1962), 1-16. Nicol's most recent summary of the ecclesiastical events of the years 1261-1285 is "The Byzantine Reaction to the Second Council of Lyons, 1274," in G. J. Guming and D. Baker (edd.), *Studies in Church History*, 7 (Cambridge, 1971),

113-46. This useful synthesis does not carry events beyond 1285, however, and deals only briefly with the restoration of Orthodoxy. All these articles are now conveniently collected in *Byzantium: Its Ecclesiastical History and Relations with the Western World* (London, 1972); see also Nicol's survey, *The Last Centuries of Byzantium, 1261-1453* (London, 1972). H. Evert-Kapessowa's four principal studies on the period are: "La sociéte Byzantine et l'union de Lyon," *BS*, 10 (1949), 28-41; "Une page de l'histoire des relations byzantino-latines: Le clergé byzantin et l'union de Lyon (1274-1282)," *BS*, 13 (1952-1953), 68-92; "Une page des relations byzantino-latines I: Byzance et le St Siège à l'époque de l'union de Lyon," *BS, 16 (1955), 297-317;* and "Une page de l'histoire des relations byzantino-latines II: La fin de l'union de Lyon," *BS*, 17 (1956), 1-18.

14. S. Runciman, *The Sicilian Vespers: A History of the Mediterranean World in the Late Thirteenth Century* (Cambridge, 1958); D. J. Geanakoplos, *Emperor Michael Palaeologus and the West, 1258-1282* (Cambridge, Mass., 1959); idem, "Michael VIII Palaeologus and the Union of Lyons," *Harvard Theological Review*, 46 (1953), 79-89.

15. B. Roberg, *Die Union zwischen der griechischen und der lateinischen Kirche auf dem II. Konzil von Lyon* (1274) (Bonn, 1964).

16. *Das Papsttum und Byzanz* (Berlin, 1903).

17. A. Laiou, *Constantinople and the Latins: The Foreign Policy of Andronicus II 1282-1328* (Cambridge, Mass., 1972). See also J. Gill, *Byzantium and the Papacy 1198-1400* (New Brunswick, N.J., 1979), where Blachernae is treated in less than two pages. This substantive study by a distinguished scholar in the field is designed to update Norden. As such, its title may be misleading, since it is chiefly concerned with the Latin West and its attitude toward Byzantium.

18. See Troitskij's obituary by E. Kurtz, *BZ*, 11 (1902),692-93.

19. I. E. Troitskij, *Arsenij i Arsenity,* ed. J. Meyendorff (London, 1973), introduction (no pagination). This reprint is based on the journal edition published during the years 1867-1872. For Gregory's patriarchate, see pp. 231-318.

20 It was not used, for example, by V. Laurent; cf. "Les grandes crises religieuses à Byzance. La fin du schisme arsénite," *Académie Roumaine. Bulletin de la Section Historique,* 26 (1945), 255n1, where it is referred to as outdated; see also I. Sykoutres, "Concerning the Schism of the Arsenites" (in Greek), *Hellenika*, 2 (1929), 289.

21. "Toward a History of the Dispute on the Question of the Procession of the Holy Spirit" (in Russian), *Khristianskoe Chtenie,* 69 (1889), pt. 1, 338-77, 581-605; pt. 2, 280-352, 520-70. The *Tomus* can be found in vol. 69 (1889), pt. 1, 344 66; and *On the Procession* in vol. 69 (1889), pt. 2, 288-352. A translation by Troitskij of Gregory's important *Autobiography,* including several letters addressed to the emperor, Andronicus, also exists in the earlier volume of *Khristianskoe Chtenie,* 50 (1870), pt. 2, 164-77. These, too, are little known.

22. *History of the Schism* (Leipzig, 1866); *Orthodox Greece* (Leipzig, 1872). Both works are written in Greek. On this historian's achievement, cf. the notes in *Theologia,* 2 (1924), 277-81, and 17 (1939), 183-84.

23. Published in Cologne, 1648.

24. For material published by S. Salaville and V. Laurent since these scholars wrote, cf. the reference by Meyendorff, in Troitskij, *Arsenij,* intro., n. 7.

25. A. D. Zotos, *John Beccus, Patriarch of Constantinople, New Rome, the Latinizer* (in Greek) (Munich, 1920); reviewed by V. Grumel, "Un ouvrage récent sur Jean Beccos, patriarche de Constantinople," *EO*, 24 (1925), 26-32.

26. Zotos, *John Beccus*, pp. 82-83: "No one in the Eastern Church fought and struggled with such zeal for the union of the Churches; no one, among the Latin-minded, supported Latin doctrine with such a large series of compositions, with such rich theological arguments, and with such an abundance of biblical quotations, as did John Beccus....His works reveal him to be both a studious searcher of Scripture...and an eminent Greek scholar and Byzantine author."

27. See Evert-Kappesowa, "Byzance et le St Siège," 298: "Délibérément, j'ai laissé de côté les questions dogmatiques, car ce n'est guère la justesse d'un dogme religieux qui me préoccupait ici, mais plutôt l'attitude d'un groupe social envers ce dogme tel quel."

28. V. Laurent and J. Darrouzès, *Dossier Grec de 1' Union de Lyon* 1273-1277 (Paris, 1976); V. Laurent, *Les Regestes des actes du Patriarcat de Constantinople.* I: *Les actes des Patriarches,* fasc. 4; *Les regestes de 1208 à 1309* (Paris, 1971); idem, "Les grandes crises religieuses à Byzance: La fin du schisme arsénite," 225-313; idem, "La chronologie des patriarches de Constantinople au XIIIe siècle (1208-1309)," *REB*, 27(1969),129-50; idem, "Notes de chronologie et d'histoire byzantine de la fin du XIIIe siècle," *REB*, 27 (1969), 209-28. Laurent's early study of the Council of 1285 is basic: "Les signataires du second synode des Blakhernes," 129-49. For a complete list of articles, see the "Bibliographie du P. Vitalien Laurent," *REB*, 33 (1974), 343-70.

29. Actually, the distant founder of this practice was Leo Allatius, himself a convert to Catholicism and one of the first to publish Beccus' work. See Leo Allatius, *Graeciae Orthodoxae*, I-II (Rome, 1652-1659), the edition of all of Beccus' important writings; idem, *De Ecclesiae occidentalis atque orientalis perpetua consensione libri tres* (Cologne, 1648), especially cols. 727-82, for the discussion on Beccus and the Union of Lyons. The recruitment by scholars of John Chrysostom, Theodore of Stoudios, Andrew of Crete, and Photius to support papal primacy or the Immaculate Conception of Mary are other cases in point; e.g., see M. Jugie, "Saint Jean Chrysostome et la primauté de Saint-Pierre," *EO*, 11 (1908), 5-15, 193-202; S. Salaville, "Quae fuerit Sancti Theodori Studitae doctrina de Beati Petri Apostoli deque Romani Pontificis primatu," *Acta Academia Velehradensis*, 6 (1910), 123-34; idem, "La primauté de Saint-Pierre et du pape d'après Saint Théodore Studite (759-826)," *EO* 17 (1914), 23-42; A. Marin, *Saint Théodore* (Paris, 1926); M. Jugie, "Saint André de Crète et l'Immaculée Conception," *EO*, 13 (1910), 129-33; idem, "Photius et l'Immaculée Conception," *EO*, 13 (1910) 198-201. See also J. Pargoire, *l'Eglise byzantine de 527 à 847* (Paris, 1905), pp. 189,295. For this practice, cf. Meyendorff, *Byzantine Theology*, pp.58, 147.

30. "Les signataires du second synode des Blakhernes," 130.

31. V. Laurent, "Un polémiste grec de la fin du XIIIe siècle: La vie et les œuvres de Georges Moschabar," *EO*, 28 (1929), 139; idem, "Planude, Maxime," *DTC*, 12, pt. 2 (Paris, 1935), col. 2250.

32. See Laurent's review, in *BZ*, 50 (1957), 541-42, of M. Sotomayor's "El patriarca Becos según Jorge Paquimeres (semblanza histórica)," *Estudios Ecclesiásticos*, 31 (1957), 327-58.

33. E. Candal (ed.), *Oratio dogmatica de unione Bessarionis* (= Concilium Florentinum, Documenta et Scriptores, series B. vol. VII, fasc. I; Rome, 1958), lix*n*1 ("martyr of union") Evert-Kapessowa, "Le clergé byzantin et l'union de Lyon," 75-76: "Richement doué par la nature,

d'une rare intelligence, d'une belle stature éloquent, instruit—Jean Veccos est incontestable-
ment une des figures les plus remarquables du XIIIè siècle byzantin...Leur [unionists] catholicisme tirait sa source non pas d'une conversion mais d'une tolérance tout à fait exceptionelle à
leur époque"; G. Hoffman, "Patriarch Johann Bekkos und die lateinische Kultur," *OCP,* 11
(1945), 164 ("hero's death"); cf. V. Laurent, "La date de la mort de Jean Beccos," *EO,* 25
(1926), 319 ("the great confessor"). See also the valuable articles by G. Dagron, J. Darrouzès,
D. Stiernon, and J. Gouillard in *Actes du Colloque international du Centre National de la Recherche Scientifique: 1274, Année charnière. Mutations et continuités* (Lyon-Paris 30 sept-5 oct
1974) (Paris, 1977).

34. "Les signataires du second synode des Blakhernes," 134. Pachymeres was never an apologist for
     the unionists. Yet apart from his mistrust of theWest, his detailed contemporary narrative more
     often contains the sounder verdict when compared to Georges Metochites' valuable, but seldom
     objective, polemical account. On Pachymeres' objectivity, cf. Sotomayor, "El patriarca Becos,"
     327-58; G. Ostrogorsky, *History of the Byzantine State* (Oxford, 1968), pp. 418—19; and
     Laiou's "essay on sources" in *Constantinople and the Latins,* pp. 345-48. Pachymeres served un-
     der the patriarchs Beccus and Gregory, but seems never to have been anything else but a deacon.
     On this and his years as a student (together with Gregory), in the sixties of the century, at the
     school of George Acropolites, see the preface of V. Laurent, in R. P. E. Stephanou (ed.), *Quadriv-
     ium de Georges Pachymère* (= Studi e Testi, 94; Vatican City, 1940), xxvii.

35 "Les grandes crises religieuses à Byzance. La fin du schisme arsénite," 274; idem, "Les signataires
    du second synode des Blakhernes," 129.

36. Pelikan, *The Spirit of Eastern Christendom.* The present writer has profited greatly from this
     truly balanced and masterful exposition of Eastern Christian thought.

37. F. Cayré, "George de Chypres, *DTC,* 6, pt. 1 (Paris, 1920), col. 1234 ("mediocre theologian");
     F. Dölger, in *The Cambridge Medieval History,* IV, pt. 2 (2nd ed.; Cambridge, 1967) 220 ("a
     theologian of inferior talent"); E. Candal, "Progresso dogmatico nelle definizioni trinitarie del
     Concilio II di Lione e del Fiorentino," *Divinitas,* 5, fasc. 2 (1966), 338 ("the new error"), K.
     Krumbacher, *Geschichte der byzantinischen Literatur* (Munich, 1897), 98 ("As a dogmatician
     he was not a match for his adversaries").

38. See his text *On the Arsenite Schism,* in J. Darrouzès (ed.), *Documents inédits d'ecclésiologie byz-
     antine* (Paris, 1966), p. 400.

39. Laurent, "Les signataires du second synode des Blakhernes," 141-42.

40. See the text in *PG* 142.129A—B.

41. Pelikan, *The Spirit of Eastern Christendom,* p. 280.

42. Laurent, "Les signataires du second synode des Blakhernes," 140; idem, "Théodore Mouza-
     lon," *DTC,* 10, pt. 2 (Paris, 1929), col. 2582 ("heretic patriarch"); idem, *Les "Mémoires" du
     Grand Ecclésiarque de l'Église de Constantinople Sylvestre Syropoulos* (= *Concilium Florentinum,
     Documenta et Scriptores,* series B, vol. IX; Rome, 1971), 343n2.

43. See letter 152, in S. Eustratiades (ed.), *Ekklesiastikos Pharos,* 4 (1909), 108.

44. For another famous Byzantine, who "craved for secular immortality," see I. Ševcenko, "Theo-
     dore Metochites, the Chora, and the Intellectual Trends of his Time," in P. S. Underwood
     (ed.), *The Kariye Djami,* IV (Princeton, 1975), 19-55, esp. 50-55.

1

CUIUS REGIO, EIUS RELIGIO

The patriarchate of Gregory II has its own prehistory and dynamics. The Latin occupation of Constantinople on 12 April 1204 and Michael VIII's religious policy set the stage for what occurred in the 80s of the thirteenth century under Gregory's rule. Generally, the Fourth Crusade of 1204 transformed the century into an unqualified "time of troubles." It rent the organizational fabric of the state, challenged the Byzantine faith, dislocated and confused the Byzantine Church, and signaled the beginning of a campaign of compulsion and force.[1] On the other hand, Michael's policy of forced union led only to opposition, violence, and then persecution. Finally, the loss sustained by the Church from the invasions of the Turks, "Byzantium's natural enemy" (to borrow patriarch Gregory's phrase), should not be forgotten.[2] By Andronicus' reign, Anatolia, the hub of Greek Christianity, was practically reduced to vanishing point. A rapid review of some of these events is desirable, if we are to understand the ecclesiastical setting Gregory inherited on the eve of his elevation.

A. Church History and the Fourth Crusade

The fall of the capital city of Constantinople to the Fourth Crusade was a major turning point in the long history of Eastern Christendom. Most dates, it is true, have little specific significance as cut-off points in the continuum of history; 1204 is a rare exception. The creation of the Latin empire of Constantinople, and the election of a Latin patriarch shortly after was a violent break with the Byzantine past. The city and empire, for the first time since its foundation in 330, was in foreign hands. Neither emperor nor patriarch ruled any longer in the God-guarded city of Constantine.

But if the Byzantines were stunned by the loss of Constantinople and most of Greece, they did not yield. Theodore Lascaris soon became the conscious champion of Byzantine imperial power in Nicaea, where he established headquarters and set up his empire-in-exile. True, the new empire's legitimacy and continuity with the past was questioned. Even so, Theodore's links with the Byzantine court—he was the son-in-law of the dead emperor, Alexius III—and his establishment of Nicaea as the place of residence of the patriarch rapidly made him the symbol of Byzantine resistance and imperial tradition.

This resistance, coupled with Latin weakness, achieved its goal some fifty-seven years later. Indeed, Henry of Flanders, the successor of the first Latin emperor, Baldwin I, implicitly recognized Nicaean rule in a treaty with Lascaris by 1216. Further, by the 20s of the century, the emperor, John Ducas Vatatzes, had managed to push the Latins out of Anatolia. Latin rule was henceforth centered in Constantinople and its suburbs. Finally, in 1259, the Latin forces of Greece suffered a major defeat at Pelagonia, and two years later, in July 1261, Constantinople fell to the Byzantines of Nicaea. A month later, the founder of Byzantium's last dynasty, Michael Palaeologus, was crowned in the Hagia Sophia. No longer could the legitimacy of the empire of Nicaea be in doubt. The restoration of the ancient capital pronounced it lawful.

Be this as it may, the effect of this half-century of Latin ecclesiastical and political colonialism was little short of disastrous for the Byzantine Church.[3] Pope Innocent III was undoubtedly initially displeased at the Crusade's excesses. Eventually, however, he came around to the idea that it was really God who had transferred the empire of Constantinople from the proud, disobedient, and schismatic Greeks to the humble and devout Latins.[4] The Crusade, therefore, was anything but "accidental." On the contrary, it was a "mysterium"—God's very instrument to punish the Greeks.[5] Suffice it to say, the newly conquered Byzantine territory with its patriarchate could in the event be incorporated into the institutional fabric of the Western Church. All that was needed was a Latin patriarch—the new embodiment of the previously rebellious patriarchate. Evidently the vexing problem of union was no more.

Such was the necessary conclusion of Innocent's views. Thus, when the patriarch, John X Camaterus, died in exile in 1206, and the Greek clergy of the capital asked permission to elect their own patriarch, Innocent ignored the appeal. Integration, not autonomy, *cuius regio, eius religio,* was to be the new order of things.[6] Predictably, even the layman, who had none of the theologian's insight, was quick to grasp the ecclesiastical dimension of Rome's monarchical claims.[7] If papal insensitivity appears surprising today, it was no less so to the Byzantines of the thirteenth century.[8]

The major result of the Fourth Crusade, however, was not the dislocation and confusion experienced by the Byzantine Church (which, for the most part, managed to survive by compromise and nominal submission), but the impact it had on Christian unity. The papal policy of Latinization only served to strengthen the schism—it did not contain it, as Innocent had hoped. And although he appeared convinced, by 1213, of Byzantine devotion—*Ecclesia Graeca...ad devotionem Romanae Ecclesiae est reducta*[9]—he could not have been further from the truth. As it turned out, the possibility of anything approaching complete agreement was by then more remote than ever. Latin domination not only steered Byzantium irreversibly toward 1453, it also triggered the final *de facto* separation of the Churches. The thirteenth century, then, is "the crucial period for the evolution of Christianity"[10]—the moment of division in the history of united Christendom. Nowhere is this erosion of Christian unity more graphically illustrated than in Gregory's own patriarchate, when direct communication between the two Churches virtually ceased. Although this was not unconnected with Michael's religious policy and the Union of Lyons, its causes, nevertheless, were rooted in the Fourth Crusade.[11]

Clearly, papal foreign policy in the East had failed. The military solution to union had not worked. It is against this background of failure that the numerous negotiations, experimental pourparlers, and embassy exchanges between the popes and Nicaea should be viewed.[12] If the military method for union could not work perhaps political negotiation would. The abundant union deliberations of the mid-thirteenth century all point in this direction. Innocent IV not only negotiated with Vatatzes, but exchanged embassies. So did his successors. Characteristically, however, these informal preliminary conferences were little more than diplomatic maneuvers on the part of the Lascarids of Nicaea. Their aim was primarily the end of Byzantine exile and the restoration of Constantinople.[13] As it happens, when this was achieved in 1261, the policy was quickly set aside—but not for long. For 1261 also had the effect of reviving the threat of a repetition of 1204, especially with the accession in Italy of Charles of Anjou in 1266.

Michael VIII was thus forced to continue Lascarid religious policy. He realized that ecclesiastical union alone could neutralize the Western justification of aggression. As Pachymeres notes, were the Byzantines to become "sons of Mother Church " Angevin hostility would automatically disappeare.[14] In point of fact, Michael's labors to convince Patriarch Joseph I and his synod of the political benefits of union included reminders of the earlier Lascarid attempts to mend the schism. Nor did he hesitate to point out that his situation was far more urgent, since there was no other way to win the pope's sympathy except by speaking and acting thus.[15] His efforts were to bear fruit at the Council of Lyons in 1274.

The observation that the reign of the first Palaeologus belongs more to the Lascarids of Nicaea than to his own house is fully justified.[16] On the strength of Michael's religious policy alone, this would be true, since, in the end, it was Michael's implementation of Lascarid diplomacy that united the two Churches and converted Byzantium into a "papal protectorate." At the same time, it saved his dynasty and aborted a Western coalition and a repetition of 1204 by Charles of Anjou. His entreaties with the pope, for the moment, had succeeded.[17]

In summary, the policy adopted by the papacy and the Byzantine court by mid-century, after the military solution had failed, was one of political negotiation. Simply put, the papacy pledged to guarantee the safety of the Byzantine state from Western aggression in return for the ecclesiastical submission of the Byzantine Church. It was a product of pure political calculation, a "package deal," by which the Byzantines were to buy security at the cost of obedience. However, this elaborate plan had its flaws. For it was dependent on the exaggerated belief that the emperor had the power to impose his decision on the Church, and on the willingness of the Byzantines to accept what their government had negotiated. Both assumptions were illusory. Both were also the basis of Lyons. The result was that "1274, like 1054, became one of the great years in which nothing happened."[18]

B. *Michael VIII's Union Council*

By and large, there is no need to repeat the lengthy and delicate diplomacy by which the Union of Lyons was effected in 1274. The story of Michael's complex negotiations with five popes has already been told amply and cogently.[19] A few points need to be stressed concerning these events, however, since they form the prologue to the patriarchate of Gregory II, and affect the life of the Byzantine Church and the course of Byzantine theology. Indeed, much that happened in this period only gained full momentum in Gregory's patriarchate.

If at the second Council of Lyons the papacy was present in full force, the same cannot be said for the Byzantine Church and its delegation of three. Among the three, the scholar-diplomat George Acropolites, Michael's prime minister, was the only delegate of some distinction. Little could be said of the other willing instruments of Michael's policy, the clerics Germanus III, a former patriarch, and Theophanes, bishop of Nicaea.[20] At any rate, in less than a fortnight after their arrival, union was solemnly concluded in the cathedral of Lyons at the fourth session of the council, 6 July 1274

It was during this session that Acropolites read the emperor's profession of faith, in which he acknowledged, accepted, received, and confessed not only the primacy, but azymes,and the *Filioque.*[21] After a reading of two more letters, one from the sixteen-year-old Andronicus II and another from the bishops who had accepted Michael's plans, Acropolites, the imperial plenipotentiary, again in the emperor's name, promised to renounce the schism and to recognize the primacy.[22] Following this oath, the creed was sung in Latin by the pope; it was then repeated in Greek by the ex-patriarch, Germanus, and the other Byzantines. Although they had recited the words *qui ex Patre Filioque procedit* three times a week before at a pontifical mass (29 June), they nevertheless again repeated them twice.[23]

The Latin account of the proceedings, known as the *Notitia brevis* or *Ordinatio*, has little else to report on the participation of the Byzantines at this famous "ecumenical" conclave. Suffice it to say, no debate or any sort of dialogue took place at Lyons. In fact, even Michael's profession of faith, strictly speaking, was not promulgated or discussed by the council. It was first drafted by Clement IV in March 1267 for Michael's adoption, and then imposed on him by Gregory X in 1272; finally, at the fourth session, it was accepted by the council and inserted in its *acta.* Equally, the major bone of contention, the procession of the Holy Spirit—technically the only theological constitution enacted by Lyons—had been the object of a detailed definition in the second session.[24] It had been agreed upon long *before* the Byzantines had even set foot on French soil. The Greeks' "error" had been condemned without their approval or presence.

Predictably, later unionists, like Manuel Calecas, were to argue for the Union decree's ecumenicity on the grounds that it was issued and ratified in the presence of both the Greeks and the Latins.[25] Contemporary Byzantines knew better, however. It is not accidental that they thought of Lyons as little more than a "mockery and a fraud,"[26] the words heard by the Latin friars on the streets of Constantinople. If historians differ about the way in which union was achieved at the later Council of Florence (1439), they do not differ about the Council of Lyons. Whereas Byzantine and Latin bishops had actually sat together as Fathers at the Council of Florence, such was not the case at Lyons.[27] True, *private* theological conversations between the three Byzantine delegates at Lyons and Latin theologians should perhaps not be ruled out. All the same, it seems safe to assume that no formal public debate of any kind ever took place at Lyons. Lyons was not convened to bring about union, but to ratify the *reductio Graecorum*.[28]

Finally, it should be noted that the Byzantine Church was, in reality, not even represented at Lyons. None of the four Eastern patriarchs had sent representatives or were themselves present. Moreover, none of the prominent theologians of the period, such as Beccus, Mouzalon, Gregory of Cyprus, Holobolus, or Planudes, were sent or even considered for the mission. Strictly speaking, the three delegates represented the emperor, not the patriarch or the members of his synod, the majority of whom had opposed the union. As for the ex-patriarch, Germanus, his presence in France was highly irregular. What was involved was a personal delegation and a personal submission—a formal ratification of what had already been arranged by the emperor and the papal nuncios in Constantinople.[29]

Undeniably Michael had his difficulties. He knew of the concrete psychological and theological difficulties that had to be overcome if the "peace of the Churches" was to be achieved. He was equally aware of the difficulties raised by doctrinal discussions. Perhaps, as a youth, he had witnessed the pourparlers at Nymphaeum in 1234, where the two opposing groups failed to reach any common ground, and ended instead by accusing each other of heresy. No doubt, his fears of theological discussion were real and, in fact, help explain his insistence to the clergy and synod that union would be strictly a canonical matter. As he stated in a chrysobull of December 1273, the Church need make only three formal concessions—papal primacy, the right of appeal, and liturgical commemoration. Indeed, he was eager to "guarantee" that union would be based on three conditions only.

> That the most holy bishop of Rome as ecumenical pope and successor on the apostolic throne is the supreme and first bishop; that to him as being superior belongs ecclesiastical decision on a judgment given here, which a condemned man, considering himself unjustly treated, will not accept; and thirdly, that his name be commemorated in the holy diptychs....On these conditions, then, we agreed; on these, we decided that union should be concluded, so that, in other words, our holy Church should remain without change in all the dogmas and customs transmitted to it from of old.[30]

For all that, an overwhelming number of clergy remained unconvinced. It is remarkable, as one scholar has put it, that any Byzantine delegation went to France at all.[31] For few could be persuaded to believe that the Orthodox faith would remain unchanged or "untouched by innovation," as Michael had stated in an earlier report of 1273.[32] Spearheading the opposition was the patriarch, Joseph I, himself. In a counter-memorandum, or *Response*,[33] to the last-mentioned imperial report, the patriarch was quite daringly explicit. In substance, he argued that peace could never be achieved, unless the theological issues separating East and West (such as the controversial interpolation to the creed) were first discussed in an open council. Specifically, he was unable to be a party to a settlement that did not first air out these difficulties freely and openly, and in the presence of all the patriarchs.[34] Besides, union could not be restricted to questions of protocol, the traditional prerogatives of the popes, since even these canonical concessions could not be accepted without discussion.[35] The patriarch, nevertheless, noted that the Church should not view the Latins as enemies, or detest them, "although they are always raving at us. [After all] they were formerly our brothers, reborn brothers of the same font of holy baptism; if they are sick, if they are eccentric, they nevertheless merit more pity than hate. We need to be merciful, to love them, to pray for them."[36]

Even more eloquent was the synodal opinion that followed in June of the same year, and which was signed by the synod, apart from its more "prudent prelates," as Pachymeres notes.[37] It was probably written by one of the patriarch's colleagues. Like the earlier document, this, too, was not impressed by the possible political dividends of Lyons. The calling of an ecumenical council to discuss the dogmatic issues is again emphasized, as is the idea that such discussion would be the necessary preliminary to acceptance of any of the three items. The council would be attended by the patriarchs and all the body of the hierarchy everywhere. "But if this does not come to pass—far be it for me to think so—and the Church's scandal remains without remedy, then neither the commemoration of the pope, nor the papal primacy, nor the right of appeal can ever have my approval, for fear I may be found in communion with those whose faith I have previously condemned."[38]

It is significant to note that the council mentioned both by the patriarch and by the author of the synodal opinion, was an old request. This was the conventional way (in conformity with the practice of the Church during the first millennium of its history), to solve such problems as the reunion of the

Churches. As the author of the synodal encyclical put it, the council would be convoked "according to the practice in force in the past."[39] Typical, too, was the ecclesiological perspective of these documents. The insistence on the participation or representation of all five patriarchates was, for its authors, a tangible ecclesiological sign of a council's catholicity.[40] In a broader sense, it was their way of rejecting the unilateral "package deal" of Lyons, and of guaranteeing a genuine dialogue.

By and large, the emperor could not accept such advice, even if Joseph was speaking for the Byzantine majority. He knew Rome was against debate. The pope had already decided these matters; they were no longer open to discussion. Debate would constitute an implicit rejection of papal authority. And this Rome could not tolerate. Michael's only alternative, therefore, was violence and the harassment of the opposition. According to Pachymeres, this was done for the explicit purpose of frightening the clergy.[41] Thus, at a synod of 24 December 1273, a very modest section of the hierarchy—less than one-third of the total number—agreed to the union, but only on the basis of the three concessions. All theological discussion was to be excluded.[42] Their collective letter of submission was eventually dispatched with the delegation to Lyons.[43] Shortly after these events, the patriarch repaired to the monastery of the Peribleptos (11 January 1274) from where, with his privileges still intact, he continued to manage the affairs of the Church. He promised to resign, however, should the emperor's delegation to Lyons succeed in its mission.[44]

C. *John XI Beccus and the Unionist Effort*

All the same, Michael was able to find a replacement, a spirit kindred to his own, in the *chartophylax* John Beccus. Beccus' opportune conversion to unionism was the turning point in the emperor's efforts to win over the "veto-proof" patriarch and synod. Perhaps no name is more closely associated with Lyons, and no conversion to unionism more celebrated than that of Beccus. True, initially he had been one of Patriarch Joseph's staunchest allies; he had even been accused of leading him and the synod by the nose.[45] Equally, he had often waxed eloquently in the emperor's presence against the Latins. His speech on one such occasion early in 1273 (repeated reference to it has made it famous) got him into a great deal of trouble. It was then that he announced to the emperor that the "Italians," because of their doctrine of the double procession, were *de facto* guilty of heresy, even if they had never been officially or technically labeled as such by a council.[46]

The emperor was of course angered, particularly since he had known Beccus' virtues and ability, and had hoped to win him over to his side. (In 1268, he had dispatched him and Patriarch Joseph to the Serbian court of Stephen Uros, while, in 1270, he sent him on an even more important diplomatic mission—namely, to the court of Louis IX of France.[47]) In fact, Beccus was removed from the Hagia Sophia, where he had taken refuge from the emperor's anger, and was incarcerated in the prison of Anemas.[48] Not for long, however: Michael was never fully reconciled to the loss; shortly after the imprisonment, the theological works of the recently deceased Nicephorus Blemmydes were sent to Anemas for Beccus to read.[49] Beccus was quickly converted, released, and eventually elected to the patriarchate, 27 May 1275. (Earlier in the year, Patriarch Joseph had abdicated upon the return of the imperial delegation from Lyons.[50]) In Gregoras' memorable phrase, "the former double-edged sword against the Latins" had gone over to the opposition.[51]

On the whole, it is useless to deny (as is often done) either the sincerity or the reality of this moment in Beccus' religious evolution.[52] In the final analysis, Pachymeres' reconstruction appears believable. "Because he was truthful, he was not afraid to confess his ignorance [about the doctrine of the procession]. The reason was that he was occupied with secular studies; neither was he familiar with Holy Scripture nor had he studied it."[53] In other words, Beccus had gone along with the then current view in Byzantium, and had not personally investigated the question, absorbed as he was with scholarly activities. During his imprisonment, however, he pondered the question and was genuinely converted. Although the historian does not agree with Beccus' new theological insight, he does seem to believe in his sincerity.

So important was Beccus in Michael's efforts to enforce the Union of Lyons, that it is interesting to speculate what would have happened during those eight years without his backstairs adviser. For the work of persuasion was left almost entirely in Beccus' hands. Pachymeres notes that, once Beccus was promoted, the emperor was less and less solicitous about the affairs of the Church because he knew these were now in the hands of a capable director, "full of experience and abundant wisdom."[54] If there was someone who could end the long-standing schism, it was he.[55]

Yet, if anything was accomplished during those eight years of misplaced optimism, it was that the schism was made more profound and the conflict more violent, as Cantacuzenus later said.[56] Byzantine society was thoroughly unhinged. The opposition was so pronounced that at the solemn proclamation of the union, at the liturgy sung on 16 January 1275, the *Filioque* was omitted.[57] (It was also not an accident that the liturgy was celebrated in the imperial chapel, without a blaze of publicity, and without a patriarch.) To be sure, Michael took pains to crush the resistance, making the 70s one of the most unrestful in the history of the Byzantine Church. Even the peaceful Joseph was not spared. For "security reasons," he and his closest confidants were separated and deported.[58]

Arguably, Michael's knowledge that some of the opposition was related to the question of the legitimacy of his dynasty—having usurped the Lascarid throne—increased his fears and his willingness to condone measures of imprisonment, flogging, exile, and blinding. And yet, it is necessary to note the basic religious complexion of this reaction as reflected in its composition. It included individuals of the royal blood, members of the senate, the episcopal circle, the provincial episcopate, church officials, priests, and monks, as well as simple laymen.[59] In short, it was not restricted to any one institution or segment of society,[60] such as the non-conformist fanatic monks, or the pro-Lascarid Arsenites, or the deposed patriarch's followers, the Josephites.[61] Essentially, the general character of the opposition explains why it could not be silenced, and why sanctions and excommunications were of little use. Indeed, the theological debate, which the emperor had hoped to avoid, soon broke out in earnest.[62] Those who "persevered in the schism" flooded Beccus' patriarchate with letters and pamphlets in their attempt to discredit the union. They wanted to make no secret of the fact that the Latins were guilty of heresy regarding the *Filioque*.[63]

Beccus' initial reaction to this extensive literary activity and agitation was to remain calm. Yet, he eventually lost his patience, and soon set out to defend the *Filioque's* orthodoxy and to promote the union. In a matter of weeks Beccus became Byzantium's most voluble defender of the Latins, resulting in a number of his own compositions and the calling of numerous synods.[64] At these meetings he attempted to show with iron determination, according to Pachymeres, that the preposition ἐκ (*Filioque*), used by the Latins to explain the procession of the Holy Spirit, was equivalent to the preposition διά (*ex Patre per Filium*), used by the Greeks. That the two were interchangeable was shown by

Scripture, which used the phrase "born from a woman" (ἐκ) to mean through a woman (διά), or again "created through God" to mean "from God." In sum, to confess procession "from the Son" or "through the Son" was to profess an identical creed.[65] For, although the terminology or expression of the two traditions differed, the two were nonetheless equivalent and, indeed, legitimate. On the whole, it made no difference whether one recited the creed in its original fourth-century form or with the Latin interpolation.[66] Obviously, too, if identity of faith existed between Rome and Constantinople, then the Latins could not be heretics.

As we should expect the imagination of almost all churchmen before long became riveted on the trinitarian context of the phrase "from the Father through the Son." This phrase, which served Beccus so well, and which remained at the center of discussion until the end of Gregory's own patriarchate, was well enough known. Its meaning and significance had been placed firmly on the agenda of Byzantine theologians long before Beccus. Its trinitarian context had not gone unnoticed, for example, at Nymphaeum (1234).[67] Then, too, Nicephorus Blemmydes' focus on the question is well known,[68] as is his decisive influence on Beccus, who was actually following the course charted by the monk from Ephesus.[69] Originally, even Patriarch Joseph's *Response* of May 1273 had included a discussion of the troublesome phrase. However, he opted for the traditional view, noting that it signified the temporal mission of the Spirit through the Son, and not its eternal procession. All the same, he also pointed out that the great difference in meaning between the prepositions barred anyone from equating the phrase "through the Son" with the Latin "from the Son." There was, indeed, nothing surprising in the Fathers' use of the phrase; its importance was not to be exaggerated. "The fact that some Fathers have also said that 'the Spirit proceeds through the Son' is not at all astonishing; because the Spirit is not 'from the Son' and 'through the Son, inasmuch as the difference in meaning between the two prepositions is too great."[70]

For all that, the patriarch's theological insight was conveniently ignored by Beccus, who, as we have seen, made a concerted effort to persuade anyone who would listen to his interpretation. Even so, he was singularly unsuccessful and instead managed to alienate almost everyone. This included even those partisan bishops who had complied with the emperor's union, but who had nevertheless managed to get the emperor to promise that all theological discussion would be avoided. "Our most holy emperor guaranteed [that]…if there is an attempt to lead any one of us to overstep these three items [appeal, commemoration, and primacy], the agreement would be set aside immediately."[71] In brief, Beccus' effort had angered and confused, rather than converted. Michael's fragile union was about to collapse.

On the whole, however, the failure should not be laid solely at Beccus' door. The papacy soon suspected the emperor of duplicity, and began to make new demands on the Byzantine court. That these demands seriously jeopardized the Byzantine effort, and any measure of unity that had been achieved is now generally recognized.[72] Pope Nicholas III (1277-1280), for example, insisted that the interpolated creed be adopted in Byzantium, and that oaths acknowledging papal primacy be imposed on all the Byzantine clergy. As a further sign of compliance, it was suggested that a permanent papal cardinal-legate be established in the Byzantine capital.[73] To the old papal thesis of obedience, a new note of uniformity was added. "Unity of faith," wrote Nicholas in his memorandum to his legates, before they left for Constantinople, "does not permit diversity in its confessors or in confession,...especially in the chanting of the creed."[74]

In a very real sense, Nicholas' demands, which threatened the integrity of Byzantine custom, were as unwelcome to the unionists as to the Orthodox.[75] Both agreed it was too much to request the recitation of the *Filioque* of everyone. It was one thing for the emperor to do so (it was public knowledge that he had professed it at Lyons through his ambassadors), and another for the entire Church suddenly to begin chanting it in the liturgy. In short, the bishops, and many of those who had opposed the union, soon realized their fears had come true. Not surprisingly, Michael was forced to fabricate episcopal signatures in his attempt to convince Pope Nicholas of his efforts to force the union on his subjects.[76]

Michael's improvisations, however, were unable to turn the papal tide. Nicholas' successor, Pope Martin IV, finally took the step Michael feared most. On 3 July 1281, at Orvieto, he concluded an alliance with Charles of Anjou for the restoration of the Latin empire of Constantinople. Michael was excommunicated three months later.[77] The political solution, Rome realized, had not worked out. Yet, a repetition of 1204 never came. The empire and the dynasty were saved by the Sicilian Vespers, the rebellion that broke out in Palermo, 30 March 1282, against Charles of Anjou. The Union of Lyons, like the Angevin campaign, had collapsed like a house of cards.[78] Michael lived just long enough as a witness to both. He died on 11 December 1282.

Summary and bleak as the preceding events may seem, they will at least have served to show that Christendom unquestionably fared badly as a result of the Fourth Crusade and the Union of Lyons. From the point of view of the papacy, it was little more than a momentary Pyrrhic victory.[79] Neither the military (1204) nor the diplomatic (1274) solutions to reunion had survived its architects. Sadly, the lesson that union could not be achieved without the cooperation of the Byzantine Church was ignored. The failure was attributed to Byzantine faithlessness, not to the emperor's inability to put the Byzantine Church and its patriarch in his pocket. The case for the Byzantine Church, however, is different. Seen from the perspective of the bitter experience of 1204, Lyons was a significant chapter in its struggle to preserve its identity. On the whole, the chief beneficiary was the Byzantine Church, whose prestige and authority was appreciably strengthened by its efforts to retain its freedom.[80] Significantly, Michael's successor quickly realized that it was no longer expedient to be as independent either of the patriarch or of the synod. The Church became increasingly the focal unifying point against the state. In due course, its own alternative proposal to union—the way of genuine dialogue—was to gain greater currency in both the papal and the imperial court.

An equally notable thread in this development, however, is the fact that Lyons was to serve as a point of departure for one of the most fruitful and creative theological reactions known to Byzantium. Beccus' labors, his round of synods and the pamphlet propaganda of the 70s were only the prolonged prelude, as Pachymeres rightly notes, of the theological debate that came later in Gregory's patriarchate.[81] By then, the theological questions raised in Beccus' reign had taken on a breathless urgency. The violent reaction against Lyons, which followed on the threshold of Gregory's election, was paralleled by a great deal of discussion. Foremost in the debate was the new patriarch himself, a leading representative of Byzantine learning and a theologian of considerable competence. It is to this theologian's early career, before he changed his name from George to Gregory on his promotion to the See of Constantinople, that we now turn.

NOTES

1. All Orthodox bishops were required to take an oath of obedience to the pope and his "Catholic successors." Additionally—as a further sign that the Churches were united— they were asked to commemorate the pope and the new Latin patriarch in the daily liturgy: *PL* 215.135B (Book II, no. 21). See also R. L. Wolff, "Politics in the Latin Patriarchate of

Constantinople, 1204-1261," *Dumbarton Oaks Papers,* 8 (1954), 226-28. A detailed comparison of the *Provinciale Romanum* and six Byzantine *Notitia episcopatum* has conclusively shown that the Byzantine hierarchical organization was greatly modified and restructured; see idem, "The Organization of the Latin Patriarchate of Constantinople, 1204-1261; Social Administrative Consequences of the Latin Conquest," *Traditio,* 6 (1948), 48ff.; J. Lognon, *L'empire latin de Constantinople et la Principauté de Morée* (Paris, 1949), p. 137; idem, "L'organisation de l'Eglise d'Athènes par Innocent III," in *Mémorial Louis Petit* (Bucharest, 1948), pp. 342ff.

2. See Gregory's *Eulogy on Michael VIII,* in J.-F. Boissonade, *Anecdota Graeca e codicibus regiis,* I (Paris, 1829), 335; quoted by A. Ducellier, "Mentalité historique et realités politiques: L'Islam et les Muselmans vus par les Byzantins du XIIIe siècle," *Byzantinische Forschungen,* 4 (1972), 40. On the changes in Asia Minor, see S. Vryonis, *The Decline of Medieval Hellenism in Asia Minor and the Process of Islamization from the Eleventh Through the Fifteenth Century* (Berkeley, 1971), p. 258: "It is surely true that this late thirteenth and fourteenth century period is the period of final, critical change in the ethnic and religious configuration of Anatolia."

3. See the comments of the archivist of the patriarchate at the Synod of Nymphaeum in 1234, in P. G. Golubovich, "Disputatio Latinorum et Graecorum seu relatio apocrisariorum Gregorii IX de gestis Nicaeae in Bithynia et Nymphaeae in Lydia," *Archivum Franciscanum Historicum,* 12 (1919), 451-52.

4. *PL* 215.456A (Book 7, no. 154); Innocent's letter to the emperor, Theodore Lascaris, dated 1208, is even more explicit: *PL* 215.1372C (Book II, no. 47). Cf. also J. Gill, "Innocent III and the Greeks: Agressor or Apostle?" in D. Baker (ed.), *Relations Between East and West in the Middle Ages* (Edinburgh, 1973), pp. 95-108; W. Norden, *Das Papsttum und Byzanz* (Berlin, 1903), pp. 195-96. For Innocent's misgivings concerning the Crusade, see especially *PL* 215.701A (Book 8, no. 136)

5. *PL* 215.641A (Book 7, no. 154)

6. The sixteenth century Reformation phrase is applied to the Latin conquest by H.-G. Beck in H. Jedin (ed.), *Handbuch der Kirchengeschichte.* III, pt. 2: *Die mittelalterliche Kirche* (Freiburg, 1968), 151.

7. See now the splendid systematic summary of the evidence by D. M. Nicol, "The Papal Scandal," in D. Baker (ed.), *Studies in Church History,* 13 (Oxford, 1976), 141-68.

8. W. de Vries, "Innocenz III (1198-1216) und der christliche Osten," *Archivum Historiae Pontificiae,* 3 (1965), 87ff

9. *PL* 215.903c (Book 16, no. 106); see also *PL* 215.902D (Book 16, no. 105); quoted in Norden, *Das Papsttum und Byzanz,* p. 243nI.

10. G. Alberigo, "L'œcuménisme au moyen âge," *Revue d'Histoire Ecclésiastique,* 71, nos. 3-4 (1976), 365.

11. The Crusaders' contribution to Christian division is especially emphasized in the works of F. Dvornik, G. Every, S. Runciman, and J. Meyendorff; see also the rewarding exposition of P. Lemerle, "Byzance et la Croisade," X. *Congresso Internazionale di Scienze Storiche, Relazioni,* 3 (Florence, 1955), 617: Le Schisme n'a pas encore séparé les deux mondes chrétiens: c'est au contraire *à cause* de 1204, et de ce qui suivit, que le Schisme prendra son importance et sa signification."

12. Ch. Papadopoulos, "Attempts at Union of the Churches During the Period of the Latin Occupation in Constantinople (1204-1261)" (in Greek), *Theologia*, 14 (1936), 21ff.

13. I. Sakellion, "The Unpublished Letter of the Emperor John Ducas Vatatzes to Pope Gregory, Discovered at Patmos" (in Greek), *Athenaion*, I (1872), 369-78.

14. Pachymeres, I, 410.

15. Ibid., I, 397, 374-75. For Michael's two major speeches to the clergy, see Pachymeres, I, 386-88, 457-59; on his motives, see B. Roberg, *Die Union zwischen der griechischen und der lateinischen Kirche auf dem II. Konzil von Lyon* (1274) (Bonn, 1964), p.24; M. Viller, "La question de l'union des églises entre Grecs et Latins depuis le concile de Lyon jusqu'à celui de Florence (1274-1438), *Revue d'Histoire Ecclésiastique*, 17 (1921), 260-305, 515-33.

16. P. Lemerle, *Histoire de Byzance* (Paris, 1969), p. 114. According to Lemerle, the accession in 1282 of Andronicus II (not Michael) marks the true beginning of the Palaeologan dynasty and the Byzantine decline.

17. Pachymeres, I, 359: "And he entreated with the bishop of Rome not to permit Charles to carry out his plans or to allow Christians to crusade against Christians."

18. For this summary, see the balanced and penetrating analysis of R. W. Southern, *Western Society and the Church in the Middle Ages*, vol. 2, The Pelican History of the Church, ed. O. Chadwick (London, 1970), pp.78, 73.

19. Roberg, *Die Union von Lyon;* D. J. Geanakoplos, *Emperor Michael Palaeologus and the West 1258-1282* (Cambridge, Mass., 1959); S. Runciman, *The Sicilian Vespers. A History of the Mediterranean World in the Late Thirteenth Century* (Cambridge, 1958); and now K. M. Setton, *The Papacy and the Levant (1204-1571). I: The Thirteenth and Fourteenth Centuries* (Philadelphia, 1976).

20. For the Latin representation, see J.-B. Martin, *Conciles et bullaires du diocèse de Lyon, des origines à la réunion du Lyonnais à la France en 1312* (Lyons, 1905), pp.xxix-xxxi; L. Gatto, *Il Pontificato di Gregorio X* (1271-1276) (Rome, 1959), 127ff.; F. Vernet, "IIe Concile œcuménique de Lyon," *DTC*, 9, pt. 1 (Paris, 1926), cols. 1376-77. For the Greek delegation, see Pachymeres, I, 384; Metochites, VIII, pt. 2, 34. Two laymen, Nicholas Panaretus and George Berrhoiotes, were also part of the delegation but never made it to Lyons; their ship disappeared in a storm off the southern coast of Greece: Pachymeres, I, 396.

21. Mansi, XXIV, 74; see now A. L. Tautu, *Acta Urbani IV, Clementis IV, Gregorii X (1261-1276)* (Pontificia commissio ad redigendum codicem iuris canonici orientalis, Fontes, series III, vol. 5, tom. I; Vatican City, 1953), no. 41, p. 117; Roberg, *Die Union von Lyon*, pp. 239-43 (a new edition of the confession); also cf. Michael's own letter to Pope Gregory X, ibid., 227, and the older edition by L. Delisle, "Notice sur cinq manuscrits de la Bibliothèque Nationale et sur un manuscrit de la Bibliothèque de Bordeaux," *Notices et extraits des Manuscrits de la Bibliothèque Nationale*, XXVII, 2 (Paris, 1879), 154-58.

22. Mansi, XXIV, 73; Roberg, *Die Union von Lyon*, p. 242; Tautu, *Acta Urbani*, no. 48, p. 134; O. Raynaldus, *Annales ecclesiastici*, XXII (Bar-le-Duc, 1870), a. 1274, no. 18, pp. 328-29. Cf. the important article by Charitakis, "Catalogue of Dated Codices of the Patriarchal Library of Cairo" (in Greek), *Epeteris Hetaireias Byzantinon Spoudon*, 4 (1927), 135-36.

23. A. Franchi, *Il Concilio II di Lione (1274) secondo la Ordinatio concilii generalis Lugdunensis* (Rome, 1965), pp. 91-92. See the recent narrative of the proceedings in J. Gill, *Byzantium and the Papacy, 1198-1400* (New Brunswick, N.J., 1979), pp.133-39.

24. On the first constitution dealing with the procession and its probable promulgation at the second session, see Vernet, "IIe Concile de Lyon," col. 1379. The Greeks arrived on 24 June, nearly seven weeks after the opening of the council on 4 May; see Franchi, *Il Concilio II di Leone*, pp. 79-80. On Michael's confession, see I. N. Karmiris, "The Latin Confession of Faith of 1274 Attributed to Michael VIII Palaeologus" (in Greek), *Archeion Ekklesiastikou kai Kanonikou Dikaiou*, 2 (1947), 127-47. For an analysis of the sources of the confession, see H. Wolter and H. Holstein, *Lyon I et Lyon II. VII: Histoire des Conciles Œcuméniques*, ed. G. Dumeige (Paris, 1966), 163-64.

25. Manuel Calecas, *PG* 152.172A: "Denique in Lugdunensi concilio, Graecis Latinisque congregatis, haec sententia promulgata est: quam plurimis in locis Graecis Latinisque inscriptam litteris et libris, facile qui quaerit, invenit." See Vernet, "IIe Concile de Lyon," col. 1383.

26. Pachymeres, I, 458, 456.

27. For the view that Latin and Byzantine metropolitans sat in Florence "as true members of the Council," see J. Gill, "Greeks and Latins in a Common Council: The Council of Florence (1438-9)," *OCP,* 25 (1959), 286-87.

28. Alberigo, "L'œcuménisme au moyen âge," 377.

29. Cf. what Barlaam of Calabria said to Pope Benedict XII in Raynaldus, *Annales ecclesiastici,* XXV, a. 1339, no. 21, p. 160: "quia illi Graeci, qui interfuerunt isti Concilio, non fuerunt missi neque a quatuor patriarchis, qui gubernant Orientalem Ecclesiam, neque a populo: sed a solo imperatore qui conatus fuit facere unionem vobiscum ex vi, et non voluntare." See also the opinion of A. Fliche, "Le problème oriental au second concile œcuménique de Lyon," *OCP,* 13 (1947), 483; and D. J. Geanakoplos, "Bonaventura, the Two Mendicant Orders, and the Greeks at the Council of Lyons (1274)," in D. Baker (ed.), *Studies in Church History,* 13 (Oxford, 1976), 198-204, and esp. 210.

30. Greek text in *Dossier de Lyon*, 317; and in J. Gill, "The Church Union of the Council of Lyons (1274) Portrayed in Greek Documents," *OCP,* 40 (1974), 14; Michael's three points or "chapters" (πρωτεῖον, ἔκκλητον, καὶ μνυμόσυνον), are discussed, at length, in Pachymeres, I, 371, 374-75, 386, 395. See also Metochites, VIII, pt. 2, 35; Gregoras, I, 125; and D.J. Geanakoplos, "Michael VIII Palaeologus and the Union of Lyons (1274)," *The Harvard Theological Review,* 46 (1953), 80ff.

31. D. M. Nicol, "The Byzantine Reaction to the Second Council of Lyons, 1274," in G. J. Cuming and D. Baker (edd.), *Studies in Church History: Councils and Assemblies,* 7 (Cambridge, 1971), 120.

32. See A. Demetracopoulos, *History of the Schism* (in Greek) (Leipzig, 1866), p. 67.

33. The *Response* was recently published by Darrouzès and Laurent, with a detailed analysis and a French translation, in *Dossier de Lyon*, 134-301; see the earlier analysis by J. Skruten, "Apologia des Mönchpriesters Job gegen die Argumente zugunsten der Lateiner," *Bulletin de l'Institut Archéologique Bulgare,* 9 (1935), 326-30. Extracts only in Demetracopoulos, *History of the Schism*, pp. 58-60, and J. Dräseke, "Der Kircheneinigungsversuch des Kaisers Michael VIII. Paläologos," *Zeitschrift für wissenschaftliche Theologie,* 34 (1891), 332-35; Laurent, *Regestes,*

no. 1400. The patriarch's ghost writers were the historian Georges Pachymeres and the monk Job Iasites; see Pachymeres, I, 380. George Metochites, VIII, pt. 2, 37, notes that the patriarch was also under the influence of the emperor's sister, the nun Irene-Eulogia. On Iasites, see L. Petit, "Job Iasites," *DTC*, 8, pt. 2 (Paris, 1925), cols. 1487-89.

34. *Dossier de Lyon*, 365,17.

35. *Dossier de Lyon*, 190ff. Cf. the letter sent by the monks of Mt. Athos to Michael in 1275, which adopts a similar position on the three items; and especially on the daily liturgical commemoration of the pope; see *ibid.*, 419.

36. *Dossier de Lyon*, 299.

37. Pachymeres, I, 382; text in *Dossier de Lyon*, 303ff. See also V. Laurent, "Le serment antilatin du patriarche Joseph Ier," *EO*, 26 (1927), 405-406; Laurent, *Regestes*, no. 1401.

38. *Dossier de Lyon*, 313.

39. Ibid., 313

40. Byzantine requests for a common council in the thirteenth century are discussed by Y. Congar, "1274-1974: Structures ecclésiales et conciles dans les relations entre Orient et Occident," *Revue des Sciences philosophques et théologiques*, 58 (1974), 362-65; see the detailed discussion for the fourteenth century in D. M. Nicol, "Byzantine Requests for an Œcumenical council in the Fourteenth Century," *Annuarium Historiae Conciliorum*, I (1969), 69-95. It is not surprising that Rome's rejection of the idea of an open council eventually convinced the Byzantines that the root cause of the schism was to be found in Rome's refusal, and not in Byzantium's inability to agree to take second place after Rome. See Neilus Cabasilas, *The Cause of the Schism in the Church*, PG 149.685B. The papal posture was also vigorously rejected early in the thirteenth century by the patriarch John X Camaterus; see A. Papadakis and A.-M. Talbot, "John X Camaterus Confronts Innocent III: An Unpublished Correspondence," *BS*, 33(1972), 36, 37, 39-40; see also Y. Congar, "Quatre siècles de désunion et d'affrontement. Comment Grecs et Latins se sont appréciés réciproquement au point de vue ecclésiologique," *Istina*, 13 (1968), 140-43.

41. Pachymeres, I, 392-94.

42. See the synodal acceptance in *Dossier de Lyon*, 321-23; and Gill, "The Church Union of the Council of Lyons," 18-21; for the text of the chrysobull, which defined the conditions of union and gave the bishops guarantees, see ibid., *OCP*, 40 (1974), 12-18; and *Dossier de Lyon*, 317-19

43. New edition by Roberg, *Die Union von Lyon*, 235-39; early edition by Delisle, "Notice sur cinq manuscrits de la Bibliothèque Nationale," 150-54; and Mansi, XXIV, 74-77.

44. Pachymeres, I, 386; see the patriarch's πιττάκιον in *Dossier de Lyon*, 323; and in Gill, "The Church Union of the Council of Lyons," 20-22; Laurent, *Regestes*, no. 1409. The bishops' letter to the pope (see note above) makes explicit mention of the patriarch's promise to resign: F. Dölger, *Regesten der Kaiserurkunden des oströmischen Reiches* (565-1453). III: *Regesten von 1204-1282* (Munich-Berlin, 1932), no. 2004.

45. Pachymeres I, 377 (the accusation was made by the emperor's regular representative at the synod, George Acropolites).

46. Ibid., I, 376. Cf. the similar remarks in Patriarch Joseph's *Response, Dossier de Lyon*, 141, and in an anonymous text of 1275, ibid., 335.

47. Pachymeres, I, 350-55, 361-64; Dölger, *Regesten*, III, nos. 1953, 1954, 1968.

48. Pachymeres, I, 378.

49. Ibid., I, 381.

50. The delegation returned on 9 January 1275, when, in the terse phrase of Pachymeres, I, 399, "the Patriarch Joseph's name ceased to be commemorated"; Gregoras, I, 125. Beccus' actual enthronement occurred a week after his election, on the Sunday of Pentecost, 2 June 1275. In addition to Beccus' name, the synod had given the emperor the name of another candidate, Theodosius, titular patriarch of Antioch; he was not chosen: Pachymeres, I, 403. On Theodosius' background, see Pachymeres, I, 436-37; and Ch. Papadopoulos, *History of the Church of Antioch* (in Greek) (Alexandria, 1951), pp. 952-53.

51 Gregoras, I, 130.

52. V. Nikolsky, "The Union of Lyons. An Episode from Medieval Church History, 1261-1293" (in Russian), *Pravoslavnoe Obozrienie*, 23 (1867), 33; Demetracopoulos, *History of the Schism*, p. 62; A. D. Zotos, *John Beccus, Patriarch of Constantinople, New Rome, the Latinizer* (in Greek) (Munich, 1920), pp. 40ff. For a recent opposing view, see Beck, *Die mittelalterliche Kirche*, p. 225: "To me, it hardly seems possible that his conversion was political in nature for we know that, in prison, Beccus read the work of a Byzantine theologian...Nicephorus Blemmydes by name." See also R. Souarn, "Tentatives d'union avec Rome: un patriarche grec catholique au XIIIe siècle," *EO*, 3 (1895-1900), 236; and L. Bréhier, "Jean XI Beccos," *Dictionnaire d'Histoire et de Géographie Ecclésiastique*, 7 (Paris, 1934), 357. Cf. the recent discussion in Gill, *Byzantium and the Papacy*, pp. 152-59.

53. Pachymeres, I, 38, and Gregoras, 1, 129; these passages are discussed by V. Grumel, "Un ouvrage récent sur Jean Beccos, patriarche de Constantinople," *EO*, 24 (1925), 28. See also M. Sotomayor, "El patriarca Becos según Jorge Paquimeres (semblanza histórica)," *Estudios Eclesiásticos*, 31 (1957), 339, 354.

54. Pachymeres, 1, 403; according to Gregoras, I, 130, he had become "all things to the emperor, his voice, his hand, his very pen, whether speaking, writing, or theologizing on his behalf." Cf. Zotos, *John Beccus*, pp. 26-27.

55. This is Michael's reason, as reported by Pachymeres, I, 403, for nominating Beccus as patriarch.

56. John Cantacuzenus, *Historiae*, III, ed. L. Schopen (Bonn, 1832), 59; also, J. Meyendorff, "Projets de Concile Œcuménique en 1367: Un dialogue inédit entre Jean Cantacuzène et le légat Paul," *Dumbarton Oaks Papers*, 14 (1960), 162.

57. Pachymeres, I, 399; Gregoras, I, 130. The concessions made at this liturgy (it was the feast of St Peter in Chains) were the commemoration of Pope Gregory's name in the litany "as supreme pontiff and ecumenical Pope of the apostolic Church," and the reading, in Latin and Greek, of the epistle and gospel lessons. Neither historian mentions the *Filioque*.

58. Pachymeres, 1, 386; Joseph, who had retired to the monastery of St Michael's at Anaplous on the Bosporus, was exiled to the fort of Chele on an island at the extreme end of the Black Sea; his disciple and co-author of the *Response*, Job Iasites, was sent to Kabaia, a fort on the

Sangarius; the remaining disciples were sent to the Aegean islands. For a more general description of the persecution, see Gregoras, I, 127; and Nicephorus Choumnus, *Epitaph for Theoleptus of Philadelphia,* ed. J.-F. Boissonade, *Anecdota Graeca,* V (Paris, 1833), 200.

59. See the τομογραφία (19 February 1277) in *Dossier de Lyon,* 463; and Gill, "The Church Union of the Council of Lyons," 24; Laurent, *Regestes,* no. 1431. It is also substantiated by Pachymeres, I, 459, who reports that the opposition included the emperor's two sisters, Eulogia and Maria,five nieces, and two nephews, John and Andronicus Palaeologus. Other eminent dissidents, reported by the historian, were the prime minister's son, Constantine Acropolites, Theodore Mouzalon, and John Cantacuzenus: Pachymeres, I, 494-96. See the case histories itemized in the report made for the papal legation of Nicholas III by Ogerius, Michael's protonotary, in R.-J. Loenertz, "Mémoire d'Ogier, protonotaire, pour Marco et Marchetto nonces de Michel VIII Paléologue auprès du Pape Nicholas III. 1278 printemps-été," *OCP,* 31 (1965), 374-408; V. Grumel, "En Orient après le IIè concile de Lyon. Brèves notes d'histoire et de chronologie," *EO,* 24 (1925), 321-25; D. M. Nicol, "The Greeks and the Union of the Churches: The Report of Ogerius, Protonotarius of Michael VIII Palaeologos, in 1280," *Proceedings of the Royal Irish Academy,* 63, sect. C, I (1962), 11-16, Laurent, *Regestes,* no. 1435; F. M. Delorme and A. L. Tautu, *Acta Romanorum pontificum ab Innocentio V ad Benedictum XI (1276-1304)* (Pontificia commissio ad redigendum codicem iuris canonici orientalis, Fontes series III, vol. 5, tom. II; Vatican City, 1954), no. 23, pp. 50-55.

60. See Beccus' own description of the reaction, in *De depositione sua. Oratio* I, *PG* 141.952-53; H. Evert-Kappesowa, "Une page de l'histoire des relations byzantino-latines: Le clergé byzantin et l'union de Lyon (1274-1282), *BS,* 13 (1952-1953), 68-92; idem, "Une page de l'histoire des relations byzantino-latines II: La fin de l'union de Lyon," *BS,* 17 (1956), 1-18.

61. I. Sykoutres, "Concerning the Schism of the Arsenites" (in Greek), *Hellenika,* 2 (1929), 306-317.

62. The τομογραφία, in Gill, "The Church Union of the Council of Lyons," 24, excommunicates all those who labored "to the best of their power to overthrow Christianity"; *Dossier de Lyon,* 463; and Beccus' letter to Pope John XXI, in *Dossier de Lyon,* 479-85; and in Gill, *OCP,* 40 (1974), 34-41. The early edition of this letter was made by V. Laurent, *Unité de l'Eglise.* 12 (1934), 266-70; idem, *Regestes,* no. 1432.

63. Pachymeres, I, 415-16. The polemical work of these confessors and martyrs (such as Meletius and Hierotheus) is, for the most part, still unedited. See L. Petit, "Mélèce le Galésiote ou le Confesseur, *DTC,* 10, pt. 1 (Paris, 1929), cols. 536-38; H.-G. Beck, *Kirche und theologische Literatur im byzantinischen Reich* (Munich, 1959), pp. 678-79. Meletius was actually sent to Rome by Michael, who asked the Pope personally to punish the confessor; see his *vita,* in *Gregorios Palamas,* 6 (1921), 620. His poem *Against the Latins* is now published in *Dossier de Lyon,* 554-63.

64. We have the offical report of the proceedings of one of these synods held on 3 May 1280: *PG* 141.281-89; and Mansi, XXIV, 365-73. On Beccus' compositions, see Beck, *Kirche und theologische Literatur,* pp. 681-83. Prior to this, Beccus' own non-unionist friend, the grand *oeconomus,* Theodore Xiphilinus, had tried to convince him not to ˙nswer any of his theological adversaries nor to contradict them in any way: Pachymeres, I, 416, 476; Laurent, *Regestes,* no. 1430. Beccus' promise to Theodore, however, was broken. See also Gregoras, I, 130; and Zotos, *John Beccus,* pp. 27-29.

65. Pachymeres, I, 481. Cf. Gill, *Byzantium and the Papacy,* pp. 152ff.

66. See Beccus' other letter to Pope John XXI written in 1277, in A. Theiner and F. Miklosich (edd.), *Monumenta spectantia ad unionem ecclesiarum graecae et romanae* (Vienna, 1872), p. 24; Laurent, *Regestes* no. 1433.

67. A. Papadopoulos-Kerameus, "The Unpublished Synodal Definition Enacted by the Synod Held at Nymphaeum in the Year 1274" (in Greek), *Ekklesiastike Aletheia*, 3 (1882), 72-74; also edited, with a Latin translation, in Golubovich, "Disputatio Latinorum et Graecorum," 466-70; Laurent, *Regestes*, no. 1273.

68. V. Grumel, "Nicéphore Blemmydès et la procession du Saint-Esprit," *Revue des sciences philosophiques et théologiques*, 18 (1931), 636-56; M. Jugie, "Bulletin de littérature byzantine: Nicéphore Blemmide et ses écrits," *EO*, 17 (1914), 153-56; A. Demetracopoulos, *Orthodox Greece* (in Greek) (Leipzig, 1872), pp. 36-37, and the important article of M. Candal, "Nueva interpretación del 'per Filium' de los Padres Griegos," *OCP*, 31 (1965), 8. See also M. V.-J. Barvinok, *Nicephorus Blemmydes and his Works* (in Russian) (Kiev, 1911).

69. Pachymeres, I, 476-77; II, 27; see also V. Laurent, "Théodore Mouzalon," *DTC*, 10, pt. 2, col. 2583. An opposing view is given in Zotos, *John Beccus*, pp. 20-23.

70. Response, *Dossier de Lyon*, 161.

71. See the chrysobull in Gill, "The Church Union of the Council of Lyons," 18; Pachymeres, I, 483; Laurent, *Regestes*, no. 1446.

72. V. Grumel, "Les ambassades pontificales à Byzance après le IIè Concile de Lyon (1274-1280)," *EO* 23 (1924), 437ff.

73. See the detailed discussion of Pope Nicholas' memorandum in Geanakoplos, *Emperor Michael Palaeologus and the West*, pp. 315ff.

74. J. Gay, *Les Registres de Nicolas III* (Bibliothèque des Ecoles Françaises d'Athènes et de Rome; Paris, 1904), col. 128B; quoted in Zotos, *John Beccus*, p. 54; and Geanakoplos, *Emperor Michael Palaeologus and the West*, p. 313. See also Delorme and Tautu, *Acta Romanorum pontificum*, no. 35, p 72.

75. See Michael's profession of faith, and his letter to Pope Gregory X requesting that the creed be left as it was, in Roberg, *Die Union von Lyon*, pp. 243, 227. The imperial delegation had, of course, accepted the definitive dogmatic statement *Cum sacrosancta*, which the Council of 1274 had issued in the sixth and final session. See Franchi, *Il Concilio II di Lione*, p. 137; for the Greek translation, see *Dossier de Lyon*, 324-25; and Gill, "The Church Union of the Council of Lyons," 22. Yet, the council did not insist that the Byzantines add the *Filioque* to the creed. Admittedly, the sources are completely silent about Gregory's response to Michael's request that Rome pledge to respect the integrity of Byzantine custom. Thus, the possibility exists, as Vernet believed, "IIe Concile de Lyon," col. 1388, that the pope may have imposed the addition on the Byzantines. This is unlikely. Both Latin and Greek sources (Pachymeres, for example) could not have remained silent on such a point.

76. Pachymeres, 1, 461; Sotomayor, "El patriarca Becos," 338. Beccus' involvement in this forgery remains uncertain; Pachymeres himself says that he did not know if it involved the patriarch.

77. Geanakoplos, *Emperor Michael Palaeologus and the West*, pp.337-42.

78. That which alone survived the union was its symbol: two processional crosses set up on the high altar of St John's Cathedral at Lyons to commemorate the event of 6 July 1274; but even this was eventually destroyed by the Huguenots in 1566; see L. Bégule, *Monographie de la Cathédrale de Lyon* (Lyons, 1880), p. 94; see esp. Vernet, "IIe Concile de Lyon," col. 1389.

79. See C. Andersen, "Geschichte der abendländischen Konzile des Mittelalters," in H. J. Margull (ed.), *Die ökumenischen Konzile der Christenheit* (Stuttgart, 1961), p. 139

80. Nicol, "The Papal Scandal," 160.

81. Pachymeres, 1, 482.

2

GREGORY OF CYPRUS: THE SCHOLAR

The new, highly gifted patriarch of Constantinople was not unknown, at either the imperial or the patriarchal curia at the time of his consecration, 11 April 1283.[1] He was, in fact, well known long before he was to cross swords with his predecessor, Beccus, and to become his principal theological adversary. The patriarch's voluminous correspondence reflects this quite well. His list of correspondents—in an age of letter writers he was one of the most accomplished—reads like a "who's who" in late-thirteenth century Byzantium. Moreover, Gregory was an enthusiastic participant in that impressive intellectual revival, the so-called second Byzantine renaissance of the thirteenth century. Unlike Beccus, who never ventured outside theology, Gregory was a leading representative of this movement, which he himself described as an "expansion of knowledge" and "a literary revival."[2] Gregory is a major figure in Byzantine literature and, like Photius, belongs as much to the history of scholarship as to ecclesiastical history.

A. *Early Training and Career*

Two crucial sources for understanding Gregory's personality and career, both before and after 1283, are his own correspondence and his *Autobiography*. In view of the importance these assume, both in the controversy in which he became involved and for his early career, a brief description may be justified. Nearly half of Gregory's original collection of 242 letters (excluding those of an indeterminate nature) was written while he was patriarch; the others date before 1283.[3] Thus, their importance as a private and official dossier can hardly be exaggerated.[4] The letters written before he came patriarch, for example, are full of insights into his personality, his studious temperament, and his deep-seated humanism. His love of books is, to quote but one example, touchingly conveyed in a letter to Isaac of Ephesus who had presented him with a manuscript as a gift. He notes how he, as a lover of books, often turned to the manuscript, and marveled at the miracle of his friend's separation from his valuable possessions.[5] And yet, as a precious primary source, this private dossier has not been tapped as much as it should be. The same may be said of the official section, the letters of his patriarchate (nos. 128-140), to which we must turn when other contemporary sources are silent, brief or confused.[6]

Pachymeres' narrative of the events of Gregory's patriarchate would clearly be incomplete and abbreviated without the information provided by this section of the correspondence. Its importance is further enhanced by the fact that the *Autobiography* seldom mentions the patriarchate, save for one or two allusions.

Gregory's *Autobiography* has, of late, been described as a "precious witness of the constituent humanism of the Byzantine soul."[7] He is indeed one of the few prominent figures in Byzantine intellectual history—other rare examples are Psellus and Blemmydes—to have left us anything autobiographical. The work covers his first thirty-three years, up to the point when, as he says, his studies came to an end.[8] Thus, it contains little about his activity as patriarch. Actually, even the story of his early years is deliberately tailored, since it was originally intended as an introduction to his collected letters.[9] Yet, despite its introductory and reflective tone, this brief work, distinguished by both style and simplicity, is of the greatest importance. It is our principal source of information about his early youth, the "academic" background of the times (of which so little is known), and the urgent premium he had placed on the acquisition of education early in his life.[10]

Gregory was born in Latin-occupied Cyprus in 1241/2, forty-nine years after its occupation by the Lusignans in 1192. Under their rule, the island was to play a role of some importance in thirteenth-century crusading history. According to his own testimony, although his parents and grandparents were among the leading Greek families of the island, they nonetheless suffered equally with the others on the arrival of the Lusignans. Gregory adds that his "train of descendants" hailed entirely from Cyprus.[11] True, Beccus, from his exile in Brusa, was later to condemn Gregory as a non-Greek, or as one born and raised among "Italians."[12] But this has little foundation in fact. Gregory was from a distinguished Cypriot family, and was as much "a Roman of Roman parentage and upbringing" as Beccus himself claimed to be; he had no need to advance his way into Byzantine circles by adopting Byzantine dress and speech.[13]

No more striking proof of this exists than his own enthusiastic description of his wanderings in search of Greek learning. He began his education under the watchful eye of his parents, who first sent him to the local grammar school. He finished this elementary training, he informs us, at a very early stage. Shortly after, at age nine, when his natural gift for learning became clear, he was sent to Nicosia to pursue advanced training.[14] The lack of com-

petent Greek teachers, however, obliged him to enroll instead in the school of
the Roman archbishop of Nicosia where instruction was in Latin. This school
had opened shortly after 1248 when the archbishop was ordered, by a visiting
legate from Rome, to open two schools in his cathedral, one for grammar, and
another for theology. Apparently, the Church and the monasteries were, until
then, the only institutions on the island providing instruction.[15] Here, he was
taught grammar and Aristotelian logic. Even so, it was only an "introduction,"
since the limited time at his disposal, coupled with his difficulties with the "foreign and bastard"[16] Latin language, impeded his progress. In any event, during
those four or five years at Nicosia, Gregory must have acquired some rudimen-
tary knowledge of Latin. At the age of fifteen, he returned home.

His thirst for knowledge was not yet fully quenched, and, once at home,
he asked to be sent to the schools of Nicaea. At Nicaea, he had heard, could be
found an abundance of wise men; one could actually see ancient Athens.[17]
(The court of Nicaea, the Byzantine government-in-exile, had in fact been
something of an intellectual refuge for scholars; many had fled there after the
capture of Constantinople in 1204.) But, because of his youth, he was denied
the request. The eastern tip of the island of Cyprus, however, lies less than sev-
enty miles off the coast of Syria; two years later, he took ship and, after stop-
ping in Acre ("Ptolemais"), sailed north to Anaea where he disembarked for
nearby Ephesus.[18] At Ephesus, he hoped to study with the famous Nicephorus Blemmydes, the man whose writings were to play, as we have seen, a significant role in Beccus' conversion. He "was said to be the wisest man, not
only among Greeks, but among all men."[19] But Blemmydes, who had an inflexible nature, would not allow him to approach his monastery. That Gregory was poor and a foreigner may have had something to do with the
rejection.[20] He was thus obliged to go to Nicaea, and arrived there shortly after a six-month journey. From there, he traveled to Thrace, where Michael
VIII was trying to recover Constantinople from the Latins.

Shortly after, he returned to the Nicene capital and took up the study of
grammar and poetry. To his dismay, however, his teachers, besides being super-
ficial, were incapable of teaching him anything else. His amusing remarks are
highly instructive, for they show that Nicaea's reputation as a center of Greek
learning has been exaggerated. "I was despondent...for I had crossed a conti-
nent only to be taught declensions, the formation and irregularities of verbs, the
abduction of Tyndareus' daughter, how the city of Priam fell, and about a pro-

longed war fought for the sake of a woman."[21] Education at Nicaea, then, allegedly encouraged by the emperors, was, in the main, of a secondary level. The
only instruction on an advanced level in such subjects as logic and philosophy
was offered by Blemmydes at Ephesus. Gregory would later describe this period
as a time when education was everywhere neglected and letters endangered.[22]

Additional information on Gregory's stay in Nicaea is also provided by a
letter from a friend of long standing, the Josephite monk Methodius. Methodius wrote the letter when Gregory had become patriarch, twenty-five years
after their sojourn together in Nicaea.[23] (Methodius himself was to become
metropolitan of Cyzicus only after Gregory's patriarchate.) Among the bits of
information offered by his friend is the revealing detail that Gregory had seriously thought of embracing the monastic life when at Nicaea, and had actually visited a monastery for that purpose.[24] Unaccountably, Gregory does not
mention this youthful impulse or the fact of a trip to Trebizond—likewise revealed by Methodius—either in his letters or in his *Autobiography*. This information is nevertheless reliable, and sheds further light on Gregory's youth as
well as on his later career, when, on his elevation to patriarch, he accepted the
monastic tonsure.

The academic situation at Nicaea and the thought of his parents, whose
tears he had made light of, caused him to return to the port of Anaea. He did
not take ship to Cyprus, however, but instead traveled to Constantinople,
which, by then, had been recovered by Michael VIII. It was then that his od-
yssey ended as a student of George Acropolites, the former tutor of Theodore
II Lascaris, and the head of a newly reopened school in the capital. It was under Acropolites, who had been fortunate enough to have studied under Blemmydes, that the future patriarch, for the next seven years (1267-1274),
received his most extensive humanist training.[25] This consisted of the study of
Aristotle's philosophy, Euclid's geometry, and Nicomachus' arithmetic. His
tastes were clearly Aristotelian, for he notes that he learned to admire Aristotle
like no other thinker.[26] And although he was the youngest of a large group of
students (he says he was then twenty-six), he did not allow his elders to sur-
pass him, but quickly set the standard. Before long others were imitating his
compositions.[27]

Curiously, Gregory makes no mention of any theological training. He refers only to the secular education he received under Acropolites. It has been
suggested that he was also enrolled in the school in the orphanage of St Paul's

church.[28] This institution was reopened in 1265-1266 when the rector, Manuel Holobolus, was put in charge.[29] This establishment was separate from the school of Acropolites.[30] Quite possibly, Gregory followed Holobolus' lectures as well as those of Acropolites. It is clear from his correspondence that he knew Holobolus well. At least one letter addressed to the rector indicates that Holobolus supported Gregory in his theological struggle against Beccus.[31] In 1285, as we will see, it was Holobolus who was given the privilege of opening the Council of Blachernae that was to condemn Beccus and adopt Gregory's theology. Given the silence of the sources, however, and the school's unsettled status—it is not certain whether it was a patriarchal school, or whether theology was taught there—the connection remains unconvincing. True, Gregory later displayed an uncommon theological maturity which would indicate that he was not a stranger to the discipline; as scholar, stylist, humanist, and seasoned theologian, Gregory was to have few peers. But this in itself was not unusual; a theologian without formal training was a familiar phenomenon in Byzantium. We should not indeed forget the large Byzantine "capacity for dealing with abstract ideas," as one scholar has put it.[32] Gregory, it seems, had this in abundance.

In any event, his industry and elegance of style did not go unnoticed. Among literary circles, perhaps nothing was more prized than an involved precious style. And, in that, Gregory especially shone.[33] Gregoras observes that "he brought to light and, as it were, gave a new lease on life" to the Attic tongue and Greek literature, both of which had been in limbo far too long.[34] Indeed, this exceptional competence soon pushed the "restorer of Atticism" into teaching, a vocation he was to continue until his accession to patriarch. Gregory taught at the patriarchal school—he lectured on the Epistles of St Paul—as well as at the monastery of Christ the Incomprehensible; it is there, in the neighborhood of another great monastery, that of the Pantocrator, that he lived for many years.[35] Two of his most polished and urbane students, Theodore Mouzalon and Nicephorus Chumnus, later became Andronicus II's chief ministers of state.[36] Mouzalon, in addition, was to play a prominent role by the side of his teacher at the Council of Blachernae in 1285. Maximus Planudes, the translator of Augustine, may have also been one of his students.[37] All these students corresponded with Gregory and, like the princess Theodora Raouaina Palaeologina, cousin of Andronicus, seemed to "hang upon his every word."[38] Significantly, it was at Theodora's foundation, the little monastery of Aristine near St Andrew in Crisei, that Gregory retired in 1289.

Competence, however, was also a guarantee of advancement in the re-stricted circle of Byzantine court officials and clerics. Although he may have been reluctant because of his unmitigated passion for books (this is his own phrase), he soon joined the ranks of the palace clergy.[39] This ordination to *protapostolarius,* first reader for the Prophesies and Epistles in the imperial chapel, probably occurred during his study with Acropolites during the patri-archate of Joseph I.[40] It was on the whole in line with his earlier desire to be-come a monk.

This consideration brings us to the revival of asceticism and spirituality in these decades, namely the movement that parallels the classical interests of the scholars who crowd the closing decades of the thirteenth century. In general, these years have often been condemned as a period of anti-Latin phobia, in-ternal schism, useless discussion, and theological conservatism.

> But, a secular tradition, the result of Photius' *Mystagogy,* gave to the Byzantine error on the procession of the Holy Spirit *a Patre solo* the aspect of a national dogma...The religious dispute thus became a vogue as much as a need experi-enced by the entire nation; a theological madness possessed the Byzantine capi-tal. Amid the sacred outcries, accusations of scandal, few vigilant ears picked up the noise of Moslem arms extending from Trebizond to Nicaea along a border as fluctuating as the tides of the Bosporus.[41]

In brief, churchmen were so wrapped up in barren or unedifying wrangles that the more pressing danger from the Moslem was ignored.

The controversies of the cleric and the fanatic doubtless did contribute to the mental climate of the age, and, at times, even paralyzed initiative.[42] All the same, however, a genuine religious revival was at the time also taking place. The far-from-marginal creative contribution in spirituality, ecclesiology, the-ology, and church government made by some of the very same people in-volved in those years of "theological madness," should be emphasized. Suffice it to say, the labors of Theoleptus of Philadelphia, Patriarch Athanasius, and Gregory of Cyprus, to name only the most important, are not without merit.[43] The confusion and turmoil that was so much a pattern of thirteenth-century Byzantine society must not be allowed to obscure the authentic achievement of these churchmen. On the contrary, they deserve far more attention than they have hitherto received.

The inclusion of Gregory's name among those contributing to the spiri-tual movement may seem somewhat anomalous. As a devotional writer, he does not measure up in spiritual stature either to Theoleptus or to his successor, Athanasius, who was eventually canonized; his hagiographic *encomia* and *vitae*, for example, are no more than formal studied exercises with little of the spiritual in them.[44] Even if one thinks of Gregory primarily as a professional scholar, however, his position in the revival would still be secure by virtue of his contribution to the field of speculative theology. Ultimately, his formulations were an attempt to rediscover, in an authentic manner, the patristic legacy, and to achieve an identity of thought with the Fathers of the Church. It is doubtful if this goal differs substantively from that of Athanasius or Theoleptus. It may be that, in his efforts to open the way to "a dialogue in depth between Greek and Latin theology,"[45] he surpassed them. As it happens, this very theology was to prepare the way for the other major spiritual movement of the fourteenth century—hesychasm. In fact, it is in the context of "immediate forerunner"[46] of hesychasm that we can best appreciate his theological and historical significance. He is a crucial link to Palamite theology and the hesychast movement, even if he cannot be identified in traditional hesychast categories.[47] Suffice it to say, the posthumous praise lavished on Gregory by fourteenth-century hesychast theologians and patriarchs is eloquent testimony of this.[48] Contemporaries certainly recognized the relation between his formulations and those of Gregory Palamas. (It is, incidentally, not without interest that the circumstances and disputes which came to surround Gregory II as patriarch show unmistakable parallels with those involving Gregory Palamas some fifty years later.)

Gregory, then, had a foot in both the spiritual and the classical renaissance and, as such, constitutes a striking example of an unprecedented phenomenon of the time. By the late thirteenth century, to put it otherwise, the pursuits of the scholar and the theologian, of the Hellenist and the monastic, did not seem so incompatible with each other as they had in the past.[49] In the monastic schools, for example, such as that of the Incomprehensible, Greek learning was taught by both monks and laymen;[50] for the moment, at least, the two traditionally tension-ridden groups in Byzantium had achieved a symbiosis.[51] As principle theologian, patriarch, and participant in the Palaeologan renaissance Gregory was the very embodiment of this phenomenon.

B. Gregory and Unionism

It remains to examine Gregory's role in the feverish union plans of Michael VIII. These took place in the years when Gregory was a student and then professor in the capital. As court cleric and intellectual, he could not but involve himself in what was the great issue of the day. Besides, in the highly competitive milieu of the Byzantine court, there was little choice. To insist that he had a choice in the matter is an uninformed suggestion at best.[52] However, his involvement has been thought to have been less than honest. Specifically, he has been accused of being, above all, a "clever politician"[53] and a "perfect courtier,"[54] both at Michael's and then at Andronicus' court, when he prudently changed his views to go along with the prevailing winds of 1283.

All of these views have been based almost exclusively either on Beccus' contemptuous criticism or on what can hardly be called an unimpeachable source—George Metochites humorless *Dogmatic History:*

> I shall not narrate his bad qualities in detail, since that would involve more than I propose to do in the present project. Yet, like a fox, he has used cunning and pretense to conceal the real wolf within. Besides, he is shrouded in darkness, being a non-native to our region and of counterfeit birth....he clearly involved himself in ecclesiastical discussion and was willing to compromise, and used skilled speech and compositions....nevertheless, he did not adhere to these [unionist] views...for he undertook this ecclesiastical employment to further his own interest, as subsequent events show, certainly he treated the matter differently at the time when it was first raised. Now [as patriarch] following the prevailing wind, he is against it so as to secure his own tyrannical dignity.[55]

Evidently, some questions need to be asked concerning Gregory's role in the union negotiations of Michael VIII. What, for example, was the nature of his assignment and the compositions he is alleged to have written under Michael? Was he a unionist or was he, perhaps, a "double agent" for the Orthodox?[56] If he was a unionist did he not arouse Orthodox suspicion by leaving the pro-unionist camp in 1283? Finally, how did he himself account for the lapse, if lapse it was? To set the context for a proper evaluation of his position, a brief review of the various shades of religious opinion that had formed during the government's union negotiations is necessary.

One of the largest parties shaping Byzantine opinion at the time was composed of the traditionalists. These individuals have been variously identified as either unenlightened rigorists or reactionaries, or even as Orthodox. They were found among the monks, among the followers of Patriarch Joseph (the Josephites), and, above all, among the Arsenites. Such active but diverse members as the monk Job Iasites, John Chilas of Ephesus, and George Moschabar (the last two would later be among Gregory's major critics) were all traditionalists. Not unpredictably, the party's wide composition, distaste for compromise, and ability to mobilize public opinion explain why it became Michael's and Beccus' greatest concern.

Above all, the group was noted for its passionate adherence to the patristic tradition, and conviction that the Church should set its face against any traffic with the West inasmuch as the Latins were heretics.[57] Their position on the *Filioque*, as we should expect, was all too clear—procession was from the Father alone. That they accused the unionists of being short on patriotism and of being the very cause of division in the Church is not surprising.[58] However, there were many in this group who were willing to counsel moderation. We have already seen an eloquent exponent of this attitude in Patriarch Joseph. He was certainly less suspicious of theological speculation and would have welcomed a genuine dialogue with the West, if that were possible.

Another group, in opposition to the above, was that which advocated the practice of prudent accommodation, or *oikonomia*. Its members were to be found in some numbers in the court, and in those members of the episcopate who had accepted the terms of union early in 1274. The eight signatories of Beccus' synod of 3 May 1280 (one of the few whose minutes we possess) give us some idea of the composition of this group among the higher clergy.[59] To these eight should be added those elevated to the episcopate by Beccus.[60] On the whole, this group of moderates was not entirely convinced of the Latin's orthodoxy. Equally, they were united in their opposition to any union that would result in an interpolated creed, or a change in the Church's custom or rites. In short, they believed their position to be tenable as long as the doctrinal integrity of the Church remained unimpaired. Specifically, the concessions they were willing to make were for the benefit of the state. As Pachymeres puts it, these men were unionists in appearance only, and had agreed to union solely on a canonical (not a theological) basis. Acceptance of the right of appeal to the pope was permissible; a changed creed was not.[61]

Union under such terms was wholly unacceptable to a third group, the diehard unionists, who constituted Beccus' immediate circle. Their posture was an unqualified acknowledgment of Roman doctrine.[62] "We rightly identify the Latins as orthodox; yes, I call those of the Roman Church (I shall never cease from doing so) like-minded in faith....We accept them as brothers, as our own kin, and we embrace them as being foremost and more honorable than others."[63] Beccus himself, as we have seen, was not some secret sympathizer of the Latins; he held very pronounced views on the fundamental identity of the two traditions, even if he opposed, together with the moderates, an interpolated creed and changed customs.[64] Clearly, what was involved was more than a sense of moderation, or "exceptional tolerance," in doctrinal matters.[65] Essentially, the attitude and spirit that informed this group differed alike from the traditionalists and from the moderates. Indeed, Beccus' train of thought so alarmed those of the moderate wing, who had signed the union for political reasons, that the unionist effort was seriously jeopardized.[66]

What, then, was Gregory's standing among these parties or positions of rigorous orthodoxy, theological relativism, and determined unionism? Both Gregoras and Pachymeres confirm Metochites' claim that Gregory did indeed favor the unionist party line, and that, together with Manuel Holobolus, the rector of the patriarchal school, and Constantine Meliteniotes, the imperial archdeacon, he was commissioned by the emperor to draw up arguments in its favor.[67] From what is known of the activities of Meliteniotes, who was a unionist, it is clear that, in contrast, Gregory's and Holobolus' contribution was modest; indeed, the rector's attitude cost him a great deal of ignominy and suffering.[68] As for Gregory, we are told little other than the fact that he was a member of the commission which labored to represent the "Italians" as "blameless" in doctrinal matters.[69] Nor has his literary effort in this area, if it ever existed, survived.[70] Furthermore, certain documents which could conceivably be helpful (by their very nature and subject matter), contain nothing on the question. Thus, his *Eulogy on Michael VIII* makes no allusion whatever either to his literary activity or to the events surrounding Lyons.[71] In addition, his own personal explanation of his conduct and opposition to Michael's policy, read publicly in all the churches of the capital a fortnight after his consecration as patriarch, has not survived. This text, it should be noted, was actually a companion piece to (but separate from) the text of deposition of the unionist bishops; it was issued by the synod and read on the same day, 26 April 1283. Neither text survives.[72]

Gregory's justification, or at least the tenor of this lost document, is probably reflected in another work of his own pen, the *Eulogy on Andronicus II*, written in 1284, the year following the above-mentioned text. "And we made a decision [that of Lyons] and an agreement, but not in the spirit of God, or through his approval...and, contrary to our conviction, we went along for the duration of ten years, for which we became an example, a reproach, a joke, and a mockery to the nations and to those around us. For the decision (Oh, the shame !) changed that which was set securely, and altered the boundaries set by our fathers."[73] In short, like the young emperor, Andronicus (whose behavior during his joint rule with his father the patriarch is here trying to defend), Gregory, too, was hostile to the negotiations. The whole enterprise appeared misguided—"contrary to his convictions"—and yet, he had no choice in the matter in view of the emperor's restraining orders. Similar sentiments are expressed in his *Autobiography*, when he speaks of "innovations in theology"—an allusion to Michael's policy and, no doubt, a reasonable reflection of his own feelings at the time.[74]

On balance it seems that Gregory's shadowy allegiance to Lyons, and his suggestion that he had little choice in the matter, may be what shielded him in 1283. In view of the emotional atmosphere in the capital during the deposition of Beccus (and the punishment meted out to other unionists), it is difficult to see how he could have escaped disgrace. Given the deposition of many of the bishops at the time (there was actually some difficulty in finding non-unionist prelates to consecrate Gregory),[75] the new patriarch's past would certainly have aroused the suspicion of conservative circles. The force of popular suspicion was not yet spent. There is not, however, a shred of evidence of any storm of protest or opposition to his ordination! Again, Pachymeres notes that Gregory was present at the deposition of Beccus (8 January 1283), along with Manuel Holobolus, Patriarch Athanasius of Alexandria, and Theodore Mouzalon.[76] All were known to have had serious doubts about the wisdom of Michael's policy; Holobolus and Mouzalon were even beaten and humiliated in Michael's reign for their lack of "ardor" in the matter.[77] Athanasius, who presided, was the only one who had been complacent during those years; yet, he was in no way a die-hard unionist.[78] In short, all had cause to object to Gregory's presence. And yet, they did not.

That Gregory had credibility, and was somehow considered one of the uncompromised, is even more cogently illustrated by his relations with the Arsenites,[79] who consistently refused to recognize the official hierarchy, including the three patriarchs who had succeeded their founder, Arsenius. In their eyes, the ecumenical throne had been vacant since Arsenius' deposition in 1265. This rigorous canonical position had, as its complement, Arsenite hatred of Michael's unionist policy, which, for them, had positively compromised Orthodoxy. Evidently, any tolerance shown toward "one of Michael's principle collaborators"[80] would have been unthinkable. For all that, when the non-Arsenite and non-monastic Gregory was raised to the patriarchate, they did not object or harangue him for his unionist activity under Michael VIII. They did not even declare him guilty by association, although they would have done so had they any reservations about his past. On the whole, their silence on the matter was as much the result of Gregory's deft diplomacy in handling them as the fact that they did not think of him exclusively as a thoroughgoing sympathizer of union.

Finally, it is also expressly stated in the sources that Gregory, who had been ordained reader by Patriarch Joseph, had this patriarch's personal blessing, and, indeed, numbered among his admirers many Josephites.[81] This, again, would serve to indicate that people did not think of him in terms of unionism. And yet, just as he cannot be identified exclusively with the Arsenites, neither can he be described exclusively as a Josephite.[82] Significant, too is the fact that his successor. St Athanasius—an implacable adversary of Rome—had no doubts about Gregory's election to the patriarchate or his right to that throne; indeed, he is quite articulate on this very point.[83] Had Gregory been convinced of the wisdom of the Union of Lyons, as were the unionists, he would not have been able to escape either Athanasius' or Joseph's condemnation, let alone that of the Arsenites.

It is not accurate to look upon Gregory as the ardent unionist turned redcoat, as Metochites and Beccus insist. True, he was, like Beccus, receptive to union, but here the similarity stops. Whereas Beccus was willing to accept a union negotiated in fear, Gregory was not. On the contrary, he was convinced that this type of union was the great collective illusion of his day. This, in fact, is the implicit and explicit motif of all his major works; it explains his passionate and articulate opposition. Gregory became increasingly aware, particularly after 1283, that union would have to be "in the spirit of God," that is, it would have to be based on a free dialogue or a negotiated agreement.

It would be faulty reasoning to give a false impression of a complex situation by conflating Gregory's position before and after 1283. Even so, what he had to say on Lyons, on unionism, and, especially, on the *Filioque* issue after 1283 must be taken into consideration. It will give a fuller portrait of Gregory, and may possibly shed light on his freedom of movement immediately after Michael's death. Unlike many of his ultra-conservative contemporaries, Gregory, while patriarch, was unwilling merely to isolate or fossilize formulas; he could not see how the formal repetition, coordination, and systematization of patristic loci constituted theology. He was, in simple terms, far from content with the argument from authority. That kind of rigorism, he recognized, blocked any genuine dialogue. This explains his determination to face the issue squarely, and find a solution that would satisfy both sides—the hardy conservatives as well as Beccus' radical unionist circle. If, indeed, the doctrine of procession "from the Father alone" was incontrovertible (as the traditionalists argued), then the phrase "through the Son" (the battle cry of the unionists) had also to be justified theologically. After all, the unionists were claiming, that the patristic expression "through the Son" was simply the Greek Fathers' shorthand way of summarizing the *Filioque*.

It is within this framework that Gregory's thought finds much of its historical attraction. It is to his credit to have recognized in the *Tomus* that the patristic evidence cannot be reduced solely to Photius' exclusive formulation "from the Father alone." His solution was to resolve the impasse in terms of an eternal manifestation (ἔκφανσις ἀΐδιος) of the Spirit through the Son. It was a formulation that was both seminal and original. At any rate, in Byzantine theological literature, there is probably no text like the *Tomus*, in which the Byzantine assessment and solution of one of the richest phrases in the Greek patristic vocabulary is so impressively stated. This said, the patriarch cannot be seen as the blind enemy of Beccus. That he labored—allegedly out of sheer jealousy—to outdo his doctrinal adversary is a possible interpretation.[84] A more careful investigation, however, indicates that the *raison d'être* for Gregory's theology has deeper roots. It cannot be dismissed as peripheral.

Gregory's interpretation is admittedly intricate and difficult to understand. (As we shall see, his contemporaries had a similar difficulty.) A comprehensive and systematic analysis of his theology has never been attempted. It is obviously easier to maintain a hostile posture toward Gregory, to repeat Beccus invective that Gregory was being pseudo-scientific,[85] to reduce his doctrine of the eternal manifestation into a "meaningless expression" by intentionally repeating contemporary Arsenite argument,[86] or to arrive at the comforting conclusion that the unionist position has never been refuted by its critics, either then or since.[87] But such conclusions would be true only if we ignore the patriarch's scrupulous reading of the Fathers, his incisive rejoinder in the *Tomus*, and his teaching on the real distinction between procession and manifestation, essence and energy.[88]

And yet, in a very real sense, it is Beccus' theological competence which is wanting. Certainly he made a concerted effort to bring into agreement the numerous Greek patristic texts, which spoke of the Spirit's procession "through the Son," with the Latin *Filioque*. At the same time, he proposed that the former was the patristic systematization of the Latin doctrine. He argued in point of fact that the different trinitarian expressions "from the Father through the Son" and "from the Father and the Son" were identical; the Greek and Latin Fathers were in complete agreement. However this willingness to accommodate the two traditions, which, for him, were neither exclusive nor contradictory, was neither ingenious nor a solution to the problem. In the final analysis, it was little more than a compilation of patristic proof-texts in favor of the Latin view, a compromise rather than a solution. The boy wonder of late-Byzantine theology was, for the most part, an "anthologist." This being so, it is not surprising that, at Blachernae, Gregory went to some pains to impress upon his opponent the danger of handling quotations apart from their correct interpretation.[89] As he noted elsewhere, the theologian cannot lay violent hands on a text—on the assumption of correspondence—and proceed to apply it to that which is inapplicable.[90]

Beccus was equally unable to grasp the deeper dimensions of the division between East and West. Fundamentally, his views were an attempt to downgrade the basic dogmatic difference between the two traditions. For these, according to him, in no way compromised the unity of the faith. Indeed, the difference was over a matter of words, not over substance.[91] This, in fact, was the origin of the schism.[92] Curiously, the major role which the progressive growth of papal authority played in the separation is never mentioned in any of his writings, nor is the question of papal primacy ever discussed. Finally, we should note that Beccus' view, which has been described as "an approach of the greatest importance,"[93] always remained a minority view. Even in the fourteenth century when unionism became a constant feature of the Byzantine landscape, it never once constituted a movement within the Byzantine Church, but was only the conversion of certain Orthodox to Catholicism.[94] Beccus' speculations never entered the mainstream of Byzantine medieval theology. By contrast, Gregory's formulations were eventually absorbed by hesychasm in the fourteenth century.

Present scholarly opinion on Gregory justifies itself by the exclusion of Gregory's name from the *Synodicon*, by the hesitation and lack of unanimity on the part of some bishops regarding the *Tomus*, by the rear-guard action he had to wage against reactionary currents (for whom the door to innovation and change was closed), and by the opposition of the Arsenites, George Moschabar, his student Mark, and the bishop of Ephesus. No amount of theological subtlety, no softening of the dark side of the picture, can mask what is amply documented by the sources. (At one point, before the celebration of the liturgy at the Hagia Sophia, Gregory actually despaired of his own safety and had to ask for police protection against the pro-Arsenite crowds![95]) All this, as we should expect, has cast a shadow on Gregory's theological achievement.

None of these developments actually supports the routine blanket condemnation of Patriarch Gregory and his theology. As we shall see, even the omission of Gregory's name from the catalogue of patriarchs has its explanation. Likewise, it is necessary to stress that most of the shadows in Gregory's career were *atheological* in nature. As one writer summed it up, "envy would not allow success to this excellent bishop of God, who governed the Church with such care and intensity of spirit, and the opposition slandered this fine shepherd who eventually relinquished the ship's rudder and resigned his throne."[96] In short, theological considerations do not always explain Gregory's stormy patriarchate. It is surely significant that the formal theological decision of 1285 was actually never reversed and survived all opposition. Nor did Gregory accept stepping down and resigning on any grounds other than the non-theological reasons he himself gave. Significantly, his opponents accepted this condition.

It is ultimately within this framework that Gregory's commitment to union—either before or after 1283—must be located. His attempt to solve the *Filioque* must be seen in this light. Unlike Beccus (who saw it only as a trifle in the path of dogmatic reconciliation), Gregory realized that the doctrine was, in fact, an absolute obstacle and the cause of the schism. It was because of this obstacle that the Latins "were, from the beginning, accused by our Church, and for which the schism occurred."[97] In the end, the solution was not to minimize the doctrinal differences, but to solve them; otherwise, any union—without genuine dialogue—was doomed to failure. This is why, in his judgment, Lyons was a "worthless union" and a "misleading accommodation."[98] In summary, Gregory was receptive to union—this was always his position both before and after he became patriarch. Redcoat, he was not; that is a label he would have disowned.

As for Gregory's ambition, it should be noted that Pachymeres does not see anything unusual in Gregory's elevation to the patriarchate in 1283. To say that Gregory prudently cast his lot for the restoration of Orthodoxy in order to be on the winning side and to gain the patriarchate, or to "secure his own tyrannical dignity," is to read what is not there. Nor does the historian ever emphasize Gregory's love of power, or the fact that he owed his "usurpation" to the Arsenites(!), as Metochites declares.[99] On the contrary, a focus of Pachymeres' narrative of Gregory's years as patriarch is the disquieting effect the new patriarch's theology had on the unionists.[100] One wonders if this is not the root cause of their campaign to defame him. There is, further, the fact that Pachymeres' portrait of Gregory is confirmed by Gregory's own conviction that he was "shoved" on the patriarchal throne.[101] He did not covet, as he wrote elsewhere, the exercise of "envied authority," or the leadership with which God had visited him.[102] This he said to Methodius, who had taken him to task for his collaborative work under Michael, and for his attempts to bring about the reconciliation of the Arsenites. Of course, this may be the well-worn theme of humility so dear to the medieval mind; and yet, we are struck by the intensity and sincerity of this particular exchange with his correspondent. Gregory was, by temperament, a scholar who prized tranquillity, which he knew would be shattered on his elevation in 1283.

This is not to say that Gregory was totally free of faults. Pachymeres is aware of them, as is Gregory himself. Gregory, for example, notes his impatience with those who would abuse him. "I do not rejoice in power or in the use of violence.... nevertheless, should anyone attempt to injure me, I would not easily endure it."[103] Nor was he always ready to listen, as his relations with the Arsenites indicate.[104] And then, too, his choice of friends was seldom fortunate. Again, his impatience with mediocrity is often very glaring. His evaluation of Moschabar or Gerasimus of Heracleia was far from flattering; and his remarks on Methodius' attempts to write classical Greek—"a gingerbread Demosthenes"—are as revealing for their vanity as for their lack of charity.[105] Gregory certainly suffered from many of the limitations of his class, and yet, he could be tolerant and charitable. Nor was he always impatient. One of Gregory's longest letters is addressed to the above-named friend Methodius, the monk whose continuous attacks the patriarch had to endure.[106] Railing against and abusing others (particularly those who have never harmed us), writes the patriarch, is seldom becoming to a monk; no doubt, your wicked tongue, which will remove you from the love of God and men, will continue to spread its poison. Nevertheless, the patriarch concluded by noting that he had no intention of persecuting or harassing Methodius. Indeed, the patriarch abandoned any attempt at defending himself against the accusations of his friend and made no effort to stop him.

In conclusion, the hollowness of Metochites' shrill rhetoric and Beccus' offensive against the "Cypriot upstart" should be laid to rest, if not qualified. Surely, their portrait is inconsistent not only with independent evidence, but also with what we know of Gregory's own temperament, teaching, and activity both before and after 1283. Finally, it is worth emphasizing that Gregory cannot be pegged down to any one party line, whether it be that of the unionists, the moderates, the intransigent traditionalists, the Josephites, or the Arsenites.[107] Earlier, it was noted that Gregory's contribution to the vigorous ascetical and spiritual revival paralleled the classical renaissance. In effect, it is in the years of his patriarchate, and not before, that both of these movements first picked up momentum and came into full swing.[108] Gregory's kinship is more with these "trends," to which he made major contributions, than with any group mentioned above. More to the point, we cannot label or place Gregory in some neatly circumscribed compartment. The reality was more untidy. Such is the way of history (and of theology, for that matter).

NOTES

1.   No attempt is made here to give a detailed biography of Gregory. Only such factors and events are stressed which help in understanding the years of his patriarchate, and which helped mold the man who was to ascend the patriarchal throne in 1283. For brief biographical material with bibliographies, consult the following: *Threskeutike kai Ethike Enkyklopaideia*, 4 (Athens, 1964), cols. 731-34 (S. G. Papadopoulos); *DTC*, 6, pt. I (Paris, 1920), cols. 1231-35 (F. Cayré); *Dictionnaire de Spiritualité*, 6 (Paris, 1967), cols. 922-23 (J. Darrouzès); W. Lameere, *La tradition manuscrite de la correspondance de Grégoire de Chypre* (Brussels Paris, 1937) pp. 1-3, and n. I; A. F. von Pauly and G. Wissowa (edd.), *Real-Encyclopädie der classischen Altertumswissenschaft*, 7 (Stuttgart, 1912), cols. 1852-57; and T. Voigtländer, "Gregor von Cypern. Aus der Kirchen- und Schulgeschichte des 13. Jahrhunderts," *Zeitschrift für die historische Theologie*, 43 (1873), 449-62.

2.   *Eulogy on Michael VIII*, in J.-F. Boissonade, *Anecdota Graeca e codibus regiis*, I (Paris, 1829), 353-54 (πλατυσμὸς ἐπιστήμης, ἀναβίωσις, ὡς εἰπεῖν, λόγων).

3.   Edited by S. Eustratiades, *Ekklesiastikos Pharos*, I (1908), 77-108, 409-39; 2 (1908), 195-211; 3 (1909), 5-48, 281-86; 4 (1909), 5-29, 97-128; 5 (1910), 213-26, 339-52, 444-52, 489-500; this is a partial edition only (197 letters). Cf. Lameere, *La tradition manuscrite*, pp.197-203, who lists 242 letters for the original collection. An incomplete listing is included in *PG* 142.421-31; F. Fatouros, "Textkritische Beobachtungen zu den Briefen des Gregorios

Kyprios," *Rivista di Studi Byzantini e Neoellenici,* N.S. 12-13 (1975-1976), 109-16. See the useful remarks of J. Darrouzès, *Recherches sur les* Ὀφφίκια *de l'Église byzantine* (Paris, 1970), 454-56. The three other major collections of letters by patriarchs are those of Photius, Nicholas I, and Gregory's contemporary and successor, Athanasius I. For Gregory's other compositions, see the old but useful description of G. A. Fabricius, *Bibliotheca Graeca sive notitia scriptorum veterum Graecorum,* VIII (Hamburg, 1802), 57-62. Unlike Lameere, M. Treu (who wanted to publish a systematic edition of the letters) and Eustratiades (their first editor) do not seem have known the exact number of the letters, or the principal manuscripts involved.

4. Lameere, *La tradition manuscrite,* is an exhaustive study of the manuscript tradition of this important dossier preserved in some 32 manuscripts (six are lost); see the review of this "model study" by R. Guilland, *BZ,* 40 (1940), 461-64.

5. Ed. Eustratiades, *Ekklesiastikos Pharos,* I (1908), 415-16 (letter 9); cf. the description of late-thirteenth-century literary society by I. Ševcenko, "Theodore Metochites, the Chora, and the Intellectual Trends of His Time," in P. A. Underwood (ed.), *The Kariye Djami,* IV (Princeton, 1975), 23: "...this was a society whose members loved books, professed an insatiable thirst for knowledge, and showed it in their actions."

6. The numbering here is from Lameere, *La tradition manuscrite,* p. 200. Eustratiades' division is necessarily different, since his is only a partial edition; the patriarchal dossier of his edition begins with letter 115, *Ekklesiastikos Pharos,* 3 (1909), 47.

7. A. Garzya, "Observations sur l'Autobiographie de Grégoire de Chypre," *in Praktika tou Protou Diethnous Kyprologikou Synedriou,* II (Leucosia, 1972), 36. The *Autobiography* is edited with a French translation in Lameere, *La tradition manuscrite,* pp. 176-91. See also the valuable commentary of Rubeis, *Vita,* cols. 17-220, and J. Irmscher, "Autobiographien in der byzantinischen Literatur," *Studia Byzantina,* II (Berlin, 1973) (= Berliner byzantinistische Arbeiten, 44), 3-11.

8. *Autobiography,* in Lameere, *La tradition manuscrite,* p. 187; see G. Misch, "Ein Patriarch von Konstantinopel über seinen Bildungsgang," in *Geschichte der Autobiographie,* III, pt. 2 (Frankfurt am Main, 1962), 892-903; idem, *Zeitschrift für Geschichte der Erziehung und des Unterrichts,* 21 (1931), 1-16.

9. For the use of the *Autobiography* as an introduction to his letters, cf. the patriarch's letter to his former student, friend, and first minister of the empire, Theodore Mouzalon, ed. Eustratiades, *Ekklesiastikos Pharos,* 4 (1909), 113 (letter 155); and Lameere, *La tradition manuscrite,* p. 9.

10. F. Fuchs, *Die höheren Schulen von Konstantinopel im Mittelalter* (Leipzig, 1926), pp. 54ff; L. Brehier, "L'enseignement classique et l'enseignement religieux à Byzance," *Revue d'histoire et de philosophie religieuses,* 21 (1941), 34-69; idem, "Notes sur l'histoire de l'enseignement supérieur à Constantinople," *Byzantion,* 3 (1926-1927), 73-94; F. Schemmel, "Die Schulen von Konstantinopel von 12.-15. Jahrhundert," *Berliner philologische Wochenschrift,* XXV, 236, No. 8 (1925), 236-39.

11. *Autobiography,* in Lameere, *La tradition manuscrite,* p. 177. On the date of his birth, see Rubeis, *Vita,* col. 34C; Darrouzès, "Grégoire II," *Dictionnaire de Spiritualité,* 6: 922.

12. Pachymeres, II, 88-89; similar thoughts are echoed by Metochites, VIII, pt. 2, 36-37, quoted below, p. 44.

13. Pachymeres, II, 89.

14. *Autobiography*, in Lameere, *La tradition manuscrite*, p. 179; Rubeis, *Vita*, col. 34D.

15. G. Hill, *A History of Cyprus*, III (Cambridge, 1948), 1067 (with references).

16. *Autobiography*, in Lameere, *La tradition manuscrite*, p. 179.

17. Ibid.; Fuchs, *Die höheren Schulen*, p. 55.

18. *Autobiography*, in Lameere, *La tradition manuscrite*, p. 181. For the identification of Anae, a port near Ephesus, see W. Müller-Wiener, "Mittelalterliche Befestigungen im südlichen Jonien: III, Kadikalesi (Anaia) und Kusadasi (Scalanova)," *Istanbuler Mitteilungen*, 11 (1961), 65-85.

19. *Autobiography*, in Lameere, *La tradition manuscrite*, p. 181; cf. H. Hunger, "Von Wissenschaft und Kunst der frühen Paläologenzeit," *Jahrbuch der Österreichischen byzantinischen Gesellschaft*, 8 (1959), 126.

20. This suggestion was made by M. Angold, *A Byzantine Government in Exile* (Oxford, 1975), p. 32. On his family's poverty, see Gregory's letter to Theodore Mouzalon, ed. Eustratiades, *Ekklesiastikos Pharos*, 4 (1909), 22-24 (letter 136).

21. *Autobiography*, in Lameere, *La tradition manuscrite*, p. 183.

22. Eulogy on Michael VIII, in Boissonade, *Anecdota Graeca*, I, 352. See, however, Ševcenko, "Theodore Metochites," 24*n*31, who believes this dearth of knowledge, as reported by Gregory, should not be taken as an absolute rule, even if there must have been something to the revival under Michael VIII.

23. Edited in *Dossier de Lyon*, pp. 518-27. The letter (dated 1286-1288) was previously unknown, except for the brief quotations in V. Laurent, "Héraclée du Pont: Métropole et ses titulaires (1232/50-1287)," *EO*, 31 (1932), 321-22. See Gregory's answer to Methodius, ed. Eustratiades, *Ekklesiastikos Pharos*, 4 (1909), 108-109 (letter 152); Laurent, *Regestes*, no. 1535 (no date given).

24. Dossier de Lyon, p. 521.

25. Autobiography, in Lameere, *La tradition manuscrite*, p. 185. Acropolites is also mentioned in Gregory's *Eulogy on Michael VIII*: see Boissonade, *Anecdota Graeca*, I, 352. See also R. Magdalino, "A Translation and Commentary on George Acropolites' History" (diss. King's College, University of London, 1978), pp. 29ff.

26. Autobiography, in Lameere, *La tradition manuscrite*, p. 185; see also Nicephorus Blemmydes in A. Heisenberg (ed.), *Curriculum vitae et carmina* (Leipzig, 1896), xxii-xxiii; Fuchs, *Die höheren Schulen*, p. 56.

27. *Autobiography*, in Lameere, *La tradition manuscrite*, p. 187.

28. A. Sopko, "Gregory of Cyprus: A Study of Church and Culture in Late Thirteenth Century Byzantium" (diss., King's College, University of London, 1979), ch. II.

29. Pachymeres, I, 283-84; quoted in M. Treu, "Manuel Holobolos," *BZ*, 5 (1896), 543. Fuchs, *Die höheren Schulen*, p. 58; see also K. Vogel's chapter on Byzantine science in J. M. Hussey (ed.), *The Cambridge Medieval History*, IV, pt. 2 (Cambridge, 1967), 275, who notes (

following Pachymeres) that the orphanage was basically a grammar school. The appointment was made under Patriarch Germanus (1265/1266).

30. The sources are stingy in yielding any concrete information on this school's status. Thus, Darrouzès, *Recherches sur les* Ὀφφίκια, p. 111, is critical of H.-G. Beck, *Kirche und theologische Literatur im byzantinischen Reich* (Munich, 1959), p. 704, for using the title "rector of the patriarchal school": "Sommes-nous informés de l'existence et du statut de cette école?" Actually, the title was used earlier by V. Laurent, "Un polémiste grec de la fin du XIIIe siècle: La vie et les ceuvres de Georges Moschabar, *EO*, 28 (1929), 133n6. For the early period, the school's existence is upheld by R. Browning, "The Patriarchal School at Constantinople in the Twelfth Century," *Byzantion*, 32 (1962), 176-77.

31. Ed. Eustratiades, *Ekilesiastikos Pharos*, 3 (1909) 288-90 (letter 122); letter 96 is also addressed to Holobolus, ibid., 3:29.

32. K. M. Setton, "The Byzantine Background to the Italian Renaissance," *Proceedings of the American Philosophical Society*, 100, No. 1 (1956), 23.

33. For Gregory's style, see Ševcenko, "Theodore Metochites," 21-22.

34. Gregoras, 1, 163; Ephraem, *Imperatorum et Patriarcharum recensus*, ed. I. Bekker (Bonn, 1840), p. 414 (lines 10,333-346); see also Nicephorus Chumnus' enthusiastic praise of Gregory in Boissonade, *Anecdota Graeca*, III, 367-69. For the Byzantine tendency to Attic archaism with reference to Gregory, see E. Kriaras, "Diglossie des derniers siècles de Byzance: Naissance de la littérature néo-hellénique," *Proceedings of the XIIIth International Congress of Byzantine Studies* (London, 1967), 283-99.

35. See his letter 20 ed. Eustratiades, *Ekklesiastikos Pharos*, I (1908), 422-23: "Whoever delivers the books should look for us not at the archives—he will not find us there—but at the monastery of the Savior, also called the Incomprehensible, where we live. If, after this, he is still lost, he should go to the great monastery of the Pantocrator and inquire either for George of Cyprus, or for the monastery. In any case, we are neighbors with Pantocrator and are known to the community for many years." See also the preface by V. Laurent, "Le quadrivium et la formation intellectuelle sous les Paléologues," in P. Tannery, *Quadrivium de Georges Pachymère* (= Studi e Testi, 94 [1940]), xixn5; on the identification of the monastery of the Incomprehensible with Kalenderhane, see the reservations of C. Striker and Y. D. Kuban, "Work at Kalenderhane Camii in Istanbul: First Preliminary Report," *Dumbarton Oaks Papers*, 21 (1965), 267; C. Wendel, "Planudea," *BZ*, 40 (1940), 408-409. See also Laurent, "Un polémiste grec," 133.

36. On the office of "prime minister" (μέγας λογοθέτης) in the empire, see R. Guilland, "Les logothètes: Études sur l'histoire administrative de l'Empire byzantin," *REB*, 29 (1971), 5-115, esp. 106-10; and V. Laurent, "Notes de titulature byzantine 4: Le logothète du trésor sous les premiers Paléologues," *EO*, 38 (1939), 368-70. On Chumnus' intellectual formation, see J. Verpeaux, *Nicéphore Choumnos homme d'État et humaniste byzantin* (ca. 1250/1255-1327) (Paris, 1959), 27-33; for Mouzalon, see Gregory's letter addressed to him, ed. Eustratiades, *Ekklesiastikos Pharos*, 2 (1908), 204 (letter 60), and ibid., 3:27 (letter 91); see also Beck, *Kirche und theologische Literatur*, pp. 679-80. The chronology of Mouzalon's career, and particularly his death in the spring of 1294, is discusses by J. Verpeaux, "Notes chronologiques sur les livres II et III d'Andronico Paléologo de Pachymère," *REB*, 17 (1959), 168-70.

37. S. Runciman, *The Last Byzantine Renaissance* (Cambridge, 1970), p. 59; Beck, *Kirche und theologische Literatur*, pp. 686-87, W. O. Schmitt "Lateinische Literatur in Byzanz: Die Übersetzungen des Maximus Planudes und die moderne Forschung," *Jahrbuch der Österreichischen byzantinischen Gesellschaft*, 17 (1968), 127-47.

38. Gregoras, I, 178. For Gregory's correspondence with the princess, most of which is unedited, see S. Kugeas, "Zur Geschichte der Münchener Thykydides-handschrift Augustanus F," *BZ*, 16 (1907), 588-609. See Ševčenko, "'Theodore Metochites," 22n21, for a criticism of Kugeas' edition of one of Gregory's letters to the lady. The Eustratiades canon contains only three of the eighteen letters sent to Raoulaina: *Ekklesiastikos Pharos*, 5 (1910), 450-52, 489-90 (letters 187, 188, 189). For a brief sketch, see D. M. Nicol, *The Byzantine Family of Kantakouzenos (Cantacuzenus) ca. 1100-1460* (Washington, D.C., 1968), pp. 16-19; and R. Guilland, *Recherches sur les institutions byzantines*, I (Berlin, 1967) (= Berliner byzantinistische Arbeiten, 35), 224; and S. Phassoulakes, *The Byzantine Family of Raoul-Ral(l)es* (Athens 1973), pp 25-27.

39. Autobiography, in Lameere, *La tradition manuscrite*, p. 189.

40. Pachymeres, II, 42; for a description of the office, see pseudo-Kodinos, *Traité des Offices*, ed. J. Verpeaux (Paris, 1966), pp. 193-94; Rubeis, *Vita*, cols. 56-58.

41. V. Laurent, "Les signataires du second synode des Blakhernes (été 1285)," *EO*, 26 (1927), 129-30; cf. also idem, "Grégoire X (1271-1276) et le projet d'une ligue antiturque," *EO*, 37 (1938), 272.

42. It should be added that, despite their insistently parochial concerns, Andronicus and the Byzantine population were keenly aware of the Turkish danger, a fact attested by the emperor's personal four-year sojourn in Anatolia (1290-1293), and now forcefully underscored by A. Laiou, *Constantinople and the Latins: The Foreign Policy of Andronicus II 1282-1328* (Cambridge, Mass., 1972), p. 22. This concern for Anatolia is described by Laiou as the single greatest difference between the emperor, Andronicus, and his father Michael, and was the "backbone of Andronicus' foreign policy." George Metochites, X, pt. I, 327-30, argues that the emperor's purpose in going to Asia Minor was to speak with the exiled unionist leaders. This is only partially true, of course; see Laiou, *Constantinople and the Latins*, pp. 76-77. Again, the claim that Orthodoxy at this time had become virtually synonymous with Byzantine "nationalism," much like "papal" with "Frankish," needs to be qualified. The term "nationalism" is not only inapplicable in the context of thirteenth-century Byzantium, it is incompatible with the new territorial, judicial, and universalist position that the patriarchate eventually assumed in the fourteenth century.

43. On Theoleptus, see J. Meyendorff, "Spiritual Trends in Byzantium in the Late Thirteenth and Early Fourteenth Centuries," in *The Kariye Djami*, IV, 95ff.; idem, *Introduction à l'étude de Grégoire Palamas* (Paris, 1959), ch. I; see also below, p. 168. On Athanasius, see R. Guilland "La correspondence inédite d'Athanase, patriarche de Constantinople (1289-1293; 1304-1310)," *Mélanges Charles Diehl*, I (Paris, 1930), 121-40; also N. Banescu, "Le patriarche Athanase I et Andronic II Paléologue, état religieux, politique et social de l'Empire," *Académie Roumaine. Bulletin de la Section Historique*, 23 (Bucharest, 1942), 28-56; and A.-M. Maffry Talbot, "The Patriarch Athanasius (1289-1293; 1303-1309) and the Church," *Dumbarton Oaks Papers*, 27 (1973), 13-28; and now idem, *The Correspondence of Athanasius I, Patriarch of Constantinople: Letters to the Emperor Andronicus, Members of the Imperial Family, and Officials* (Washington, D.C., 1975).

44. Cf. Darrouzès, "Grégoire II," 922.

45. D. Knowles aud D. Obolensky, *The Middle Ages*. II: *The Christian Centuries: A New History of the Catholic Church*, edd. L. Rogier et al. (Freiburg, 1968),326.

46. Meyendorff, *Introduction à l'étude de Palamas*, pp. 25ff. One of the first scholars to make the link between Gregory II and Palamas was the Italian Dominican Bernard M. de Rubeis (1687-1775); see *Vita*, cols. 110C, 138C.

47. For a similar problem with another "forerunner," Athanasius, see Talbot, *The Correspondence of Athanasius I*, p. xxix: "Nor is there any hint in his writings that he was a forerunner of hesychasm, or a master of the 'psycho-technical ' method of prayer, as he is described by Gregory Palamas." The problem is also discussed by J. Boojamra, "The Ecclesiastical Reforms of Patriarch Athanasius of Constantinople (1289-1293; 1303-1309)" (diss., Fordham University, 1976), pp. 199 201.

48. See below, Ch. 8.

49. Verpeaux, *Nicéphore Choumnos*, p. 181; Meyendorff, "Spiritual Trends in Byzantium," 96. See also A. Tuilier, "Recherches sur les origines de la Renaissance byzantine au XIIIe siècle," *Bulletin de l'Association Guillaume Budé*, 3 (1955), 75; see also N. G.Wilson, "The Church and Classical Studies in Byzantium," *Antike und Abendland*, 16 (190), 68ff.

50. These monastic schools, a development of thirteenth-century Byzantine education, were separate from the state university and the patriarchal school, both of which were reopened under Michael VIII.

51. J. Meyendorff, "Society and Culture in the Fourteenth Century: Religious Problems," *XIVe Congrès International des Études Byzantines. Rapports,* I (Bucharest, 1971), 56.

52. See F. Vernet, "IIe Concile œcuménique de Lyon," *DTC*, 9, pt. 1 (Paris, 1926), col. 1388: "Il n'est pas douteux non plus que les évêques étaient libres de résister au désir impérial."

53. H. Evert-Kapessowa, Une page de l'histoire des relations byzantino-latines, II: La fin de l'union de Lyon," *BS*, 17 (1956), 11.

54. Cayré, "Georges de Chypre," *DTC*, 6, pt. I (Paris, 1920), col. 1231.

55. Metochites, VIII, pt. 2, 36-37. Gregory's friend Methodius also accuses Gregory of collaboration and partisanship, but the terms and the frame of reference are entirely different; see *Dossier de Lyon*, p. 521.

56. Dossier de Lyon, p. 91.

57. See Beccus, *On the Union of the Churches of Old and New Rome, PG* 141.24A.

58. See George Metochites' account, in C. Giannelli, "Le récit d'une mission diplomatique de Georges le Métochite et le Vat. Gr. 1716, in H. Laurent, *Le Bienheureux Innocent V (Pierre de Tarentaise) et son temps* (= Studi e Testi, 129 [1947]), p.424- See also, for their attitude, the letter attributed to Athanasius of Alexandria, in *Dossier de Lyon*, pp.338-45, and 41-45 (editor's comments).

59. Mansi, XXIV, cols. 365-73 (= *PG* 141.281-89); see also V. Grumel, "Le IIe concile de Lyon et la réunion de l'église grecque," *DTC*, 9, pt. 1 (Paris, 1926), col. 1400.

60. Beccus, *De depositione sua. Oratio I, PG* 141.965A-B.

61. Pachymeres, I, 480; the historian's comments are borne out by the deliberately vague and imprecise language (in which these bishops couched the concessions they made on the primacy and the rights of the Holy See) of their letter to the pope in 1274; see above, p. 22-3.

62. The rise of the unionist movement—Λατινοφρονία—is more accurately dated to Beccus than to Nicephorus Blemmydes (his contemporary), or to Nicetas of Maroneia in the twelfth century: both Blemmydes and Nicetas have often been considered for the honor; see M. Jugie, *Le Schisme byzantin: Aperçu historique et doctrinal* (Paris, 1941), p. 254. Cf. the review of this work by A. Michel, *BZ*, 45 (1952), 408-17. Evert-Kapessowa, "Une page de l'histoire des relations byzantino-latines, II," 1, states that the traditionalists were recruited from the monks, the peasants, and the small landowners, while the unionists came from the great wealthy landowners eager to preserve their property and perpetuate feudalism. In view of the actual composition of the two groups, this sociological distinction is untenable. See especially Laiou, *Constantinople and the Latins*, p. 21.

63. Constantine Meliteniotes, *On the Procession of the Holy Spirit Through the Son. Oration I, PG* 141.1041D, 1044A

64. Beccus' *professio fidei* of 1277 contains an unconditional acceptance of the *Filioque*: see the text in A. Theiner and F. Miklosich (edd.), *Monumenta spectantia ad unionem ecclesiarum graecae et romanae* (Vienna, 1872), p.26; Latin translation in F. M. Delorme and A. L. Tautu, *Acta Romanorum pontificum ab Innocentio V ad Benedictum XI (127-1304)* (Pontificia commissio ad redigendum codicem iuris canonici orientalis, Fontes, series III, vol. 5, tom. II; Vatican City, 1954), no. 18, p. 39.

65. As has been suggested by H. Evert-Kappesowa, "Une page de l'histoire des relations byzantino-latines: Le clergé byzantin et l'union de Lyon (1274-1282)," *BS*, 13 (1952-1953), 74-76; B. Roberg, *Die Union zwischen der griechischen und der lateinischen Kirche auf dem II. Konzil von Lyon* (Bonn, 1964), 113n47, also objects to this interpretation, and insists that Beccus had, in fact, accepted the *Filioque*.

66. Cf. the tense atmosphere in one synod described by Pachymeres, I, 483, 479; on the factions in Beccus' circle, see M. Sotomayor, "El patriarca Becos, según Jorge Paquimeres (semblanza histórica)," *Estudios Eclesiásticos*, 31 (1957), 336.

67. Pachymeres, I, 374; Gregoras, I, 130; Metochites, VIII, pt. 2, 36-37. Rubeis, *Vita*, col. 66B.

68. Pachymeres, I, 394; see Treu, "Manuel Holobolos," 545; A. Heisenberg, *Aus der Geschichte und Literatur der Paläologenzeit* (Munich, 1920),pp. 112-14.

69. Pachymeres, I, 378-79.

70. The titles of documents 4 and 7 (a declaration of loyalty to Michael VIII by the ἄρχοντες of the imperial palace, and an imperial chrysobull about union), published recently by J. Gill, "The Church Union of the Council of Lyon (1274) Portrayed in Greek Documents," *OCP*, 40 (1974), 12-19, 32-35, and *Dossier de Lyon*, pp. 315-19, 475-77, indicate that they were composed by one "Cypriot." The two compositions were, no doubt, written in the seventies. The titles, however, were not part of the original and were written later, either by their compiler or by the scribe. Hence, to attribute them to Gregory is unwise. Their largely formal, non-theological content further increases the difficulty of identification. J. Darrouzès, in *Dossier de Lyon*, p. 23, ingenuously suggested that Gregory's ex-archivist and sworn opponent, George Moschabar, may be responsible for their publication.

71. Boissonade, *Anecdota Graeca,* I, 313-58; Verpeaux, *Nicéphore Choumnos,* p. 35, suggests that this is explained by the fact that the *Eulogy* was written before 1274.

72. Metochites, VIII, pt. 2, 103, 104. I follow Laurent, *Regestes,* no. 1463, who argues that the patriarch's apology was read in the churches along with the deposition, but was not an appendix, nor was it incorporated in the synodal deposition. Grumel, "Le IIe Concile de Lyon," cols. 1404-1405, hypothesized that it was an appendix to the deposition and was lost in the course of the manuscript tradition; moreover, he identified the deposition with the text published by S. Pétridès, "Sentence synodique contre le clergé unioniste (1283)," *EO,* 14 (1911), 133-36.

73. Boissonade, *Anecdota Graeca,* I, 381.

74. *Autobiography,* in Lameere, *La tradition manuscrite,* p. 187.

75. Pachymeres, II, 22-23, 42-45; Gregoras, I, 163-65.

76. Pachymeres II, 25

77. Ibid., I, 496,394

78. See below, p. 123.

79. Cf. Troitskij, *Arsenij,* esp. pp. 231-32. For further discussion and bibliography on this movement, see below, p. 68.

80. *Dossier de Lyon,* p. 91

81. Pachymeres, I, 43; II, 152; see also Metochites, VIII, pt. 2, 96-97, who, however, sees such friendship as part of Gregory's grand strategy to secure his candidacy to the patriarchal throne; Troitskij, *Arsenij,* 232; Rubeis, *Vita,* cols. 56D-58C.

82. Pachymeres, II, 720 (glossarium of P. Possinus). See also the letter of Methodius, a Josephite, who reproaches Gregory, while patriarch, for his favoritism of the Arsenites, in *Dossier de Lyon,* pp. 518ff. A second letter, known only from the patriarch's rejoinder, ed. Eustratiades, *Ekklesiastikos Pharos,* 5 (1910), 221 (letter 171), contained similar accusations.

83. Talbot, *The Correspondence of Athanasius I,* pp. 6, 303 (letters 2 and 115). True, he refers once to his predecessor as the "impious George" for his activity under Michael; however, his implacable attitude toward anything Latin explains this.

84. As is believed by Cayré, "Georges de Chypre," col. 1231; cf. the derisory approach of M. Candal, "Nueva Interpretación del 'per Filium' de los Padres Griegos," *OCP,* 31 (1965), 5, 10.

85. See E. Candal, "Progresso dogmatico nelle definizioni trinitarie del Concilio II di Lione e del Fiorentino," *Divinitas,* 5, fasc. 2 (1966), 338: "l'altra teoria posteriore [of Gregory] potra forse presentarsi corredata da un maggiore apparato pseudo-scientifico, perche pretende di essere la spiegazione di un celebre passo del Damasceno..."

86. V. Laurent, "Les grandes crises religieuses à Byzance: La fin du schisme arsenite," *Académie Roumaine. Bulletin de la Section Historique,* 26 (1945), 263.

87. J. Gill, *The Council of Florence* (Cambridge, Mass., 1959), 249n2.

88. A recent example that does precisely this is B. de Margerie, *La Trinité Chrétienne dans l'histoire* (Paris, 1975), pp. 223-43.

89. Pachymeres, II, 94.

90. *On the Procession of the Holy Spirit*, PG 142.289C. In the *Tomus*, PG 142.243D-244A, he equates Beccus' methodology to twisting ropes of sand and building houses therefrom; it was like obtaining the shadow instead of the body.

91. Beccus, *Treatise on Peace*, in *Dossier de Lyon*, p. 431.

92. Beccus, *Apology*, PG 141.1016B-C.

93. H.-G. Beck, *Die mittelalterliche Kirche*. III, pt. 2: *Handbuch der Kirchengeschichte*, ed. H. Jedin (Freiburg, 1968), 157.

94. A. Schmemann, *The Historical Road of Eastern Orthodoxy* (Chicago, 1966), p. 253.

95. See his letter to Theodore Mouzalon, ed. Eustratiades, *Ekklesiastikos Pharos*, 5 (1910), 214 (letter 168).

96. *ita Athanasii*, ed. A. Pantocratorinus, in *Thrakika*, 13 (1940), 87.

97. *Tomus*, PG 142.244D.

98. Ibid., 244D

99. Metochites, VIII, pt. 2, 96.

100. Pachymeres, II, 111.

101. *Autobiography*, in Lameere, *La tradition manuscrite*, p. 187.

102. Ed. Eustratiades, *Ekklesiastikos Pharos*, 4 (1909), 108 (letter 153).

103. Ibid., 3:48 (letter 115).

104. See his remarks to the emperor, Andronicus, ibid., 4:17 (letter 133).

105. Ibid., 5:216-17 (letter 170).

106. Ibid., 217 (letter 171)

107. Cf. A. D. Zotos, *John Beccus, Patriarch of Constantinople, New Rome, the Latinizer* (in Greek) (Munich, 1920), p.58; Troitskij, *Arsenij*, 231-32.

108. Ševcenko, "Theodore Metochites," 23, notes that the classical revival was in full swing in the eighties and nineties.

3

THE SEARCH FOR STABILITY

Andronicus' haste in reversing his father's religious policy in 1283 was prompted by his desire to bring peace to the troubled ecclesiastical situation. The earlier description—brief though it was—served to show how critical the situation had really become. In light of this, there were many in high places eager to convince the young emperor that his attachment and loyalty to Orthodoxy had to be made public quickly if his throne was to be saved. The future and security of the dynasty depended on the liquidation of Lyons. Likewise, the new emperor may have wished to soothe his conscience since he had openly applauded the union with Rome during his father's reign. His letter and the Latin profession of faith (which he had signed) had been read at the fourth session of Lyons.[1]

> Once the mourning was over, he made the restoration of the Church his first and most important task. For, while his father was alive, he concealed his concern for the Church—like good seed in rich soil for the winter. And when spring, as it were, arrived, he showed by his deeds who he really was. Thus, heralds and royal edicts were sent everywhere announcing the good news of the restoration of the Church, bringing home those who, for their zeal, had been exiled, or had suffered some other serious injury.[2]

But if Andronicus was, in principle, convinced the Union of Lyons was indefensible (as this passage suggests), he also knew it could no longer be justified politically. The Sicilian revolt had actually removed the Western pressure and the threat of Charles of Anjou. Charting a new course would not be difficult.[3]

A. *The Restoration of Orthodoxy*

On Christmas Day 1282—exactly two weeks after his father's death—Andronicus disclosed his attitude by refusing to attend the liturgy in which Beccus would have participated.[4] The following day, the patriarch was removed to the monastery of the Panachrantos after his collaborator, Constantine Meliteniotes, had been dispatched to inform him of the emperor's plans.[5] On 31 December, his predecessor, Joseph I, was reinstalled in the patriarchal palace.[6] A few days later, a patriarchal sentence of deposition was issued against Beccus, Theophanes of Nicaea, Constantine Meliteniotes, and Beccus' other lieutenant, the archdeacon George Metochites. The bishops and clergy who had accepted the union were suspended for three months.[7] Finally, on 8 January 1283, the ex-patriarch appeared before a synod at Hagia Sophia at which Patriarch Athanasius of Alexandria presided, since Joseph was very ill.[8] Beccus submitted a signed Orthodox profession of faith—later, Gregory was to incorporate this verbatim in the *Tomus* of 1285—which contained his resignation, and his promise never to attempt to recover the priesthood.[9] This did not mend matters, however, and he was soon exiled to Brusa. His colleague, Constantine Meliteniotes, was imprisoned in the monastery of the Pantocrator in Constantinople, while George Metochites remained under arrest in his own house.[10]

Modern apologists have advanced the idea that these deliberations, which condemned Beccus, were disciplinary in nature and did not deal with Beccus' heresy.[11] Yet, Pachymeres notes that the members of the assembly did not "allow the former patriarch to go uncondemned; in fact, they accused him of heresy."[12] Moreover, according to Metochites, his writings were explicitly condemned and burned by the councils.[13] Again, in the profession of faith given to the council, Beccus took pains to explain the "dogmatic absurdities" found in his writings and, particularly, the attribution of "cause" (αἴτιος) to the second person of the Trinity (in addition to the Father). Further, he noted that his errors were "of a dubious nature and at variance with sacred and holy doctrine, and, this being so, *the synod had them condemned.*"[14] Indeed, he himself was ready—before God, his awesome angels, and before the holy and sacred synod—to renounce them all: "From the bottom of my heart, without deceit, without hiding one thing and saying another, I turn away from, I reject, and I cast them out, because they lead to the ultimate destruction of the soul."[15] Obviously this was more than a simple question of discipline.

The choice of Joseph as patriarch to succeed the deposed Beccus was not difficult. As we have seen, he had been Beccus' immediate predecessor and had resigned because the Union of 1274 had been negotiated without his approval. His second enthronement was the very embodiment of restored Orthodoxy. (Not surprisingly, several months after his death, he was canonized for his opposition to the religious policy of Michael VIII.) But more significantly, Joseph and his circle, the Josephites, who eventually came to surround him, were, for the most part, supporters of the Palaeologan dynasty, unlike the pro-Lascarid Arsenites, who thought of the dynasty as usurpers.[16] That Andronicus had good reason to reinstate Joseph is patently clear.

But Joseph's health was failing, and on 23 March 1283 he died.[17] A successor was found quickly, however, in Gregory II of Cyprus, who was, in turn, invested with the patriarchal dignity on Palm Sunday, 11 April 1283.[18] Gregory's candidacy may have been suggested by Theodore Mouzalon, Gregory's former student and now the new prime minister of the empire. He was probably equally responsible for the restoration of Orthodoxy and the punishment of some of the unionist hierarchy.[19]

One of the first tasks of the new patriarch was to hold a synod on Easter Monday, 19 April, one week after his consecration. It is significant that the direction of this synod, which assembled at the church of the Virgin of Blachernae and which was presided over by the new patriarch, was allowed to fall into the hands of Andronicus of Sardis, the newly appointed confessor of the emperor and a determined Arsenite.[20] That this maneuver was designed by the young emperor and the new patriarch to give the Arsenites some satisfaction and, conceivably, to reconcile them to the Church and the dynasty, goes without saying. But this momentary solidarity of Orthodox, Josephites, and Arsenites ("the schismatics were out in full strength"[21]) was likewise rendered possible by their past common opposition to Lyons, and by their suffering under Michael VIII.

Essentially, this synod was convened to deal with the unfinished work of the brief second patriarchate of Joseph. The question of what to do with Andronicus' widowed mother, Theodora, and the even more delicate canonical matter of the unionist hierarchy, had not been fully resolved.[22] For starters, the dowager empress was asked for a written confession of faith in which she repudiated her past, and condemned her late husband's religious policy. She gave assurances, moreover, that she would never request memorial services or ecclesiastical burial for her excommunicated husband. Through this solemn and public retraction, her name was again restored and commemorated in the liturgy, along with that of her son.[23] As for the compromised clerics, it was eventually resolved to depose all those bishops who had, in fact, accepted or supported the union with Rome, regardless whether they had received orders before or during Beccus' patriarchate. This resolution which is no longer extant, but which had a large circulation, was read in all the churches of the capital the following Sunday, 26 April.[24]

This was not a general condemnation incorporating all clerical ranks. Such a condemnation was not issued until twenty months later, in January

1285. It is this last synodal *Decision* which, in effect, deposed all those bishops, priests and deacons who had supported the union and persecuted the Orthodox. Additionally, bishops (apart from certain exceptions made by the synod) who had been elevated to the episcopate during Beccus' patriarchate were deposed. Finally, all clerics who had been personally ordained by Beccus in Constantinople were suspended, while those ordained outside the capital (but not by him) were permitted to retain their clerical rank.[25] This, too, was a further attempt by Patriarch Gregory to strengthen his hand in dealing with the Arsenites, who would have been pleased with these belated suspensions.

These anti-unionist trials of the hierarchy, and particularly the powerful passions released at the purge of 1283, have not had a good press. In fact, they have been routinely described as a "reign of terror" and as a "brigand's synod."[26] It has even been suggested that the truly determinant factor in the collapse of Lyons and the principal perpetrators of the purge were the rigorist monks of Byzantium.[27] And yet, to label these events as the work exclusively of Arsenite and Josephite fanatic monks, and to place the blame for the failure of Lyons on them, is surely an oversimplification and would ignore the wide composition of the opposition. It also does not take into account the widespread belief within all Byzantine ranks that Lyons was a "fraud." Ultimately, the denunciation of theological opponents and the outbursts of anger and persecution were but the logical outcome of some eighty years of Latin ecclesiastical colonialism. It was in fact but the natural postscript to Lyons and the papal policy of *cuius regio, eius religio.* Forced union (not fanaticism) was the key to Lyons' failure.

Considering the sequel to these events, the exile of the unionists, and the fate of Beccus and of unionism in general, the attitude and role of the new patriarch is of the greatest importance. Gregoras' comments on this point are of some interest. He notes, for example, that in ambitious talents (like Gregory's) the motive of emulation and envy against fellow craftsmen is always present. Gregory was among the most celebrated Greeks of his age; even so, he was also expecting to distinguish himself among the famous patriarchs. Fearing that Beccus' dazzling talent and eloquence would cheat him of these honors—"he had been overtaken by the eloquence of that man in disputations"—he promoted Beccus' banishment in no small way.[28]

In general, Gregoras' charge that Gregory furthered Beccus' banishment is serious. And yet, it cannot be accepted at face value. Besides, the burden of responsibility for Beccus' and his collaborators' exile must not be placed solely at Gregory's door. Gregory could hardly be expected to do much about the above-mentioned prevailing atmosphere. Moreover, the more reliable and contemporary Pachymeres expressly states that Gregory, who presided over the assembly of 1283, was displeased with most of what went on, and did not hesitate to say so in private. Pastoral prudence, Gregory reflected, called for a milder attitude.[29] The evidence linking Beccus' condemnation and exile in January 1283 directly with Gregory is, moreover, non-existent. The decision, as we have seen, was made by the synod during Joseph's patriarchate. This is equally true of Beccus' subsequent exile in 1285 (Gregoras, in his general remarks, does not distinguish this from the events of 1283). Here again, the decision was made by the synod; it was not the exclusive decision of the patriarch. One suspects that Gregoras' interpretation is a product of his literary imagination, if not an over-simplification of what actually happened.

It is under these circumstances that Gregory assumed his new duties as patriarch. His previous peaceful existence as productive scholar and teacher was clearly over. A "free man and a philosopher" he was no longer.[30] His busy, but short, teaching career was at an end. But canonical questions and the emotional atmosphere in the capital were not the sum total of the problems he had inherited. As he reflected later, he soon found himself deeply immersed in the life of the Church and in "difficulties" few of his predecessors ever knew; the exaltation, of which he was the object, was in inverse proportion to his expectation.[31]

There were good grounds for thinking that the repudiation of the enforced Union of Lyons, the personal recantation of Beccus and the purge of his faithful friends would bring about the desired peace and stability. Equally, the Arsenite faction—the very embodiment of "accuracy" in matters doctrinal—should have been delighted with the restoration of Orthodoxy and the deliberate good will shown it by the new imperial and ecclesiastical administration. And yet, this was not to be. The difficulties of which Gregory speaks arose from the very same cross-currents that had been a major source of division in the past. Neither Beccus, in his distant exile, nor the Arsenites saw fit to desist from disturbing the already troubled waters of the Church.[32] The divisions, in fact, soon hardened into even greater hostility toward the Church and its representatives.

B. *Elements of Opposition: Arsenites*

Of all the elements to oppose Gregory, however, the Arsenites must easily rank as the most unscrupulous.[33] The campaign they eventually launched against the new patriarch must be judged callous and in every way destructive. It concerned not only his theological contribution (that would later be embodied in the *Tomus*), but his right to the patriarchal throne. All in all, Gregory could hardly afford to ignore this zealous element which was now commanding such wide popular support (it had actually grown in numbers since 1265).[34] Their importance in Gregory's patriarchate and particularly the role they played in his resignation six years later, can hardly be exaggerated. Indeed, it has not always been appreciated. It is not surprising, to be short, that from the very first days of his enthronement, the liquidation of the Arsenite schism was one of Gregory's major concerns.

The Arsenite view, as noted earlier, was that the uncanonical and arbitrary deposition in 1265 of Arsenius by the emperor, Michael VIII, had made all subsequent nominations to the patriarchate invalid.[35] This being so, both Gregory and his immediate predecessor, Joseph I, were usurpers. For some Arsenites, in fact, the case of Arsenius and Joseph (the former's successor) was analogous to the old case of Ignatius and his successor Photius—both Joseph and Photius were usurpers. To be sure, the Church was able to counter this argument by pointing out that both Photius and his adversary, Ignatius, had long since been listed in the *Synodicon,* and were numbered among the Orthodox patriarchs![36] Besides—so the official hierarchy would argue—irregular imperial depositions did not necessarily invalidate new elections or ordinations to the patriarchal throne. Irregularity of elections or depositions could not lead to a general rejection of the hierarchy of the Church; only if Orthodoxy had been compromised would this be possible. As such, the Arsenite schism was inexcusable.

Decisive arguments such as these, however, seem to have had few results. Very early in the debate, the Arsenites attempted to answer them by claiming that Joseph had been excommunicated by Arsenius for usurping his throne. Naturally, if this were true, it would not only make Orthodox arguments untenable, it would also make all of Joseph's decrees, acts, and ordinations null and void. Indeed, the entire hierarchy's authority would be compromised and contested. Contemporaries, of course, did not believe in the excommunication by Arsenius. In fact, they saw it for what it was—a fabrication of Arsenius' partisans. (Joseph himself rejected the idea and considered it an Arsenite invention.) For all that, it continued to be the basis and source of their agitation and hostility to the hierarchy until the accession of Gregory.[37]

Fortunately, conditions were such at the beginning of Gregory's reign that a rapprochement was possible. Not only were Michael VIII and Joseph dead, but the other "usurper," Beccus, was also out of the way and in exile. Not since 1265 had conditions been so favorable for the recognition of a new patriarch;[38] the hierarchical structure of the Church could again be set right. Indeed, the Arsenites thought they might even be able to negotiate their own share of the spotlight, and have one of their own placed on the patriarchal throne. For the most part, this goal, which is amply documented for 1283, 1289, and again for 1303, was born in Gregory's patriarchate.[39] The fact, however, that they were never permitted to choose a new patriarch (it was never more than a fleeting possibility) failed to shake their confidence. On the contrary, it only fanned the flames of their ambition, and prevented the disintegration of their ranks. It even caused the sect to grow.

Gregory was not their choice in 1283. And yet, the opposition did not become immediately evident. Possibly, Gregory's ordination by Gerasimus of Heracleia may have had something to do with it.[40] For although Gerasimus was not yet a full party member, as it were, he was to espouse their cause shortly after he signed the *Tomus* in 1285. More significant, however, was the fact that Gerasimus' own canonical status (he had not been a unionist) made Gregory's consecration indisputably canonical. (As noted earlier, Gregory's own unionist activity does not seem to have stirred much controversy.) Finally, the emperor's and the new patriarch's deliberate attempt to win their active good will and to avoid a collision course should not be underestimated. The tactful handling of their leaders, such as Andronicus of Sardis, who was made confessor to the emperor and was then permitted to preside in judgment over the unionist hierarchs at the Council of 1283, is a case in point.[41] This was no small achievement, since Andronicus himself had his eye on the patriarchal throne. Equally, the above-mentioned canonical actions of 1283 and 1285 against those who were still suspected of unionist sentiments further served to neutralize any opposition.[42]

Increasingly, however, Gregory came to realize that it would not all be smooth sailing. Theirs was, after all, an unlikely, if not wholly precarious, partnership. Besides, Gregory was determined to be master in his own house.

Indeed, the erosion of his authority began when the Arsenites realized just
months after his consecration that he was not prepared to play the part for
which they had cast him—neither he nor the Church could be manipulated.
The decisive point came with the resolve to raise the deceased patriarch, Joseph, to sainthood for his struggle against Michael's misguided religious policy.[43] It was a bold assertion of Church independence, and a direct challenge
to their sectarian views on Joseph. Actually, Gregory turned a deaf ear to Arsenite clamor—under no circumstances was he willing to rescind the decision
concerning Joseph's commemoration.

One thread in this important development was the emperor Andronicus'
personal decision to support the Church. He, more than anyone else, was aware
of the movement's violent and intractable attitude toward his father. It was Michael, after all, who had usurped the throne and had blinded the legitimate Lascarid heir, John IV; and it was on this that Arsenius had subsequently based his
excommunication of Michael. To put it briefly, Andronicus knew too well that
Arsenius' deposition (and the schism that followed the excommunication of his
father) was, from the beginning, associated with the dynastic issue. Arsenite
policy was implicitly anti-Palaeologan, if not always solidly pro-Lascarid. As far
as the Arsenites were concerned, he, too, was merely another "unnatural emperor," another usurper.[44] (Joseph's lifting of his father's excommunication was
naturally ignored by them, since Joseph himself was thought a usurper and an
excommunicate.) Legitimacy and religious sanction, then, were major issues for
Andronicus. Besides, it was Joseph who had provided him with his own legitimacy when he anointed him co-emperor in 1272.[45] The canonization of his
benefactor was a matter that touched him vitally.

Given the obduracy of the Arsenites, the situation soon became critical,
especially since they had never actually recognized the new patriarch. The
passions released by the announcement of Joseph's canonization only served
to underscore this point. It was primarily for this reason that Gregory and the
emperor decided to extend to them a final olive branch at Adramyttium during Lent 1284.[46] The Council of Adramyttium was the single most important effort made in Gregory's patriarchate to bring about a reconciliation.
Here, after much discussion, the two sides unexpectedly decided to resolve
their differences, and to accept the judgment of heaven, by submitting the issue to a test by fire. It was agreed that if both documents (one contained the
arguments of the official Church, the other those of the Arsenites) were con-
sumed in the flames, the Arsenites would have to recognize Gregory's canoni-

cal election. As we should expect, this is precisely what happened.[47] To be sure, Gregory and the emperor were relieved—the schism had at last ended.

Characteristically, however, on the following day, the majority of the Arsenites refused to accept the decision; only a minority had capitulated. True to form, even those who rallied to the patriarch refused to yield on the question of Joseph's canonization.[48] Shortly thereafter, Gregory issued an excommunication against those who had broken their solemn promise to abide by the decision.[49] As he was to note later that year, their only virtue was to be in opposition and schism. "They do not examine whether their resistance serves or pleases God; on the contrary, they believe it is far more virtuous and preferable to be at variance and in opposition. In doing so, the Body of Christ is pitifully maimed and torn asunder."[50]

Gregory, however, was determined to find a permanent common ground and to bind the majority to the Church. The pourparlers were thus prolonged until the end of the year; he did not return to Constantinople until early December. Predictably, this phase of the negotiations, too, produced precious little in results. Likewise, the emperor's subsequent order to have Arsenius' body returned to Constantinople, where it was interred in the monastery of St Andrew (after a solemn celebration of the liturgy in the Hagia Sophia), did not produce the expected results.[51]

All the same, the differences were still negotiable. Gregory continued to correspond after Adramyttium with the important Arsenite Athanasius Lependrenus, from whom he expected assistance.[52] Also, he was still willing to make concessions to those Arsenites who were already reconciled to the Church. And yet this situation could not last, particularly after the excommunication of the patriarch by the pro-Arsenite Gerasimus of Heracleia. After this event, no attempt to bridge the cleavage between the two sides could succeed—at least as long as Gregory remained patriarch.

Gerasimus, as we have seen, had been untouched by unionism, and so was chosen to ordain Gregory in 1283. That he was a simple unlettered monk, and a non-unionist, pleased the Arsenites. Though he himself had not joined the dissidents he had, no doubt, sympathized with them, as his background and subsequent behavior show.[53] As a further concession, he was appointed Gregory's own spiritual father.[54] In 1285, Gerasimus was one of Gregory's supporters who signed the *Tomus*; his name is second on the list of metropolitans.[55] Even so, relations eventually became strained, especially after Joseph's canonization and the colloquies at Adramyttium, both of which had displeased Gerasimus. Further, his diocese of Heracleia was an Arsenite stronghold, and this may have convinced him to embrace their cause.[56]

Shortly after 1285, therefore, this "light-minded"[57] and fanatical bishop made the astonishing decision to excommunicate the head of the Church, his patriarch. Having consecrated him, he perhaps thought he could depose him, too. Moreover Gerasimus managed to get an equally "unlettered" colleague, Neophytus of Brusa (another dissident center), to sign the excommunication. Neophytus, too, it must be noted, had signed the *Tomus*.[58] The patriarch, of course, promptly had the two excommunicated.[59] To paraphrase Gregory, both metropolitans had now voluntarily joined the schismatics.[60]

The Arsenites' grudge against Gregory could only have been strengthened by this episode. It reminded them that Gregory had at one time supported the unionist policy of Michael VIII. It seems that Gerasimus had based his excommunication on the fact that his spiritual son, Gregory, had deliberately concealed his pro-Latin sentiments from him; he had not told him that he had prayed with the unionists under Michael![61] What had been forgotten at Gregory's accession was now conveniently revived.

The truly unfortunate result of these excommunications, however was that Gregory, too, became still another uncanonical and excommunicated patriarch. Until 1310, the Arsenites would continue to hold to the view that Gregory's tenure of the patriarchate was likewise uncanonical; in their eyes, the patriarchal throne had been vacant from 1255 to 1310, that is, from the deposition of Arsenius to the accession of Patriarch Niphon. Gregory's remark, that the selection of Gerasimus as head of the see of Heracleia had been a total disaster for the Church, was not an exaggeration.[62]

But this was not all. After Gregory's excommunication by one of their own nothing could assuage the Arsenites except his resignation. It is, in fact, a goal on which they were to lavish all their attention. The savagery with which they pursued and harassed the patriarch is astonishing. The weapons they chose, violence and rioting, were both direct and effective, as Gregory's grim account of the possibility of a riot at the Hagia Sophia illustrates. In a letter addressed to Theodore Mouzalon, the patriarch warns the first munister of the empire that the "demagogue Gerasimus" and his crowd of partisans planned to disrupt the services on the following Sunday. Their goal was to injure and insult the patriarch as he celebrated the liturgy. Theodore is urged to be sure to have sufficient police present to prevent the confrontation, should any materialize. The emperor, too, was to be informed.[63] Plainly, the rebel bishop had been able to carry on the struggle against his patriarch not only in his own diocese, but in the capital as well.[64] In the face of such opposition, it is remarkable that Gregory was able to retain his position as long as he did.

C. *Elements of Opposition: Beccus*

If the Arsenites were set on a collision course with Gregory early in his patriarchate, so were the unionists. Historians are agreed on Beccus' honesty of character, and the fact that he generally remained true, until his death in 1297, to his unionist persuasion.[65] This is true enough. Nevertheless, Beccus' anxiety for the Churches, and his hope for the day when there would be "neither Greek nor Latin,"[66] was also sustained by a stiff-necked attitude, and an impetuous and opinionated nature. His scornful and polemic posture is richly documented, by both Pachymeres and Metochites.[67] His "sudden defection" in 1283, when he signed the anti-unionist profession of faith—it was acknowledged as a sign of weakness by his own supporters[68]—was, for him, a bitter pill to swallow.

Thus, he could not consign himself or his unionist platform to obscurity, nor accept the fact that for eight years he had labored to redirect the course of Byzantine theology and had failed. Increasingly he came to believe that another hearing would vindicate his theological position. At the outset, he labored to win the active sympathy of the hierarchy; finally, he launched a clever and calculated propaganda campaign that resulted in the calling of the Council of Blachernae in February 1285. Unfortunately for him, however, he ran head-on into a stone wall of theological opposition. The tide of feeling against him and his theology had not yet ebbed. It was—put briefly—a grave tactical mistake. For that which he thought was theologically unassailable was eventually publicly and unconditionally anathematized from the pulpit of Hagia Sophia by the very council he had seen fit to call. Beccus had joined the fellowship of heretics.

It was at Brusa, where Beccus had been confined following his disgrace in 1283, that the campaign was launched for an open and full discussion of his theology. Neophytus, the newly-elected bishop of Brusa (Gerasimus' partisan), provided the immediate provocation—early in 1284, he ordered his flock to abstain from meat for several days as an act of atonement for the liturgical commemoration of the pope's name during Beccus' tenure.[69] It appears,

however, that the Brusans refused to take this fast of expiation in stride. Instead they chose to vent their rage on the ex-patriarch. Being of a touchy sus-
ceptibility himself, Beccus moved quickly by heaping scorn on both
Neophytus and Patriarch Gregory. One of his speeches, given in the courtyard of the monastery where he was lodged, is preserved by Pachymeres. It
was addressed to the assembled crowd:

> What is wrong with you that you abuse me and avoid me who am Roman and
> of Roman parentage and upbringing, while you receive with honors a man [Pa-
> triarch Gregory] who is of Italian parentage and upbringing? And not only that,
> but even in his very dress and speech, he has wormed his way into our customs.
> If you oppose my beliefs, let the emperor convoke a council, and, when all are
> gathered, hear my views. If, in the opinion of wise and pious men, and the scrip-
> tures, I am proven wrong, all well and good. Otherwise, why follow the igno-
> rant and the vulgar and accuse me of the worst?[70]

Beccus was looking for a confrontation. In fact, this verbal attack was not
the only way in which he made his wishes known. Meliteniotes informs us
that Beccus "wrote an encyclical letter from Brusa, where he was exiled, which
he even dispatched to the army, requesting another trial and another court of
justice for he had reasonably categorized the previous one as a band of rob-
bers."[71] Pachymeres makes no mention of this letter. Even so, its content (also
summarized for us by Metochites)[72] differs in no way from Beccus' courtyard
speech, since it contains his fear of being branded a heretic, denounces the
"intruder" in the patriarchate and, finally, urges a public hearing on the matter. Possibly Pachymeres had Beccus' letter in mind when he reported his harangue in the courtyard; he thus saw no need to mention the letter he had just
summarized. In any event, the latter, which apparently was "circulated everywhere," including Constantinople, soon had the desired result. Shortly afterward, under tight security and, no doubt, isolation,[73] the ex-patriarch was
brought to Constantinople to wait the convocation of the council he had requested.[74]

Beccus' letter was sent just before the beginning of Lent, 22 February
1284, when the patriarch and the emperor were to journey to Adramyttium
to mediate with the Arsenites.[75] Likewise, the incident at Brusa had probably
occurred sometime before February and not during Lent, when it seems unlikely that Neophytus would have imposed an additional fast on the city. It
would appear, then, that Beccus began his campaign for a hearing approxi-
mately a year after his condemnation, when the Church was still hopelessly

divided by the Arsenites. The important and difficult negotiations with this faction were just then getting under way. The synchronization of these events, the possibility that he was trying to make capital of Gregory's difficulties with the schismatics, and the wanton calumny directed at the patriarch (who had neither harassed nor silenced Beccus at Brusa) were surely irresponsible. He may have been following the unstable internal condition of the Church, and then resolved to use it to his advantage.

Beccus' campaign did not help matters. At the outset Gregory appears to have been greatly alarmed at the turn of events, and so informed the emperor in a letter dated 20 December 1284.[76] After describing the activities of the Arsenites (hopes for their reconciliation had dimmed considerably by then) he notes that Beccus, too, had not resisted adding to the confusion. A reading of Beccus circular, he continues, would convince anyone of this; indeed, the letter had caused people in the capital to become even more divided, and some were now prepared to defend him, while others wanted to punish him for his insolence. If the situation was to be contained, the patriarch advised, the proposed synod had to meet soon. A similar urgent note, in which the potentially dangerous situation is again emphasized, was sent to Theodore Mouzalon.[77] Gregory's further request for the emperor's return in this second missive is explained by the fact that the emperor had not returned to the capital after the events at Adramyttium, early in 1284.

Gregory was initially reluctant to follow Beccus' request and expose the precarious peace of the Church to any excessively strong test, or "new judges and new courts," as he put it.[78] This, as his letters plainly indicate, was the result of an honestly endured anxiety for the Church.[79] He knew that, this time, the confrontation with Beccus would be painful, even decisive. Besides, he was familiar with Beccus' nature, so bent on martyrdom. Increasingly, however, he saw that the only way to resolve the issue and end the unionists' campaign of calumny against him was to call a synod.[80] This was certainly the view of government officials who had decided to give Beccus a hearing. It was not long after the arrival of the emperor in Constantinople, mid-January 1285, that the synod held its first session in the palace of Blachernae.

This Council of 1285 should be distinguished from the earlier assembly of January 1283, which had merely deposed Beccus. Whereas the discussion of 1285 was devoted entirely to the doctrine of the procession of the Holy Spirit, the early meeting of 1283 was limited to procuring an Orthodox profession of faith from Beccus. It avoided any debate. Moreover, 1285 was not just another "trial,"[81] as in 1283, when the guilty were cross-examined without any defense; neither was it a mere interrogation where the judges "served as skewers" for roasting Beccus—to quote the unionist Theoctistus of Adrianople.[82] In fact, government officials were determined this would not happen.[83] If some historians, therefore, have found fault with the *modus procedendi* of 1283, they cannot do so for 1285. True, the end of the first session, after both sides had presented their views, did become a shouting match. This was only momentary, however, since the emperor would have none of it, and quickly put an end to the session. In the history of the Byzantine Church, the Council of Blachernae remains one of the most detailed discussions of the procession. It cannot be dismissed as some rabid anti-unionist convocation.

It should finally be emphasized that both Pachymeres and Metochites agree that it was the ex-patriarch himself who seized the initiative and called the meeting of 1285. And although the unionists were by now a minority, in contrast to the large delegation of official theologians present, their cause was not jeopardized as in 1283, when it was useless to resist. (If the Arsenites were in control of the deliberations in the spring of 1283, it was not so in 1285 when Gregory himself presided.) Further, existing evidence leaves little doubt that in 1285 they were given a fair and lengthy hearing. The emperor, Andronicus, was to make a concerted effort to mediate peace and bring the parties to agreement.

In general, the first two years following the restoration of Orthodoxy and the accession of Gregory as patriarch were far from peaceful—the forces of rebellion and unrest were not yet spent. We have seen how the initial show of solidarity of Josephites, Arsenites, patriarch, and emperor, early in 1283, proved to be only a facade. The delicate theological and canonical problems—as the case of the Arsenites and the unionists illustrates—became increasingly complex. The search for stability, however, was not yet over. The Council of Blachernae was to prove a major effort in this direction.

NOTES

1. On Andronicus' scrupulous handling of ecclesiastical matters and his relations with his patriarchs, see J. Gill, "Emperor Andronicus II and Patriarch Athanasius I," *Byzantina*, 2 (1970), 18.

2. Gregoras, I, 159-60. His hostility to the union while he was co-emperor was probably not unknown to the Patriarch Beccus, with whom he had many conversations; see Pachymeres, I, 501.

3. Pachymeres, II, 22.

4. According to Pachymeres, II, 16, the "pretense" used for not appearing at the solemn liturgy was the recent death of his father.

5. Pachymeres, II, 19; the historian notes that Beccus demanded a bodyguard during his departure in order not to give the impression that he was abandoning his throne. Gregoras I, 160; M. Sotomayor, El Patriarca Becos, según Jorge Paquimeres (semblanza histórica)," *Estudios Ecclesiásticos,* 31 (1957), 342ff.

6. Beccus, *De depositione sua. Oratio I, PG* 141.935c, 956A-B, 906A-C; Metochites, VIII, pt. 2, 90-91. On Joseph's second patriarchate, see V. Laurent, "La chronologie des patriarches de Constantinople au XIIIè siècle (1208-1309)," *REB,* 27 (1969), 145, 146; and idem, "Mélanges: I. Les dates du second patriarcat de Joseph Ier (31 XII 1282-av. 26 IV 1283)," *REB,* 18 (1960), 205-208.

7. Beccus, *De depositione sua. Oratio I, PG* 141.953C, 960A; Pachymeres, II, 21-22; Metochites, VIII, pt. 2, 90; Laurent, *Regestes,* no. 1453.

8. Here I follow the chronology of Laurent, *Regestes,* no. 1455.

9. *Tomus, PG* 141.237B-238B; the entire text is quoted by A. K. Demetracopoulos, *History of the Schism* (in Greek) (Leipzig, 1867), 81-83; it was taken from A. Banduri, *Imperium Orientale sive Antiquitates Constantinopolitanae,* II (Paris, 1711), 944-45; see Troitskij, *Arsenij,* 221-23, for a Russian translation of the text. H. Evert-Kapessowa, "Une page de l'histoire des relations byzantino-latines, II: La fin de l'union de Lyon," *BS,* 17 (1956), 9, states that the synod also had Metochites, Meliteniotes, and Theophanes of Nicaea condemned. This is incorrect. We have seen that their condemnation had been carried out by patriarchal decision several days before the synod met.

10. Metochites, VIII, pt. 2, 126; see also R.-J. Loenertz, "Théodore Métochite et son père," *Archivum Fratrum Praedicatorum,* 23 (1953), 188; and Troitskij, *Arsenij,* 273-74.

11. V. Laurent, "Les signataires du second synode des Blakhernes (été 1285)," *EO,* 26 (1927), 142; this view is echoed by Evert-Kapessowa, "Une page de l'histoire des relations byzantino-latines, II," 8*n*38: "...mais il ne faut pas oublier que la question de la procession du St Esprit ne fut point discutée à ce synode, ce qu'on reprocha à Veccos ce n'était pas l'hérésie mais une faute de discipline."

12. Pachymeres, II, 27.

13. Metochites, VIII, pt. 2, 93.

14. *Tomus, PG* 141.237B.

15. Ibid., 237C. See also S. S. Mpilales, *The Heresy of the Filioque.* I: *Historical and Critical Review of the Filioque* (in Greek) (Athens, 1972), 366-67.

16. See below, pp. 69ff.

17. Pachymeres, II, 37-38.

18. Pachymeres, II, 42-43; Gregoras, I, 165. On the chronology of Gregory's patriarchate, see Laurent, "Mélanges: I. Les dates du second patriarcat de Joseph Ier," 206; and idem, "La chronologie des patriarches de Constantinople au XIIIè siècle," 146-47. On Joseph's canonization, see below, n. 43.

19. Pachymeres, II, 14-15; Metochites X, pt. I, 319-22. Pachymeres also notes that the advice of Andronicus' aunt, Eulogia, was equally crucial in persuading Andronicus to change his father's policy. For a general review of the selection of patriarchs in Byzantium, see the helpful summary of L. Bréhier, "Le recrutement des patriarches de Constantinople pendant la période byzantine," *Actes du VIe Congrès international des études byzantines* (Paris, 1950), 221-28; see also the important comments of Troitskij, *Arsenij,* 232-33.

20. Pachymeres, II, 50-54; Gregoras, I, 171-72; Metochites, VIII, pt. 2, 98-104; Demetracopoulos, *History of the Schism,* 81-83. On Andronicus of Sardis, see R. Aigrain, "Andronic de Sardis," *Dictionnaire d'Histoire et de Géographie ecclésiastiques,* 2 (Paris, 1914), cols. 1774-76; and I. Sykoutres, "Concerning the Schism of the Arsenites" (in Greek), *Hellenika,* 2 (1929), 285-86.

21. Pachymeres, II, 52.

22. Ibid., II, 51.

23. Ibid., II, 55, S. Pétridès, "Chrysobulle de l'impératrice Théodora (1283)," *EO* 14 (1911), .25-28, is in fact the fifth edition of Theodora's confession (with French translation), not the first, as is claimed (p. 25); on the earlier editions of J. Iriarte (= *PG* 144.792-94), C. Simonides, A. Demetracopoulos, and J. Dräseke, see L. Petit, "Mélanges II: La profession de foi de l'impératrice Théodora (1283)," *EO,* 18 (1916—1918), 286-87.

24. Laurent, *Regestes,* no. 1463; the case of the patriarchs, Athanasius of Alexandria and Theodosius of Antioch, who were in the capital and were among the compromised, was also dealt with, but individually. Athanasius' name was struck from the diptychs, while Theodosius proffered his resignation. See Pachymeres, II, 55-56.

25. See the text edited by Demetracopoulos, *History of the Schism,* pp.84-86; and by S. Pétridès, "Sentence synodique contre le clergé unioniste (1283)," *EO* 14 (1911), 133-36. This document of 1285 has been habitually identified (by Demetracopoulos, Pétridès, Grumel, Bréhier) with the decision of the Synod of Blachernae in 1283, probably because both deal with the same canonical question. Laurent, *Regestes,* no. 1485, has, however, demonstrated that the text in question is in fact the later resolution of January 1285; his argument is supported by Pachymeres, Metochites, and Gregoras, who place this more comprehensive *Decision* immediately after the events of Adramyttium, which we know occurred in Lent 1284. Moreover, Pachymeres' paraphrase is strikingly similar to the extant text.

26. V. Grumel, "Le IIe concile de Lyon et la réunion de l'église grecque," *DTC,* 9, pt. 1 (Paris, 1926), col. 1404; L. Bréhier, "Andronic II," *Dictionnaire d'Histoire et de Géographie ecclésiastiques,* 2 (Paris, 1914), col. 1783; H. Wolter and H. Holstein, *Lyon I et Lyon II.* Vol. VII of *Histoire des Conciles Œcuméniques;* ed. G. Dumeige (Paris, 1966), 223; C. Diehl et al., *L'Europe orientale de 1081 à 1453* (Paris, 1945), p. 222.

27. J. Gill, *The Council of Florence* (Cambridge, Mass., 1959), p. 14; see H. Evert-Kapessowa, "La société byzantine et l'union de Lyon," *BS,* 10 (1949), 28ff., who says that the monastic element alone had the daring to oppose the emperor; and L. Bréhier, "Attempts at Reunion of the Greek and Latin Churches," *The Cambridge Medieval History,* IV: *The Eastern Roman Empire 71 7-1453,* edd. J. R. Tanner et al. (New York, 1923), 614: "Henceforward, the monks dominated the Greek Church, and, from this epoch onwards, the higher ranks of the clergy were almost exclusively recruited from among them. It was the monks who fanned the flame

of popular hatred against the Westerners. Forced into an attitude of sullen nationalism, they showed that they preferred the ruin of the empire to union with Rome."

28. Gregoras, I, 168

29. Pachymeres, II, 53-54: "Gregory, it appeared, was displeased with most of what was going on; nevertheless, he followed and complied with the decision. But secretly he did not hesitate to call their synod a wicked council."

30. *Autobiography* in W. Lameere, *La tradition manuscrite de la correspondance de Grégoire de Chypre* (Brussels-Paris, 1937), p. 187.

31. Ibid., 187.

32. See Gregory's letter to the emperor, Andronicus, ed. Eustratiades, *Ekklesiastikos Pharos*, 4 (1909), 12 (letter 132).

33. On the Arsenites, see Sykoutres, "Concerning the Schism of the Arsenites," *Hellenika*, 2 (1929), 257-332; 3 (1930), 15-44; 5 (1932), 107-26; V. Laurent, "La question des Arsénites," *Hellenika*, 3 (1930), 463-70; Troitskij, *Arsenij*. See also below, n. 37.

34. Pachymeres, II, 112.

35. Sykoutres, "Concerning the Schism of the Arsenites," *Hellenika*, 2 (1929), 270. On Arsenius, see S. Eustratiades, "The Patriarch Arsenius Autorianus (1255-1260 and 1261-1267)" (in Greek), *Hellenika*, I (1928), 78-94.

36. The case is argued well in John Chilas' antirrhetic *On theArsenite Schism*, ed. J. Darrouzès *Documents inédits d'ecclésiologie byzantine* (Paris, 1970), p. 98, and esp. p. 382 (Greek text).

37. V. Laurent, "L'excommunication du Patriarche Joseph Ier par son prédécesseur Arsène," *BZ*, 30 (1929-1930), 490; idem, "Les grandes crises religieuses à Byzance: La fin du schisme arsénite," *Académie Roumaine. Bulletin de la Section Historique*, 26 (1945), 259: "Dans une précédente étude j'ai écrit que l'histoire de cette excommunication était sujete à caution. Aujourd'hui je n'hésite pas...à affirmer qu'elle a été inventée de toutes pièces pour les besoins de la cause." For the text on which the excommunication was based, see Eustratiades "The Patriarch Arsenius," 89-94; and the discussion in Sykoutres, "Concerning the Schism of the Arsenites," *Hellenika*, 2 (1929), 312-32.

38. G. P. Schiemenz, "Zur politischen Zugehörigkeit des Gebiets um Sobesos und Zoropassos in den Jahren um 1220," *Jahrbuch der Österreichischen byzantinischen Gesellschaft*, 14 (1965), 232.

39. Pachymeres, II, 138-39, 349-57; see also A.-M.Maffry Talbot, "The Patriarch Athanasius (1289-1293; 1303-1309) and the Church," *Dumbarton Oaks Papers*, 27 (1973), 17-18.

40. Pachymeres, 11, 42-45; Gregoras, I, 164-65; Troitskij, Arsenij, p. 235.

41. See above, p. 64.

42. See above, p. 65.

43. The text is lost; see Laurent, *Regestes*, no. 1461; see also idem, "Les grandes crises religieuses," 257-60. The canonization is, likewise, mentioned in Methodius' letter to Patriarch Gregory in *Dossier de Lyon*, p. 525. R. Macrides, "Saints and Sainthood in the Early Palaeologan Period,"

The Byzantine Saint, ed. S. Hackel (London, 1981), pp. 79-81, has recently argued against Joseph's canonization. In any case, it does not affect the argument.

44. I. Ševcenko, "The Imprisonment of Manuel Moschopoulos in the Year 1305 or 1306," *Speculum*, 27, No. 2 (1952), 156

45. F. Dölger, "Die dynastische Familienpolitik des Kaisers Michael Paläologos," *E. Eichmann Festschrift* (Paderborn, 1940), 183; A. Laiou, *Constantinople and the Latins: The Foreign Policy of Andronicus II 1282-1328* (Cambridge, Mass., 1972), 1n1.

46. Pachymeres, II, 83; Gregoras, 1, 166-67, 173-74; Laurent, *Regestes*, no. 1470.

47. Pachymeres, 11, 62.

48. Ed. Eustratiades, *Ekklesiastikos Pharos*, 4 (1909), 105-106 (letter 149).

49. Laurent, *Regestes*, no. 1472.

50. Ed. Eustratiades, *Ekklesiastikos Pharos*, 4 (1909), 104 (letter 147); Laurent, *Regestes*, no. 1478

51. Pachymeres, II, 85-86; Gregoras, 1, 167.

52. Ed. Eustratiades, *Ekklesiastikos Pharos*, 4 (1909), 103-104, 104-105 (letters 147 and 148); Laurent, *Regestes*, nos. 1478 and 1491; both letters are addressed to his "friend" Lependrenus. See also Sykoutres, "Concerning the Schism of the Arsenites," *Hellenika*, 2 (1929), 304-305.

53. Schiemenz, "Zur politischen Zugehörigkeit," 232, believes Gerasimus was already a party member.

54. Pachymeres, II, 45.

55. Laurent, "Les signataires du second synode des Blakhernes," 144.

56. Ed. Eustratiades, *Ekklesiastikos Pharos*, 4(1909), 105 (letter 149); 5 (1910), 221 (letter 171).

57. Ibid., 5:214 (letter 168).

58. Laurent, "Les signataires du second synode des Blakhernes," 146.

59. Pachymeres, II, 133; Laurent, *Regestes*, no. 1499.

60. See Gregory's letter to the monk Methodius, in *Ekklesiastikos Pharos*, 5 (1910), 221 (letter 171)

61. Pachymeres, II, 133.

62. Ed. Eustratiades, *Ekklesiastikos Pharos*, 5 (1910), 214 (letter 168).

63. Ibid., 214-15 (letter 168); Laurent, *Regestes*, no. 1492; I. Sykoutres, "Methodius the Monk and Gregory of Cyprus" (in Greek), *Hellenika*, 5 (1932), 125-26.

64. See Sykoutres, "Methodius the Monk and Gregory," 126; Laurent, "Les grandes crises religieuses," 275.

65. Pachymeres, II, 28.

66. Metochites, VIII, pt. 2, 3 and 46.

67. Evidence in Pachymeres, II, 114: "Beccus had a constant longing to oppose him [Gregory] who had provoked him"; see also ibid., 88-89; I, 405-408, 450; cf. Zotos, *John Beccus,* pp.14-15.

68. Metochites, VIII, pt. 2, 92.

69. Pachymeres II, 88; Troitskij, *Arsenij,* p. 271.

70. Pachymeres II, 88-89; 0. Raynaldus, *Annales ecclesiastici,* 22 (Bar-le-Duc, 1970), a. 1284, no. 44, p. 544.

71. Codex Paris. gr. 1303, fol. 86^v.

72. Metochites, VIII, pt. 2, 121. Laurent, *Regestes,* no. 1474, suggests that the text of this letter is to be found in *PG* 141.949-69 (Beccus' *De depositione sua. Oratio I*). See, however, the objections of J. Gill, "Notes on the De Michaele et Andronico Palaeologis of George Pachymeres," *BZ,* 68 (1975), 300n13.

73. Laurent, *Regestes,* no. 1487 (a synodal decision—text lost—ordering th complete isolation of Beccus).

74. Pachymeres, II, 89; Metochites, VIII, pt. 2, 122-23.

75. Metochites, VIII, pt. 2, 121.

76. *Ekklesiastikos Pharos,* 4 (1909), 11-15 (letter 132); Laurent, *Regestes,* no. 1474; idem, "Les signataires du second synode des Blakhernes," 132-33.

77. *Ekklesiastikos Pharos,* 4 (1909), 22-24 (letter 136); see also 3 (1909), 296 (letter 130); Laurent, *Regestes,* no. 1476.

78. *Ekklesiastikos Pharos,* 4 (1909), 11 (letter 132).

79. Cf. the view of Metochites, VIII, pt. 2, 122-23.

80. *Ekklesiastikos Pharos,* 5 (1910), 224-26 (letter 173); Laurent, *Regestes,* no. 1486. See also *Ekklesiastikos Pharos,* 5:296 (letter 130).

81. J. Gill, "John Beccus, Patriarch of Constantinople 1275-1282," *Byzantina,* 7 (1975), 262; see also Metochites, VIII, pt. 2, 161.

82. Pachymeres, II, 25

83. Metochites, VIII, pt. 2, 123.

4

THE COUNCIL OF BLACHERNAE

Although the official text of the *acta* of the Council of Blachernae has not survived, we are reasonably well informed about its deliberations, from the lengthy contemporary testimony of Pachyrneres and Metochites[1] and the short (but misleading) summary of the historian Gregoras.[2] Although the accounts of Metochites and Pachymeres preserve a substantial part of the proceedings (neither is actually a complete or verbatim report), they digress at times into personal exposition or polemic; this makes it difficult to distinguish what is official text and what is not. But, it is perhaps more pronounced in Metochites, Beccus' redoubtable ally, who does not hesitate to indulge in such digressions in order to refute Patriarch Gregory or Theodore Mouzalon, the council's main spokesmen. On the other hand, Pachymeres seldom permits himself this luxury. In fact, his account of the first session—the only one for which we have a complete description—appears to be an accurate record of the proceedings, for the stormy debate it describes has the ring of authenticity, and his account is supported by Metochites. Possibly the compressed nature of the narratives is due to the council's lengthy deliberations, which may have forced the historians to conflate or summarize.[3]

A. *Cappadocian and Augustinian Trinitarian Thought*

The inclination to summarize may, in fact, be the reason why the narratives fail to provide exact dates, either for the council's deliberations or for the publication of the *Tomus*. This imprecision is further intensified by those manuscripts of the *Tomus* with long superscriptions which give the date of the council as 1291/92 when, of course, Gregory had resigned and was, in fact, dead![4] This, in turn, would explain why the secondary literature, which is based in large part on Pachymeres, often places the council anywhere between 1283 and 1285, while the composition, signing, and publication of the *Tomus* is placed between 1286 and 1288.[5] Fortunately recent scrutiny of the sources (including the discovery of an unpublished text of Constantine Meliteniotes) has resolved the difficulty, and need be sketched here only in the briefest outline.[6]

It is clear that the council and the *Tomus* must be placed in the year 1285, and not before. Earlier it was mentioned that one of Gregory's letters indicates that the emperor was not in Constantinople on 20 December 1284, whereas the patriarch himself had returned from Adramyttium.[7] Moreover, it is highly unlikely that the time-consuming preparations for the council would have been made in the last days of December 1284, that is, immediately after the patriarch's return. The council, then, was held sometime after mid-January 1285, after the emperor had returned, when sufficient time had passed to allow the necessary preparations to be made. The argument is strengthened by the unpublished text of Meliteniotes, who states clearly that the deliberations began on the first day of Lent,[8] which would rave been 5 February 1285.[9] This information, coupled with Metochites' observation that the final, fifth session was held six months later, would give us five sessions, of which the first four were held in February and the fifth in August 1285.[10]

It is after these five sessions were held that the synodal decree, the *Tomus*, was written for none had been drawn up during the actual debates. Gregory, who was assigned this important task, finished his draft at the end of August, when he had the members of the council—after a public reading of the text in Hagia Sophia—endorse the document with their signatures. At the outset, the document was signed by the emperor, the patriarch, most of the council's participating episcopal circle, and some of the ecclesiastical officials of the Great Church. The document was a solemn declaration of faith and included eleven anathemas aimed directly at the unrepentant John Beccus, Constantine Meliteniotes, and George Metochites.

The Council of Blachernae, then, had two quite separate phases. The first, in February, included four sessions and was given over to a hearing of both parties, although neither side managed to convince the other. The second, in August, was for the most part formal, and included the deposition of the unionist Theoctistus of Adrianople, a public and solemn reading of the text of the *Tomus*, and the signing ceremony that followed.[11]

Before considering the discussions in detail, their nature and theme must first be understood. This long debate, which engaged Byzantine theologians for some six months in the year 1285, may well seem to some as little more than a fruitless and endless verbal exercise. In the past, the above-mentioned historical narratives have, in fact, led scholars to lament the air of pathetic unreality involved; others conclude that the debate was only over terminology—a self-contained phenomenon dealing with no material or substantive issue. This view ignores Beccus' point that faith is dependent, not on words, but on their meaning.[12] Speaking more generally, the conventional political explanation of the schism—in vogue among historians today—embraces not a little of this attitude. Religious issues were really almost always peripheral—so the interpretation runs. If we probe beneath the surface of the terminology, however, we will see how deceptive and misleading this picture can be.

The Council of 1285 was anything but a self-contained debate dealing with verbal formulas. Its focus was exclusively trinitarian, and dealt with two major approaches to the Trinity—the Augustinian and the Cappadocian—which, in the course of the Middle Ages, had established themselves in East and West. Suffice it to say that the Byzantines were duty-bound to defend their own Cappadocian approach to the Trinity when challenged in the aftermath of Lyons with the doctrine of the eternal personal procession of the Holy Spirit from the Father and the Son, as from one single principle. As one recent observer notes: "The *real* significance of the *Filioque* quarrel consisted in the fact that the two sides held to a different approach to God. The East refused to identify God's being with the concept of 'simple essence,' while the West admitted this identification on the basis of Greek philosophical presuppositions."[13] To be sure, the two paths involved not only what may be called "theological method,"[14] but also basic differences in the doctrine of God itself.

Historically, the trinitarian theology of the Byzantine Church was first enunciated in the fourth century at the Council of Nicaea. Athanasius of Alexandria was its original champion, while the Cappadocian Fathers, Basil the Great, Gregory of Nyssa, and Gregory of Nazianzus, brought the process to its conclusion.[15] As is well known, it was their technical theological definition—that God is one essence in three hypostases, or persons—that led to the final defeat of Arianism at the close of the fourth century. This permanent achievement became increasingly the ultimate standard and source for all subsequent speculation on the Trinity in Byzantium. Characteristically, the foundation of this terminology was biblical and soteriological. For it is as Father, Son, and Spirit that God has chosen to reveal Himself in salvation-history, and to be experienced by man. God is a Trinity of persons who is first met in Scripture as three agents of salvation and only then acknowledged as one God. This, says Gregory of Nazianzus—in defending himself against his critics—was neither monarchism (Judaism) nor tritheism (Hellenism).[16] On the contrary, it was ultimately true to man's experience of the mystery of the deity as revealed in Scripture and the incarnation of Christ. For it is in the coming and revelation by Christ of His own person, or hypostasis, that the other two hypostases in turn are revealed and manifested to us. As such, the *personal* revelation of God in Scripture is the point of departure for all trinitarian theology, both for the Cappadocians and for all Byzantine theology. God may never be reduced either to the unity or to the single common essence of philosophical speculation.

By contrast, a very different line of development is observed in the West.[17] Instead of starting with the three hypostases—the personal diversity in God—and then passing to the consideration of the one essence, the West first considers the one essence, and then arrives at the three hypostases. Latin theology, then, is inclined first to consider the nature and then to proceed to the agent. If the Cappadocians experienced God as three persons before they met Him as one God, the Latins experienced Him as one God before they met Him as three persons.[18] This is, in fact, the approach of Augustine, whose *De Trinitate,* written in 414,[19] was afterward widely accepted by almost every Latin writer in the West. The Carolingian theologians of the eighth century are forever referring to this work in their anti-Byzantine polemic to justify the addition to the Creed. But, his influence also extended to the scholastics of the high Middle Ages—namely, Anselm, Peter Lombard, and Aquinas.[20] Not surprising, it is Augustine's terminology which probably lies behind the definition of the Council of Lyons.[21] To be sure, both paths were legitimate as long as both refrained from attributing any priority, either to the one essence, or to the three hypostases. To assume a supremacy of the essence over the three hypostases, or, *mutatis mutandis,* of the three hypostases over the one essence, would be a denial of the trinitarian personalist experience as the ultimate revelation of the nature of God.

An essential element in the theology of the Cappadocian Fathers is their theory of the relations of the three persons to one another, and the principle of *causality* that this involves. It is the key to understanding the subsequent rejection by Byzantine theology of the *Filioque* clause. The doctrine in question insists that the *origin* of the persons within the deity is not the common essence, but the hypostasis of the Father—the unique cause and principle of the unity of both the Son and the Spirit. For the Father is not only unbegotten, He is without cause (ἄναρχος). As Patriarch Gregory was to say: "The hypostasis of the Father is the source of divinity, and the natural principle, and the root of Son and Spirit."[22] Specifically, the one real point of distinction within the deity is causality, which is to be identified with the Father, the first cause;

from this one cause—the guarantee of the unity of the three—the other two are derived.[23] Or, as Gregory of Nyssa (in a passage that would be discussed extensively at Blachernae) notes: "The difference between them is by way of 'cause' and 'caused,' and by this alone can we conceive of one Being distinguished from the other, namely, by the belief that one is 'cause' and another from the 'cause.' In the case of those who are from the cause, we recognize a further difference; one is derived immediately from the first, and the other through that which comes immediately from the first."[24] The argument that this doctrine of causality, or "monarchy" of the Father, masks a potentially dangerous subordinationism, is countered by the fact that the concept of time is inapplicable to the eternal life of God.

In comparison, the West attributes the causal dependence on the Father by the the Son and the Spirit to the one common essence. The focus is no longer on the hypostasis of the Father, as ἄναρχος ἀρχή, the origin of the persons in the Trinity, but on the common essence; the result is that the persons within this one essence are defined in terms of their mutual relations. Thus, when we speak of God, it is in reference to His essence, but, when we speak of Father, Son, or Holy Spirit (or the act of begetting or sending), we are speaking "relatively" of His relations. Specifically, it is a shift of emphasis (for which Augustine is responsible) to a philosophically conceived unity and essence of God, in which the three persons have lost their distinctiveness by being transformed into mere relations. In this perspective, not only has the essence assumed a logical priority to the person of the Father, but the trinitarian concept of God (in which the Father is the principle of unity and the unique cause—according to His hypostasis—of Son and Spirit) becomes "irrelevant and unintelligible."[25] The personal God of revelation has become a philosophically impersonal essence.

It is not difficult to see how this emphasis leads directly to the *Filioque*. For the creative role in the deity is, perforce, attributed to the one essence shared by the Father and the Son, not to the hypostasis of the Father. As such, the Holy Spirit is said to be caused by both the Father and the Son. The staunch opposition to this doctrine by the Byzantine Church is quite understandable. For "either one is forced to destroy the unity by acknowledging two principles of Godhead, or one must ground the unity primarily on the common nature, which thus overshadows the persons and transforms them into relations within the unity of the essence."[26] The difference between this essentialist perspective, on the one hand, and the personalist orientation, on the other, is evident. Suffice it to say, it served as the point of departure for the debate of 1285.

From all accounts, this discussion, which began on 5 February 1285 in the *triclinium* of Alexius Comnenus in the palace of Blachernae, was the work of a large and imposing assembly. The emperor, sitting on a "royal couch inlaid with gold," was accompanied by numerous notable laymen, by many officials, and by the whole Senate. Adding authority to the proceedings was Theodore Mouzalon, Gregory's former student, now first minister of the empire, who was an accomplished theologian and intervened actively in the proceedings. Manuel Holobolus, the public orator of the Hagia Sophia and head of the school in the orphanage of St Paul's church, was also present. In addition to the patriarch of Constantinople, Gregory II, the gout-ridden Athanasius of Alexandria also attended; since he was ill, he followed the deliberations from his bed, which had to be brought into the hall. He had been a refugee in the capital ever since 1275 because his see was in the hands of the Mamelukes. Present also were the hierarchy (the assembly technically was a synod of the episcopate of the patriarchate of Constantinople) and a large crowd of monks.[27] The saintly Athanasius, future patriarch and successor of Gregory, was also there.[28] So, too, was George Moschabar, Gregory's archivist, who fancied himself a theologian.[29]

By comparison, the opposition was small. A few days before the opening of the council, Beccus had requested that two of his former associates, the bishops of Cyzicus and Nicomedia, be invited to help in the defense. This, however, was impossible, since both were in exile. As a result, Constantine Meliteniotes and George Metochites were recruited for the job; both had been in prison in Constantinople ever since their condemnation early in 1283.[30]

B. *Beccus' Explanation*

The tension-laden synod was officially opened by the public orator, Manuel Holobolus. He began gingerly by sketching Beccus' past, and then proceeded to ask him to explain his 1283 profession of faith (its ink had not yet dried), his resignation, and request for pardon. Finally, he requested Beccus to explain if, by convening the synod, he meant to imply that these things were now invalid. Beccus replied by underscoring his conviction that he had been a victim of injustice, that his submission and resignation had been prescribed by circumstances, and that these had permitted no alternative at the time.[31] According to Gregoras, his twofold aim was to bring the synod around to a more benevolent attitude and to show how harsh and inequitable his treatment, in fact, had been.[32]

At this point, his partisans, Meliteniotes and Metochites, were asked—this time by the patriarch—what they thought of Beccus' apology regarding his teaching and conduct, since they, too, had signed professions of faith. Rather than answer the patriarch directly, however, the archdeacons chose to ignore the question altogether; instead, they launched into a discussion of their theological position and of the patristic witness supporting that position, namely, John of Damascus.[33] By so doing, they determined the subject and heart of the debate of the council's first session.

The deacons' first move was to show the frequency of the phrase "from the Father through the Son" in the patristic literature, and to note that the Fathers believed not only that the Spirit was imparted, given, and sent, but that it even proceeded "from the Father through the Son." Indeed, this last phrase was the equivalent of the Latin *Filioque*. This was shown by St John of Damascus' use of the term "projector" (προβολεύς), which was a synonym for the term "cause" (αἴτιος): "The Father is the projector, through the Word, of the manifesting Spirit."[34] Suffice it to say, if "projector" is understood to mean "cause," then the Father is, perforce, through the Son, the Spirit's cause, or source of existence.[35] Even so, this did not mean that the Son was either cause or joint-cause of the Spirit. For, we do not consider the Son as being cause in the procession of the Spirit, or even joint-cause; on the contrary, we condemn and excommunicate any who say so. What we do say is that the Father is cause of the Spirit through the Son, for the word 'projector' is understood in the sense of cause."[36]

Theodore Mouzalon was not convinced and quickly told the deacons that what they were, in fact, saying was that the Son was a cause in the procession and that the Spirit also had its existence from the Son. Indeed, by insisting that procession was "through the Son," they were really arguing that procession from the Father was somehow imperfect and that the Father could not project the Spirit, unless the Son was first generated. "Is the Father such an imperfect cause that He needs...the Son as joint-helper and joint-cause?"[37] Plainly, their argument could denote only one thing—that the Son was being transformed into a cause.[38] This, in turn, would mean that they saw no difference between the traditional formula of the creed and the doctrine of double procession confessed by the Roman Church at Lyons.[39]

The embarrassing reference to a "second cause," raised by Mouzalon, was countered by the argument that no one believed in three Gods, even though the Father, the Son, and the Holy Spirit were each said to be perfect God. So, just as there are not three Gods, there are not two causes. Likewise, the deacons added, another argument against the notion of a "second cause" was the fact that, in theology, it was not permissible to speak of a time interval between "cause" and "caused," even if it is said that the Son is "begotten" of the Father. For all three persons coexist simultaneously—none being posterior or inferior to the others. As a consequence, the deacons could not accept Mouzalon's ill-advised conclusion; they would stand by their pious definition, for the word "projector" meant "cause" to the exclusion of any other possible interpretation.[40]

An attempt to resolve the impasse created by the Damascene text was then made by the archivist, George Moschabar. His solution was one of rejection—since many of the manuscripts did not contain the controversial text, the passage must be an interpolation, and therefore spurious. Mouzalon would have none of it, however, and whispered in the archivist's ear—he was obviously seated nearby—that this would undermine the strength of their argument. Besides, he added, the passage was to be found word for word in the authorized collection of patristic texts, the *Arsenal* or *Sacra Hoplotheca* of Andronicus Camaterus.[41] No doubt, too, as Pachymeres notes, the assembly was reluctant to renounce the Damascene authorship; the very same thirteenth chapter, which contained the passage, also contained a "powerful weapon" against the Latin *Filioque*, namely, the text: "We speak of the Holy Spirit as from the Father, and we call it the Spirit of the Father, yet *we do not speak of the Spirit as from the Son*."[42] And if this great patristic witness prohibited, even once, the phrase "from the Son," then the Latin solution—the alternative "through"—was altogether forbidden. The solution was not to abandon the text, but to see to its proper and correct interpretation.[43] Patriarch Gregory agreed. Later, he was to include this argument, and the new "weapon" from the Damascene, in the *Tomus*, along with still another Damascene passage—"the Father alone is the cause."[44]

This instinct to accept the text's authenticity (the "editions" of the Fathers and of Scripture were, in the main, in private hands, and were not supervised or controlled by the Church)[45] has been reinforced by modern scholarship. Actually, the question of authenticity involves almost the entire thirteenth chapter of the *Orthodox Faith* of St John of Damascus. Moreover, the text which was discussed at the council itself—found in the same chapter—does not exist in the oldest manuscripts, but only in a few of the latest date. All the same, the latest editor of the work notes that, in terms of grammar, content, and arrangement, the "appended" chapter conforms with the rest of the work; indeed, there is little reason, in light of the manuscript tradition, to doubt its Damascene origin.[46]

In general, Mouzalon was representing the view of the council's membership when he agreed with the archdeacons (and not with Moschabar) that the passage was, in fact, authentic.[47] He added, however, that the unionists should not expect him also to accept their peculiar interpretation. For the Spirit does not have its source of existence "from the Father through the Son," since this would be tantamount to the Latin doctrine of procession "from the Father and the Son." The Latins, at least, preserved the equality of the two persons, whereas the deacons' interpretation created havoc among the hypostases in the one procession of the Holy Spirit. What could be worse, he asked, than saying that the Son is one source and the Father another?[48]

According to Pachymeres, the opposition was, for the most part, reduced to silence, and was forced to take refuge under the authority of John of Damascus; it could only reply that it should not be blamed for the supposed anomaly. Any accusation of heresy or innovation ought to be directed at St John himself. Besides, they had all unanimously opposed Moschabar and agreed that St John's words were genuine, not apocryphal. Either the Damascene *testimonium* was wrong or it was not, in which latter case, it had to be accepted as it was.

At this point, Patriarch Gregory felt moved to register a protest by pointing out that to quote the Fathers and accept their texts as genuine was not enough, for the same is equally true of Holy Scripture, whose acceptance must also be accompanied by its *correct interpretation*. For example, it is stated in Scripture that the Father is greater than the Son.[49] Suffice it to say, acceptance of this seemingly contradictory verse is not enough, unless it is also interpreted in an Orthodox sense. Likewise, acceptance of the Damascene quotation cannot be accompanied by a distorted exegesis. Besides, patristic texts cannot contradict each other—the saints neither err nor disagree—since, by virtue of their mutually intertwining nature, they form the separate pieces of one chain. This being so, they have to be in harmony with each other, with the common consensus of the Fathers, and with the totality of the faith.[50]

According to Gregory, three ground rules were needed for the interpretation of all patristic texts. The text had to be genuine and not spurious; it had to be accompanied by a consistent or accurate interpretation; and, finally it had to be reinforced or confirmed by additional evidence from other Fathers. The text they had selected was genuine—true enough. For all that, they had not been able to show that their interpretation of St John's *testimonium* was fundamentally faithful to the catholic and unanimous tradition of the Church. On the contrary, the facts suggested that their interpretation was not in accordance with tradition; what they had done was to attach their interpretation to the patristic literature, regardless of the facts. The result, Gregory concluded, was pure distortion of John of Damascus.[51]

The logical force of Gregory's argument may have surprised the deacons, who answered Gregory's three points by asking the patriarch for a different interpretation of the disputed text. The latter obliged by pointing to the existing dogmatic legislation of the Church—the common creed. This, said Gregory, expressed quite sufficiently the true faith, when it stated that the Holy Spirit proceeds from the Father. The archdeacons responded that in this they did not disagree, for that, likewise, was their hope of salvation. Mouzalon then interjected that if this was so, and if they accepted the age-old credal statement of the Church, why did they need to introduce the modification "through the Son"? To this, the archdeacons "replied that the unity and the peace of the Churches demanded it.[52]

It was at this point that Beccus, who until then had been silent, took the floor to plead for his friends, the archdeacons. It seems that the first minister's reasonably moderate and logical attitude had impressed Beccus, and he said so. Then, in a dramatic *volte-face*, he announced that he was willing to stop using the daring expression "through the Son," if the assembly would only accept the defense offered by his associates against the accusation of heresy. Mouzalon, however, was not impressed either by the promise or by what he perceived to be sheer flattery. He quickly ordered the ex-patriarch to refrain from using his charms on him. Beccus replied that flattery was not his intention—"God forbid"[53]—and proceeded to buttress and defend the interpretation of the Damascene text given earlier by his friends. For the most part, Beccus accomplished this with further quotations (this time from Gregory of Nyssa), as well as with a number of classic patristic comparisons. And although he feared to explain by metaphor the unexplainable, nevertheless, he would follow, he said, the example of the Fathers as his solid support.

He began by bringing to the attention of the assembly the fact that the Fathers had often used the images of sun, rays, and light, as well as spring, river, and stream, to explain the procession of the three divine persons.[54] Thus, it is said that the rays are directly from the sun, while light is from the sun through the rays. Translated theologically, this simple truth would mean that the Father (sun) is the cause, while the Son (rays) is from the cause. To further the argument and to confirm John of Damascus, Beccus then proceeded to quote from Gregory of Nyssa's *Letter to Ablabius*: "The difference between those who are from the cause is that, whereas one proceeds immediately from the first, the other proceeds through that which comes immediately from the first." If this is so, then the Father is the first cause of the Holy Spirit, while the Son is the second, as indicated by the word "through" (διά). Or, more briefly, the Holy Spirit proceeds through the Son who is directly from the Father—the first and principal cause.[55]

Beccus' opponents then asked if he meant by this that the Holy Spirit proceeded immediately from the Father and from the Son, because if this was so, then the procession of the Holy Spirit would be somehow separated from the generation of the Son. For the witness of Scripture concerning the Son—"thou Father art in me, and I in thee"[56]—was equally true of the Spirit, since it, too, was in the Father, and the Father in the Spirit and in the Son, as was the Son in the Spirit. Or was it possible, they reflected, that you believe differently?

Beccus quickly endorsed their exposition, and confirmed that the Spirit proceeded directly from the Father as did the Son, and that neither procession nor generation was to be thought separate. Both the Spirit (light) and the Son (rays) proceeded from the Father (sun), but the Spirit (light) proceeded from the Father (sun) through the Son (rays). As such, the Son (rays) acted as an intermediary. Hence, Gregory of Nyssa says, "while the intermediate position of the Son preserves His only-begotten attribute, it does not separate the Spirit from His relation to the Father."[57] This being so, the preposition "through" (διά), employed by Gregory of Nyssa and John of Damascus, denoted the intervention or interposition—between the Father and the Spirit—of the Son. This, in turn, was what the Latins meant when they used the preposition "from" (ἐκ), the one permitting us to explain the other.[58]

Beccus and his associates were convinced thee the *testimonia* of the Damascene and of Nyssa meant the same thing as the *Filioque*—they were to be understood in a causal sense. Ultimately, the use by the Fathers of the expression "procession through the Son" was connected with the cause of the procession of the Spirit, or with "theology" proper; it was not connected with the "economy," which, for traditionalists, meant a sending in time of the Spirit by the Son. As the deacons had noted at the beginning of the session, the expression involved more than the imparting, giving, or sending of the Spirit. Indeed, the expression was related—it was identical—to the existence of the Spirit through the Son.[59] As such, the Son's mediating position necessarily involved Him in the procession of the Spirit. In short, both Father and Son had a role in the procession, which was at once *mediate* and *immediate*. By stoutly maintaining that the mediatory or intermediary position of the Son in the procession was causal, Beccus was introducing the category of double procession or second cause into the thought of St John of Damascus. Even before the Council of Blachernae, Beccus had taught and spoken of a caused cause, of a "direct" and "removed" principle of causation.[60] This particular interpretation is, likewise, exemplified by the unionist Theoctistus' exegesis of the Damascene's prohibition, "We cannot speak of the Spirit as from the Son." This, the bishop reflected, did not forbid anyone from using "through the Son" in a causal sense; the only intention of the passage was to underline the fact that the Son was not the principal cause.[61]

Be this as it may, modern exegesis notes that the category of "second cause" is totally non-existent, in terms either of words or of ideas in St John's thought. Indeed, the facts suggest that the *Filioque* cannot be found (as the unionists maintained) in the Damascene.[62] This, it seems, was the view of St. Thomas Aquinas, who, likewise, saw the Greek Father as an opponent, rather than a partisan of the *Filioque*. Patriarch Gregory, after quoting most of the Damascene passages in the third rebuttal of the *Tomus*, and noting the unequivocal attitude of these words, sums it up thus: "For both of these views to be true is impossible."[63]

C. The Orthodox Case

In any event, when Beccus had finished, the staunch traditionalist, Athanasius of Alexandria, decided to undertake the defense, sick though he was. As we should expect, the refugee patriarch admonished Beccus for his senseless factionalism, and for teaching something that was not the traditional faith of the Church. Indeed, he could prove this by the assembly's lack of familiarity with his beliefs. It would be to your advantage and the peace of the Church, the patriarch added, to abandon such teaching. At this suggestion, Beccus promptly noted that the question was far more grave, since he and his friends were being accused of heresy. Even so, this was all to the good, Athanasius quickly replied, for the assembly was in the right and the Church understandably hostile; in the final analysis, he had strayed outside the narrow bounds of Orthodoxy; what was in question was doctrinal novelty. Surely, they were being innovators insofar as theological expression was concerned. All the same, he would again extend his invitation to unite with the common faith of the Church. Only then would peace—the object of everyone's desire and especially the emperor's—become a reality.[64]

The patriarch was suggesting that all attempts to explain the Damascene text be dropped. The only safe procedure, in fact, was to return to the traditional ways of the Church. For all deviations or modifications of patristic pronouncements were forbidden. Typically, the patriarch's speech was little more than the impassioned outcry of a traditionalist, of a man who conceived of the past statically and formally, as a repetition of things once delivered to the saints. Tradition, simply put, could not be used in any viable or expanding way. Suffice it to say, Athanasius' argument was not new: it had been used in 1276 to express a similar hostility toward any discussion that might endanger the faith.[65] A correspondingly conservative spirit had been exhibited in 1283, when Beccus had been admonished to refrain from trying to comprehend the vast ocean of theology by rational means.[66] In a sense, the patriarch's solution was but an alternative to Moschabar's earlier rejection of the Damascene text.

It is not surprising that Gregory should, at this moment, have felt the need to balance matters, and to show how tradition could be used in a living way. Instead of attacking his colleague, however, he took up Beccus' objection to the accusations of heresy and turned to the central point in the debate—the argument that the preposition "from" (ἐκ) used by the Latins was the equivalent of the preposition "through" (διά) found in many of the Greek Fathers. To argue in this way, reflected Gregory, and to say that the *Filioque* was interchangeable with the Greek patristic *per Filium*, was absurd, given the fact that "from" and "through" were not identical. The two prepositions must not be confused, either alone or as they are used by St Gregory of Nyssa. Specifically, to proceed "through the immediate cause" was not the same as proceeding "immediately from the first cause." The grammatical infelicity, not to say frivolous nature, of such an interpretation was plainly manifest. "If the Spirit is from the immediate one [the Father], how can it also be from the first [the Son], who proceeds from the immediate one? Similarly, if it is from the first, how can it be from the immediate one?"[67] The complexity and confusion that ensues from such an exposition, Gregory concluded, undermined theology itself. As such, the accusation leveled against Beccus could not be dismissed so summarily.

Oddly enough, Beccus and his associates were ready to agree by noting that what they had done was, indeed, daring. Nevertheless, all they were asking was to be pardoned, since they had been prompted not by vanity, novelty, or curiosity, but by the desire to bring an end to the division between the Latin and the Greek Churches. And, since both Churches had been obstinate in defense of their positions, the only solution was to emphasize the absence of any real difference between the two creeds. Beccus and his friends should not have been defrocked, accused of total apostasy, or condemned as heretics for their ecumenical efforts. Lastly, when they were deposed in 1283, the holy chrism and the churches of the capital should not have been reconsecrated, as if these had been profaned.[68]

Gregory, who was not finished in his attempt to balance matters, continued by reinforcing his simple lesson in philology with a doctrinal exposition of the disputed Damascene text. He commenced by producing a passage from Beccus' writings in which it was clearly stated that the Holy Spirit received its existence through the Son. In other words, "through" was understood to mean "existence," that is, causality. Gregory then insisted that such language had never been used by the Fathers, and was certainly not supported by any of their writings. Simply put, "through," as in the προβολεύς phrase, did not mean the personal hypostatic existence of the Holy Spirit. This is not quite what the Fathers had in mind.

> The recognized doctrine is that the existence of the all-Holy Spirit is from the Father. This is what is meant whenever "procession" from the Father is used; it signifies that the Spirit has its natural and eternal existence from Him. This is unquestionably—so we maintain and believe—the meaning of the term "procession." As for the prepositions in the phrase "from the Father through the Son," the first "from" denotes existence-procession, while the second "through" denotes eternal manifestation and splendor, not existence-procession..."through," then, denotes eternal manifestation in contradistinction to eternal procession.[69]

The theological notion of causation—αἰτία—was to be understood in an absolute sense, and had to be ascribed to the Father alone, as the Cappadocians had affirmed; any intervention by the Son in the procession was ruled out.

Further, distinctions such as "first" or "second cause" or "caused cause" were unacceptable. Causation was not susceptible to either participation or division (sharing) with the Son; as Gregory was to say later in the *Tomus*, the Son was not the cause—either separately or with the Father—of the Holy Spirit. Hence, the expression "through the Son" was neither synonymous nor coextensive with the Latin *ex Filio* (*Filioque*).[70]

Gregory agreed with Beccus that the economic explanation—an emission in time of the Spirit by the Son—which the traditionalists were advocating was inadequate and unsatisfactory. For it failed to express the abiding relationship outside time of the second and third person of the Trinity. Nevertheless, the solution was to be found not in Beccus' device of "equivalency," but in the concept of a timeless or *eternal* (as opposed to temporal) manifestation of the Spirit by the Son. That is, the Spirit was sent in time by the Son, yet it was manifested and revealed through Him in eternity as well. One could say that the formula "through the Son" was expressive of the permanent relationship that exists between the Son and the Spirit as divine hypostases outside time, as well as the emission of the Spirit in time. However, on neither the intra-trinitarian nor the economic level can the Son be said to be the *cause* of the Spirit. For the Spirit receives from the Father that which pertains to its existence; that which it receives from the Son pertains to its timeless manifestation.[71]

To this, the opposition replied that they accepted the double equation, existence-procession, but could not fathom how, in the same context, "through" could have two meanings; it could only denote the Spirit's natural and eternal existence. Besides, the Fathers never drew any such distinction between the procession and eternal manifestation.[72] It was clear that the unionists could not be budged from their position.

Beccus then tried to turn the tables on the assembly by claiming that it, too, was guilty of heresy, that is, of the same thing he had been accused of. Yet, as far as he was concerned, such error was slender grounds for accusations of heresy, or excommunication. Asked what he meant by this—it had obviously aroused everyone's curiosity—Beccus gleefully proceeded to read from an anonymous text which apparently contained a number of questionable doctrinal statements. These the assembled theologians immediately rejected by taking to task the author, who hastened to confess with embarrassed excuses.

The author, as it turned out, was none other than the patriarchal archivist, George Moschabar.

It is possible that Beccus may have thought the text had belonged to Gregory, in which case he would certainly have disconcerted the synod. This is, in fact, what Pachymeres implies. But such hopes were not fulfilled, for the work was actually Moschabar's. Besides, the synod, unhesitatingly and without embarrassment, saw to the text's general condemnation. "Scarcely had they read it, when they repudiated and denounced the work, very nearly condemning the author himself."[73]

Although this composition has not come down to us (Pachymeres fails to identify it), we can assume that its content dealt with Moschabar's personal explanation of the preposition "through" in terms of "with" or "together." We are reasonably well informed of this explanation, since Gregory was to criticize it later as being "even more slippery" than Beccus' own error.[74] That this may well have been the doctrinal error of the condemned text is supported by Beccus' contention that he was not alone in suggesting other prepositions for the phrase "through the Son"; others, too had gone about doing the same thing. And if Moschabar could be excused, so could he, for he, at least, had the unity of the Churches at heart.[75]

Beccus' maneuver failed to sow any division among the bishops, or to have the assembly's theologians rally to his cause. This uncomfortable realization, however, did not deter him. He would take a different tack. If neither side was willing to budge, he would propose a new compromise-program for agreement. He began by noting that he, too, was a lover of peace, and that he wanted to speak frankly and simply. It was his fondest desire, he added, to unite himself with all those present at the synod—the Orthodox bishops, clergy, monks, laymen, and the two patriarchs—rather than continue in schism and isolation. Like them, he professed, as universally valid and Orthodox, the doctrine that the "Spirit proceeds from the Father," since it was the very words of the Fathers, of the Savior Himself, and of the Second Ecumenical Council.

All the same, he also accepted the notion that "the Spirit proceeds from the Father through the Son," since this, too, was based on the authority of the Fathers, as well as the testimony of the Seventh Ecumenical Council. Beccus was referring to Patriarch Tarasius' use of the phrase "through the Son" at the Council of 787.[76] (It had played an important role in Beccus' conversion, and had become a major proof-text of his theology.[77]) This being so, they should not oblige him to renounce a doctrine whose antiquity was beyond dispute. That, to him, seemed unreasonable, especially when they themselves had hardly considered it.[78] Perhaps the solution lay in drawing up a profession of faith, a *tomus*, which would explicitly exclude and repudiate the formula "through the Son." This they could then both accept, conscious though they both might be of rejecting a portion of the patristic tradition. He then added derisively that any hesitation on their part would be reasonable and understandable, given the awesome responsibility involved in any repudiation of the Fathers.[79]

The patriarch's party promptly answered that they were surely not responsible for the expression; they had not used it. On the contrary, he and his colleagues, who had used it, should also reject it. Beccus then responded that he could not see what harm or inconvenience it would cause if they were to adopt his suggestion. As we should expect, this calculated irony soon transformed the assembly into a shouting match, and even the patriarch lost his composure; everyone's patience was threadbare. Finally, Beccus turned to the emperor, Andronicus, who, till then, had refrained from interfering in the proceedings, and, in a loud voice, swore that peace would never be restored as long as Gregory remained patriarch.[80] Gregory had the good sense to ignore this final petulant gesture.

The emperor, however, did not. Indeed, he was furious with Beccus, and in a voice trembling with anger, soundly chastized him for his vain efforts at ecumenism, and for his continual disturbance of the Church. Had he not done enough harm in the past? Was he not now guilty of all the tumult and shouting that was disrupting the unity of the one Church, for which Christ Himself had shed His own blood?[81] Plainly, even the emperor had realized that Beccus' tiresome protest of innocence had not been honest. Visibly displeased at the failure of the council to restore peace, he quickly brought the session to a close.

NOTES

1. Pachymeres, II, 88-103 (= Mansi, XXIV, 595-608); Metochites, VIII, pt. 2, 132-61.

2. Gregoras, I, 169-71.

3. The existing secondary literature on the council is either incomplete or misleading. Thus, M. Sotomayor, "El patriarca Becos, según Jorge Paquimeres (semblanza histórica)," *Estudios*

Ecclesiásticos, 31 (1957), 346-49, often skirts many points or omits mentioning them altogether. A far more valuable account is Troitskij, *Arsenij*, 273-86.

4. See examples of such introductory superscriptions in Laurent, *Regestes*,no.1490, esp. p. 282 and 283; for their explanation, see idem, "Les signataires du second synode des Blakhernes (été 1285), *EO*, 26 (1927), 131*n*2.

5. See the discussion in Laurent, "Les signataires du second synode des Blakhernes," 130.

6. V. Laurent, "Notes de chronologie et d'histoire Byzantine de la fin du XIIIè siècle," *REB* 27 (1969), 217-19. The author here rejects his dating of the council made in his earlier article, "Les signataires du second synode des Blakhernes," 130-34 (summer 1285), and proposes instead February-August 1285.

7. See above, pp. 75ff.

8. Codex Paris. gr. 1303, fol. 88^r (not fol. 87^v, as noted by Laurent, "Notes de chronologie," 218); this valuable text is a verbose refutation of the *Tomus*, which is quoted at length.

9. Laurent, "Notes de chronologie," 218, interprets the first day of Lent as Ash Wednesday, 7 February 1285. The Byzantine liturgy, however, does not know the Latin Ash Wednesday—Great Lent in Byzantium always began on *Monday*; thus, the date must be moved up to Monday, 5 February 1285.

10. Metochites, VIII, pt. 2, 166.

11. Ibid., VIII, pt. 2, 166. Theoctistus had been ordained by Beccus; see V. Laurent, "La liste episcopale du *Synodicon* de la métropole d'Adrianople," *EO*, 38 (1939), 23-24.

12. See A. D. Zotos, *John Beccus, Patriarch of Constantinople, New Rome, the Latinizer* (in Greek) (Munich, 1920), pp. 76-77. Cf. Beccus, *On the Union of the Churches, PG* 141.17B.

13. J. Meyendorff, *Byzantine Theology* (New York, 1979), p. 188. For the history of the *Filioque*, see idem, "At the Sources of the Filioque Quarrel" (in Russian), *Pravoslavnaia Mysl'*, 9 (1953), 114-37; and the old, but still helpful and complete, account of H. B. Swete, *On the History of the Doctrine of the Procession of the Holy Spirit from the Apostolic Age to the Death of Charlemagne* (Cambridge, 1876); M. Jugie, *De processione Spiritus Sancti: Ex fontibus revelationis et secundum Orientales dissidentes* (Rome, 1936); B. de Margerie, *La Trinité chrétienne dans l'histoire* (Paris, 1975), pp. 223-43; H.-G. Beck, *Kirche und theologische Literatur im byzantinischen Reich* (Munich, 1959), pp. 306-21; T. de Régnon, *Études de théologie positive sur la Sainte Trinité*, II (Paris, 1892); J. Pelikan, *Development of Doctrine: Some Historical Prolegomena* (New Haven, 1969); idem, *The Christian Tradition: A History of the Development of Doctrine.*, II: *The Spirit of Eastern Christendom (600-1700)* (Chicago, 1974), 183-98, 275-78; S. S. Mpilales, *The Heresy of the Filioque*. I: *Historical and Critical View of the Filioque* (in Greek) (Athens, 1972), pp. 31-96, 113-61; I. Chevalier, *S. Augustin et la pensée grecque: Les relations trinitaires* (Fribourg, 1940).

14. Pelikan, *The Spirit of Eastern Christendom*, p. 193. See also idem, "The Doctrine of *Filioque* in Thomas Aquinas and its Patristic Antecedents," *St Thomas Aquinas Commemorative Studies*, I (Toronto, 1974), 335: "One needs to ask whether the difference underlying the *Filioque* was merely one of 'protervia' and 'ignorantia,' even merely one of differing attitudes toward tradition and authority. Was it not ultimately a clash between two views of the Godhead and two means of salvaging monotheism within the framework of the Trinitarian dogma?"

15. For a convenient summary of the Cappadocian synthesis, see Meyendorff, *Byzantine Theology,* pp. 180-89; idem, "La procession du Saint-Esprit chez les Pères orientaux," *Russie et Chréti-enté,* 3-4 (1950), 158-78; V. Lossky, *The Mystical Theology of the Eastern Church* (London, 1957), pp. 44-66; and idem, "The Procession of the Holy Spirit in the Orthodox Triadology," *The Eastern Churches Quarterly,* Suppl. 7 (1948), 31-53, an essay included in idem, *A l'image et à la ressemblance de Dieu* (Paris, 1967). G. L. Prestige's *God in Patristic Thought* (London, 1952) has been described as one of the best introductions in English.

16. *Oratio* 45, *PG* 35.628C.

17. See especially de Régnon, *Études de théologie positive sur la Sainte Trinité,* I (Paris, 1892), 433; the critical study of I. V. Popov, *Personality and Doctrine of the Blessed Augustine* (in Russian), I (Sergiev Posad, 1917); Margerie, *La Trinité,* pp. 159-72; and Chevalier, *S. Augustin et la pensée grecque,* pp. 27-36.

18. T. R. Martland, "A Study of Cappadocian and Augustinian Trinitarian Methodology," *Anglican Theological Review,* 47 (1965), 256; J. S. Romanides, "Filioque" (in Russian), *Messager de l'Exarchat du Patriarche russe en Europe occidentale,* 89-90 (1975), 89ff.

19. P. Brown, *Augustine of Hippo* (Berkeley-Los Angeles, 1967), p. 282.

20. J. N. D. Kelly, *Early Christian Creeds* (London, 1960), p. 359; A. Segovia, "Equivalencia de fórmulas en las sistematizaciones trinitarias griega y latina," *Estudios Eclesiásticos,* 21 (1947), 438. See also M-J. Le Gouillou, "Réflexions sur la théologie des Pères grecs en rapport avec le *Filioque*," in *L'Esprit Saint et l'Eglise,* Actes du symposium organisé par l'Académie Internationale des Sciences Religieuses (Paris, 1969), 195ff.

21. G. Every, *Misunderstandings Between East and West* (London, 1965), pp. 44-47, protests against the idea that Augustine was the leading representative of the Latin theory in the West by pointing out that other defenders of the *Filioque* (William of St Thierry, for example) were not distinctly Augustinian, and that Augustine's disciples were far more Augustinian than he was. Every himself, however, gives the lie to his qualification by noting (p. 46) the identity of the Lyons definition with Augustine's own formulations.

22. *On the Procession of the Holy Spirit, PG* 142.271A; *Tomus, PG* 142.241A.

23. J. Pelikan, *The Christian Tradition: A History of the Development of Doctrine.* I: *The Emergence of the Catholic Tradition (100-600)* (Chicago, 1971), 223.

24. *To Ablabius,* ed. W. Jaeger, *Gregorii Nysseni opera dogmatica minora,* III, pt. 1 (Leiden, 1958), 56. H. B. Swete, *The Holy Spirit in the Ancient Church: A Study of Christian Teaching in the Age of the Fathers* (London, 1912), p. 252, notes that it is doubtful "whether any subsequent writer, in East or West, has approached nearer to a satisfactory statement of the relation which, according to the laws of human thought, the divine persons may be conceived to hold toward one another."

25. Martland, "A Study of Trinitarian Methodology," 257.

26. Lossky, *Mystical Theology,* p. 58. For a defense of the Latin view, see T. Camelot, "La tradition latine sur la procession du St Esprit 'a Filio' ou 'ab utroque'," *Russie et Chrétienté,* 3-4 (1950), 179-92. See also Pelikan, "The Doctrine of *Filioque* in Thomas Aquinas," 336: "Most doctrines of the Trinity can be characterized as tending toward either the tritheistic or the modalistic heresy. The Cappadocians and their successors had to strain to avoid the first, while western theologians often manifested some inclination toward the second."

27. Pachymeres, II, 89-90. On Patriarch Athanasius II, see now E. Trapp, *Prosopographisches Lexicon der Paläologenzeit,* I (Vienna, 1976), no. 413. Gregory specifically requested the presence of Athanasius at the council; see his letter to the emperor in *Ekklesiastikos Pharos,* 5 (1910), 226 (letter 173).

28. Joseph Calothetus, *Vita Athanasii,* ed. A. Pantocratorinus, *Thrakika,* 13 (1940), 87; Trapp, *Prosopographisches Lexicon,* I, no. 415.

29. His position of archivist of the patriarchate was previously held by the unionist Constantine Meliteniotes; see J. Darrouzès, *Recherches sur les* Ὀφφίκια *de l'Eglise Byzantine* (Paris, 1970), p. 114.

30. See above, p. 64 n. 10.

31. Pachymeres, II, 90.

32. Gregoras, I, 169

33. Even so, we do know their view of the question put to them by Gregory; elsewhere, Metochites, VIII, pt. 2, 90, 92, deplores his own and Beccus' lack of heroism in 1283, and notes that their sudden defection "was a sign of weakness, they should have suffered to the last for their cause." Like Beccus, however, he adds that resistance was unwise.

34. *De fide orthodoxa,* ed. B. Kotter, *Die Schriften des Johannes von Damaskos,* II (Patristische Texte und Studien, 12; Berlin, 1973), 36 (= *PG* 94.849B); Pachymeres, II, 91; Jugie, *De processione Spiritus Sancti,* pp. 188-89.

35. Pachymeres, II, 91; Metochites, VIII, pt. 2,149-52.

36. Pachymeres, II, 91. See also Metochites, VIII pt. 2, 158, 159. This argument seems to be identical with the triple excommunication—an attempt to ward off any accusation of heresy—which Beccus had tacked onto the *Synodicon* while patriarch. The three anathemas according to Pachymeres, II, 32, were against those who maintained that the Son was the cause of the Holy Spirit, against those who affirmed that the Son was a joint-cause with the Father, and finally, against those who knowingly maintained communion with such as spoke or believed this way. This addition, which Pachymeres alone mentions (but which need not be dismissed), is not found in the most recent edition of the *Synodicon* by J. Gouillard, "Le Synodikon de l'Orthodoxie: Édition et commentaire," *Travaux et mémoires,* 2 (1967). See also J. Gill, "Notes on the De Michaele et Andronico Palaeologis of George Pachymeres," *BZ,* 68 (1975), 300-301: and Rubeis, *Vita,* col. 84C.

37. Metochites, VIII, pt. 2, 155. Photius used this same argument in his letter 24 to the metropolitan of Aquileia, *PG* 104.801C ("if the procession from the Father is perfect, what is the need of a second procession....if it is imperfect, who will tolerate such absurdity?"); quoted in R. Haugh, *Photius and the Carolingians: The Trinitarian Controversy* (Belmont, Mass., 1975), p. 134.

38. Pachymeres. II, 91

39. This argument is neatly elaborated in the *Tomus* by Patriarch Gregory, *PG* 142.240D.

40. Pachymeres, II, 92; cf. ibid., 31.

41. Ibid., 92; Troitskij, *Arsenij,* p. 276. The *Arsenal's* only partial edition comprises the long extracts found in Beccus' *Refutation Against Andronicus Camaterus*, *PG* 141.396-613 (the

Damascene text is located at 593C); Rubeis, *Vita,* col. 105C. For a summary of its contents, see A. K. Demetracopoulos, *Orthodox Greece* (in Greek) (Leipzig, 1872), pp.25-29; and J. Hergenröther, *Photius, Patriarch von Constantinopel,* III (Regensburg, 1869),810-14.

42. Pachymeres, II, 109

43. Pachymeres, II, 110; for this text, see *De fide orthodoxa,* ed. Kotter, *Die Schriften des Johannes von Damaskos,* II, 30 (= *PG* 94.832B). Actually, this second Damascene text is in book I, chapter 8 of *De fide orthodoxa,* not in book I, chapter 13, as Pachymeres has it.

44. *Tomus, PG* 142.240A-B. If the unionist interpretation of the text was correct, Gregory argued, then "John of Damascus would never have said—in the exact chapter—that the only cause in the Trinity is God the Father, thus denying, by the use of the word 'only,' the causative principle to the remaining two hypostases. Nor would he have said elsewhere, 'and we speak likewise of the Holy Spirit as the Spirit of the Son, yet we do not speak of the Spirit as from the Son'." See also Beccus, *De depositione sua. Oratio* II, *PG* 141.996C-1001B; not surprising, this explicit passage and denial of the formula "from the Son" by the Damascene was also discussed at Florence. Cf. also Jugie, *De processione Spiritus Sancti,* p. 188. See also various interpretations of the text in *PG* 94.831-34.

45. Darrouzès, *Recherches sur les* Ὀφφίκια, p. 433.

46. B. Kotter, *Die Überlieferung der Pege Gnoseos des hl. Johannes von Damaskos* (Studia Patristica et Byzantina; Ettal, 1959), 148. This new edition of St John's *opera* is the work of the Byzantine Institute of the abbey of Scheyern in Bavaria, which has already published three of the eight volumes anticipated. The question of authenticity is also dealt with more briefly by J. Grégoire, "La relation éternelle de l'Esprit au Fils d'après les écrits de Jean de Damas," *Revue d'histoire ecclésiastique,* 64 (1969), 747.

47. Moschabar momentarily agreed, but later returned to his point of view.

48. Pachymeres, II, 93; Troitskij, *Arsenij,* p. 277.

49. John 14:28.

50. Pachymeres, II, 93.

51. Pachymeres, II, 93-94; Troitskij, *Arsenij,* pp. 278-79. This familiar principle, that the Fathers basically must be in agreement with each other, was later used by the Byzantine delegation at Florence—if we accept the view recently expressed—as "both the explanation and the justification of their accepting union." See J. Gill, *The Council of Florence* (Cambridge, Mass., 1959), p. 231; also E. Boularand, "L'argument patristique au concile de Florence, dans la question de la procession du Saint-Esprit," *Bulletin de littérature ecclésiastique,* 63 (1962), 196-99.

52. Pachymeres, II, 94.

53. Ibid., 95

54. For the source of these comparisons and Gregory's use of them, see below, pp. 130ff.

55. Pachymeres, II, 95; Metochites, VIII, pt. 2, 147-48. O. Raynaldus, *Annales ecclesiastici,* 22 (Bar-le-Duc, 1870), a. 1284, nos. 45-46, pp. 545-46; Rubeis, *Vita,* col. 106B. For the quotation, see *To Ablabius,* ed. Jaeger, *Gregorii Nysseni opera,* III, pt. I, 56.

56. John 17:21.

57. *To Ablabius, Gregorii Nysseni opera*, III, pt. 1, 56.

58. Pachymeres, II, 96-97; Troitskij, *Arsenij*, p. 281.

59. Patriarch Gregory correctly identified this as the foundation stone of unionist theology; see his *Apology, PG* 142.258B-C.

60. See his profession of faith of 1283, *PG* 142.237B; and *On the Union of the Churches of Old and New Rome, PG* 141.64C: "For, what is essentially from the essence of the Father (and is not from the Father immediately) has the Son as a medium."

61. Theoctistus' brief commentary on the Damascene will be found in A. Dondaine, "'Contra Graecos.' Premiers écrits polémiques des dominicains d'Orient," *Archivum Fratrum Praedicatorum*, 21 (1951), 435.

62. Grégoire, "La relation éternelle de l'Esprit au Fils," 751: "Jean de Damas emploie cette expression [διὰ Ὑιοῦ] sans en fournir l'ombre d'une explication. Nous savons seulement qu'elle ne peut avoir un sens causal, et qu'elle diffère significativement du ἐξ Ὑιοῦ."

63. *Tomus, PG* 142.240A-B. See especially Pelikan, "The Doctrine of *Filioque* in Thomas Aquinas," 333-34, for the "unequivocal sound" of the Damascene's words. Cf. also Meyendorff, "La procession du Saint-Esprit," 171-72.

64. Pachymeres, II, 97; see also Ch. Papadopoulos, *History of the Church of Alexandria* (in Greek) (Alexandria, 1935), pp. 568-69.

65. See the letter attributed to Athanasius in *Dossier de Lyon*, pp. 338-45.

66. Pachymeres, II, 27. On this particular point, see Zotos, *John Beccus*, p. 65, and Grumel's review of Zotos' work in *EO*, 24 (1925), 29.

67. Pachymeres, II, 97-98. W. Jaeger, *Gregor von Nyssa's Lehre vom Heiligen Geist* (Leiden, 1966), p. 149, agrees, and notes that Beccus' efforts to equate the two prepositions would have seemed strange to Gregory of Nyssa.

68. Pachymeres, II, 98.

69. Metochites, VIII, pt. 2, 135. Pachymeres does not mention Gregory's speech or his reading from Beccus' writings.

70. *Tomus, PG* 142.236C. Cf. Gregory's *Apology, PG* 142.258C: "And since it is not a question of identity, the great foundation of Beccus' thesis—along with the other absurdities that followed—collapses."

71. Cf. M. V.-J. Barvinok, *Nicephorus Blemmydes and His Works* (in Russian) (Kiev, 1911), pp. 166-67; Gregory's theology is discussed in more detail below, Ch. 5.

72. Metochites, VIII, pt. 2, 136-37. Metochites at this point abandons his narrative and launches into an elaborate refutation of Gregory's speech. However, it is not part of the deliberations of the assembly.

73. Pachymeres, II, 98.

74. An explanation of his views, together with Gregory's criticism, is given below, p. 152-3; cf. Jugie, *De processione Spiritus Sancti*, p. 324.

75. Pachymeres, II, 98. M. Jugie, *Theologia dogmatica Christianorum orientalium ab Ecclesia Catholica dissidentium,* II (Paris, 1933), 355n2.

76. Tarasius, *Epistola ad Summos Sacerdotes,* Mansi, XII, 1122 (= *PG* 98.1416C-D): "and [I believe] in the Holy Spirit...which proceeds from the Father through the Son, which, too, is and is acknowledged God." This letter was read at the Council of 787, and was subsequently incorporated into its *acta.* See also Raynaldus, *Annales ecclesiastici,* 22, a. 1284, no. 47, p. 546. The entire passage is quoted by the monk Mark in his *Report to the Synod;* see below, p. 231-32. For its use by other theologians in the period 1250-1453, cf. Troitskij, *Arsenij,* p. 283n4. Like Beccus, many western theologians such as Margerie, *La Trinité,* p. 228, believe that this eighth-century text already points to the Western *Filioque.*

77. Pachymeres, II, 28. The other major texts were from Maximus the Confessor, John Damascus, Nicetas of Maroneia, and Nicephorus Blemmydes. According to Pachymeres, I, 476-77, it is these five who "allegedly" convinced Beccus of the identity of the Greek and "Italian" formulations. Maximus, John of Damascus, and Tarasius are also mentioned in connection with Beccus by an anonymous text edited in *Dossier de Lyon,* p. 533.

78. Pachymeres, II, 99-100.

79. Ibid., 100-101.

80. Ibid., 101.

81. Ibid., 102.

5

THE FAITH OF BLACHERNAE

Earlier, it was noted that the closing of the first session of Blachernae by the emperor did not put an end to the council. Three more sessions were to follow shortly afterward. These, too, however, produced little in the way of a real meeting of minds—Beccus would not throw in the towel. The council then adjourned, only to meet again in August when it proceeded, by common consent, to commission Gregory to write its *Tomus*.[1] These deliberations are not extant. Nevertheless, it has been argued that the council, after rejecting Moschabar's, Athanasius', and Beccus' solutions to the Damascene *testimonium*, adjourned in disarray because it was unable to find an acceptable alternative "on the spur of the moment."[2] It remained permanently paralyzed and defenseless until August, when it tried to redress the deficiency by way of Gregory's *Tomus*. Pachymeres, on whom some of this information is based, notes that all the Orthodox could think about was this embarrassing text.[3]

A. *The Council is Adjourned*

Even so, this is not the whole truth. The *Tomus*, for example, is a substantive and extensive examination and refutation of unionist theology. It is decidedly not an exegesis of a single isolated proof-text. Of its eleven anathemas, only one, the third, deals entirely with the Damascene text while the ninth touches briefly on the meaning of "projector" (προβολεύς). Equally, the *Tomus* includes most of the unionist arguments, which had been presented at the synod and which required some reply. Certainly, the document is not a systematic account of the council's deliberations; yet, much of its material may actually correspond with the debate of the last four sessions. Thus, the points in excommunications three through seven were discussed in the first session; those in eight, nine, and ten may well be the points raised in the subsequent four sessions for which we have no narrative account.

More to the point, it must be emphasized that the centering point of the *Tomus*' component parts is Patriarch Gregory's explanation of the doctrine of the eternal manifestation. The text of the *Tomus*, in short, does not concentrate on the Damascene *testimonium*, nor does it endow it with undue importance; it approaches the problem from a larger trinitarian context. Its focus is the timeless manifestation of the Holy Spirit. This was the very same doctrine which the council had heard in the course of its first meeting, and which had left Gregory's theological abilities untarnished. It is for this reason, as well as for his literary reputation, that the council *unanimously* agreed to have the patriarch draft the appropriate conciliar statement of its deliberations. In other words, there *was* a solution at hand, a solution that was both familiar and recognizable to those who signed the *Tomus* in August 1285.

The *Tomus'* deeper theological foundations, coupled with its general evidence, is an alternate and, perhaps, better guide than Pachymeres or Metochites to the events following the first session of Blachernae. (It is arresting that Gregoras is totally unaware of the council's alleged confusion, and does not even mention the Damascene text.) In sum, it is doubtful if the council was rendered as defenseless and inarticulate as has been alleged. Pachymeres, in his recollection of events, overstates the truth. As Gregoras admits, Gregory and Mouzalon had, in fact, "stemmed the violent tide of Beccus' guilty tongue and prevented falsehood from triumphing over truth."[4]

But there is also evidence to suggest that the quotation from Gregory of Nyssa and John of Damascus, which supposedly confused the Council of Blachernae had been used by Beccus long before 1285. There is, in sum, compelling information that Beccus' theology (along with its proof-texts) and the general thrust of his ideas had already been forged in the crucible of his patriarchate. In effect, we have a very succinct statement of his "errors" two years before Blachernae—namely, in his profession of faith of 1283. Although the Damascene text is not quoted directly, its theological context (as he understood it) is very much in evidence. The thesis of a "direct" and a "remote" cause, together with the corresponding idea that the Father and the Son constitute a single cause from which the Spirit has its being, are included in the confession.

> I said, for example, that the Holy Spirit had, as cause of its personal existence, the Father and the Son, and that this doctrine was in harmony with the formula which declares that the "Spirit proceeds from the Father through the Son." In the final analysis, this means that the Spirit has two causes, and that both the direct and the remote principles of causation were implied. That is, the Son is as much the cause of the existence of the Spirit as the meaning of the preposition "through" allows. And, since all these doctrines are found in my own writings and speeches, they are mine, for no one else had thought and written these. Additionally, I said that the Father and the Son [together] constitute a single cause of the Spirit from whom, as from one principle and source, the Spirit has its being.[5]

It follows that this theology must have been known to many of the theologians at the Council of Blachernae, including, of course, the patriarch, who saw fit to incorporate Beccus' profession of 1283 in the body of the *Tomus.*

But Pachymeres, too, gives the lie to his own interpretation. The historian, after describing the disgrace of Beccus on the death of Michael VIII in 1282, gives a long exposition of Beccus' theology *prior to 1282.* In this analysis, he not only notes Beccus' use of Gregory of Nyssa, and his belief in the identity of "from" and "through," but emphasizes his approval of the Latin *Filioque* as well. He then adds significantly: "The summit of his daring was to discover that the theologically profound John of Damascus, in the thirteenth of his theological chapters, said, 'the Father is projector, through the Word, of the manifesting Spirit,' and to take the word 'projector' to mean 'cause' to the exclusion of any other possible interpretation.[6] The Damascene had already been used by Beccus in the *Filioque* debate before both his disgrace and the Council of Blachernae.[7] At any rate, the text could not have been so totally surprising as to confound Beccus' critics in 1285.

Significantly, this conclusion is corroborated in a very striking way by still another reference from the same historian. This particular passage is a description of a council Beccus held in 1280, while still patriarch, in which—so we are informed—he used the same staples from Gregory of Nyssa and John of Damascus. It seems, in fact, like a miniature Blachernae. We are given Moschabar's suggestion (here made by some of the bishops) that the text from St John of Damascus was not genuine. We are further informed that, while some took the term προβολεύς to denote παροχεύς, still others saw it as an expression of the eternal manifestation of the Spirit by the Son.[8] (It is in this passage, by the way, that Pachymeres makes his own views known—a rare instance, indeed—about Beccus' efforts at persuasion prior to his disgrace; he compares the views with people of poor appetite, who upon eating too much, end in vomiting everything. The better part of wisdom, he adds, would have been to endure the opposition patiently.[9])

Lastly, it should be noted that the Damascene text is found in some of Beccus' pre-1282 treatises, such as the *Refutation Against Andronicus Camaterus,* and in the first letter to Theodore of Sugdea. That it is not found in all of his early works is not, of course, proof that he had not used it.[10] As for the quotation from Gregory of Nyssa used at Blachernae, it is found in the above two works as well as in *On the Union of the Churches of Old and New Rome* and in *The Procession of the Holy Spirit.* All these are pre-1282 texts.[11] Again, it is difficult to see how the Council of 1285 was polarized by a text which had been used in synodal meetings, as well as in Beccus' works long before 1285. In short, the long adjournment of the council cannot be explained solely by the alleged sensation caused by the introduction of the Damascene text in the proceedings of the first session. (As noted above, it is doubtful that the text continued to be the principal topic of discussion in the sessions that followed; the evidence of the *Tomus* indicates the contrary.) Similarly, it cannot be explained solely as the result of the Church's inability to come up with an interpretation of the text; Gregory had offered a solution as early as the first session.

In light of all this, the prorogation of the council may have been a deliberate move by the patriarch, the bishops, and the emperor to give Beccus and his companions an opportunity to rethink their position before any irrevocable decision was made. Gregoras' suggestion that once Beccus had realized that he was not going to receive any sympathy from the official Church, he "openly repudiated the union" is incorrect.[12] The fact is, he remained "inflexible,"[13] as Pachymeres notes, and as the subsequent exile and eleven excommunications of the *Tomus* indicate (there never was a full or a semi-reconciliation).[14] Quite possibly, this is precisely what the council wanted to avoid and may be the reason why it prorogued the council as long as it did.

There is, further, the fact that the council was well aware of unionism's divisive nature. Pachymeres notes that it had split the Church for over a decade by causing a schism that was as deep as that which, only yesterday, had divided Greeks and Latins.[15] It is not unreasonable to believe that a desire to end this disunity forced the council to extend the adjournment. It is of a piece with that search for stability which had eluded Gregory's relations with the Arsenites from the beginning of his patriarchate. Significantly, this is supported by the emperor's frequent personal messages to the imprisoned at the Cosmidion monastery; he repeatedly asked the condemned to reconsider their position for the peace of the Church.[16] It is further corroborated by the conciliatory posture adopted by the *Tomus* itself. Its repetitious note of reluctance to condemn those who had been born and nurtured in the Church[17] is too pronounced to be interpreted as rhetoric, as the conventional expression of a formal ecclesiastical text.

Another avenue of approach to the events of 1285 and the Damascene text is to weigh the alleged confusion of the council against its actual overall achievement. True, during the deliberations, neither side had been able to disarm the other's objections. Very few were willing—apart from Gregory and Mouzalon—to be enlightened or to join in genuine theological conversation; instead, each strove to outdo the other with every conceivable subtlety.[18] Certainly, Moschabar and the patriarch of Alexandria, with their barren attitude toward tradition, were not ready to indulge in free discussion. Regrettably, Beccus, too, for all his acknowledged gifts and willingness to enter into dialogue, could not always hide his intense irritation at his failure to alter the synod's views materially. Pachymeres notes that, instead of cooperation, both sides wished only to uphold their own position; the emperor's long but admirable speech, at the close of the opening session, was thus, in vain, and produced not the slightest change in the views of those present.[19]

Yet it is not true to suggest that the council was without results. Roman theology, for example, did well by Beccus in the deliberations. Theological exchange—the absence of which served to negate the ecumenicity and validity of Lyons in the eyes of most Byzantines—was not lacking in 1285. That the Roman doctrine of procession *ex Patre et Filio* was permissible on theological grounds, that no difference existed between the Nicene formula and that of the Roman Church, that "through" and "from" were interchangeable, and that this was allegedly sustained by the Greek patristic tradition were capably and determinedly presented by Beccus in open and full synod. Indeed, Beccus' definition of the doctrine of double procession, defended at Blachernae, was not much different from the doctrine of Lyons—*ex Patre et Filio tanquam ex uno principio*. Lyons' precision alone was lacking.[20] Facts even suggest that Beccus may have known the dogmatic decree that enshrined the dogmatization of the *Filioque*. We possess, for example, a literal translation in Greek of the original Latin text of the decree *Cum sacrosancta*, endorsed at Lyons, 17 July 1274.[21] The text was probably brought back to Conntinople by George Acropolites' delegation.[22] Typically, authors raised in the Western tradition often describe Beccus' literary output as the very spirit of "Catholic" literature in Byzantium.

Correspondingly, Beccus' position was not left unanswered. Blachernae is at once both the reaction and rejection of the Roman formulation of 1274 by way of Beccus' own condemnation. For that which Lyons declared to be the revealed truth—the irreversible *de fide definita* of the Church of Rome—was solemnly rejected by Byzantium; in answering Beccus, the council registered its views on Lyons as well. This is one of the council's principal achievements.

> We reject the recently established union [of Lyons] which provoked God's hos-
> tility toward us. For this union divided and ravaged the Church under the pre-
> tense of harmless accommodation.... We also render void their dangerous
> doctrine concerning the procession of the Holy Spirit...[for the Son] is not, ei-
> ther separately or with the Father, the cause of the Spirit; for the all-Holy Spirit's
> existence is not "through the Son" and "from the Son.".…This Beccus, and any-
> one who agrees ever to receive those members of the Roman Church, who re-
> main intransigent concerning those doctrines, for which they were from the
> beginning accused by our Church, and for which the schism occurred...that is,
> prior to this misleading accommodation and worthless union [of Lyons]...we
> subject to the terrible penalty of anathema.[23]

A more conclusive condemnation of Lyons in a Byzantine document will be difficult to find. Plainly, the habitual assumption that Byzantium never made any definitive pronouncement on the Union of Lyons or the doctrine of the *Filioque*
(apart from the famous *Mystagogy* of Photius and the familiar anathemas scattered in pamphlet propaganda), is inconsistent with the evidence of 1285.

The substance of this achievement, of course, lies in the answer given to
Lyons. It will be recalled that at the close of the first session of the council,
Beccus had proposed to renounce his theological stand if the opposition, in
its turn, also rejected all the patristic affirmations of procession "through the
Son." He suggested, in fact, the drafting of a document which would embody
this position. Beccus, to be sure, was being ironic since almost everyone knew
that the familiar formula was Orthodox and authentic. Rejection could never
be a consideration. Nevertheless, the council and Gregory took up the challenge, both in the deliberations and in the *Tomus* that followed. The result
was the rejection of Beccus' interpretation of the formula, and the creative development of its patristic meaning in terms of an eternal manifestation. This,
in effect, was accomplished by the *Tomus*' eleven accusations and the accompanying Orthodox rebuttals, each of which closes with an identical formula-
like excommunication of the ex-patriarch, John Beccus, the ex-archivist,
Constantine Meliteniotes, and the ex-archdeacon, George Metochites. And
although this new and "precise" definition of the Orthodox faith[24] went even
further than Photius' own interpretation, the synod solemnly endorsed and
confirmed it.

Some scholars mourn the fact that the *Tomus* was never proscribed by any
subsequent official investigation of the Byzantine Church.[25] But this is to forget that the *Tomus* was not some *pièce d'occasion* or mere polemic, but a con-

ciliar and dogmatic statement—one of the most important of late-thirteenth
century theology. The *Tomus* was sealed and settled both by a lawfully summoned synod and by imperial decree. Clothed with the council's approval, it
became the textually and officially determined Orthodox position on the procession—a στήλη εὐσεβείας, as the text itself notes, of the Orthodox faith.

B. *Photius and the Unionists*

It remains for us to identify the "proof-laden reply"[26] of Patriarch Gregory. To
do so we need first to look briefly at the state of the debate prior to the thirteenth century; we must briefly examine Photius' own contribution, to see
how his *Mystagogy* had affected discussion in post-ninth-century Byzantium;
we have to ask if Photius' "official" reply to Rome was a sufficient and exhaustive treatment, as was frequently claimed; finally, we need to examine unionism's criticism of Patriarch Photius to see why it was so sharply critical of those
who held to his interpretation. The problem, after all, was centuries years old.

As we should expect, Patriarch Photius was faithful to the Greek patristic
tradition.[27] His views on the *Filioque*—it is the first major refutation of the
doctrine by a Byzantine—are Cappadocian in detail and inspiration. True, the
canonical issue implied by the arbitrary addition to the common creed, did not
escape him. All the same, the focus of his argument was on the content of the
addition. He was particularly disturbed by the fact that this entailed an understanding of the Trinity as simple essence, in which essential unity had primacy
over personal diversity; the three persons were reduced to internal relations
within the single deity. Such a priority of the essence over the three hypostases
was positively improper and inadmissible.[28] For, like the Cappadocians, he attributed the cause and origin in the deity, not to the essence, but to the hypostasis of the Father. It is the Father who is the principle of unity in the Trinity.
Procession, in fact, was from the Father alone—*a Patre solo.* Although this formula was verbally novel, it was, for the most part, nothing more than an affirmation of the Cappadocian teaching of the Father's "monarchy."[29]

At the same time, Photius did recognize the fact that the Spirit may be
said to proceed *temporally* through or from the Son.[30] This sending of the
Spirit in time, to the world, was not related to the timeless procession of the
Spirit by the Father, but to the Spirit's work in the economy of salvation; it
was temporal and economic, not theological. In short, it was related to the
Trinity's economic activity of creation and redemption, and expressed the
temporal or cosmic emission—accomplished time—of the Spirit from or

through the Son. Photius, it is true, had not read Augustine. And yet, he realized, as his refutation indicates, that, behind the Latin addition and the Byzantine's objection, lay two different lines of trinitarian development; this insight, coupled with his arguments concerning the relativization of the hypostases and the destruction of the Father's monarchy, explains the popularity of the *Mystagogy*. From the ninth to the thirteenth century, it was the focus of all discussion on the *Filioque* in Byzantium.

Arguably, this was unfortunate, since the view that the Spirit proceeds from the Father only, had the result of blocking any discussion of the eternal relationship of the Spirit to the Son. Photius had failed to address this issue of the lasting or permanent relationship existing between Son and Spirit as divine hypostases. He had not gone beyond the notion of *a Patre solo*. Procession, for his part, was proper to the paternal hypostasis only. Nor had he given any thought, as we shall see, to the patristic expression "through the Son." His successors followed suit, and instead concentrated on the gifts, or the charismata—χαρίσματα—of the Spirit as they are distributed temporally. In short, the eternal and abiding relationship of the Son to the Spirit was ignored. The discussion was on the gifts in isolation from the Spirit's eternal existence. Increasingly, moreover, the general discussion became a matter of text collecting on the part of both Greeks and Latins—for the purpose of disarming their opponents—rather than a genuine theological exchange. It was a self-defeating dialogue that was more apt to confuse than to clarify a still unresolved issue. Significantly, when Gregory tried his hand at a solution, it was not to this post-ninth-century literature that he turned, but to the early Fathers. He neither quotes nor mentions any theologian later than Patriarch Tarasius.[31]

Beginning with the thirteenth century, things changed. It is best to start with Nicephorus Blemmydes, unionism's forerunner. Initially, Blemmydes supported the Byzantine position, both by his writings and by his active participation in the pourparlers with Latin representatives in 1234 and again in 1250. The Latin notion of co-causality—two causes were implied by the *Filioque*—was unorthodox and blasphemous. After 1250, however, he abandoned his traditional position. In two treatises, one addressed to James, archbishop of Bulgaria, and the other to Theodore II Lascaris, he embraced the Latin exegesis, or, at least, came very close to it. As one scholar notes, the two texts contain all the essentials of Catholic dogma.[32] The letters—both were written in the fifties—are particularly important for their decisive role in the subsequent religious evolution of Beccus. It is in these texts that Beccus found his proof for the equivalency of the trinitarian formulas "through" and "from."

Specifically, he assumed, along with Latin exegesis, that the relationship between the Son and the Spirit involved the essential procession, not just their consubstantiality. In other words, he recognized that the Son had a real participation in the eternal procession of the Spirit, and acknowledged Him as a necessary element or essential intermediary in that procession. He insisted, however, that this did not mean that the Spirit proceeded from the Son, as from a first principle. The formula *ex Filio* was to be rejected, since this would make the Son a principle distinct from the Father, who alone was the emitting or producing power. This, he argued, was the meaning of the phrase "procession through the Son." Blemmydes, as we should expect, could not avoid the still actively debated question of the charismata and necessarily introduced these into his exegesis. However, in order to remain consistent with his scheme, and to avoid isolating them from the eternal existence of the Spirit, he was led to identify them with the Spirit's person, or hypostasis. The formula "through the Son" did not designate a mission in time only. Indeed, no difference existed between the charismata and the procession of the Spirit from the Father and the Son.[33]

We have already seen, in the exposition of the discussion at Blachernae, that Beccus was even more consistent. There is no need to repeat his explanation again, except to note that whereas Blemmydes refused to accept the Latin formula *ex Filio*, Beccus did not. On the contrary, he followed Blemmydes' argument to its conclusion by equating "from" with "through." The result was to affirm at Blachernae the Son's essential intermediatorship in the procession of the Spirit. "Through the Son" designated a medial position of essence or, more precisely, the Spirit's eternal procession, not its mission in time, as traditionalists attached to Photius affirmed. The *Filioque*, as such, was both proper and legitimate.

This was, of course, the position against which Photius had expended so much effort in the ninth century. As such, Photius' contribution and role in the schism could not easily be ignored by the unionists. Beccus' attempts to dislodge Photius from his position in Orthodox polemics, and to single him out as the agent personally responsible for the division in the Church, should not cause surprise.[34] In Beccus' judgment neither the *Filioque* nor any other abuse attributed to the Roman Church by Photius was the cause of the Photian schism. Instead, its origin was Photius' own "emotions," and "anger" at his excommunication by the Roman pontiff. Ambition, not doctrine, was the root of the problem. The *Filioque* was only a pretext. This, certainly, was not sufficient motive for the extension of the schism—so fatal to the unity of the Churches. Furthermore, the papal legates at the Council of 879 had not acquiesced in Photius' request that the addition be suppressed. In fact, Photius made a formal repudiation of his previous position.[35] Finally, Photius was wrong in his insistence that the creed had been altered by the Roman Church—the addition neither subtracted from nor added to the creed's original meaning; the interpolation was wholly in consonance with the sense, if not the wording, of the original credal statement of the fourth century.[36]

There are those who would argue that Beccus was the first among Byzantines to use the "historical method" in discussing the schism, and in assessing Photius' role in it.[37] By so doing, he assumed the noble task of dispelling the prejudices and uncritical spirit of his compatriots.[38] Such a view, however, requires amendment. The misrepresentation involved in Beccus' explanation of the crisis which set Photius against Rome is, in fact, considerable. It not only is too simple to be historical, it involves gross distortion. It is well known, for example, that the Council of 879 solemnly confirmed the original text of the creed, that it recited it without the addition, and that it condemned anyone who would corrupt or compose another confession, either by addition or by subtraction. Photius, moreover, made no formal repudiation of his position.[39] As for his attitude toward the *Filioque*, recent scholarship has shown that Photius was never rigorously anti-Latin.[40] His stand toward the doctrine cannot be explained either as a pretext or the result of personal frustration. He considered it serious and far from trivial.

In conclusion, Beccus' historical assessment of Photius has little to do with dispelling the prejudices or the distorted views of his fellow Byzantines. Beccus' reconstruction is an attempt to undermine his opponents' rightful contention—that the Latins ultimately violated their signatures and promises of 879 when, early in the eleventh century, they adopted the *Filioque*.[41] In fact, the unionists had every reason to attack Photius—they knew that he was against what they were desperately trying to promote for a decade. In attacking Photius, the unionists were defending themselves.

C. *The* Tomus: *Trinitarian Personalism*

But what is Gregory's place in this historical framework within which, as has been said, no new element had been introduced since the ninth century? What new dimension did he add to the "official" theological mainstream charted by Photius in the ninth century? In what particular way was the doctrinal statement, enshrined in the *Tomus*, a reply and a rejection of Lyons? In what sense did Gregory go further than his contemporaries in answering his unionist adversaries? To answer these questions we shall need to concentrate on Gregory's argument as developed in the *Tomus*, although we will draw, when necessary or useful, on his other texts as well; the *Apology, Confession,* and *On the Procession of the Holy Spirit* are, in the main, an apologetic restatement of the *Tomus*.

The text begins with a lengthy preamble which actually is a summary of the events leading to Blachernae in 1285. The confusion and division which plagued the Church in Beccus' patriarchate, the text notes, were brought about by the Union of Lyons, and Beccus' attempts to impose it under the pretense of harmless concession. Despite Beccus' solemn promises, however, the alien doctrine of the *Filioque* was introduced into Byzantium, and for eight years flourished like the plague. God in His mercy then raised up the emperor, Andronicus, who re-established Orthodoxy and had the doctrine condemned. If the Church was to avoid straying from the path of faith, however, it was urgent that the Orthodox doctrine be rigorously defined; Beccus' foreign faith must be refuted and condemned if the safety and security of the Church were to be guaranteed. "It is, likewise, commendable and truly salutary, and the work of superior planning, to attend to the future safety of the Church and, in every way, to secure its stability, so that if someone hateful to God should again attempt to disturb it, he will be shown to be acting in vain, because he will be repelled by the unshakable words of our faith."[42]

This declaration of intent is followed by the synod's profession of faith—a detailed variation of the creed.[43] In addition to the familiar articles, mention is made of the veneration due the holy images, the immaculate Mother of God, and the saints. We are then informed how Beccus eventually rejected his heresy, and in 1283 gave an Orthodox profession of faith to the synod handling his case. The verbatim text of his signed profession is then given so that everyone can judge whether the lapsed Beccus had been justly condemned. He had hardly tasted that synod's compassion, however, when he returned to his old ways and continued his literary activity. The spirit of error had departed from him only momentarily. Indeed, even "the new Moses," the emperor, Andronicus, was unable to bring him to his senses. "It became clear from his words (he did not say anything that is true), and from his actions (he made no attempt to hide his wickedness), that he is so closely united with heterodoxy that no words could convince him to renounce his position."[44] The new Synod of 1285 was thus forced to render its decision. The substance of Gregory's theological argument is then given—with persuasive brevity and simplicity—in the form of eleven accusations and their rebuttal.

The logical starting point underpinning Gregory's argument is the fundamental Cappadocian distinction between the one essence and the three hypostases in the deity.[45] In the one essence, there is no division, difference, or multiplicity; it is one, and it is common to all three. As such, it is perfectly correct to say that the Spirit is of the essence of the Father, just as it is to say that the Spirit is also of the essence of the Son.[46] There is no division of the essence in God; each person possesses the whole essence in a manner that is personal and unique to himself. On the other hand, what is said of the consubstantiality of the three persons cannot be said of their hypostatic attributes—unbegottenness, generation, and procession. These are what differentiate or distinguish the one from the other. They are their incommunicable "mode of origin" or mode of subsistence—τρόπος ὑπάρξεως.[47] Thus, the Father's mode of origin is without principle or beginning (ἄναρχος) in character, while the Son's is generative and the Spirit's is processional.[48] This mode of origin simply serves to distinguish the three, and thus to indicate that the Father is not the Son, nor the Son the Holy Spirit, nor the Holy Spirit the Father. Nor do these individuating properties reveal what the mode of origin is.

Within this framework, the hypostasis of the Father holds a special position inasmuch as it is from this hypostasis that the Son and the Spirit receive their personal subsistence. That is to say, it is the origin or cause of the other two; better still, it is the eternal source of all being and action in the internal life of the Trinity. Causality, then, must be ascribed to the person of the Father to the exclusion of the other two: "There is no other hypostasis in the Trinity except the Father's, from which the existence and the essence of the consubstantial [Son and Holy Spirit] are derived. According to the common mind of the Church and the aforementioned saints, the Father is the foundation and the source of divinity, and the only cause."[49] To clinch the argument—a central affirmation of the Cappadocians—Gregory quotes Gregory of Nazianzus: "Everything the Father is said to possess, the Son likewise possesses, except causality."[50] Correspondingly, John of Damascus, in asserting that the only cause in the Trinity is God the Father, denies, by the use of the word "only," the principle of causality to the other two hypostases.[51]

In Gregory's analysis—as with the Cappadocians—the Father, who is the unique source, does not constitute a substitution for the essence. It is not a question of attributing a priority to the Father over the essence; nor does the Father's monarchy imply, as a consequence, any inferiority or posteriority for the Son and the Spirit. The Father generates the Son and projects the Spirit, not as inferiors, but as His equals in "perfection" and "superabundance." Because "that which the Father is, essentially the Son and the Spirit are likewise."[52] Thus, in speaking of the persons and the essence, we cannot say that one proceeds from the other, or that one is posterior or subordinate to the other. Persons and essence are established eternally, that is, at the same time, and are, in fact, co-equal, co-eternal, co-essential, and co-equal in glory.[53]

Correspondingly, although the Spirit is said to be consubstantial with the Father and with the Son, and is the Spirit of both, it does not follow that the Spirit is also from the hypostasis of the Son. For the Father is the cause only by virtue of His hypostasis—of His personal identity—not by virtue of the common essence, of which it has never been said that it generates or projects.[54] More specifically, the Spirit can only be from the hypostasis of the Son if the Father and the Son constitute not only one essence, but also one hypostasis.[55] Given the ultimate "monarchy" of the Father and the incommunicability of the hypostatic attributes, however, such a premise is inadmissible nonsense.

In general, Gregory's thought is based on the biblical-personalist approach of Photius and the Cappadocians who, as has been said, first see God as a trinity of persons subsisting in the divine essence, and then confess Him to be essentially one God. Moreover, it is the person of the Father (as opposed to some abstract essence) who provides the concrete principle of unity without in any way undermining the ultimate equality of the three. This basic patristic perspective is revealed by Gregory when he writes: "It is not because we say that the Son and the Spirit are of the essence of the Father that we confess the Father as their principle and cause; on the contrary, it is because He is the natural principle and cause of those who *subsist* essentially from Him—in an impassable and eternal manner—that they are of His essence."[56] The Father, then, is the source of their common possession of the same essence, and, indeed, the pledge of their unity. Trinitarian unity is grounded in the person of the Father, not in some philosophically conceived abstract essence of God.

Gregory's argument was intended to form the basis of his refutation of the doctrine of Lyons, namely, that the eternal procession of the Spirit is from the Father and the Son, not as from two principles or two causes, but as from one single principle. Indeed, rebuttal numbers seven and eight of the *Tomus* address themselves directly to this issue. In brief, Gregory realized that the doctrine of Lyons stemmed logically from the Western view that the essence is the source of all divinity and the principle of unity. As such, procession is an activity of the common essence, not of the hypostasis of the Father, whence follows necessarily the notion that the Son, being consubstantial with the Father is, likewise, the Spirit's essential cause. The consequences of this confusion between persons and essence—between personal diversity and essential identity in God—Gregory argues, are theologically unsound: first, because the Spirit itself would have to be the cause of someone else, since it, too partakes (like the Son) of the Father's nature; second, because there would logically be an increase in the number of the cause, since "as many hypostases as share in the nature must likewise share in causality"; and, finally because the common essence and nature would be transformed into the cause of the hypostasis.[57] Gregory is, of course, fully aware that the Latin doctrine excludes the participation of the Son and Father in the procession, "as from two principles and two causes"; the Spirit is said to proceed from the Son only in the sense implied by the preposition "through."[58] Even so, the above inadmissible consequences in no way lose their force. The monarchy of the Father simply cannot be reduced to the notion of a double principle in the Trinity. For "the Son is not the cause—either separately or with the Father—of the Spirit, because the Spirit does not have its existence 'through' or 'from' the Son."[59]

To substantiate his case further, Gregory also mentions, in the tenth rebuttal of the *Tomus*, the incongruous unionist argument of the parallel between Christ and the Virgin as "fountain of life." The argument was used to support a double principle of procession and was probably originally discussed in the latter session of Blachernae; this would explain its absence in Pachymeres' account of the first session. "The Virgin is so called [fountain of life] because she lent living flesh to the only begotten word with a rational and intellectual soul, and became the cause of mankind born according to Christ. Therefore, those who understand life to be in the Holy Spirit will think of the Son as the fountain of life in terms of cause."[60] Hence their argument, notes

Gregory, for the "participation" of the Son with the Father in the procession of the Spirit. The argument, Gregory adds, is entirely inept.

Quite simply, the Virgin's title "fountain of life" means that she was the cause of His holy flesh, that is, Christ received His existence—according to His humanity—from His mother, the Theotokos; it is from her that real life came.[61] As Gregory argues elsewhere, Christ is consubstantial with us, inasmuch as He has received—when born of the Virgin—our common essence and nature. To say that He received His existence from each of us as well, however, is absurd. "The man-according-to-Christ is said to be co-essential with us men, and to be of our essence and nature; and yet, His existence is not from the hypostasis of each one of us, for He exists from the Virgin mother from whom He has received that which is ours."[62] Ultimately, then, the primacy of the person of the Father as the unique source of the Spirit (as opposed to the common essence) is reflected in the birth of Christ itself. For it is from the person of the Virgin, not from the common essence of all men, that He received His existence; the trinitarian antinomy of essence-hypostasis is thus confirmed by Christology. If anything, it authenticates the Orthodox interpretation, rather than the Latin notion of a double principle.

Ultimately, then, theological personalism is the tradition to which Gregory was passionately bound. We need only peruse his two major works, the *Tomus* and *On the Procession,* to recognize the continuity of the monarchical perspective of the Greek Fathers, and the thoroughly personalist approach to trinitarian theology they embody. Patriarch Gregory's theology was traditional. This is true of his own personal contribution, which, in fact, broke new ground. For Gregory's doctrine of the divine and energetic manifestation, which he saw enshrined in the formula "through the Son," was ultimately grounded on his profound grasp of the antinomy between unity and personal diversity in Cappadocian thought.[63] It is this which opened the path to his understanding of the interpenetration, or περιχώρησις of the three divine persons.

Until the thirteenth century, as we have seen, theologians were content with three basic ideas: Photius' formulation of an eternal procession of the Spirit from the Father alone; the Spirit's economic sending from the Son; and the accompanying temporal distribution of the charismata by the Spirit. These ideas, however, failed to address the question of the relationship of the Spirit and the Son outside time, as expressed in the formula "through the

Son." For, although patristic literature spoke of an immediate procession from the Father, and of the Spirit's temporal sending, it also spoke of the Spirit as proceeding through the Son. For example, what did Cyril of Alexandria really mean—asks Gregory—when he said that the Spirit "proceeds substantially from both, that is, from the Father and the Son"?[64] Indeed, even Tarasius—as Beccus carefully pointed out at Blachernae—had employed the expression "through the Son" in the Seventh Ecumenical Council of 787. And then, of course, the Damascene had said: "The Father is the projector through the Word of the manifesting Spirit." Moreover, why is the Son often called "the image of the Father," while the Spirit is called the "image of the Son" ?[65] Again, what does Scripture imply when it notes that the "Spirit of God" is the "Spirit of Christ," or the "Spirit of the Son"?[66] Finally, what does St John the Evangelist mean when he says that Christ "breathed on them and said: Receive the Holy Spirit"?[67]

As Gregory's friend Theodore Mouzalon put it, we could follow either one of two extremes. We could accept Beccus' thesis that such proof-texts were a legitimate expression of the Latin *Filioque* and give them a causal interpretation; or, we could reject them and adopt Photius position by opposing the eternal procession of the Spirit from the Father to its temporal sending "from the Father through the Son."[68] Suffice it to say, Gregory—like Mouzalon—found both solutions wanting. One was an "interpolation of the apostolic faith,"[69] while the other had failed to provide an effective counter to explain how the Spirit is said to "come from both." That is to say, if the phrase could not be taken literally—as Beccus wished—neither could it be reduced to Photius' exclusive formulation of *a Patre solo*. Arguably, the patriarch would have agreed with the modern contention that Photius' theology "was not a happy point of departure for any evaluation of the Byzantine viewpoint."[70] For although Photius was a dedicated patristic scholar, the fact remained that the phrase "through the Son" had never carried any weight with him. The traditional insistence on the temporal distribution of the gifts—in isolation from the existence of the Spirit—did not eliminate the issue. In short, the doubts raised by the texts remained unresolved. Only if we spoke of an eternal illumination or manifestation of the Spirit by the Son—without making the Son responsible for the Spirit's origin—could the unionist interpretation of the formula be countered. So Gregory believed.

This interpretation, however—and here Gregory is insistent—must conform with "patristic traditions and the common beliefs about God and things divine." This alone was to be the guiding principle and criterion of interpretation; we must not, like Beccus, alter, distort, or refuse to adhere to the true intention of the patristic texts.[71] Nor must we rush arrogantly past their meaning in order to invent our own. For he "does not look at the aim that the author had in mind, but arrogantly passes over the purpose and desire, and even the express intent of the author's statement and adheres to the word." Such methodology, Gregory was convinced, obtained only the shadow instead of the body: it was like twisting ropes of sand and building houses therefrom.[72]

D. *The* Tomus: *Eternal Manifestation*

Gregory, then, was willing to accept those expressions of the post-Nicene theologians, such as Maximus the Confessor, Tarasius, John of Damascus, and Cyril of Alexandria, that the Spirit exists through the Son and from the Son.[73] To say that the Spirit exists from or through the Son did not mean, however, that it also had its existence from or through Him.[74] A distinction had to be made between existing (ὑπάρχει) and having existence (ὕπαρξιν ἔχειν). At the outset, we should note that the distinction is both valid and fundamental to Gregory's trinitarian theology. It helps us to differentiate between two separate realities in God—one, referring to the Spirit's cause, which concerns its eternal personal mode of origin from the Father alone; the other, referring to the divine life itself of the Spirit, or to its eternal manifestation, which concerns the Father and the Son. True, the fine distinction between existing and having existence is a subtle one. (Beccus—along with some modern commentators[75]—saw it as a contradiction, or a senseless distinction.) And yet, according to Gregory, the alternative would have meant reading the Fathers out of context, and nullifying the immutable monarchy of the Father (which these same theologians clearly advocated). In short, he would be abandoning the only guiding principle in the interpretation of the Fathers.

In general, Gregory argued that, if the Spirit received that which pertains to its subsistence "immediately and exclusively" from the Father, it also finds its reason for subsisting or its manifestation in the Son.

> The phrase of saint John of Damascus, "the Father is the projector through the Son of the manifesting Spirit"...clearly denotes the manifestation—through the intermediary of the Son—of the Spirit, whose existence is from the Father.

> Those who affirm that the Paraclete, which is from the Father, has its existence (ὕπαρξιν ἔχειν) through the Son and from the Son...propose as proof the

phrase the Spirit exists (ὑπάρχει) through the Son and from the Son. In certain texts [of the Fathers] the phrase denotes the Spirit's shining forth and manifestation. Indeed, the very Paraclete shines forth and is manifest eternally through the Son, in the same way that light shines forth and is manifest through the intermediary of the sun's rays; it further denotes the bestowing, giving, and sending of the Spirit to us.

According to the common mind of the Church and the aforementioned saints, the Father is the foundation and the source of the Son and the Spirit, and the only source of divinity, and the only cause. If, in fact, it is also said by some of the saints that the Spirit proceeds through the Son, what is meant here is the eternal manifestation of the Spirit by the Son, not the purely [personal] emanation into being of the Spirit, which has its existence from the Father.[76]

In trinitarian theology, therefore, two distinct realities are involved. If one level of reality denotes the *internal* life and nature of the Trinity itself—its self-existence—the other denotes the *external* life or self-revelation of God Himself, as it reveals perpetually the glory and "splendor" that is common to the trinity of persons in the Godhead. (For every externalization in the order of the manifestation of the divine life includes the three—the Father, the Son, and the Holy Spirit.) God, in short, exists not only in His essence but outside His essence. But, since this antinomy is, in truth, a distinction within God's very being (both the manifestation and the timeless procession are *eternal*), the divine manifestation, as such, is neither alien nor "without" God.

More specifically, the patriarch's ideas involve the distinction between the essence and the energy, or the incommunicable and unknowable essence of God and His participable and perceivable energy, or life. Plainly, the divine manifestation is dependent on the consubstantiality of the Son and the Spirit; the Son shares the co-essential nature of the Spirit eternally. It is not the essence that is revealed by God's manifestation, however, but the divine life. Thus, the proof-texts of the unionists, namely, the divergent phrases of the Fathers, of Cyril, of John of Damascus, of Maximus the Confessor, and of Tarasius are references to the revealing or energetic processions of the Trinity, not to the Spirit's personal procession. As Gregory puts it: "The great Maximus, the holy Tarasius, and even the saintly John [Damascene] recognize that the Holy Spirit proceeds from the Father, from whom it subsists in terms of its hypostasis and the cause of its being. At the same time, they acknowledge that the Spirit is given, revealed, and, manifested, comes forth, and is known through the Son."[77] Gregory's theological output—terse and slight though it may be—is one of the clearest expressions in all Byzantine literature of this theological antinomy between the unknowable divine essence and the eternal revelation in the Spirit, for which God goes out of His essence. It is this that is meant—insists the *Tomus*—in all patristic literature.[78]

But it is not the *Tomus* alone which contains this distinction. Elsewhere, in an attempt to defend himself against those who had accused him of muddling the notion of the hypostatic procession by his distinction, Gregory notes the following:

> We say that the Holy Spirit exists immediately from the Father and through the Son. Whatever our opponents may say, the fact remains that we do not abolish the procession "through the Son" by accepting the immediate procession, any more than we suppress the immediate procession by accepting the procession "through the Son." Indeed, we affirm the immediate procession, because the Spirit derives its personal hypostatic existence, its very being, from the Father Himself and not from the Son, nor through the Son. Were this not the case, the Son would also be indisputably the cause of the Paraclete, a fact which is impious and which was never said or written by any of the Fathers. For all that, we say that the Spirit proceeds through the Son, and this without destroying our faith in the immediate procession. For, on the one hand, it proceeds and has its existence from the Father, of whom is born the Son himself; while, on the other, it goes forth and shines through the Son, in the same manner as the sun's light is said to go forth through its rays, while the sun remains the light's source, the cause of its being, and the natural principle of its origin; and yet, the light passes forth, emanates, and shines through the rays from which it derives neither being nor existence. And, although the light passes through the rays, it in no wise derives the origin of its being through or from the rays but immediately and exclusively from the sun—whence the rays themselves, through which the light is made manifest.[79]

Gregory again insists on the distinction, by carefully noting that neither the immediate procession nor the manifesting procession can be abolished. The immediate procession concerns that order of the divine life in which the notion of a double principle is excluded. For the Father is the only cause from whom the Spirit's origin is "immediately and exclusively" derived without the Son's active mediation; as in the case of the sun and its rays, the Son can be neither joint-cause nor joint-contributor.[80] It is not from the rays that the light derives its being or existence but from the sun. In the order of God's eternal manifestation, however, the Son's participation poses no problem; for, in the energetic life of the Trinity, the Spirit "goes forth and shines through the

Son," independent in its origin of the Son's hypostasis. For the sun remains the light's source and the source of its being.

Needless to say, within this context—the order of God's eternal manifestation— the scriptural and patristic references to the Spirit as the eternal "image of the Son" or the "Spirit of the Son" acquire their full force. One could even say legitimately that this revelation of the manifesting Spirit is from the Father and from the Son—*Filioque*. For in Gregory's theological scaffolding, the traditional metaphor of the sun and its rays was transformed. While the Son is the rays from the Father, "the Spirit is the boundless circumference of the Father within which the uncreated light of the Trinity is carried."[81] There is no separation. The light, splendor, and radiance belong to all three persons. Even so, the personalism of Byzantine theology remains inviolate. It in no wise "destroys the faith," as Gregory notes, for the Spirit continues to derive both "its being and its existence" from the person of the Father. Clearly, the patriarch's "great task of reconciling the Damascene proof-text by giving it an Orthodox sense"[82] was realized, but only as a consequence of the distinction he introduced between the essence and the divine life of God.

It was noted earlier that Gregory's notion of the Spirit as "energy" or the "gift" of the Son is dependent on the consubstantial nature of the Son and the Spirit. This point is forcefully made in the patriarch's discussion of Cyril of Alexandria. The proof-texts used by Beccus from this Father, Gregory points out, deal exclusively with the notion of consubstantiality. When the Fathers say that the Spirit is the "Spirit of God" as well as the "Spirit of Christ," or that it "proceeds substantially from both" (according to Cyril), they "mean that the Spirit proceeds from the Father, and that it is inseparably one with the Son with whom it is naturally united and consubstantial."[83] That is to say, the Spirit proceeds from the Father—it has its "perfect procession" from Him—and is joined to the Son in unity by reason of their mutual consubstantiality. For, if the Son were the Spirit's cause and principle, how could the Spirit be said to "proceed perfectly" from the Father? This is the voice of Cyril, notes Gregory.[84] What is being expressed is the consubstantiality of the Trinity, or "the unity and unchangeableness of the divine essence," as Maximus the Confessor put it.[85]

Nevertheless, Gregory is at some pains to stress that what is being sent or given by the Son cannot be identified with the essence, the procession, or the hypostasis of the Spirit. What, then, is it that is being sent and in which we "participate"? What is it that is being imparted to those who are "well-disposed to receive the Spirit? Better still, what did Christ communicate to His apostles when He breathed on them and said "receive the Holy Spirit"? None other, says Gregory, than the "gifts" and the "energies" of God, which, as Athanasius and Cyril insist, come from the Father and from the Son in the Holy Spirit.[86] Gregory then defines these energies, sent through the Son, by noting that they are God's sanctifying grace, or "manifestation," or "benefaction," which is "rightly called gift or energy." And as these gifts are the gifts of the Spirit, so are they the Son's. For the operations of the Spirit are, likewise, the operations of the Son, and there is nothing, says Athanasius, which is not perfected through the Word in the Spirit.[87]

In the *Tomus*, Gregory is just as explicit, particularly in rebuttal number ten dealing with the title "fountain of life" that was discussed earlier. After explaining what this title meant in relation to the Theotokos, he has this to say about its meaning in relation to Christ:

> As for the Son, He is the fountain of life because He became the cause of life for us who were dead to sin because He became as an overflowing river to everyone; and because, for those who believe in the Son, the Spirit is bestowed as from this fountain and through Him. This grace of the Spirit is poured forth, and it is neither novel nor alien to Scripture, were it to be called by the same name as the Holy Spirit. For sometimes an act (ἐνέργεια) is identified by the name of the one who acts, since frequently we do not refuse to call "sun" the sun's own luster and light.[88]

What the patriarch wishes to emphasize is that the label "fountain of life" has nothing to do with the "participation" of the Son with the Father in the Spirit's procession, as argued by the unionists.[89] On the contrary, the Son is the fountain, or "cause," for the outpouring toward us of sanctifying grace, which is "bestowed *from* this fountain and *through* Him." Moreover, this grace, or energy of the Spirit, is itself called spirit just as the sun's light is often called "sun." Not surprisingly, Gregory Palamas conveyed the exact same theological meaning when he noted, some fifty years later, that "spirit" (πνεῦμα, without the article and without capitalization) is the flowing of divinity, which we receive from Father through the Son in Holy Spirit.[90] With both theologians, then, the Spirit goes forth and shines as sanctifying energy manifesting itself *ex Patre Filioque*.[91]

This manifestation, however, Gregory hastens to emphasize, is separate from both God's person and essence, for the divine is alone participable through its energies and manifestation. That is to say, God is unparticipable apart from His external revelation, or energies, or charismata, through which He is exclusively known. Otherwise, Christ, in breathing on His apostles, would have given them the very essence and hypostasis of the Spirit. And that, of course, would be the falsehood perpetuated by Blemmydes. In addressing his opponents, Gregory has this to say:

> If this enhypostasized essence of the Paraclete is both gift and energy (ἐνέρ-γεια), do we—who partake of the gift and for whom the gift and illumination operate—share and receive the essence? And, what truth is there in him who says that the divine is participable alone in its energies and illumination? As regards what St Athanasius says—that the coming down of the Holy Spirit is realized in the energies and divine power—what value will that have? None, I believe—if you are right![92]

In short, Gregory differentiates between the hypostasis of the Spirit and the energy, between the person of the Spirit and the eternal gifts received at Pentecost—at "the coming down" of the Holy Spirit. As one scholar notes (reflecting on the contribution of Gregory II and Gregory Palamas), Pentecost is not an incarnation of the Spirit, but the communication or the bestowing of the gifts of divine or uncreated grace.[93] And rightly so, for the divine, as Gregory emphasizes, is alone participable through its *eternal* (and, therefore, uncreated) energies. God is not limited solely to His essence, but interacts with creation through the eternal and uncreated character of His radiance, or manifestation. Gregory implies that if it were otherwise, and we followed Beccus' argument and admitted no differentiation there would be no energetic manifestation of the Trinity outside the essence. "Indeed, it would be difficult even to enumerate the theological absurdities that follow."[94] Gregory's view, in general, is a denial of the validity of the Latin position. For, if we admit, as Latin theology does, no distinction in the Trinity outside the essence, and uphold only the divine simplicity, then everything outside the essence must be created.

Theologians and scholars familiar with late-Byzantine theology, will have noticed the striking similarity between the above exposition and the subsequent fourteenth-century Palamite conception of God. Patriarch Gregory's unwillingness to limit God to His essence, and his insistence that it is through the energy that God is made manifest, are the main threads from which the theological fabric of Palamas is woven. Gregory's elaboration of God's glory and radiance is identical to that experienced by the hesychasts some fifty years later. Equally, Palamas' emphasis on the direct experience of the divine light—as a real and attainable possibility—is never doubted by the patriarch. He did not, it is true, explain in detail this reception by man of God's divine light, as Palamas was to do. But that is only because Gregory's main concern and focus was on the internal life of the Trinity and, particularly, on the relationship existing outside time between the Son and the Spirit. His formulations were a direct response to the *Filioque* controversy, while Palamas' dealt principally with man's participation in the new life—hence, his existential theology and spirituality. In conclusion, the idea that Palamite theology was developed during the controversy with Barlaam, and that this theological system was, for Palamas' supporters, a new revelation—*eine neue Offenbarung*—is hardly tenable.[95]

One point in this brief exposition of Gregory's theology needs further emphasis. This is his view of the charismata and the temporal procession of the Spirit. Gregory's position is quite clear—there can be no isolation between these and the Spirit's eternal manifestation, or existence. "The Spirit is [economically] imparted, given, and sent through the Son to those who are well-disposed to accept it...Likewise, it is manifested, shines, and revealed eternally [in its eternal existence]."[96] We are, thus, speaking of an identical phenomenon—one is the expression of the other. In arguing this point—particularly in the *Apology*—Gregory's emphasis on the *eternal* nature of the manifestation is crucial. "If the Spirit is eternally the Spirit of the Son and is called the Spirit of the Son—for it is through Him that it is revealed—then he who acknowledges this reality and says that the Spirit is revealed through the Son must perforce admit that it is also revealed eternally."[97] In brief, the manifestation is eternal, or uncreated, or beyond created being, inasmuch as the Spirit is eternally the Spirit of the Son by whom it is sent and revealed. That is to say, God has always existed—independently of the created world—both in His unknowable essence and outside His essence or energies. Indeed, this is a reality that would be, even if creation did not exist to receive it. As Mouzalon notes, the manifestation is "eternal and pre-eternal."[98] Obviously, if this is so, then the manifestation cannot be restricted exclusively to the economic realm—that is, to the temporal mission of the Spirit, or the charismata. On the contrary, the eternal manifestation is the supra-temporal aspect of the charismata. As such, the terms ἐνέρ-γεια, δωρεά, and χάρις are all synonyms for ἔκφανσις. The "manifestation" of Gregory's theology *is* the charismata.

Such, then, are Gregory's principal ideas as found in the synodal statement of 1285 and in his apologetic tracts. In drawing the threads together, he solemnly brings the document of 1285 to its conclusion by noting that Beccus' doctrine, which he and the Church had addressed, was in reality a departure from all ecclesiastical prudence, and constituted slander against the saints; although Beccus confidently affirmed that it was the Fathers' very thought, in effect, it was his own fabrication.

> Certainly, the doctrines of the above-listed and already expelled individuals are filled with blasphemy, malice, and fall short of all ecclesiastical prudence. Even if Beccus, the father of these doctrines—or someone among his zealous supporters—confidently affirms that these teachings are the thoughts of the saints, in reality, we must suppose him a slanderer and blasphemer of the saints. For where have the God-bearing Fathers said that God the Father is, through the Son, the cause of the Spirit?...Where did they say that the Paraclete has its existence from the Father and from the Son? In what text did they teach that the one essence and divinity of the Father and the Son is the cause of the Holy Spirit's existence? Who, and in which of his works, ever prohibited anyone from saying that the hypostasis of the Father is the unique cause of being of the Son and the Spirit? Who, among those who believe that the Father is the cause of the Spirit, has taught that this is by virtue of the nature, not by virtue of the hypostasis? And who has failed to maintain this as the characteristic that distinguishes the Father from the other two hypostases? Finally, who says that those other teachings, about which he has lied by insulting the Fathers, belong to the Fathers?[99]

Gregory then adds that both the authentic wheat of the Gospel and the future of the Church must be guaranteed against such prickly thorns and weeds. And since counsel had not sufficed, the synod roundly anathematized and excommunicated their fabricators together with all those who, now or in the future, would dare re-establish the act of the Union of Lyons, and again impose these doctrines on the Church.

A final comment with which to conclude this short account of Gregory's theology concerns the simile of the sun with its rays and light found throughout his work, and especially in the *Tomus*. (The omnipresent word ἔκφανσις, of course, is itself derived from the word for light.) To begin with, what has been called a "gross comparison"[100] in reference to the deity was also used by Beccus on several occasions, including Blachernae. Moreover, this and various other images from nature are traditional, and were first used in the third century by Tertullian in *Against Praxeas*.[101] They were then adopted and used by numerous writers of the fourth and subsequent centuries, including the greatest theologian of the Trinity Gregory of Nazianzus![102] Equally, it is useless to insist that Gregory—as deeply learned as he was—had actually taken this useful and far from clumsy comparison "literally," as it has been claimed.[103] Nor did he transform the Son, by the use of this simile, into a sort of inactive conduit in the procession of the Holy Spirit.[104]

This is certainly an inaccurate, even prejudiced reconstruction of Gregory's thought. In fact, Gregory's formulation of the mystery of the Trinity's life *ad extra* involves a mutual sharing jointly and equally *from* the Father *through* the Son *in* the Holy Spirit; it implies a "bond of interdependence and reciprocity"[105] which is hardly one of inactive participation. For the charismata belong to all three persons. In other words, what is communicated and participated in the "energy" is the *trinitarian* life of God. This energy and operation (Gregory's own terms) are neither alien to the divine essence nor exterior to God. They reflect the common life of the three persons, or the "interpenetration" or "co-inherence" of the three divine hypostases. Gregory, it is true, does not employ the patristic term of the divine περιχώρησις. And yet, this is precisely what is conveyed in his concept of the eternal manifestation. It is also eloquently expressed in his *Confession*, in a passage of genuine intuition, when he declares that the Spirit "accompanies" the Son through whom its eternal splendor is made manifest. "The Spirit is co-essential with God the Father, and with the Son, with whom it is united in the Father whom it accompanies, and through whom it shines forth, is manifest, and is revealed."[106]

The above-mentioned negative criticism is understandable if its Western perspective and incompatibility with Gregory's theology are recognized. For the West, to repeat, has not always maintained the genuine apophaticism of Byzantine theology, or the antinomy between the essence and the energy which open the way to the co-inherence and energetic manifestation enshrined in Greek patristic thought. As such, Gregory's "new theory" or "new error"—based on the decisive authority of the Fathers—is neither novel nor unusual, as Beccus and many modern commentators claim.[107] Its foundations lie deep in patristic soil; it is an organic development of patristic thought—a theological scaffolding that allows us to discover and locate the intuitions of the Greek Fathers. As we have seen his masters are not the theologians of the post-ninth-century period, but the early Fathers: John of Damascus, Cyril of Alexandria, Athanasius, Gregory of Nyssa, and Maximus the Confessor. Thus, it is not the *Tomus'* theological novelty or discontinuity with the past that should be emphasized, as much as its profound doctrinal grasp and fidelity to tradition. Such was the faith of Blachernae.

NOTES

1. The *editio princeps* of the *Tomus*, based on codex Parisinus gr. 1301, fols. 87^r-102^v, was made by A. Banduri, *Imperium Orientale sive Antiquitates Constantinopolitanae,* II (Paris, 1711), 942-49, and reprinted in Migne, *PG* 142.233-46. Since the Migne reprint is the most accessible, all references to the *Tomus* will be made from this edition. See also Laurent, *Regestes,* no. 1490. O. Raynaldus, *Annales ecclesiastici,* 22 (Bar-le-Duc, 1870), a. 1284, no. 44, p. 544. The signatures of the *Tomus,* published by V. Laurent, "Les signataires du second synode des Blakhernes (été1285)," *EO,* 27 (1927), 143-49, are based on codices Ambros. gr. 653 and Dionysiou 150. Paris. gr. 1310 does not contain signatures. For the first translation into English of the *Tomus,* see Appendix A. The Russian translation was done by I. E. Troitskij, in *Christianskoe Chtenie,* 69, pt. 1 (1889), 344-66.

2. Laurent, "Les signataires des Blakhernes," 135; idem, "Un polémiste grec de la fin do XIIIè siècle: La vie et l'œuvre de Georges Moschabar," *EO,* 28 (1929), 138: "En effet, celui-ci n'était qu'un long commentaire du fameux passage de saint Jean Damascène allégué par les catholiques et dont on n'avait pu, séance tenante, fournir une explication suffisante." See also J. Gill, "Notes on the De Michaele et Andronico Palaeologis of George Pachymeres," *BZ,* 68 (1975), 296, idem, "John Beccus, Patriarch of Constantinople 1275-1282," *Byzantina,* 7 (1975), 263; F. Cayré, "Georges de Chypre," *DTC,* 6, pt. 1 (Paris, 1920), col. 1232.

3. Pachymeres, II, 108ff.

4. Gregoras, 1, 170. See also ibid., 176-78, for Blachernae and its proceedings.

5. *Tomus, PG* 142.237B-C.

6. Pachymeres, II, 31

7. See G. Hoffman, "Johannes Damaskenos, Rom und Byzanz (1054-1500)," *OCP,* 16 (1950), 179, 181, who notes that, in the twelfth century, Nicetas of Maroneia drew material from the Damascene, but not in any active or polemical way; Beccus alone did this, and was thus the first Byzantine to place the Damascene in the forefront of the *Filioque* debate.

8. Pachymeres, I, 482.

9. Ibid., I, 479.

10. For a different interpretation, see Gill, "Notes on the De Michaele of George Pachymeres," 297, who believes (*a*) that, before 1285, Beccus had not brought the quotation from the Damascene into clear prominence, because his pre-1282 works do not support such a conclusion; and (*b*) that Pachymeres gave the quotation too large a space in his description of the Council of 1285, as well as in his account of Beccus' pre-1282 theological activity. In short, Beccus' writings are a safer guide than Pachymeres'.

11. For the dating of Beccus' work, see L. Bréhier, "Jean XI Beccos," *Dictionnaire d'Histoire et de Géographie ecclésiastiques,* 7 (Paris, 1934), cols. 362-63.

12. Gregoras, I, 170-71.

13. Pachymeres, II, 103; Raynaldus, *Annales ecclesiastici,* 22, a. 1284, no. 48, p.546.

14. M. Sotomayor, "El patriarch Becos según Jorge Paquimeres (semblanza histórica)," *Estudios Ecclesiásticos,* 31 (1957), 350-57, believes in a "semi-reconciliation"; this is not supported by

Pachymeres, Metochites, Beccus, or the evidence of the *Tomus*. Gregory notes in the *Tomus*, *PG* 142.239A, that after the council, "it became clear from his words (he did not say anything that is true), and from his actions (he made no attempt to hide his wickedness), that he is so closely united with heterodoxy that no words could convince him to renounce his position."

15. Pachymeres, I, 400-401.

16. Ibid., II, 102; cf. *Tomus*, *PG* 142.239A.

17. *PG* 142.239B-D, 244D, 246A-B.

18. So Troitskij, *Arsenij*, p. 282.

19. Pachymeres, II, 102.

20. Cf. Beccus' letter to Pope John XXI, in A. Theiner and F. Miklosich (edd.), *Monumenta spectantia ad unionem ecclesiarum graecae et romanae* (Vienna, 1872), 25-26. On the doctrine of Lyons, see E. Candal, "Progresso dogmatico nelle definizioni trinitarie del Concilio II di Lione e del Fiorentino," *Divinitas*, 5, fasc. 2 (1966), 334-44; on the correctness of Beccus' formulations vis-à-vis Roman doctrine, see M. Jugie, *Theologia dogmatica Christianorum orientalium ab Ecclesia Catholica dissidentium*, II (Paris, 1933), 345ff.; and M.-J. Le Guillou, "Filioque," *Catholicisme*, 4 (Paris, 1956), cols. 1279-86.

21. See the new edition in B. Roberg, *Die Union zwischen der griechischen und der lateinischen Kirche auf dem II. Konzil von Lyon (1274)* (Bonn, 1964), p. 247.

22. Recently published in *Dossier de Lyon*, pp. 324-25; and by J. Gill, "The Church Union of the Council of Lyons (1274) Portrayed in Greek documents," *OCP*, 40 (1974), 22, cf. V Laurent (ed.), *Les "Mémoires" du Grand Ecclésiarque de l'Eglise de Constantinople Sylvestre Syropoulos* (= Concilium Florentinum Documenta et Scriptores, Ser. B. IX; Rome, 1971), 37. This was the only dogmatic decree issued by Lyons; the remaining thirty constitutions were disciplinary in nature.

23. *Tomus*, *PG* 142.236B—C, 244D.

24. Ibid., 235B.

25. Jugie, *Theologia dogmatica*, I (Paris, 1926), 431.

26. Pachymeres, II, 111; Troitskij, *Arsenij*, p. 288.

27. Cf. the qualifying remarks of J. Meyendorff, *Byzantine Theology* (New York, 1979) p. 59. On the addition itself, see idem, "At the Sources of the 'Filioque' Quarrel" (in Russian) *Pravoslarnaia Mysl'*, 9 (1953), 114-37; V. Grumel, "Photius et l'addition du 'Filioque' au symbole de Nicée-Constantinople," *REB*, 5 (1947), 218-34; M. Jugie, "Origine de la controverse sur l'addition du 'Filioque' au Symbole," *Revue des sciences philosophiques et théologiques* 28 (1939), 369-85; J. N. D. Kelly, *Early Christian Creeds* (London, 1960), pp. 358-67.

28. *Mystagogy*, *PG* 102.289B, 313B, 313B—C.

29. Ibid., 295, 297-304. See especially V. Lossky, "The Procession of the Holy Spirit in the Orthodox Triadology," *The Eastan Churches Quarterly*, Suppl. 7 (1948), 37.

30. *Mystagogy*, *PG* 102.328-29. My discussion draws heavily upon the exposition of Meyendorff, *Byzantine Theology*, pp. 60-61, 92.

31. The literature for this period is extensive; see especially H.-G. Beck, *Kirche und theologische Literatur im byzantinischen Reich* (Munich, 1959), 306-21; S. S. Mpilales, *The Heresy of the Filioque. I: Historical and Critical Review of the Filioque* (in Greek) (Athens, 1972), 130-61, and 410-11 for an incomplete list of authors on the *Filioque*; M. Jugie, *De processione Spiritus Sancti: Ex fontibus revelationis et secundum Orientales dissidentes* (Rome, 1936), 312-19, A. K Demetracopoulos, *Orthodox Greece* (in Greek) (Leipzig, 1872), lists 111 writers who wrote on the *Filioque* from the ninth to the nineteenth century. See also the brief exposition by A. Sopko, "Palamism Before Palamas and the Theology of Gregory of Cyprus," *St Vladimir's Theological Quarterly,* 23, Nos. 3-4 (1979), 145-47.

32. M. Jugie, "Bulletin de littérature byzantine: Nicéphore Blemmidès et ses écrits," *EO,* 17 (1914), 155. The letters in question will be found in *PG* 142.534-65; 565-84. For his pre-1250 position, see P. Canart, "Nicéphore Blemmyde et le mémoire adressé aux envoyés de Grégoire IX (Nicée, 1234)," *OCP,* 25 (1959), 310-25, esp. 319-20.

33. *PG* 142.553B, 557C-D; and 540 (on the charismata). On the Western tendency to equate proceeding of the Spirit with its being sent, and "to move from the economic to the theological and back again," see J. Pelikan, *The Christian Tradition: A History of the Development of Doctrine. II: The Spirit of Eastern Christendom 600-1700* (Chicago, 1974), 193-94. For Beccus' later views on the absence of any radical difference between the eternal procession and the economic sending, see *On the Union of the Churches of Old and New Rome, PG* 141.49A-B; and *On the Procession of the Holy Spirit, PG* 141.136C.

34. See especially *On the Union of the Churches of Old and New Rome, PG* 141.96C-117D; and *Third Letter to Theodore of Sugdaea, PG* 141.324-37. See also the discussion of these texts by F. Dvornik, *The Photian Schism: History and Legend* (Cambridge, Mass., 1948), pp. 403-11; A. D Zotos, *John Beccus, Patriarch of Constantinople, New Rome, the Latinizer* (in Greek) (Munich, 1920), pp. 75-77; *Dossier de Lyon,* pp. 65-69. For Metochites' condemnation of Photius (he follows Beccus), see Metochites, VIII, pt. 2, 44.

35. *Third Letter to Theodore of Sugdaea, PG* 141.324B, 327B, 337A-B; and *On the Union of the Churches of Old and New Rome, PG* 141.17C. Cf. the anonymous tract on Beccus and Photius in *Dossier de Lyon,* p. 529.

36. This "theology of interpolation" was, in reality, an old argument of Rome, and was first expounded by Paulinus of Aquileia in the eighth century; see Kelly, *Early Christian Creeds,* pp. 364-65; and R. Haugh, *Photius and the Carolingians: The Trinitarian Controversy* (Belmont, Mass., 1975), p. 56.

37. Dvornik, *The Photian Schism,* p. 403.

38. V. Laurent, "Le cas de Photius dans l'apologétique du patriarche Jean XI Beccos (1275-1282) au lendemain du deuxième concile de Lyon," *EO,* 29 (1930), 396, 411.

39. Mansi, XVII, 520, 516: "Whosoever ventures to write anything except this sacred creed, or to add or subtract or presume to create a new dogmatic definition, is condemned and excluded from all Christian communion." See also the confirmation by Photius, *Mystagogy, PG* 102.380-81; Dvornik, *The Photian Schism,* pp. 194ff. For an alleged anathema against Photius in the *acta* of 789, see Laurent, "Le cas de Photius dans l'apologétique du patriarche Beccos," 396-415. Laurent's views have been rejected, however, by M. Jugie, "Les actes du Synode photien de Sainte-Sophie (879-880)," *EO* 37 (1938), 89-99, and by Dvornik, *The Photian*

Schism, 406-409. See also the response to Jugie's article by V. Laurent, "Les Actes du Synode photien et Georges le Métochite," *EO*, 37 (1938), 100-106.

40. See *Epistle II to Pope Nicholas*, *PG* 102.695D; quoted in Meyendorff, *Byzantine Theology*, p. 60.

41. Cf. *Dossier de Lyon*, p. 98.

42. Tomus, *PG* 142.235A-B; allusions to the malice and work of the Devil, made at the very beginning of the *Tomus*, are also made by Beccus against the Orthodox in one of his declarations; for the text, see *Dossier de Lyon*, p. 463; and Gill, "The Church Union of the Council of Lyons," 24.

43. Tomus, *PG* 142.235C—236A.

44. Ibid., 239A, and 237B-238B (= Beccus' verbatim profession of 1283).

45. Ibid., 241A, 241B, 243 C.

46. *On the Procession of the Holy Spirit*, *PG* 142.270D-271A. See also the valuable and useful analysis of this text by O. Clément, "Grégoire de Chypre 'De l'ekporèse du Saint Esprit'," *Istina*, 3-4 (1972), 443-56. For the Russian translation of this work, see Troitskij, in *Christianskoe Chtenie*, 69, pt. 2, 288-352.

47. This traditional term is used repeatedly by Gregory; see *Apology*, *PG* 142.254A, 255A, 264. For its usage by the Cappadocians, see G. W. H. Lampe, *A Patristic Greek Lexicon* (Oxford, 1961-1968), fasc. 5, pp. 1415, 1434 - 35

48. *Tomus*, *PG* 142.235C.

49. *Tomus*, *PG* 142.240D-241A; cf. *Confession*, *PG* 142.247C. See also *On the Procession*, *PG* 142.271C, where Gregory (quoting Dionysius the Areopagite) calls the hypostasis of the Father "the begetting divinity" and "the source of divinity."

50. *Tomus*, *PG* 142.241A (= Oratio 34, *PG* 36.252A). See also the quotations from Maximus the Confessor and John of Damascus in *Apology*, *PG* 142.260D-261A.

51. *Tomus*, *PG* 142.240B.

52. *On the Procession*, *PG* 142.271D.

53. *Tomus*, *PG* 142.241B; *On the Procession*, *PG* 142.271A.

54. *Tomus*, *PG* 142.235C; *On the Procession*, *PG* 142.271C-D.

55. *On the Procession*, *PG* 142.271A-B; Clément, "'De l'ekporèse'," 445.

56. *On the Procession*, *PG* 142.272A.

57. *Tomus*, *PG* 142.241D—242A.

58. Ibid., 241C-D; *Apology*, *PG* 142.253C.

59. *Confession*, *PG* 142.249A; cf. *Tomus*, *PG* 142.236C.

60. *Tomus*, *PG* 142.242D; also mentioned briefly in *On the Procession*, *PG* 142.272C. See further the unpublished refutation of the *Tomus* by the unionist Constantine Meliteniotes, codex Paris. gr. 1303, fols. 116^v-117^r. The biblical reference is to Psalm 36:9

61. *Tomus, PG* 142.242D.

62. *On the Procession, PG* 142.272C. Cf. Clément, "'De l'ekporèse'," 446-47.

63. Cf. Clément, "'De l'ekporèse'," 449.

64. *On the Procession, PG* 142.272D; cf. Cyril of Alexandria, *Thesaurus, PG* 68.148A.

65. Basil, *On the Holy Spirit, PG* 32.153A-B (= Sources chrétiennes, 17 [Paris, 1947], 198); John of Damascus, *On Images, PG* 94.1337D-1340B. Cf. Gregory's Apology, *PG* 142.262C, where John of Damascus, Tarasius, and Maximus are mentioned as using the phrase "through the Son."

66. Rom. 8:9; Gal. 4:6; Phil. 1:19.

67. John 20:22.

68. *PG*.142.291D.

69. *Tomus, PG* 142.239D. According to Mouzalon, neither extreme really "conformed with the truth": *PG* 142.292A.

70. H.-G. Beck et al., *Die mittelalterliche Kirche.* Vol. III, pt. 2 of *Handbuch der Kirchengeschichte*, ed. H. Jedin (Freiburg, 1968), 214-15: "Photius' grasp of the theology of the Trinity was not up to date. His recourse to the teaching of the Greek Fathers was, whether consciously or unconsciously, insufficient; it must be called into question, even in the case of so dedicated a student of patristics as he was. Documents such as the Creed of the Synod of 787 with the formula *per filium* carried no weight with him. Thus, his theology was not a happy point of departure for any evaluation of the Byzantine viewpoint." See idem, *Kirche und theologische Lieratur*, p. 311. Cf. also Jugie, *De processione Spiritus Sancti*, 295. For a less critical view of Photius' non-usage of the phrase, see V. Rodzianko, "Filioque in Patristic Thought," *Studia Patristica*, II (Texte und Untersuchungen, 64; 1957), 303, 308. For a reply to this article see V. Lossky, in *Messager de l'Exarchat du Patriarche russe en Europe occidentale*, 25 (1957), 54-62 (in Russian).

71. *Tomus, PG* 142.243B. Cf. the similar desire expressed in an anonymous text dealing with Beccus and Photius, in *Dossier de Lyon*, pp. 99 and 535-37 (text).

72. *Tomus, PG* 142.243D-244D.

73. *On the Procession, PG* 141.275A-D; *Apology, PG* 142.262C.

74. *Tomus, PG* 142.240B; *On the Procession, PG* 142.275D-276A.

75. M. Candal, "Nueva interpretatión del 'per Filium' de los Padres Griegos," *OCP,* 31 (1965), 12; Jugie, *Theologia dogmatica*, I, 429; Cayré, "Georges de Chypre," col. 1234; S. Runciman, *The Great Church in Capitvity* (Cambridge, 1968), p. 99.

76. *Tomus, PG* 142.240A, 240B-C, 241A. Cf. the rebuttal of Constantine Meliteniotes, codex Paris. gr. 1303, fols. 99^v, 102^v.

77. *Apology, PG* 142.262C-D.

78. *Tomus, PG* 142.240C, 241A, 242B.

79. *Confession, PG* 142.250D-251B.

80. Cf. *Tomus, PG* 142.240A. Constantine Meliteniotes, codex Paris. gr. 1303, fol. 100^r.

81 Sopko, "Palamism Before Palamas," 142.

82. Pachymeres, II, 108.

83. *On the Procession, PG* 142.288D.

84. Ibid., 273C-D.

85. Maximus the Confessor, *Letter to Marinus, PG* 91.136B; cf. H. B. Swete, *The Holy Spirit in the Ancient Church. A Study of Christian Teaching in the Age of the Fathers* (London, 1912), p.279.

86. *On the Procession, PG* 142.288B-C; *Apology, PG* 142.261C-D.

87. *On the Procession, PG* 142.288C.

88. *Tomus, PG* 142.242D-243A.

89. Ibid., 242D.

90. J. Meyendorff, *Introduction à l'étude de Grégoire Palamas* (Paris, 1959), p. 315; O. Clément, "A propos du *Filioque*," *Le Messager Orthodoxe,* 7 (1959), 24.

91. Cf. P. Evdokimov, *L'Esprit Saint dans la tradition Orthodoxe* (Paris, 1969), p.63.

92. *On the Procession, PG* 142.290A.

93. Meyendorff, *Byzantine Theology,* p. 173.

94. *Tomus, PG* 142.242C.

95. Beck, *Kirche und theologische Literatur,* p. 323: "Die hesychastischen Mönche bekamen vom geplanten Schlag Kenntnis und riefen einen der ihrigen, Gregorios Palamas, zu Hilfe, der mit überraschender Schnelligkeit ein theologisches System ausarbeitete, das seinen Anhängern wie eine neue Offenbarung dünkte. Diese ganze Theologie entwickelte sich, gleichsam im Dialog mit Barlaam."

96. *Apology, PG* 142.266C.

97. Ibid., 267B.

98. *PG* 142.290C. See also V. Lossky, *Orthodox Theology: An Introduction* (NewYork, 1978), p. 49: "The energetic manifestation does not depend on creation; it is perpetual radiance, which is in no way conditioned by the existence or non-existence of the world."

99. *Tomus, PG* 142.243 C-D. Cf. Photius, *Mystagogy, PG* 102.284.

100. Cayré, "Georges de Chypre," col. 1234.

101. "The Spirit is third from God and the Son, just as the fruit from the branch is third from the root, and as the stream from the river is third from the spring, and as the light from the ray is third from the sun." The translation is from E. Evans, *Tertullian's Treatise Against Praxeas* (London, 1948), pp. 139 (text), 237-38 (commentary). See also Mouzalon's use of Tertullian's spring-river-stream simile in *PG* 142.298D.

102. Cf. *Oratio 31, PG* 36.169B

103. Cayré, "Georges de Chypre," col. 1234.

104. Ibid., col. 1234

105. Evdokimov, *L'Esprit Saint dans la tradition Orthodoxe*, p. 60.

106. *Confession, PG* 142.249D; the term "accompany" (συμπαρομαρτεῖ) is similarly employed by Theodore Mouzalon, *PG* 142.290C.

107. Beccus, *Against the Tomus, PG* 141.863 ("newly appeared heresies"); Beck, *Kirche und theologische Literatur,* p. 685 ("a new theory"); J. Grégoire, "La relation éternelle de l'Esprit au Fils d'après les écrits de Jean de Damas," *Revue d'histoire ecclésiastique,* 64 (1969), 716 ("an entirely new theory"), M.-J. Le Guillou, in *L'Esprit Saint et l'église* (Paris, 1969), p. 229 ("a new theory"); Candal, "Progresso dogmatico nelle definizioni trinitarie," 338 ("a new error").

6

THE FIRST STORM

As a coherent doctrinal exposition of the Orthodox case, the *Tomus* was an important theological achievement. Moreover, as a well-balanced and responsible statement on Lyons and Byzantine unionism, it had achieved its goal. The search for stability was now that much closer with the formal condemnation of unionism. For as soon as his expository and exegetical responsibilities were concluded, Gregory had the *Tomus'* eleven explicit anathemas read in the church of the Hagia Sophia in the presence of his episcopal colleagues and the assembled faithful. This public reading was then followed by a signing ceremony in the imperial palace. As we have seen, this should be placed in August 1285, the month in which the synod concluded its deliberations. It was a decisive defeat for unionism; its few remaining partisans would soon be sent into exile.

A. *The Lower Clergy and the Arsenites*

The consensus reached at Blachernae soon turned out to be somewhat of an illusion when the *Tomus,* shortly after its publication, became a matter of confusion and controversy. If unionism had lost its momentum, another movement of opposition soon reared its head. The first stone came from the lower clergy, followed by that from the Arsenites. More importantly, George Moschabar, the patriarchal archivist, whose poor theological performance had provided the council with its lighter moments, soon took up their cry. As a casualty of Blachernae he could not forget. His wounded pride set in motion a web of intrigue and opposition against the settlement of 1285 that the patriarch would be unable to quash.

The council's final ceremony, mentioned above, was held in the presence of the emperor, Andronicus, and the author of the *Tomus,* Patriarch Gregory both promptly gave their approval by their signatures. These were followed by forty-one metropolitans representing not only the immediate areas of the capital, but also such distant provincial dioceses as Crete and the Peloponnese.[1] Some of these bishops, like Theodore of Bitzine and Nicephorus of Crete, had been raised to the episcopal dignity two years previously on the accession of Gregory. Others, such as Ignatius of Thessalonica and the commanding personality of Theoleptus of Philadelphia, had been monks under

Beccus, and had played a prominent role in the opposition to the union plans of Michael VIII.[2] They, too, were raised to the episcopate by Gregory. This is also the case with two other signatories—the metropolitans Daniel of Cyzicus and John Chilas of Ephesus. Both had been monks and friends of Gregory prior to 1283.[3] Advocates of moderation, or οἰκονομία, were not unrepresented, as is shown by the signature of Constantine of Derkon. Arsenite sympathizers, such as Gerasimus of Heraclea and Neophytus of Brusa, were also signatories.

Characteristically, because many of these bishops had been raised to the episcopate by Gregory, it has been argued that they were merely being compliant opportunists;[4] Their signatures were a way of obliging their patron, Gregory. In brief, their professed devotion to the *Tomus* had no substance at all, nor did they attach much importance to the prolonged theological discussion of the preceding month. It was all a question of party loyalty—a pledge of their fidelity to their benefactor. The patriarch was, in the main, demanding their support in order to satisfy his grudge against Beccus.

Occasionally, religious conviction among some bishops was conditioned by political considerations. It is hasty if not misleading, however, to insist that this was the case at Blachernae. If these bishops were motivated by subservience and not theological conviction, how is it that they tolerated Gregory for so long? One would think that they would be eager to grasp at the first opportunity to rebel *en masse* against their constraining patron. Late in 1285, when the lower clergy began to voice their objections to the *Tomus,* and early in 1286, when the self-centered and spiteful Moschabar launched his attack, would have been perfect opportunities for such a rebellion. It would certainly have been to their advantage and in character to have rebelled then. And yet, this is not at all what happened. On the contrary, it was not until late 1288 that some of these bishops chose to join Gregory's opponents—nearly *four* years after the publication of the *Tomus*! Even then it was far from an unequivocal or massive rebellion. Of the forty-one episcopal signatories, for example, only three are mentioned by name as active vocal adversaries in 1288. For the most part, the description of the episcopate during Gregory's patriarchate is a gratuitous assumption, if not an oversimplification of the facts.

In addition to the bishops, those who held official positions in the patriarchate were subsequently asked to sign. Thus, in the course of the next several months, thirty more signatures were added, twenty representing administrators of the patriarchate and ten, the clergy (seven of these being attached to the imperial chapel). Because the signatures of these last two groups were obtained gradually and not in any one full session, they are not always listed in order of precedence. Despite the public humiliation he had endured during the council, the archivist George Moschabar is among this last group of signatories, as is the historian and deacon George Pachymeres.[5] Ironically, one Manuel Acropolites is also listed. He may be the monk Melchisedec, the son of George Acropolites, chief delegate to Lyons.[6]

Curiously, the three highest ranking officials of the patriarchate—the οἰκονόμος, the σκευοφύλαξ, and the σακελλάριος—are missing from the extant revisions of the list. This does not necessarily imply, however, that the majority of the administrative hierarchy refused to sign, or that the three highest dignitaries did not.[7] Many absences could be accounted for by a temporary eclipse of the rank, by its transfer to another individual (the σκευοφύλαξ could have been attached to the σακελλάριος), or by its abolition.[8] Pachymeres, for example, at one time held the rank of teacher of the Apostles, then ἱερομνήμων (the rank listed in the *Tomus*), then πρωτέκδικος, and then δικαιοφύλαξ. Given the continuing internal difficulties the patriarchate had faced since its exile in Nicaea early in the century, this should come as no surprise. In short, "It is best not to build any hypothesis based on the silence of the documents, and the absence of a name."[9] It remains true, nevertheless, that an element of the non-episcopal ranks was unwilling to subscribe. What for Gregory was initially a labor of love was turning into a thankless task; a number of patriarchal administrators and clergy—to the undisguised delight of unionists eager to cheer them on—were refusing to sign.[10]

What accounts for this obstinate refusal of the lower clergy to commit themselves to act of 1285? Why did many of them not want to sign? If we are to believe Pachymeres, the answer may well lie in the fear and ignorance of these clergy. Specifically, they remembered Michael's Machiavellian approach to union, the successful attempts to overrule the Church, the stream of documents supporting his unionist schemes, and the violence used to extort signatures during his reign.[11] They were, in short, tired and fearful of signing any kind of document regardless of its nature. Besides, what if the wind changed and Orthodoxy was again overthrown? Would the Orthodox majority not be punished for their approval of a document that had rebutted unionism? "Should this come to pass, who will have strength enough to redeem us from the new victor's judgment!"[12] The fear that the Church might again be forced to play the game of unionism was a possibility they could not ignore. In sum, although they were aware of Michael's past caesaropapism, they were ignorant of the fact that his son Andronicus no longer had any need to play his father's game.

Yet, even after they were dissuaded from placing the *Tomus* in the same category with Michael's unionist documents (most of which were bound for papal consumption), they still scrupulously refused to follow the bishops' example. Instead, they took the tack that they were baffled by the theology enshrined in the text, especially Gregory's doctrine of the eternal manifestation. They could not see, for example, exactly how the hypostatic procession of the Spirit was to be understood apart from its eternal manifesting procession. The two, in fact, seemed identical. And if this was so, then Gregory's explanation was nothing less then Beccus' own formula; he, too, was saying that the Son was a cause in the Spirit's procession—the very notion for which Beccus had been condemned.[13] Indeed, they were being asked to sign a document that was implicitly, if not openly, favorable to the Latins and to unionism. Predictably, those who questioned the document's orthodoxy by advancing this notion of "identity" between Gregory's and Beccus' thought, persisted to the end. Others, however, did sign when their reservations were put to rest by a "written assurance" from their superiors, the patriarch and the bishops, that the notion of the eternal manifestation of the Spirit was theologically sound.[14] The thirty signatures that we have are the result of this final recommendation.[15] The *Tomus* was not altered.

Interestingly enough, traces of this incident with the lower clergy in the fall of 1285, is suggested by one of the extant manuscripts of the *Tomus*. A scribe of a fifteenth-century copy of the text notes, in a gloss at the beginning of the document, that the prototype text dealt with the heresy of the Latins, and "will be found in all the original copies." A true son of the Church, he then advises, should not be so presumptuous as to contradict the synod (of Blachernae) on this matter.[16] Conceivably, the scribe was afraid that the text's intention and content might be misunderstood by the reader. Hence his efforts in the margin to assure the text's doctrinal authority, and to caution the reader against any doubt.

That the incident with the lower clergy and administrative officials of the patriarchate delighted the unionists goes without saying. Evidence even suggests that they may have been responsible for arousing the clergy's resistance against the *Tomus*. Beccus was still in Constantinople, and, moreover, continued to oppose the Church, and especially the new official anathema embodied in Gregory's synodal refutation. Indeed, "he itched—once the *Tomus* fell into his hands—to refute him who had so provoked him."[17] Quite possibly, the search of the Cosmidion monastery for unionist polemical material may have had as its goal the verification of this connection between the unionists and the attitude of the lower clergy.[18] For it was at the Cosmidion that Beccus had been confined before he was sent to exile at the fortress of St George on the gulf of Nicomedia.[19]

Beccus' retaliatory refutation of the *Tomus*, entitled *Against the Tomus and its Recent Heresies*, was probably written at the Cosmidion before he was sent into exile.[20] Although Pachymeres is not precise on the chronology (the exile is mentioned several pages before this refutation), he does tell us that the text was circulating in the city and was generating a great deal of discussion. Its arguments, which the historian summarizes, are remarkably similar to the arguments used by the lower clergy. In substance, Beccus thought the synodal exegesis was incorrect, and declared that the alleged distinction between eternal manifestation (ἔκφανσις) and eternal procession (προβολεύς) was nonsense because they meant the same thing; "having existence" (procession-προβολή) and "existing" (manifestation-ἔκφανσις) was no distinction at all, but a tautology. For this reason, to say that "through the Son" designated the eternal manifestation was to admit the personal hypostatic procession of the Spirit from the Father through the Son. On the intratrinitarian level, ἔκφανσις could not correspond to any other reality in God: "I do not see what else the manifestation of the Spirit through the Son can denote, except its hypostatic procession from the Father through the Son."[21]

It was the same argument he had used at Blachernae. But, as with Blachernae, Beccus again could not resist the opportunity to inflict further wounds on the patriarch. He could not avoid expressing his anger and scandalous hatred for the man who had been a cowardly "traitor" to his cause. The patriarch is once again scoffed and satirized. He is even compared to a veritable sea monster from Cyprus whose voracious appetite was causing the Church to disappear. The morbidly sensitive and defeated Beccus could not relent.

The lower clergy, then, were quite likely supported, and perhaps inspired, in their opposition to the *Tomus* by unionist argument. They were also abetted, however, by the Arsenites. I have already noted the negative attitude of this influential faction toward the patriarch, and the hierarchy in general, particularly after the failure of Adramyttium to bring about a rapprochement. Thus, it would have been strange if the publication of the *Tomus* had not incited them further in their opposition to the patriarch's authority. There was good reason to object to a document which, in their eyes, was a product of a usurper emperor, an uncanonical patriarch, and a suspect hierarchy. Significantly, it has even been suggested that some of the lower clergy, who remained irreducible, even after the patriarch's written assurances concerning the *Tomus*' orthodoxy, were actually Arsenites.[22] Their refusal to sign has been seen as "striking proof" that the rift between the Arsenites and the patriarch was already irreparable by 1285.[23]

Whatever the case, one thing must be stressed. The Arsenites' attitude to the *Tomus* was not related to its actual theological merit, but was essentially grounded on their newly resumed hostility toward the patriarch. After Adramyttium they could do little else except reject Gregory's formulations; to have acknowledged them would have served the patriarch's cause. Their attitude, however, was also a reflection of their intense conservatism. They were so purist in their approach to the question of "procession through the Son" raised at Blachernae that they eventually decided to reject the traditional phrase "through the Son" altogether! The Spirit could only proceed *a Patre solo*. The evidence on this matter is quite explicit—when the patriarch finally stepped down in 1289, their two-fold demand to the emperor was "the rejection of Joseph and the doctrine of procession from the Father through the Son."[24]

B. *George Moschabar's Circle*

But there was another group, in addition to the Arsenites, the unionists, and the lower clergy, which wanted to dislodge the patriarch from his throne and bring about his fall. Undoubtedly, the chief troublemaker of this circle was George Moschabar; working in close league with him were two other patriarchal administrators, John Pentecclesiotes and Michael Escammatismenus.[25] Again, as with the Arsenites, these also did not hesitate to wage their personal, non-theological dispute on the field of dogma, and to bring the *Tomus* into the discussion. Gregory's correspondence leaves little doubt that it is this defectors circle (all three had signed the *Tomus*) which provoked the final crisis four years later and eventually cost the patriarch his throne.

George Moschabar, as we have seen, became Gregory's archivist in 1283 when this post was vacated by its previous holder, the deposed unionist Constantine Meliteniotes.[26] Probably, his theological tracts against Michael's religious policy (he had issued them anonymously to avoid persecution) were a decisive factor in his selection as the patriarch's own first minister. The post, to be sure, was the most important dignity in the patriarchal bureaucracy. Increasingly, its responsibilities went beyond those of librarian or archivist, particularly after the eleventh century. As an imperial document of this century notes, the holder was the patriarch's very mouthpiece.[27] Frequently, he was the heir-presumptive to the patriarch.

Moschabar, however, was a puzzling choice for the post. Gregory's receptive theological attitude, for example, was diametrically opposed to the theological narrowness represented by his new aide. Moreover, his pride, obstinacy, and "inconsistent spirit"[28]—the key to understanding the eventual falling-out between them—should have been a warning. And yet, Gregory did not believe these flaws would impede his work. (That he was aware of the archivist's deeper prejudices and conservatism is clear—the two had met as early as 1267, if not before.)[29] For the first two years of Gregory's patriarchate, there was, in fact, no problem. Even after the incident at Blachernae the break was not immediate.

What happened at Blachernae was decisive and eventually led to Moschabar's resignation. No incident is perhaps as illuminating as this for his ambivalent character and theological conservatism. It was then, it will be recalled that he rejected the Damascene *testimonium*: it was, after all, not found in all the manuscripts. And yet (to tell the truth), his rejection was founded on the fact that the text simply did not conform with his theological position. Quite simply, his presumptive, if not perverse, position was based more on the text's lack of correspondence with his views than on a critical examination of the manuscripts themselves. Had he the skill and the stamina—two hundred and fifty-two copies of *The Orthodox Faith* survive from the ninth to the eighteenth century—to debate this question at the highest level of palaeography and history, he might have changed his mind.[30] Not surprisingly, his argument convinced no one, least of all the minister, Mouzalon, who had to censure the patriarchal archivist.

What landed him in even greater difficulties, however, was the reading of one of his polemical tracts to the assembled theologians. This document, for which he was immediately taken to task, brought into question not only his competence as a theologian, but his interpretation of the phrase "through the Son." His interpretation did not identify "through" with the eternal manifestation, as did Gregory's, or with "from," as did the unionists, but with the preposition σύν, μετά (with the genitive), or ἅμα, which were translated as "with" or "together." For his part, the phrase "the Spirit proceeds from the Father through the Son" was equivalent to saying, "the Spirit *together* with the Son proceeds from the Father."[31] True, it was an interpretation which later Palamite theologians and Mark Eugenicus at Florence would find useful.[32] However great its subsequent popularity, it could not convince Gregory or the unionists.[33]

Pachymeres, in his recollection of the events of 1285, was correct in permitting himself a bit of fun over Moschabar. The archivist, left standing on the sidelines had, in fact, provided the one comic relief in an otherwise difficult theological discussion. All the same, Moschabar could not have seen it in this light. He had been personally and publicly chastised, if not wounded, by the unexpected turn of events. If the synod was ready to forget (it had condemned only his writings, not him), he was not. He did not, however, render his resignation as head of the patriarchal chancery at the conclusion of the council. That came sometime in 1286, *after* he had signed the *Tomus.*[34] As Gregory was to note later, "previously, not only did he [Moschabar] praise it, worship it, but he also signed it as being nothing less than the *Tomus* of Orthodoxy."[35] To be sure, this, too, casts further light on his personality. For the *Tomus* assumes the authenticity of the *testimonium* he had so vigorously opposed in the synod! Equally, his signature constitutes endorsement of a document whose theology plainly did not correspond with his own rejected reflections on the matter.

The *Tomus'* alleged theological innovation was not the occasion for his resignation. It was caused by something quite different. Although Pachymeres does not elaborate, he does stress the fact that it was the outcome of a purely private quarrel with the patriarch and was, therefore, non-theological.[36] He then adds that Moschabar's subsequent attack on the *Tomus* was his way of settling the matter with the patriarch; he and his colleagues, who joined him shortly, did their best to conceal this personal grudge. They tried to persuade everyone that what they were doing was not to avenge their private quarrel, but to establish solidly the doctrine of the Church.[37] Plainly, the motive was malicious vengeance, not a concern for doctrine. But if it was his way of settling a quarrel it was, likewise, his way of getting revenge for the humiliation of 1285 and the public chastisement he had endured at the time.

This portrait of Moschabar is supported by evidence from Gregory. Moschabar could not but become isolated, once Mouzalon and the patriarch had refused to support him at the council. In the event, Gregory's relations with his chief aide became progressively strained. Moschabar (so Gregory implies) became more polemical, and refused to listen; as a result, Gregory was finally driven to abandon him.[38] Suffice it to say, Gregory did not gladly suffer the many fools he had to deal with. "If someone can demonstrate that tolerance results in some profit, let him show it; however, the man who does not tolerate advice, or refuses to listen, is to me hateful."[39] Gregory, then, must have contributed to the final rift, although it was not his own direct doing. All the same, it is surprising that the separation from this "silly old man,"[40] as Gregory calls him, did not come earlier, either before or immediately after the council.

But if Gregory's selection of Moschabar was unfortunate, so was his choice of a successor, Michael Escammatismenus, the ραιφενδάριος of the Hagia Sophia, and a signatory of the *Tomus*.[41] After his appointment, Escammatismenus proceeded to ally himself with his predecessor. This seems to have happened almost immediately; in a letter to the metropolitan of Ephesus, dated July 1287, the patriarch is already aware of his new assistant's coalition with Moschabar and names him as the principal agitator.[42] Although he contemptuously dismissed both as quack theologians, he instinctively recognized the rebellion as serious. Indeed, he implores his correspondent to come to his aid; otherwise, the harm these men will cause by their attempt to discredit the Church will be even greater than the troubles caused previously by Beccus.[43] "Men with distorted teachings have arisen among us; and the struggle of piety does not [now] originate from Beccus' writings and speeches, and from those who rally to his aid to support him, [but from Moschabar and his friends]."[44] Clearly, Beccus, in his distant exile, was no longer a problem for the Church or the patriarch, although the dissembling campaign of his less-than-devoted assistant was. The patriarch had good reason to be apprehensive. Although Gregory in his letter mentions only Moschabar and Escammatismenus, Pachymeres adds a third name to the roster—John Pentecclesiotes, a relative of the new archivist, a deacon of the patriarchate, and a signatory of the *Tomus*.[45] Though the group was numerically small, the patriarch knew that he would be unable to scotch their calculated hostility alone. Their "babbling...insane, drunk, and inconsistent ideas" could only cause trouble.[46]

In the final analysis, the patriarch was on target—the group's inconsistent ideas (identified by Pachymeres) were the same arguments used earlier by the lower clergy and by Beccus to discredit the *Tomus*. It seems that they, too, wanted to accuse the patriarch of having identified in the *Tomus* the eternal manifestation of the Spirit with its eternal procession. This, in their view, was forbidden, for just as begetter (γεννήτωρ) was used by the Fathers to denote exclusively the cause of the Son, the traditional and parallel term προβολεὺς was used to denote the Spirit's cause or hypostatic character from the Father. Προβολή, or procession, therefore, had to be identified with the Spirit's emanation (πρόοδος), not with its manifestation (ἔκφανσις) as in the *Tomus*.[47] Simply put, they wanted procession to conform—as Beccus had argued—with common patristic usage. This the *Tomus* had not done. For it had not identified the procession either with causality or with the temporal "giving, bestowing, or providing" of the Spirit. On the contrary, the document clearly spoke of an *eternal* manifestation.[48] The historian then adds that they wanted to charge the patriarch formally by presenting Beccus as another Nessus, who had defeated Heracles even after his death.[49]

All the same, they reflected that it would not be to their advantage to use these arguments, and possibly risk being identified with Beccus and his partisans. They also realized a frontal attack on the patriarch would be unwise, because they had all signed the *Tomus*; how could they reconcile or explain their previous approval of the very document they now wanted to attack? As such, "their accusations remained between their teeth, for the signatures, which they had given to the *Tomus*, impeded them from expressing their views in daylight and out loud."[50] Still, their intrigue was not conducted entirely on the sly. Moschabar, typically, continued to defend the position he had taken at Blachernae on the non-authenticity of the Damascene proof-text. One such defense—still unpublished—exists.[51] He was, thus, openly opposing the *Tomus* and the patriarch, who had accepted the text as genuine. Similarly, he continued to broadcast his own interpretation (rejected at Blachernae) of the meaning of the phrase "through the Son." Gregory goes to some length to demolish this explanation in his *Apology* written at about this time.[52] It is unlikely he would have done so had the interpretation lain dormant after 1285. Finally, the documents, purporting to be by one "Cypriot," may have been issued by Moschabar at this time with the intention of disparaging the patriarch's unionist activity under Michael VIII.[53] If so, the attempt would have paralleled Arsenite efforts to discredit Gregory on the same grounds.

C. *Gregory's* Apology

As noted above, Gregory did make some effort to refute his critics. In addition to the plea for help sent to his bishops, he also penned a longer brief for the defense, the *Apology.*[54] And although he seems to have taken up his pen almost hesitantly, as he himself notes in the introduction to the work, the effort was a cogent refutation of the mounting criticism against the *Tomus*. The text is brief, to the point, and reads like a lecture; even the seven quotations it supplies are accompanied by a minimum of analysis. This may be due to the fact that the work was actually first sent to his friend and supporter, Theodore Mouzalon, who was asked to correct the text and give the work some polish.[55]

This document was almost certainly written sometime between the publication of the *Tomus* and 1287, that is, before the patriarch's student, Mark, or any of the bishops became involved in the controversy. Neither Mark nor any of Gregory's episcopal colleagues are mentioned in the text. Additionally, the work not only refers to the discredited Beccus, but also attempts to answer his criticism. Since, by Gregory's own admission,[56] Beccus was no longer a problem by 1287, the document must be placed just before or shortly after Beccus' exile, when he was still a source of opposition. The idea that the work was composed only after the patriarch's abdication in 1289, is highly unlikely.[57] Nor could the work be an apologetic response to John Chilas' letter to the emperor.[58] This letter was sent after this metropolitan had joined the opposition in autumn 1288.

There is, however, further evidence for the earlier date—the text is probably also aimed at Moschabar. Immediately after his reference to Beccus, Gregory notes that his defense is likewise directed at someone else whose injured vanity led to his wanton attack on the *Tomus*.

> After Beccus, another one appeared, and he, too, out of ambition composed books filled with pet words and phrases, whose meaning I do not know. And he attacked me, because I dared at the start to resist Beccus, and did not hand over the whole struggle to him, who is powerful with words; for this reason, he attacked the *Tomus* which I issued, with the consent of the Church at the time, against Beccus. And he curses it as being wrong, although, previously, not only did he praise it, worship it, but he also signed it as being nothing less than the *Tomus* of Orthodoxy. This, he did without being dragged into it, or forced by anyone.[59]

The anonymous adversary can hardly be anyone other than the ex-archivist and signatory of the *Tomus*, George Moschabar. In fact, several paragraphs

later, Gregory proceeds to a lengthy analysis (and ridicule) of Moschabar's attempt to explain "through" in terms of "with" or "together."[60] John Chilas was
also a signatory, yet he cannot be a candidate, since he did not write any
"books" against the *Tomus*. Besides, Gregory's reference to the fact that the
struggle against Beccus should have been left to someone with greater literary
talent than he, is more applicable to the humiliated theologian of Blachernae
than to Chilas. (Indeed, this sounds like a corroboration of Pachymeres' own
account of Moschabar's atheological opposition to the patriarch; both seem
to be grounded on a grudge.) Finally, for the same reasons, the anonymous
author cannot be a unionist or a partisan of Beccus.[61]

Gregory begins his brief by giving a succinct analysis of Beccus' doctrine
of the double procession. He correctly identifies the "causal" interpretation,
given by Beccus to the phrase "through the Son," as the foundation stone
upon which his tower of blasphemy is constructed. This, however, Gregory
continues, has no foundation in fact, as a reading of the Fathers indicates. For
these authors speak of the Father alone as being the cause, root, principle, and
source of both the Son and the Spirit. "Through the Son" indicates the shining forth, the revelation, or simply the disclosure or manifestation of the
Spirit by the Son; it never denotes existence which the Spirit receives from the
Father alone. All the Fathers who employ the phrase—Basil, Gregory of
Nyssa, Athanasius, etc.—explicitly prohibit a different interpretation.[62] The
patriarch here is at pains to show the non-identity of his doctrine with that of
Beccus; it is an attempt to disarm those who, like Moschabar and the lower
clergy, insisted on confusing the two.

The patriarch then calls attention to the charge that he had confused the
meaning of procession. The reply is at once simple and cogent. It is not unlike
the explanation found in the patriarch's later defenses, the *Confession* and the
πιττάκιον. Gregory first underscores the fact that the manifestation (ἔκφανσις) is never identified with the procession, or with existence (ὕπαρξις)
in the *Tomus*; nowhere is procession said to be "through the Son," whereas
manifestation is described by that phrase. Moreover, the opposition ignores
the fact that the nouns "manifestation" and "existence" are not derived from
nouns, but from the verbs "to manifest" and "to exist." These bear no resemblance to each other; it is not possible for the verb "to manifest"—which can
only mean "to reveal"—to mean "to exist," as people say it does. Those who
say that the *Tomus* describes the manifestation as existence know either little

grammar or no theology, or both.[63] Plainly, Gregory, the philologist turned patriarch, had not used words promiscuously.

It is notable that Gregory's compelling argument was aimed both at those who were insisting that the meaning of the term "procession" had been compromised, and at those who were refusing to see a difference between "having existence" from the Father and "existing" through or from the Son. Equally, he suggests that the opposition had chosen the easy path of ridicule by their refusal to look at anything other than the words themselves—they had deliberately chosen to ignore what was a valid distinction in trinitarian theology. Gregory's argument was directed at all those who would now, or in the future, speak slightingly of the distinction between ὕπαρξιν ἔχειν and ὑπάρχει found in the *Tomus*.[64]

Gregory then proceeds to discuss the nature of the "eternity" of the manifestation—clearly a fundamental component of his theology. The notion had contributed to the opinion of his detractors that he had "confused" matters. Was he not, in fact, speaking of one and the same thing by insisting that the manifestation, like the eternal procession, was equally timeless or eternal? Twice, Gregory identifies this as a major complaint.[65] The patriarch's answer is again brief. The manifestation of God is indeed non-temporal, uncreated, or eternal, because the Son and the Spirit are never said to be temporal or non-eternal. "If the Spirit is always known with the Son, from whom it is never separated, then it is also *always through* Him. How else, he asks, can this be described other than by the word 'eternal'?"[66] Moreover, Gregory continues, it is said that the Spirit is the "Spirit of the Son." This being so, the Spirit is *always* the Spirit of the Son, and is eternally manifested or revealed by Him—even if its existence is not from Him. "If the Spirit is eternally the Spirit of the Son, and is called the Spirit of the Son—for it is through Him that it is revealed—then he, who acknowledges this reality and says the Spirit is revealed through the Son, must perforce admit that it is also revealed eternally."[67]

As noted earlier, Gregory does not leave Moschabar's "strange, impious, and ridiculous explanations" untouched, even if he feels that they deserve little or no attention.[68] Grammatically speaking, σύν or μετά can never be identical or equivalent to διά as Moschabar would have everyone believe. Such transposition of words is impossible. This interpretation is impious, since it confuses the divine characteristics of procession and generation. To say "the Spirit with the Son proceeds from the Father" is tantamount to saying the Son "proceeds" from the Father. In fact, the Son can only be generated. Granted, this error is concealed when "with the Son" is said to denote existence from the Father; but even this is madness, for it would then follow that the Son had His existence from the Spirit as well.[69] Such blasphemy surpasses Beccus' own irreverence.

Such, then, was the situation by 1287—less than two years after the publication of the *Tomus*. Most of the lower clergy had been persuaded to put their weight behind the *Tomus*, together with the emperor and the bishops. In addition, unionism (as Gregory noted in his letter to John of Ephesus) was no longer of any consequence. The Arsenites, however, continued to be in schism. More importantly, they were trying to bring the *Tomus* into disrepute and to have him replaced. Equally, Gerasimus' excommunication of the patriarch (issued, as we have seen, shortly after the publication of the *Tomus*) was making the solution to the Arsenite question more difficult. There was, further, the opposition by his former aide, George Moschabar, and his circle. And yet, the situation does not seem to have been wholly out of control. True, Gregory appears apprehensive in his letter to John of Ephesus. Nevertheless, as we have seen, he was reluctant to take up his pen in his *Apology*—a sign that he was not yet unduly alarmed.[70] Possibly he took courage in the fact that Moschabar and his friends had not been able to rally anyone to their cause.

The situation became progressively worse. By the following year, the crucial support Moschabar needed had materialized. Moreover, it came from unexpected quarters, namely, from one of Gregory's professed partisans, Mark. For it was Mark's published defense of the *Tomus* that finally gave the adversaries the handle they needed against the patriarch; it also brought a number of influential bishops to their side. Indeed, once Moschabar's group had gotten hold of this work—the result of Mark's desire to join the controversy on the side of the patriarch—nothing could stop them. They thought they had the patriarch cornered, as Pachymeres notes; that which was suspect in the *Tomus*—so they alleged—was now fully disclosed in the commentary written by one of the patriarch's own disciples.[71] But Gregory, too, acknowledges the fact that it was his over-zealous supporter, a member of his following—an obscure baptized Jew and now a monk —who greatly furthered the work of these self-appointed guardians of Orthodoxy. He notes, in fact, that he and the *Tomus* came under suspicion by the hierarchy for the first time with the publication of Mark's commentary; only then did his "brother bishops" feel obliged to join the controversy on the side of the opposition.[72]

All this, however, did not happen until late in 1288. The publication of Mark's commentary probably occurred shortly before autumn 1288. Neither Gregory's first call to the bishops in April 1287[73] nor his appeal to John of Ephesus in February-March 1288[74] contains any reference to Mark. We are, moreover, informed that the bishops' opposition to Mark's text became more open at the time of John's arrival in the capital, autumn 1288.[75] The commentary, then, must be placed sometime between Gregory's appeal in February-March and the arrival of John in Constantinople. After this, the opposition could not be contained.[76]

NOTES

1. V. Laurent "Les signataires du second synode des Blakhernes (été 1285)," *EO*, 26 (1927), 143-49.

2. On Theoleptus' long episcopate, see below, p. 168; On Ignatius see V. Laurent, "La question des Arsénites," *Hellenika*, 3 (1930), 466-67

3. See below, p. 168.

4. Laurent, "Les signataires du second synode des Blakhernes," 136.

5. Ibid., 148; J. Darrouzès, *Recherches sur les* Ὀφφίκια *de l'Eglise Byzantine* (Paris, 1970), p. 533.

6. Laurent, "Les signataires du second synode des Blakhernes" 148; see also E. Trapp, *Prosopographisches Lexicon der Paläologenzeit*, I (Vienna, 1976), nos. 522, 523; for a family tree, see D. M. Nicol, "Constantine Akropolites: A Prosopographical Note," *Dumbarton Oaks Papers*, 19 (1965), 254.

7. As suggested by Laurent, *Regestes*, no. 1490, p. 285.

8. Cf. Darrouzès, *Recherches sur les* Ὀφφίκια, p. 114; in addition to the list of officials of 1285, Darrouzès discusses two other lists from the patriarchate of Beccus.

9. Ibid.

10. Metochites, X, pt. I, 323-34.

11. Cf. Chapter 2 above, Pachymeres, I, 451. The fatal consequences of Michael's policy are discussed by V Nikolsky, "The Union of Lyons: An Episode from Medieval Church History, 1261-1293." (in Russian), *Pravoslavnoe Obozrienie*, 23 (1867), 377-78.

12. Pachymeres, II, 112.

13. Ibid., 114.

14. Ibid., 113-14. Juridically, this assurance (ἀσφάλεια) may have been an oath (ὅρκος); for the terminology, see Darrouzès, *Recherches sur les* Ὀφφίκια, p. 165.

15. Metochites, VIII, pt. 2, 171.

16. Codex Athos Dionysiou 150, fol. 46[r].

17. Pachymeres, II, 114.

18. Metochites, VIII, pt. 2, 172; X, pt. 1, 320-21.

19. Metochites and Meliteniotes were confined to the Pantocrator; see Metochites VIII, pt. 2, 168. Only in exile were the three united in the same prison.

20. Pachymeres, II, 114; for the text, see *PG* 141.863-926. Later, George Metochites also contributed a refutation of the *Tomus*; for the text, see Metochites VIII, pt. 2, 179-227. Cf. also his refutations of Maximus Planudes and Manuel Moschopoulos, *PG* 141.1276-1405. For his dependence on Beccus, see S. Salaville, "Georges le Métochite," *DTC* 6, pt. 1 (Paris, 1920), cols. 1238-39. Constantine Meliteniotes' refutation, codex Paris. gr. 1303, fols. 82^r-143^r, remains unpublished; it contains extensive direct quotations from the *Tomus*. His two other "orations" on the procession are to be found in *PG* 141.1032-1273.

21. Beccus, *Against the Tomus*, *PG* 141.872D; and 865B-C, for the attack on the patriarch.

22. See Laurent, "Les signataires des Blakhernes," 138-39.

23. V. Laurent, "Les grandes crises religieuses à Byzance: La fin du schisme arsénite," *Académie Roumaine. Bulletin de la Section Historique*, 26 (1945), 264.

24. Pachymera, II, 138.

25. On Moschabar, see the excellent study by V. Laurent, "Un polémiste grec de la fin du XIIIè siècle: La vie et les œuvres de Georges Moschabar," *EO*, 28 (1929), 129-58; R. Kerr, "George Moschabar: New Light on the Transmission of One of His Chapters," *Résumés des communications, XVè Congrès international d'études byzantines* (Athens, 1976), no pagination.

26. He held the position as Beccus' archivist.

27. See the text in J. Nicole, "Une ordonnance inédite de l'empereur Alexis Comnène I sur les privilèges du chartophylax," *BZ*, 3 (1894), 19; quoted in L. Bréhier, *Le monde byzantin. II: Les Institutions de l'empire byzantin* (Paris, 1970), 399.

28. See Gregory's letter to John Chilas, in *Ekklesiastikos Pharos*, 5 (1910), 345 (letter 178).

29. Laurent, "Un polémiste grec," 133.

30. For the number of manuscripts, see J. Darrouzès in *REB*, 32 (1974), 382-83, a review of Kotter's edition of *De fide orthodoxa*.

31. M. Jugie, *Theologia dogmatica Christianorum orientalium ab Ecclesia Catholica dissidentium* (Paris, 1933), II, 355-56, 384

32. For its use by Eugenicus, see S. S. Mpilales, *The Heresy of the Filioque. I: Historical and Critical Review of the Filioque* (in Greek) (Athens, 1972), 339-40; for its use by Palamas, see A. Papadopoulos, "The Teaching of Gregory Palamas Concerning the Procession of the Holy Spirit," in J. E. Anastasiou (ed.), *The Holy Spirit* (in Greek) (Thessalonika, 1971), pp. 80-81.

33. Metochites, VIII, pt. 2, 142; X, pt. I, 355; Beccus had already rejected the interpretation in his pre-1282 work *To Theodore*, *PG* 141.304B, and in *To Constantine*, *PG* 141.389A-C. See also Jugie, *Theologia dogmatica*, II, 355n2. For Gregory's views, see below, p. 151-2.

34. The exact date is not known, but must have occurred shortly after 1285. Pachymeres, II, 115, speaks of Moschabar's attack on Gregory immediately after his mention of the lower clergy's refusal to sign the *Tomus* in 1285. See also Laurent, *Regestes*, no. 1506, and *Dossier* de Lyon, p. 23.

35. *Apology,* PG 142.253B.

36. PachymereS, II, 115

37. Ibid., 115-16.

38. *Ekklesiastikos Pharos,* 5 (1910), 346 (letter 178).

39 Ibid., 4 (1909), 17 (letter 133).

40. Ibid., 5 (1910), 345 (letter 178)

41. He had also been raifendarius under Beccus; see Metochites, VIII, pt. 2, 86; Laurent, *Regestes,* no. 1447.

42. *Ekklesiastikos Pharos,* 5 (1910), 345 (letter 178); Laurent, *Regestes,* no. 1506. See also an earlier letter sent to John Chilas of Ephesus and other metropolitans three months before (April 1287), in *Ekklesiastikos Pharos,* 5 (1910), 491 (letter 161); Laurent, *Regestes,* no. 1505. Although Escammatismenus is given such prominence, the fact is that Moschabar retained, to the end, a major voice in the opposition, even after some of the bishops had joined him. Significantly, it is he, and not Escammatismenus, who was later chosen to write the certificate of Orthodoxy demanded by Gregory before he would consent to resign.

43. *Ekklesiastikos Pharos,* 5 (1910), 346 (letter 178).

44. Ibid., 344-45 (letter 178)

45. Pachymeres, II, 115 Laurent, "Les signataires du second synode des Blakhernes." 148.

46. *Ekklesiastikos Pharos,* 5 (1910), 345 (letter 178).

47. See Pachymeres, II, 115-16.

48. Ibid., 114; cf. Beccus, *Against the Tomus,* PG 141.872C.

49. Pachymeres, II, 117 (Nessus, the centaur, was shot by Heracles with a poisoned arrow, which afterward became the cause of Heracles' own death).

50. Ibid., 117.

51. Laurent, "Un polémiste grec," 155; on the manuscript, see Th. Bolides, "Die Schriften des Georgios Moschampar und der Codex Alexandrinus 285," *Bulletin de l'Institut Archéologique Bulgare,* 9 (1935) (= Actes du IVè Congrès international des études byzantines) 268. V. Laurent, "A propos de Georges Moschabar, polémiste antilatin. Notes et rectifications," *EO* 35 (1936), 336-47, is a response to Bolides' article, which is summarized at length by Chr. Papadopoulos in *Theologia,* 14 (1936), 175-84 (in Greek).

52. *Apology,* PG 142.257A-258B.

53. See above *Dossier de Lyon,* pp. 23, 313n1.

54. PG 142.251C-267B; translation in I. E. Troitskij, *Khristianskoe Chtenie,* 69 (1889), pt. 2, 545-70.

55. *Ekklesiastikos Pharos,* 5 (1910) 350-51 (letter 183). In this letter, addressed to Theodore Mouzalon, the patriarch notifies the prime minister that he is sending him a rough, unpublished composition which he hopes he will agree to correct and even to assume authorship. Laurent,

Regestes, no. 1502, believes this to be a reference (as I do) to the *Apology.* He dates the letter 1286-1288.

56. *Ekklesiastikos Pharos,* 5 (1910) 344-45 (letter 178).

57. So Jugie, *Theologia dogmatica,* II, 363, 364.

58. So F. Cayré, "Georges de Chypre," *DTC,* 6, pt. 1 (Paris 1920), col. 1232.

60. Ibid., 257-258B; M. V.-J. Barvinok, *Nicephorus Blemmydes and his Works* (Kiev, 1911) (in Russian), p. 167.

61. As is believed by Laurent, *Regestes,* no. 1502.

62. *Apology, PG* 142.256C.

63. Ibid., 265D.

64. *Tomus, PG* 142.240B.

65. *Apology, PG* 142.265C, 266C.

66. Ibid., 266D.

67. Ibid., 267B.

68. Ibid., 257A; cf. Barvinok, *Nicephorus Blemmydes,* pp. 167-68.

69. *Apolgy, PG* 142.257C-D, M. Jugie, *De processione Spiritus Sancti: Ex fontibus revelationis et secundum Orientales dissidentes* (Rome, 1936), p. 324.

70. *Apology, PG* 142.252C.

71. Pachymeres, II, 118; L E. Troitskij, in *Khristianskoe Chtenie,* 69 (1889) pt. 1, 342.

72. See his πιττάκιον to the emperor, *PG* 142.268A.

73. Laurent, *Regestes,* no. 1510 (text lost).

74. *Ekklesiastikos Pharos,* 5 (1910), 345 (letter 179).

75. Pachymeres, II, 122, 123; on the chronology, see also Laurent, *Regestes,* no. 1513, esp. p. 307.

76. Pachymeres, II, 122.

7

MARK AND THE SYNOD

Mark's modest theological *oeuvre*, the major contributory cause of this new crisis, unfortunately has not survived. We are, however, well informed, from a variety of sources, both about its content and its role in the controversy that it generated. Besides Pachymeres' narrative, Gregory's *Confession* and πιττάκιον (his missive to the emperor, Andronicus) contain considerable information.[1] In addition, John Chilas' own letter to the emperor sheds further light on the matter.[2] More important, however, is the recent publication of a *Report* to the synod of bishops,[3] which was written, in all probability, by Mark himself. Although the document bears no name, and the end is missing, it is doubtless the work of the patriarch's student, as the internal evidence indicates.[4] The anonymous author, for example, twice refers to his former commentary as a letter (γράμμα),[5] the same word used by the patriarch, by Pachymeres, and by John of Ephesus to describe Mark s literary effort.[6]

The fact that this address to the bishops of the synod is Mark's and is, in a sense, his own personal defense, his own words, his only surviving work, gives the document added significance. It adds a new dimension to Mark's own personality, since repeated, closer scrutiny reveals that Mark eventually made a *volte-face* and rejected his previous theological attempts in defense of the *Tomus*. In the text he labors to shield himself by placing the blame for his own confusion on the patriarch's *Tomus*. He even quotes a passage from the *Tomus* to illustrate the origin and inspiration of his now lost commentary.[7] The *Report's* importance needs no demonstration.

A. *Mark's Commentary*

According to Pachymeres, Mark had been a student of Gregory's and was a frequent visitor to the patriarchate when he heard of the opposition to the *Tomus*. It is then, no doubt, that he decided to join the conflict in support of his teacher. Pachymeres notes that he did not know how or when Mark got the idea into his head.[8] In any case, his intention was to elaborate on the text and to agree with the patriarchal posture rather than to create some alien doctrinal novelty. The *Tomus* served as his point of departure. "And I accepted, or so I thought, the *Tomus* of the patriarch, and his celebrated literary style as an indisputable witness that I had not strayed from the correct path. Nor was my...commentary composed as some kind of novelty, nor as an attempt to lead people astray to an alien doctrine (God forbid!), but as an attempt supposedly at agreement with the patriarchal *Tomus*."[9]

Once the work was written, it was taken to the patriarch to read. He, it seems, read the work and then returned it. Mark, however, appears to have mistaken the patriarch's silence to mean approval because he proceeded to publish the text and to inform people that it had the patriarch's personal *imprimatur*.[10] Mark actually insists that it was with the patriarch's "permission" that the commentary was shown to some others.[11] Moreover, Pachymeres comments that the patriarch had made a "few corrections" before returning the commentary to his disciple.[12] Even so, neither Mark nor Gregory (clearly the better informed) mentions any corrections or "improvements" to the text.[13] The patriarch, in point of fact, denies ever having made such emendations. "Mark's commentary should be held not against me, but against its author; nor should I be blamed as its cause. For I deemed this labor of an uncultured non-professional unworthy of careful study, not to add that it was impossible for me to amend it when I was snowed under with more important matters."[14] But, what of Mark's comment in his *Report* that he had Gregory's "permission"? Surely that cannot be accepted as it stands. He was plainly attempting to exonerate and protect himself before the bishops, who had called him to explain his views. In fact, the entire text is little more than Mark's effort to save his own skin—clearly the key to understanding its content.

But what was it that Mark had written which caused so much public excitement and eventually led to the unforeseen defection of several of Gregory's episcopal colleagues?[15] Essentially, it was an attempt by Mark to analyze a key passage of the *Tomus*—his "indisputable witness"—which explained what the Church Fathers meant *whenever* they employed the phrase "procession through the Son." "If, in fact, it is also said by some of the saints that the Spirit proceeds 'through the Son,' what is meant here is the eternal manifestation of the Spirit by the Son, not simply the emanation (πρόοδος) into being of the Spirit whose existence is from the Father."[16] Despite the simplicity of the patriarch's language, Mark assumed (to use his own words) a double meaning in the word "procession" in this passage. And so, he labeled it ambiguous (ὁμώνυμον) In his commentary, for it seemed to him to be susceptible of double interpretation.

> It seemed to me that he had made a distinction in the term procession (ἐκ-πορεύεσθαι) between the eternal manifestation (ἔκφανσις ἀΐδιος) and the

emanation (πρόοδος) pure and simple, of the Holy Spirit as it emerges into being. And I understood him to say that, in some of the writings of the saints, its eternal manifestation through the Son is indicated by the word "procession," while the procession, pure and simple is not so indicated. Because I assumed a double meaning here in the word "procession" I called the term "ambiguous" (ὁμώνυμον), as my commentary indicates. And, if he said, as he is now saying, that the phrase "through the Son" denotes the eternal manifestation apart from the term "procession," why did he add the word "here"? For where else does the phrase "through the Son" alone, and without the term "procession," denote the existence of the Holy Spirit, so that one can say that, even if, in others, the phrase "through the Son" denotes the existence of the Holy Spirit "here," nevertheless it denotes what he called the manifestation? His concern was not (I repeat, not) with the phrase "through the Son" alone, but with the term "procession," which he said means "here" the eternal manifestation through the Son, the word "here" indicating that elsewhere the word "procession" denotes a process by which the Holy Spirit emerges into being, even though "here" it denotes the eternal manifestation.[17]

Mark thought the term "procession" could be used to signify the hypostatic character of the Spirit as it emerges into being, as well as its eternal manifestation. The term which had been used for centuries by the Church to designate the Spirit's natural existence—its origin from the Father—could now somehow be used as a synonym for describing the permanent relationship existing between the Son and the Spirit. Procession (ἐκπόρευσις) could now mean the manifestation, revelation, or shining forth of the Spirit. In sum, what Mark had done was to take a traditional and hallowed definition and give it a generalized meaning and application. Apparently, that which convinced him to reach this conclusion was the word "here," found in the text quoted from the *Tomus*. From this word he concluded that the patriarch was drawing a distinction between the passage of the *Tomus* and other patristic texts which contained the phrase "through the Son." "For, otherwise, what is the meaning of the term 'here' put in the middle [of the passage quoted]?"[18]

Given this "reading" of the *Tomus*, it is not surprising to find those who had signed it accusing the patriarch of ambiguity and shifting the blame entirely onto him. This, undoubtedly, was made easier by their recognition of the similarity between Mark's formulation of ἐκπόρευσις = ἔκφανσις, and Beccus' insistence that "from" equaled "through" (ἐκ = διά), or that ἔκφανσις meant only procession. Both could easily support an "inoffensive interpretation"[19] of those patristic texts favoring the unionist cause. Quite clearly the patriarch, as a result of Mark's "homonymy" generated from his own circle, was guilty. To those who had been opposing the patriarch, the *Tomus* now seemed all too ambiguous, if not a confirmation of Beccus' own theology.

Characteristically, once his commentary was deemed out of order, Mark tried to capitalize on this same argument in his defense by accusing his former tutor of harboring unionist doctrine. In his *Report*, he deliberately quotes Tarasius' and Maximus the Confessor's[20] use of the formula "through the Son," and then proceeds to ask the patriarch whether these two Fathers, in using the disputed phrase, were referring to the hypostasis or the manifesting emanation, brightness, and energy of the Holy Spirit.

> For if what proceeds is the manifesting emanation and brightness through the Son, it is also from the Son. It follows that, in your view, procession through the Son is procession from the Son—which is where Beccus' evil and falsehood finds its strength. For he obstinately affirms that what proceeds "through the Son" is the equivalent of proceeding "from the Son," bringing the discussion to a question of existence. Clearly, he accepts procession from the Son, and your statement strongly confirms what we wish to abolish.[21]

Mark concludes by advising the patriarch to abandon such "useless explanations," since they end not by refuting but by confirming Beccian belief. He then adds that what the phrase "through the Son" really means is the unity (conjoining) and equality of the Son and the Spirit—the two causalities in the ineffable order of the Godhead. For the Son and the Spirit (caused) proceed in unity and equality from the Father (cause).[22] The phrase, therefore, cannot be understood in a causal sense, as Beccus would have it, because, then, the unity and equality of the Son and the Father would amount to two causes.

Mark's entanglement in the controversy, his efforts in support of the patriarch, and his later withdrawal of that support are undeniably of great interest. They show how the patriarch was drawn into the controversy by the opposition, and then promptly blamed for his disciple's blunders when in truth he had little to do with them. Indeed, the only thing the patriarch could be accused of is his failure to scrutinize Mark's commentary more carefully, before it had reached other hands. In all this, the evidence provided by Mark's own *Report* is invaluable, and serves to show how ill-equipped the disciple was as a theologian; the patristic term denoting the relation between the Holy Spirit and the Father was, by way of his device of "homonymy," stripped of its original and fundamental sense. The commentary was actually "the labor of a non-professional,"[23] as Gregory rightly noted. Arguably, it explains why it was so easy for the patriarch's adversaries to place the blame wholly on the patriarch. After all, how could such a simple and unseasoned theologian as Mark have tried to mislead others? Obviously, it was an artfully unscrupulous ruse of the patriarch; an attempt to promote his doctrine by way of his student's commentary.[24]

A comparison of the passage Mark had seen fit "to seize upon" (to borrow the patriarch's phrase),[25] and the interpretation he placed on it reveals that he had, in fact, inferred things which were not in the passage. The patriarch's meaning was luminously clear—when the Fathers speak of procession through the Son, "the phrase 'through the Son' here denotes the eternal manifestation." That is to say, it was not a question of the meaning of procession (as Mark mistakenly understood it), but an explanation of the phrase "through the Son —pure and simple. As Gregory was to state later, his intention in writing this section of the *Tomus* was solely a question of the meaning of the phrase "through the Son" as used by the Fathers, as well as a rebuttal of Beccus' interpretation of the phrase; it was *not* a redefinition of the traditional term "procession."[26]

Mark not only rejected his initial position, but when cowed by the opposition to Gregory II, also denied the validity and the foundation of the patriarch's own formulations. To say that the Holy Spirit takes its subsistence—its being as divine person—in proceeding from the Father, but yet is manifested by and with the Son—for, it is the Spirit of the Son—was, for Mark, patently suspect. As he notes, "if one of the holy Fathers said this, show or prove it and we will accept it."[27] Suffice it to say, Mark's "antirrhetic" against Gregory is little more than a reversion to the traditional position on the question of the procession. Any deviation from the patristic deposit was not to be tolerated. Evidently, Mark was so afraid and intimidated by the controversy he had generated that he had to retreat to this conservative posture. It is, to put it bluntly, a deliberate rejection and disregard of virtually all of Gregory's argument; the phrase which Gregory had so impressively explored in the *Tomus*, could mean little more than what it had always meant. Adopting the adversary's position seemed to be the safest solution to his predicament.

This consideration brings us to the fact that Gregory has actually been accused of treating his student Mark somewhat shabbily by dissociating himself quickly and "arbitrarily" from him;[28] Gregory all too "joyously sacrificed" him to secure his own image.[29] This, however, scarcely seems to accord with the evidence. What, in fact, happened is made painfully clear in Mark's *Report*, where it is the patriarch who is dismissed summarily, and chastised for promoting "false" and "useless" doctrines.[30] It is Mark who turned against his patriarch and teacher. This significant shift of his affections (a fact the other sources fail to mention) is the key to understanding the text of the *Report*.

Gregory acted swiftly in disowning his disciple by openly declaring his personal innocence vis-à-vis Mark's "babbling letter,"[31] but this was an action he knew was both urgent and necessary. His previous reluctance to take up his pen against Moschabar and others could no longer be justified. The danger was now more pressing, if not greater; he had to dissociate himself from Mark and refute his questionable commentary. Hence, his brief but correctly labeled *Confession*.[32] The entire first half of this text actually takes the form of a *confessio fidei*; while the second half is a refutation of Mark's confusing commentary. In the second half the patriarch goes to the heart of the issue and by deliberately omitting unnecessary details, shows, in the most direct way possible, what the *Tomus* actually said. By the end, it is evident just where Gregory stood in relation to his disciple's commentary.

The patriarch begins by noting that the law judges only after it has heard and understood what the accused had allegedly said or done. The present confession—it is the teaching of the Church—was written in fulfillment of this goal, notably, to provide information for his would-be judges; it contains what the patriarch has always professed and defended. After giving a free rendition of the creed, with some elaboration, the patriarch goes on to reject the "false Union of Lyons," as well as its theology concerning the procession of the Spirit. For the Spirit proceeds from the Father, from whom it has its existence and essential cause. That is, the Son, who also has His existence from the Father, is not its cause, either separately or with the Father; the Spirit proceeds neither through the Son nor from the Son. The patriarch concludes by acknowledging the validity of the seven ecumenical councils and all the regional synods (together with their decrees) which the Church had received. What the Church has accepted, he accepts, and what it has condemned, he condemns and rejects.[33]

The patriarch next notes that he had been blamed and made responsible for Mark's commentary. To this, he can only respond by placing anathema on both the text and its contents. Indeed, he would willingly pronounce the same excommunication and the most awesome curses on himself, should it be shown that he had, in fact, attempted to introduce or write anything of the sort. In composing the *Tomus* (as a refutation of Beccus on behalf of the Church), he had in no wise fallen into such error for which he is reproached and slandered. "Such libel plainly harms their own soul, not me." What the patriarch acknowledged in the text was that the Holy Spirit forms an essential component of the Holy Trinity, and is perfect God, like the Father and the Son. The Spirit, moreover, proceeds from God the Father and is consubstantial with Him, and has its being in its perfection from Him. However, the Son, who is likewise begotten of the Father, accompanies the Spirit; through Him the Spirit is revealed and manifested in its splendor, while it has its existence in all its perfection from the Father.

> For I acknowledge the Holy Spirit as being an essential component of the Holy Trinity, and I know it as perfect God (just like the Father and the Son), which proceeds from God the Father, and which has its perfect being from Him; it is co-essential with God the Father (from whom it proceeds) and with the Son (who is ineffably born of the Father), with whom it is united to the Father, and whom it accompanies, and through whom it shines forth, and is manifest, and is revealed, proceeding from the Father. And, it has its perfect existence and its divine and ineffable procession from the Father—revealed as its mode of existence—which I never called homonymous.[34]

Clearly, my explanation—continues the patriarch—never implied or attached a double meaning to the term "procession"; the patriarch never wrote anything of the kind. Mark's commentary, on the contrary, is a monument to its own author, not to the patriarch; the patriarch is personally responsible neither for its content nor for its cause; its "homonymy" and its ideas are those of Mark, and should not be ascribed to the patriarch. Besides, the patriarch never studied the text carefully; he never had the time to do so, since he was overwhelmed with more important matters. Mark, in short, had betrayed the patriarch's confidence by publishing a document for which he had no mandate whatsoever. Why, then, should he be saddled with Mark's ideas?

Despite these facts, the patriarch notes criticism against the *Tomus*, and his exegesis of the phrase "through the Son," continues. The "double meaning," which the monk wrongfully and ignorantly attached to his remark, is unfounded. The patriarch, and anyone else for that matter, never understood the phrase to mean the mode of existence of the Spirit as such, except, of course, Beccus, who had interpreted the phrase to mean that the Spirit has its existence through the Son. For "through" is not equivalent to "from." Indeed, this is the very notion which the fifth rebuttal of the *Tomus*—from which the patriarch's remark was taken—attempted to refute. (The only permissible exegesis of the Fathers is that sometimes the phrase denotes the eternal manifestation or revelation of the Spirit through the Son, and sometimes the bestowing, sending, and giving of the Spirit to us. This is precisely what the passage in the *Tomus* "'through the Son' here" said. Briefly, it did not mean that the Spirit has its existence through the Son, for that would be Beccus' belief. Nor did it mean the economic sending of the Spirit only (even if this is the interpretation given it by the Fathers elsewhere) (εἰ καὶ ἀλλαχοῦ τοῦτο σημαίνει). What it did stress was the Spirit's eternal manifestation through the Son, which is parallel to, and is understood in connection with, the Spirit's coming into being from the Father (συντρέχουσαν καὶ συνεπινοουμένην τῇ ἐκ Πατρὸς αὐτοῦ εἰς τὸ εἶναι προόδῳ). True, this manifestation is parallel to and accompanies the hypostatic act of procession; even so, it is separate from this act. Such was the patriarch's faith from the beginning. There is no resemblance whatever between the patriarch's compositions, written either before or after the *Tomus*, and those of Mark.[35]

In order to complete his synopsis, the patriarch then adds that Beccus, in his attempt to prove that "through" equaled "from," also stressed that "through" merely meant a "mediate," not an "immediate" or "direct," procession. The *Tomus*, however, teaches that the eternal manifestation alone was through the Son which, of course, was to be distinguished from the "immediate" act of procession. Nevertheless, neither notion of the "immediate" or "mediate" ("through the Son") could be denied. Whatever our opponents may say, the fact remains that we do not abolish the procession 'through the Son' by accepting the immediate procession, any more than we suppress the immediate procession by accepting the procession 'through the Son'."[36] The Spirit proceeds and has its existence from the Father, but shines through the Son, in the same manner as the sun's light is said to shine through the sun's rays—the sun being the source and the cause of origin. The light's existence, or origin, is in no sense derived from the sun's rays.

In conclusion, the patriarch suggests that, as a result of the content of his *Confession*, he must be judged blameless; he will, in fact, appear so before the judgment seat of Christ itself. In short, those who continue their slander and false accusations even after the above declaration of faith, are the ones who are removed from the true and immaculate doctrine of the Church; they constitute Christianity's enemies. They, therefore, are the ones who are under judgment and the curse which the patriarch had pronounced—at the beginning of his *Confession*—upon himself.[37]

The patriarch's *Confession* is one of the most successful and succinct synopses of his entire theological construct. It is, in fact, remarkable for its cogency, brevity, and clarity. In this sense, it is unique when compared to the patriarch's other works. No doubt, he wished to make his orthodoxy public, brief, and as plain as possible. This said, the patriarch succeeds in demonstrating that the accusation of "homonymy" brought against him was not his. On the contrary, Mark's explanation paralleled Beccus' earlier misrepresentation of the *Tomus*. The confusion was clearly the result of Mark's own creation.

Not surprisingly, Gregory says as much again in his other brief defense, the πιττάκιον.[38] This was sent to the emperor, Andronicus, sometime after the arrival of John of Ephesus in the capital at the end of 1288.[39] In this very short letter, the patriarch first asks that he at least be given a hearing. Furthermore, he hopes that his episcopal colleagues will be as courteous and heedful as the emperor. As in the *Confession*, the patriarch again pronounces anathema upon himself if it could be shown that his intention was ever to write that the term "procession" was susceptible to double interpretation.[40] To clinch his case, the patriarch goes on to ask just exactly what his gain would have been in composing the *Tomus* (in which he was refuting Beccus) if his intention had been to publicize Mark's error (which conforms with Beccus' notions)! Such gain simply did not make sense. The patriarch then adds that not even a "shadow of resemblance" exists between Mark's commentary and any of his writings published before or after the *Tomus*.[41] Moreover, both the prime minister, Theodore Mouzalon, and the metropolitan, Theoleptus of Philadelphia, know this; Others insist on falsifying the patriarch's words; in short, they ignore the facts, and instead draw—arbitrarily and artificially —other conclusions. Were these individuals to compare, without passion, the *Tomus'* clarity with Mark's confusing commentary, they would be convinced.[42]

It is perhaps necessary at this point to enumerate the opposition's objections to the *Tomus*, as they are summarized in the literature and, especially, in Gregory's several counter-memoranda. The objections, it seems, were fundamentally three: (1) that the *Tomus* had confused the meaning of procession, and equated it with the manifestation (the argument from homonymy); (2) that it had declared the manifestation to be eternal or timeless; and (3) that the nature or meaning of the doctrine itself was incomprehensible.[43] As we have seen, Gregory refused to concede that he was wrong, or that the *Tomus* needed modification on any of these points. Two years previously, he had pointed out to Theodore Mouzalon that the dogmatic truth of the *Tomus* far outweighed any of the objections.[44] Suffice it to say, the exact same resolute decision to stand by his position is expressed in the two documents just reviewed. Gregory never yields to the suggestion that his exegesis had been faulty, or that he had committed any sort of error. The notion of the eternal manifestation of the Spirit from the Son was neither a 'useless' explanation nor a confirmation of Beccian belief (as Mark upholds in his *Report*), but a doctrine in full and strict conformity with the Church's faith.[45] As a result, even his own circle could not convince him to mend the text. He was willing to give assurances and explanations, but remained otherwise immovable.

It may be argued that the patriarch was being stubborn, and that his posture was, in effect, an effort to save face. This is a possibility, and yet, it is hardly compelling. Actually, his attitude stemmed from the realization that many of his doctrinal adversaries were motivated for the most part by a mindless conservatism. He suspected, for example, that their objection to designating the manifestation of the Spirit from the Son "eternal" or timeless was grounded on the traditional view that "through the Son" could only mean a happening *in time*, a temporal sending of the Spirit by the Son. And yet, to believe otherwise would be dangerously approaching Latin, or Beccian, doctrine. Indeed, they had said as much. In broad terms, it is necessary to realize that the point of departure for Patriarch Gregory's formulation of the eternal manifestation "was an attempt to enter into an understanding argument with Latin theology, and that the adversaries of Gregory...belonged to that same school of verbal polemics which for too long, unfortunately, carried on the *Filioque* controversy."[46] In the end the opposition parallels Palamas' own later critics with their "frozen theology" and "oriental scholasticism." The patriarch was determined that such a group—opposed as it was to *any* redirection of Byzantine theology—should not succeed.

But Gregory's unwillingness to compromise was also rooted in the fact that his adversaries were motivated by non-theological considerations—by hostility, pure and simple. The claim that it was Gregory's theology that brought about his fall, or that the controversy was concerned strictly "with theology, and less about personalities,"[48] is unconvincing. Factors other than the purely theological were operative. The evidence is incontrovertible. His adversaries, it is true, attempted to conceal their private quarrel by arguing that their aim was the solid establishment of the doctrine of the Church.[49] But Pachymeres who informs us of this, also tells us that it was a lie and not the real reason. Others, too, must have known. Certainly, Gregory's immediate successor, Athanasius, did; in his pithy words, not one of his own predecessors (he specifically mentions Arsenius, Joseph, and Gregory) had been forced from office for some "lawful reason."[50]

B. *The Hierarchy Joins the Opposition*

The hierarchy could not have been unaware of the opposition to the patriarch and the *Tomus* which began in late 1285. However, they did not openly join the patriarch's opponents even if many had become concerned over Mark's commentary and its possible link with the patriarch's *Tomus*.[51] As it turns out, Gregory's first call for assistance to his bishops is dated April 1287.[52] Nearly a year later, in February-March 1288, when he appealed (for the second time) to John of Ephesus to come to his aid, he was still enjoying Bishop Theoleptus' favor.[53] Arguably, John's delayed arrival in Constantinople was due to his sympathy with the opposition—he had not postponed his arrival because of the difficulties of winter travel or the death of his brother.[54] Even so, Gregory appears to be unaware of any change in his bishop's attitude—a clear indication that John had not yet voiced his views, even if he may have embraced the opposition's cause from his distant diocese.[55] It is only with John's arrival in autumn 1288 and the publication of Mark's commentary several months before, that he and "the more important" of the circle of bishops began a more organized opposition.[56] It is then that they chose to take a more careful look at the *Tomus*, signed three years previously, and the debate that it had engendered. That Mark's commentary served as their point of departure is clear.

The episcopate's unwillingness to involve itself in the controversy until very late in the debate is one of the more striking features of the years following the signing of the *Tomus* in 1285. The detractors who appeared almost immediately upon the publication of the synod's doctrinal summary came from a lesser theological element in the Church, not from the hierarchy which, even when it did enter the controversy, did not do so in a body. The latter remained, to the end, the cause of a small, if influential, minority. As Gregoras notes, not all the bishops were eager "to cast their hostile scorn on their benefactor."[57] This group lacked not only unity but theological unanimity as well; not everyone was united on the extent of Gregory's culpability or "error." Sharp disagreement persisted till the end among the three major figures—Theoleptus of Philadelphia, John Chilas of Ephesus, and Daniel Glycys of Cyzicus. In fact, the disagreement was never resolved.

Among the pillars of the opposition the metropolitan of Philadelphia ranks as the most important.[58] He was probably the most distinguished member of the episcopate in Andronicus II's entire reign. His saintly qualities and deep spirituality had already earned him a deserved reputation with the emperor; he also shared, in abundance, the esteem and confidence of the prime minister, Theodore Mouzalon.[59] Theoleptus belongs to that special group of ascetics and theologians—as does Gregory—who influenced palamism; it is he who initiated Gregory Palamas into hesychasm.[60] He was a man who possessed the power of the Holy Spirit, according to Palamas. Notable too, is his continuous concern—displayed in the course of his long career—for Orthodoxy and the unity of the official Church;[61] this explains his opposition to the religious policy of Michael VIII, his fight against the schismatic Arsenites (he refused to accept the settlement of 1310 which granted them total and unconditional absolution),[62] and his involvement in Patriarch Gregory's problems. Much of his work (apart from the excerpts found in the *Philocalia* and those edited by Salaville) remains unpublished.

Less prominent than Theoleptus were the metropolitans John Chilas of Ephesus and Daniel of Cyzicus. We should note that both bishops had reason to be grateful to Patriarch Gregory. That they eventually rose from their monastic state to become bishops of major sees in the empire was due chiefly to Gregory's initiative. Both were monks and friends of Gregory prior to his accession in the spring of 1283.[63] They were among the first to be honored by Gregory; less than two years later, their episcopal signatures are to be found in the *Tomus* of Blachernae.[64] The patriarch's shock to find them, when he was sorely in need of assistance, at the head of Moschabar's faction is thus understandable.[65] Gregoras' comments on this unforeseen turn of events are succinct and on target—the patriarch's dismay and surprise were not unlike Caesar's on his assassination at the hands of Brutus and Cassius. Instead of finding in his colleagues treasure and friends, the patriarch found only criticism and charcoal![66] Significantly, when this historian describes the crisis of Gregory's patriarchate he does not mention either the *Tomus* or the Damascene text. Instead, he explains it in terms of the hostility and scorn of Gregory's episcopal detractors—further evidence that the controversy was largely atheological in origin and inspiration.

Together with these bishops, mention should also be made of the patriarch of Alexandria, Athanasius, participant in the condemnation of Beccus in January 1283 and again at the Council of Blachernae.[67] Actually, this patriarch had been in the capital ever since the seventies.[68] Early in Gregory's patriarchate, however, his name was struck from the diptychs because he had refused to sign a document denouncing the Union of Lyons.[69] (He was asked to sign because he had supported the union in Michael's reign.) Even so, he eventually made his peace, and became a hard-line anti-unionist.[70] We have seen how, in 1285, he had advised Beccus, after publicly accusing him of heresy, to abandon his novelties by returning to the traditional faith of the Church.[71] For all that, he once again refused to give his signature—this time to the *Tomus*. His argument was that he was unfamiliar with Constantinopolitan practice, and that the matter was not one that concerned his Church. He also justified his refusal by offering to write his own confession of faith; this, he said, would be consistently Orthodox, free of suspicious or objectionable elements.[72]

Gregory's relations with Athanasius were not what he had hoped from his patriarchal colleague. It is likely, personality differences—as in the case with Moschabar—may have played a role here as well. It is significant, for example, that Athanasius refused to concelebrate with Gregory, even after he had agreed to condemn the Union of Lyons.[73] Further, he seems to have been a friend of Gregory's other adversary, John Chilas of Ephesus.[74] Overall, Gregory was not the only one to have problems with Athanasius. Under Gregory's successor, the patriarch of Alexandria was actually forced to leave Constantinople for Rhodes.[75] Significantly, both Metochites and Athanasius of Constantinople accuse him of being a troublemaker and an opportunist.[76]

As noted above, some of Gregory's opponents refused to believe that Mark alone was responsible for his commentary and, instead, wished to place the blame for its errors entirely on the patriarch; they thought the patriarch had used Mark to advertise his views. As a result, they sought to convince the bishops as well. They were not unsuccessful. Bishop Theoleptus' visit to Theodore Mouzalon was probably a result of their maneuvers.[77] Equally, Gregory's refractory attitude did not help the already tense situation. Thus some bishops thought the patriarch guilty; the problem was no longer solely a question of simple naïveté on his part.[78] Moreover, the Arsenites grasped the auspicious nature of the crisis and began pressing for Gregory's retirement, and the adoption of their conservative theological position embodied in the formula *a Patre solo.*[79]

In the face of such deliberate pressure (even his own friends were attempting to convince him to change the text of the *Tomus*), Gregory retired provisionally to the monastery of the Hodegetria.[80] No precise date can be given for this move; it may have occurred shortly before the arrival of John of Ephesus in autumn 1288, since Pachymeres mentions it immediately before he speaks of John's arrival. However, the reverse is likewise possible. In any event, Gregory realized that his power base among the bishops was weakening. In fact, with the arrival of John, some bishops took the further and more serious step and ceased commemorating Gregory's name in the liturgy.[81] To be sure, the scandal, instead of being contained, grew in strength."[82] Gregory may also have thought his move would restore peace. That, at least, is the explanation he gave to his congregation in a Sunday sermon before he retired to the Hodegetria.[83] Whatever the case, although he continued the government of the Church from his monastery, Gregory was anticipating his resignation. Later, in a letter to a bishop friendly to his cause, he would note that his retirement was "pledge" of his resignation; for the initial goal of his patriarchate, and the only reason for which he had accepted it—to give stability and unity to the Church—had not materialized.[84]

But if some of the metropolitans had refused to commemorate Gregory's name, others were more concerned about Mark's commentary. Hence the meeting mentioned earlier, in which the commentary was debated and Mark's errors duly listed and condemned by the assembled hierarchs.[85] Mark's above-mentioned *Report* was a significant consequence of this discussion. The document, as noted earlier, was a written personal retraction by Mark of his commentary, and a denunciation of his teacher, the patriarch. The text, clearly addressed to the bishops, is a statement in which Mark rejects the error of his earlier commentary requested of him by the bishops. "But, since the divine and holy synod has proscribed the commentary, I am first to reject it with all my heart, and will give such proof of my rejection as you wish it to have."[86] The bishops, in other words, requested not only the retraction of the commentary but also "proof," as the author says, of its rejection. The *Report* is this proof. Since Gregory is still referred to as "patriarch" in the text, it would appear that the synod's request and the writing of the *Report* occurred before Gregory's resignation in June 1289.[87]

A further product of this assembly is John of Ephesus' personal synodal declaration. Although the document is addressed to the emperor, its theological framework indicates that originally it may have been an extract of John's memorandum to the synod. The document is material confirmation of the metropolitan's participation in the struggle against Gregory.[88] Specifically, the text denounces the confusion Gregory had allegedly introduced by his discussion of the procession. It is, in short, an attack on Mark's "homonymy," on Gregory, and on his distinction between the hypostasis of the Spirit and the energy which is manifest through the Son. That is to say, it is a categorical rejection of Gregory's exegesis of the phrase "through the Son."

The author of the text argues that the consensus of the Church had always been that the procession was an immutable characteristic of the Holy Spirit and could not mean anything other than the natural existence of the Holy Spirit from the Father. To believe that procession sometimes denotes existence, sometimes eternal manifestation, revelation, or shining forth, is blasphemous and heretical. Equally, the common confession of the Fathers is that the projecting Father is the cause of the Spirit and of the generated Son; everyone knows that projection and procession are equivalent. Those who declare that projection sometimes denotes cause, sometimes revelation, or eternal manifestation, merit condemnation. Again, procession means existence. However, those who write that at times it designates existence and at times manifestation remove themselves from the truth and, thus, merit our hatred.[89]

Mark followed a similar traditional approach in his explanation why his "homonymy," or equivocal definition of the term "procession," was an error. In sum, he employed the objections raised by the bishop of Ephesus, and explained why the adjective "ambiguous" could not be assigned to the term "procession." Procession implies uniqueness and cannot be used ambiguously; a characteristic is always unique, whereas the term "ambiguous" is by definition a general term for many and different things. Briefly, the two are incompatible with each other.

> If the procession of the all-Holy Spirit is susceptible to double interpretation (ὁμώνυμος), [then] this does not mean its [hypostatic] characteristic and its mode of existence; but if the procession is the [hypostatic] characteristic and mode of existence of the all-Holy Spirit, which it is, in fact, then its procession is not ambiguous at all. For a characteristic always and uniquely belongs to that thing of which it is a characteristic, whereas the term "ambiguous" is the general

name of many and different things both by definition and general description; thus, the two are mismatched and incompatible. For the characteristic of something is not ambiguous, while that which is ambiguous in nature is not a characteristic at all.[90]

One wonders what role John of Ephesus played in Mark's retreat to this position. For, ultimately, both reject the expression "eternal manifestation" and adhere solely to the eternal hypostatic procession of the Spirit. The formula "procession through the Son" could only indicate the Spirit's temporal sending by the Son. Clearly, Gregory's Orthodox understanding of the trinitarian antinomy of essence-hypostasis and essence-energy or manifestation was far too complicated and novel for their fixed or "frozen" theology to encompass.

Along with these documents, mention should also be made of an unpublished, anonymous manuscript, Coislinianus 192, fols. 67^r-74^v. Internal evidence indicates that it was a response to the debate generated by Mark's commentary. The text is bound along with Gregory's *Apology, Confession*, and abdication statement taken from Pachymeres. This, together with a brief marginal note at the beginning of the text containing the name "Gregory" and "in Latinos," probably led the cataloguer to ascribe it to Gregory of Cyprus.[91] The simple style of the Greek, however, as well as its criticism of Gregory's thesis of an eternal manifestation, indicates that this is not the case.[92] In light of this, the author could be any one of the circle of bishops who opposed Gregory. Although the possibility exists that it may have been written by the bishop of Ephesus, there is no clear indication that this is so. Equally, because the tone of the attack is not as sharp as Mark's *Report*, it is unlikely that it belongs to Mark. True, the text quotes the same passage of the *Tomus* which Mark used in his *Report* and in his initial commentary in defense of the patriarch.[93] But this is used by the author only to illustrate his point. Indeed, it may indicate that the author had read Mark's commentary and had written his work as a response to Mark's interpretation of this passage. At any rate, the work was probably written in the year 1288 or soon after, probably after Mark's own commentary had been published.[94]

The text clearly belongs to a conservative, and begins by condemning all the moderns or those given to innovation in matters theological. The author then buttresses his conservatism by his insistence that the proof-texts containing the phrase "through the Son" indicate nothing other than "the oneness of nature and the essential union relation of the Son and the Spirit."[95] Actually, the first half of the text addresses Beccus (without mentioning him), since it insists repeatedly that the Father alone is cause, principle, and source of the Spirit to the exclusion of the Son. In the second half of the text, however, the author turns to the *Tomus* and to Gregory, whom he takes to task for his theological innovations and his "absurd attempt" to correct Beccus' error.[96] Although Gregory is also not mentioned by name, the allusion to "new lawgivers" who declare, by way of the *Tomus* (τομογραφικῶς), that the phrase denotes manifestation and not existence, indicates that the reference is to the patriarch.

The author, at the outset, insists that "This [interpretation of Gregory's] likewise disturbs the boundaries set by the Fathers in its attempt to heal the absurd by means of the absurd; rather than overthrowing falsehood, it becomes the origin of falsehood."[97] Specifically, the Fathers never say that the Spirit proceeds from the Son; nor is the procession ever said to denote something other than the Spirit's existence. The author then pleads that the meaning of the term "procession" must not be altered. Thus, it is not permissible to write in the *Tomus*: "If, in fact, it is also said by the Fathers that the Spirit proceeds 'through the Son,' what is meant here is the eternal manifestation, not simply the emanation."[98] For the Fathers never said the Spirit proceeds "through the Son"—this is a defective way of phrasing it—but "from the Father through the Son." Thus the term "procession" must not be altered, transformed, or modernized. This is both dangerous and daring. To be brief, procession must be ascribed to the Father, the only cause of the Spirit's hypostasis, while the term "through the Son" must be ascribed to the inseparable oneness and sharing of nature. This is what the Fathers meant to say—not "through the Son," but "from the Father through the Son.[99]

The similarity between the author's position and that of Mark and John of Ephesus is obvious. The author—like Mark—had misunderstood the passage from the *Tomus* and, indeed, employed the same argument used in the *Report* to explain his position; he seems convinced that the patriarch had altered the meaning of the term "procession." To repeat, it is tempting to suggest that the work is by Mark. It is more likely, however, the reaction of someone who had read Mark's initial interpretation of the *Tomus* and saw the erroneous twist he had given to the patriarch's words. Unfortunately, the author also drew the conclusion that Mark's interpretation was actually the patriarch's.

But what of the emperor Andronicus' reaction to this new storm center in the patriarchate? No doubt, it would be surprising if he had not been apprised of the crisis that had developed during 1288, before he had received the patriarch's own πιττάκιον. Moreover, the publication of Mark's *Report*, the patriarch's withdrawal to the Hodegetria, the arrival of the metropolitan of Ephesus in the capital, and the refusal of some of the bishops to commemorate Gregory's name in the liturgy could not have escaped him. And yet, he continued to remain in the background. This could not last long; sooner or later his intervention would be actively sought. Indeed, the bishops would ask him to arbitrate, if not intervene in the affair. If this occurred, however, and Gregory's one remaining power base was gone—along with that of his bishops and the patriarchal bureaucracy—there would be little he could do; the emperor's collaboration with the episcopate would be the final turning point. Gregory's successor expressed it well: "And pay attention, holy emperor, to why the Church has been destroyed. The insult and injustice inflicted upon the patriarchs Kyr Arsenius, Kyr Joseph, and Kyr Gregory, did not revert to them...For what lawful cause did they expel the above-mentioned patriarchs? Those who collaborate with these [bishops] will not be held guiltless by God."[100] And yet, Gregory was not going to give up so easily, even if he could no longer govern in such a climate of gathering hostility without his imperial power base.

NOTES

1. *Confession, PG* 142.247A-252C; πιττάκιον, *PG* 142.267C-270A.

2. *PG* 142.245A-246D.

3. Codex Atheniensis 1217, fols. 174r-176v; Greek text published by A. Papadakis, "Gregory II of Cyprus and an Unpublished *Report* to the Synod," *Greek, Roman, and Byzantine Studies,* 16, No. 2 (1975), 227-39 (hereafter referred to as *Report*); and idem, "Gregory II of Cyprus and Mark's *Report* Again," *The Greek Orthodox Theological Review,* 21, No. 2 (1976), 147-57 (English translation). J. Darrouzès, *Documents inédits d'ecclésiologie Byzantine* (Paris, 1966), p. 89n6, first called my attention to the existence of Atheniensis 1217.

4. The absence of the missing folio is not a recent development; it was noted long ago by J. Sakkelion, *Catalogue of the Manuscripts of the National Library of Greece* (in Greek) (Athens, 1892), p. 221. The manuscript is dated by Sakkelion to the thirteenth century. It should be pointed out that a work on stars precedes the *Report* to the synod, and becomes very confused at the top of fol. 174r, where, in the middle of the third line, a new text dealing with the Holy Spirit begins. The *Report* itself begins at the bottom of the same folio (174r).

5. Papadakis, *Report,* 236, 237.

6. *Confession, PG* 142.247; πιττάκιον, *PG* 142.267D (in the title only); Pachymeres, II, 118; John of Ephesus, in Darrouzès, *Documents inédits d'ecclésiologie*, p. 400: "heretical and foolish letter."

7. I am grateful to Professor Ihor Ševcenko of Harvard University for drawing my attention to the fact that, in the first paragraph of his *Report*, Mark quotes from the *Tomus* of Gregory (cf. n. 16 below); he offered to read the Greek text and made a number of valuable philological and palaeographical suggestions.

8. Pachymeres, II, 118.

9. Papadakis, *Report*, 236-37.

10. Pachymeres, II, 118.

11. Papadakis, *Report*, 237. M. Jugie, *Theologia dogmatica Christianorum orientalium ab Ecclesia Catholica dissidentium* (Paris, 1933), II, 363, argues that Gregory gave permission for its publication.

12. Pachymeres, II, 118.

13. As is believed by Laurent, *Regestes*, no. 1514, esp. p. 309.

14. *Confession, PG* 142.249D-250A.

15. *Ekklesiastikos Pharos*, 5 (1910), 444-45 (letter 185).

16. *Tomus, PG* 142.241A. Cf. Gregory's *Confession, PG* 142.250A.

17. Papadakis, *Report*, 236.

18. Ibid.

19. Cf. J. Meyendorff, *Introduction à l'étude de Grégoire Palamas* (Paris, 1959), p. 27.

20. Papadakis, *Report*, 238 (Tarasius, *Epistola ad Summos Sacerdotes*, in Mansi, XII, col. 1122; and Maximus, *Quaestiones ad Thalassium, PG* 90.672C).

21. Papadakis, *Report*, 238-39.

22. Ibid., 239.

23. *Confession, PG* 142.240A.

24. Cf. Laurent, *Regestes*, no. 1514, esp. p. 309.

25. *Confession, PG* 142.250A.

26. Ibid.

27. Papadakis, *Report*, 239.

28. Laurent, *Regestes*, no. 1513.

29. V. Grumel, "Le IIe concile de Lyon et la réunion de l'église grecque," *DTC*, 9, pt. 1 (Paris, 1926), col. 1408.

30. Papadakis, *Report*, 239.

31. *Confession, PG* 142.249C; the patriarch's πιττάκιον *PG* 142.268A, also refers to Mark's commentary in identical terms.

32. *PG* 142.247A-252C; for I. E. Troitskij's translation, see *Khristianskoe Chtenie*, 69, pt. 1 (1889), 370-77. Laurent, *Regestes*, no. 1514, dates the document "ca. 1289 (before June)." The text, however, is an attempt to refute Mark. A more logical publication date, therefore, would be sometime in 1288, that is, after Mark's commentary had begun to circulate and cause controversy. It is less likely, in short, that the patriarch would have waited until just before his resignation to write a refutation. Internal evidence is silent on the question. Cf. the unsubstantiated remark in *Threskeutike kai Ethike Enkyklopaideia*, 4 (1964), 731, that the text was directed against the metropolitan Theoleptus of Philadelphia.

33. *Confession, PG* 142.247A-249B.

34. Ibid 249C-D.

35. Ibid 250A-D, cf. Jugie, *De processione Spiritus Sancti*, p. 340.

36. *Confession, PG* 142.251A.

37. Ibid., 251C-252C.

38. Cf. πιττάκιον, *PG* 142.268C. For patriarchal πιττάκια, cf. J. Darrouzès, *Le Registre synodal du patriarcat byzantin au XIVᵉ siècle: Etude paléographique et diplomatique* (Paris, 1971), pp. 172-81.

39 . his text was written either at the end of 1288 or at the beginning of 1289: both the subscription and the body of the text contain references to John of Ephesus (who had arrived in autumn 1288) as an adversary. See Laurent, *Regestes*, no. 1515, esp. p. 307. The text is translated by Troitskij, *Khristianskoe Chtenie*, 69, pt. 1, 367-69.

40. Πιττάκιον, *PG* 142.268C.

41. Πιττάκιον, *PG* 142.268D; the exact same phrase was used by the patriarch in his *Confession, PG* 142.250D. For Gregory's pre-1283 work against Beccus, see the evidence in Laurent, *Regestes*, no. 1513.

42. Πιττάκιον, *PG* 142.269A.

43. Cf. Jugie, *Theologia dogmatica*, II, 362.

44. *Ekklesiastikos Pharos*, 5 (1910), 350-51 (letter 183).

45. *Confession, PG* 142.252A-B.

46. Meyendorff, *Introduction à l'étude de Palamas*, p. 30.

47. J. Gill, "Notes on the De Michaele et Andronico Palaeologis of George Pachymeres," *BZ*, 68 (1975), 296: "The 'tomos' in the end brought about the downfall of its author, who had to abdicate."

48. D. M. Nicol, *The Last Centuries of Byzantium 1261-1453* (London, 1972), pp. 104-105. Cf. also K. Krumbacher, *Geschichte der byzantinischen Literatur (527-1453)* (Munich, 1897), p.98, who notes that Gregory was forced to resign because he was not a match for his theologically superior unionist adversaries.

49. Pachymeres, II, 116.

50. A.-M. Maffry Talbot, *The Correspondence of Athanasius I, Patriarch of Constantinople: Letters to the EmperorAndronicus, Members of the ImperialFamily, and Officials* (Washington, D.C., 1975), p. 6 (letter 2).

51. Pachymeres, II, 119.

52. Laurent, *Regestes*, no. 1510 (text lost).

53. *Ekklesiastikos Pharos*, 5 (1910), 345-46 (letter 179). Cf. V. Laurent, "Notes critiques: II. La correspondance de Nicéphore Gregoras publiée par R. Guilland," *EO*, 25 (1927), esp. 359-60.

54. *Ekklesiastikos Pharos*, 5 (1910), 346-47 (letter 179), 345 (letter 178); cf. Darrouzès, *Documents inédits d'ecclésiologie*, p. 89.

55. Cf. Laurent, *Regestes*, no. 1509, esp. p. 304.

56. Pachymeres, II, 122, 123; on the chronology, see Laurent, *Regestes*, no. 1513, esp. p. 307.

57. Gregoras, II, 170.

58. See his funeral oration by Nicephorus Chumnus, in J.-F. Boissonade, *Anecdota Graecae codicibus regiis*, V (Paris, 1833), 183-239; J. Gouillard, "Théolepte, métropolite de Philadelphie, *DTC*, 15, pt. 1 (Paris, 1946), cols. 339-41; and P. Schreiner, "Zur Geschichte Philadellpheias im 14. Jahrhundert (1293-1310)," *OCP*, 35 (1969), esp. 387-88. Theoleptus' own prolific literary production (mostly unpublished) is a major source for his ecclesiology and spirituality. For his unpublished work, see S. Salaville, "Un directeur spirituel à Byzance au début du XIVè siècle: Théolepte de Philadelphie," *Mélanges Joseph de Ghellinck*, II (Gembloux, 1951), 877-87. Cf. also Troitskij, *Arsenij*, p. 295.

59. Pachymeres. II. 116.

60. Meyendorff, *Introduction à l'étude de Palamas*, p. 28 (gives sources). S. Salaville, "Formes de prière d'après un Byzantin du XIVè siècle," *EO*, 39 (1940), 1-25; idem, "La vie monastique grecque au début du XIVè siècle d'après un discours inédit de Théolepte de Philadelphie," *Etudes byzantines*, 2 (1944), 119-25.

61. S. Salaville, "Deux documents inédits sur les dissensions religieuses byzantines entre 1275 et 1310," *REB*, 5 (1947), 116-36; idem, "Une lettre et un discours inédits de Théolepte de Philadelphie," *REB*, 5 (1947), 101-15.

62. V. Laurent, "Les crises religieuses à Byzance: Le Schisme anti-arsénite du métropolite Théolepte de Philadelphie († c. 1324)," *REB*, 18 (1960), 45-54.

63. They were then residents of the Ostreidion monastery; see Gregory's letter addressed to them, *Ekklesiastikos Pharos*, 3 (1909), 288 (letter 121), Troitskij, *Arsenij*, p. 296.

64. V. Laurent, "Les signataires du second synode des Blakhernes (été 1285)," *EO*, 26 (1927), 144.

65. This surprise at Chilas' defection is emphasized in Gregory's letter to Theodore Mouzalon *Ekklesiastikos Pharos*, 5 (1910), 444-45 (letter 185); cf. also Laurent, *Regestes*, no. 1509, esp. p. 304.

66. Gregoras, II, 178.

67. Pachymeres, II, 25, 97, 120.

68. Ibid., I, 428-29.

69. Ibid., II, 55-57.

70. Metochites, X, pt. 1, 323.

71. See above, p. 169.

72. Pachymeres, II, 121.

73. Metochites, X, pt. 1, 323.

74. Pachymeres, II, 135.

75. Ibid., 203; Troitskij, *Arsenij*, pp. 301-302; cf. also A.-M. Maffry Talbot, "The Patriarch Athanasius (1289-1293; 1303-1309) and the Church," *Dumbarton Oaks Papers*, 27 (1973) 21-23. See now the letter sent to the patriarch in Rhodes by the historian Pachymeres, in A. Failler, "Le séjour d'Athanase II d'Alexandrie à Constantinople," *REB*, 35 (1977), 43-71.

76. Metochites, X, pt. 1, 323; Maffry Talbot, *The Correspondence of Athanasius I*, pp. 18-23, 163-75 (letters 7 and 69); see also Failler, "Le séjour d'Athanase II," 55ff., who notes the patriarch's independent spirit, and the ambiguous path he followed during Gregory's and Athanasius' patriarchates.

77. Pachymeres, II, 119.

78. Ibid., 121.

79. Ibid., 122.

80. Ibid.; Troitskij, *Arsenij*, p. 308. This monastery's library may well have had something to do with his choice; N. G. Wilson, "The Libraries of the Byzantine World," *Greek, Roman, and Byzantine Studies*, 8 (1967), 53-80, esp. 64; L. Politis, "Eine Schreiberschule im Kloster ton Hodegon," *BZ*, 51 (1958), 16-36. Even so, Gregory eventually transferred to a μετόχιον belonging to the monastery of St Paul on Mt. Latros; cf. Pachymeres, II, 123; and V. Laurent, "Le patriarche d'Antioche Cyrille II (29 juin 1287-c. 1308)," *Analecta Bolandiana*, 68 (1950), 314. See also R. Janin, *La géographie ecclésiastique de l'empire byzantin, pt. 1: Le siège de Constantinople et le Patriarcat Œcuménique*, vol. III: *Les églises et les monastères* (Paris, 1953), 208-16.

81. Pachymeres, II, 122.

82. Ibid.

83. Ibid.

84. *PG* 142.125C-D; this letter is not included in the Eustratiades collection. See W. Lameere, *La tradition manuscrite de la correspondance de Grégoire de Chypre* (Brussels-Paris, 1937), Plates I and II; Laurent, *Regestes*, no. 1516.

85. Papadakis, *Report*, p. 237; Troitskij, *Arsenij*, pp. 312-14.

86. Papadakis, *Report*, 237.

87. Ibid., 236

88. *PG* 142.245C-246D, this letter is edited twice in Migne; see *PG* 135.505-508. Cf. also Darrouzès' *Documents inédits d'ecclésiologie*, pp. 89ff. For a Russian translation, see I. E. Troltskij.,

"Toward a History of the Dispute on the Question of the Procession of the Holy Spirit" (in Russian), *Khristianskoe Chtenie*, 69, pt. 1 (1889), 366-67; idem, *Arsenij*, pp. 308-309n2.

89. *PG* 142.245C-246C.

90. Papadakis, *Report*, p 237.

91. R. Devreesse, *Catalogue des manuscrits Grecs* II: *Le Fons Coislin* (Paris, 1945), 166. I wish to express my gratitude to Dr. Alice-Mary Maffry Talbot for her help in the transcription of this text.

92. Coislinianus 192, fols. 71^r-72^r.

93. Ibid., fol. 72^v.

94. Devreesse, *Catalogue des manuscrits Grecs* II, 165, ascribes the manuscript to the fourteenth-fifteenth centuries.

95. Coislinianus 192, fol. 69r; see also fols. 68r, 74v.

96. Ibid., fols. 71^v-74^v.

97. Ibid. fol. 71^v.

98. Ibid. fol. 71^v (= *Tomus*, *PG* 142.241A).

99. Coislinianus 192, fol. 73^r.

100. Maffry Talbot, *The Correspondence of Athanasius I*, p. 6 (letter 2).

8

CONTROVERSY AND CONSENSUS

The emperor's collaboration took the form of a plan with which he hoped Gregory would comply. He wanted to call a meeting in which the patriarch would be given an opportunity to defend himself in the presence of his accusers. The patriarch, perhaps predictably, unhesitatingly agreed.[1] The place—the imperial residence—and the date for the assembly were promptly determined, and Gregory's adversaries were requested to prepare their case. Andronicus II, however, soon realized that such a meeting might, in fact, accomplish little in restoring peace. As a consequence, the proposed debate was forthwith canceled by the emperor.[2] It was then that the dissidents convinced the emperor to request a letter of abdication from the patriarch. Mark's commentary, they argued, coupled with the patriarch's own desire to still the storm of disunity, would suffice as reasons for the request. This message was dispatched to the Hodegetria by two of Gregory's more distinguished students, the historian George Pachymeres and Nicephorus Chumnus.[3]

A. *Conditional Resignation*

The reasons given for the resignation did not include any accusations of incompetence or negligence in the management of the patriarchate.[4] Actually, independent evidence indicates that Gregory had been a "fine administrator," and, in fact, had governed the Church with considerable zeal and care.[5] Gregory himself dared anyone prove that he had been derelict in his duties, or that he had mismanaged the patriarchate.[6] Had he been asked what benefits the Church had reaped since his accession, the patriarch would, no doubt, have turned the question around. Actually, when the monk Methodius proposed this question, the patriarch promptly challenged his qualifications and asked him to show first how he had grown in Christian stature and benefited monasticism so as to become the patriarch's critic and judge. Besides, the patriarch added, to answer the question would imply boasting, and this he was not ready to do.[7]

The patriarch had the good sense not to receive the emperor's request unconditionally. Although some of the bishops had publicly slandered and satirized him for heresy, they were now secretly willing to accept him as Orthodox. As a consequence, he requested the bishops to proclaim his Orthodoxy, both openly and in writing, in the presence of the emperor, the Senate, and "all prominent monastics."[8] Only under this guarantee was he prepared to regard the matter closed and to withdraw from the patriarchate. As he wrote in a missive to an anonymous bishop: "Under no other circumstances will I abandon the leadership of the Church to anyone else. I will oppose such a move by all available means...and will impede anyone who would attempt, against my consent, to ascend the patriarchal throne."[9]

Given the attitude of some of the bishops, Gregory's response was not entirely welcome news. In a real sense, Gregory's inflexibility in turn became the occasion of the schism that followed within the episcopal circle. One group argued that such an avowed recognition of his Orthodoxy would, in effect, remove the cause for which he was being asked to withdraw; it would confirm his right to remain on the throne and he would refuse to resign. This group was led by the conservative metropolitans, John Chilas of Ephesus and Daniel of Cyzicus. The group preferred a strict canonical solution, and wished to condemn the patriarch, whose *Tomus* they had signed.[10] Theoleptus of Philadelphia, however, realized that the preservation of the internal unity and well-being of the entire Church was far more urgent, and did not agree. Moreover, by then he and his circle were convinced that Mark was to blame for the controversy and not Gregory. "They were scandalized not so much by the *Tomus* as by Mark's commentary."[11] In brief, this second group, led by Theoleptus, was prepared to recognize the patriarch, and to accept as Orthodox the notion of an eternal manifestation from the Son as enshrined in the *Tomus*. Ecclesiastical unity would be maintained. No disciplinary action of any kind was needed if the patriarch agreed to resign. To be sure, Theoleptus' involvement in ecclesiastical affairs may seem inconsistent to those who think of hesychasm as an ascetic and esoteric movement. Even so, Theoleptus' role and prominence in the resignation of Gregory shows that the movement was a genuine religious revival—an active and visible force on the local ecclesiastical level. Byzantine hesychasm was never a private sect divorced from the life of the Church.

Theoleptus' recognition of the patriarch does appear to contradict Pachymeres' earlier statement that when Mark's commentary was published, he immediately went to the prime minister, Theodore Mouzalon, to complain of the *Tomus'* errors.[12] It was at best a short-lived attitude, as is shown by his subsequent opposition to John of Ephesus. This is probably also reflected by the patriarch's statement to the emperor that both Theoleptus and the first minister, Theodore Mouzalon, were aware of the difference between his work and Mark's commentary.[13]

A sizable group of bishops was unwilling to condemn the patriarch, and, instead, preferred Theoleptus' solution. It has been suggested that this was a deliberate move on the part of Theoleptus' group to resolve an embarrassing situation—it avoided giving the advantage to the unionists, who otherwise would have made the Orthodox patriarch the butt of their derision. The bishops simply "did not dare condemn him."[14] This explanation, however, is nowhere mentioned by Pachymeres, who states that the bishops were distressed by Mark's commentary, not by Gregory's *Tomus* or unionist opinion. The historian does not hint that their goal was to find a *solution d'embarrassement.* Beccus and unionism are not mentioned by the historian. Besides, most of the unionists were not around—they had been sent into exile *four years* before. It is unlikely the bishops were overly concerned about unionist opinion.

Predictably, Theoleptus was able to rally to his support the emperor and the important ringleader, George Moschabar, the person most responsible for engineering the attack on the patriarch and the settlement of 1285. It is Moschabar who would shortly compose the document certifying Gregory's Orthodoxy! This is clear evidence that he maintained his role in the controversy, even after the bishops had become involved. More to the point, the ex-archivist's decision to join Theoleptus, and not those who wished to condemn the patriarch, is cogent proof that his campaign against Gregory was atheological in nature. Now that he had the satisfaction of seeing the patriarch placed on the defensive, he saw no compelling reason to withhold his approval. The patriarch's pending resignation was satisfaction enough. The bully's pent-up rancor had been assuaged.[15]

Among the patriarch's supporters, we should also mention Theodore Mouzalon. He, like Gregory, was opposed to the conservative cabal, which was typical of a sizable section of Byzantine medieval theology. Earlier, in discussing Blacharnae, we noted the major role he played in its deliberation, and his contribution to the condemnation of Beccus. His active participation in these events, as first minister of the empire, went beyond the call of duty, and was the result of personal conviction.[16] As the patriarch notes in one of his letters, the prime minister was nothing less than "a champion of piety, a support of faith, a pillar and foundation of the Church."[17] But this is also mirrored in the prime minister's role in the restoration of Orthodoxy in 1283, in the deposition of the unionist hierarchy and clergy. These events, in part, were carried out at his instigation.

Mouzalon was willing to serve both the cause and the *ideas* of his former teacher-turned-patriarch. we have already underlined Gregory's own willingness to trust his student with the redrafting of his *Apology.*[18] Indeed, Mouzalon must rank among the more sensitive exponents of Gregory's theology. This is illustrated by a small treatise dealing with Beccus' errors, which has been mistakenly edited (partially) under the patriarch's name.[19] Although the piece is often attributed to Gregory himself, its author is, in fact, Mouzalon.[20] The entire work is an admirable synthesis of Gregory's thought. In effect, it is a brilliant tribute to Gregory, for the former student shows a genuine grasp of Gregory's theological distinctions.

> He who wishes to think piously can say that the Holy Spirit proceeds from the Father, and that it subsists of the Father—according to the perfect expression handed down by the Savior—having the Father as principle and cause of its being. Equally, some saints note that its procession is from the Father through the Son, and they say so piously; not because the existence of the Spirit from the Father is imperfect, or that the Son is entirely its cause—either separately or with the Father. On the contrary, they wish to say that, subsisting perfectly in proceeding from the paternal essence, the Spirit accompanies the Word, and through him flows forth, shines and is revealed according to its pre-eternal and eternal splendor...It is then bestowed, and given to creation, and descends with the authority of a master to those worthy to receive it, and blows where it wills, and makes new, and sanctifies, and perfects, and deifies by graces those who accept it.[21]

The text makes it luminously clear that Mouzalon understood just how Gregory's theology was a solution to the impasse between Latin and Greek theology. In view of the fact that Mouzalon had earlier defended a more conservative attitude, his integration and grasp of Gregory's thoughts is all the more exemplary.[22]

The support Gregory received from such major representatives of the government and the hierarchy could not persuade everyone. The metropolitan of Ephesus and his faction refused to relent. Even the emperor's wrath and his pleas (their position, he said, was a disturbing and pointless exercise) could not convince them to comply. This stubbornness only made the emperor furious, and he promptly had the bishops placed under house arrest until the patriarchal crises could be settled. He was particularly angry at John of

Ephesus, who had gone so far as to write "the worst" of the patriarch to the Asiatic provinces of the empire.[23]

Events now moved quickly. Theoleptus of Philadelphia and the rest of the bishops decided to proceed with their plans; they met in the palace in June 1289 to accept Gregory's voluntary and conditional resignation. Nearly all the clergy and the monks, as well as the emperor, the senate, the patriarch, and all those "who had set in motion the attack against Gregory," were present.[24] The proceedings were opened by the metropolitan of Philadelphia, who unhesitatingly declare the patriarch Orthodox. He then noted that the root cause of the entire scandal had been Mark's commentary, which the patriarch had disowned. As such, no one could hesitate to acknowledge the patriarch's Orthodoxy. Pachymeres adds that he deliberately elaborated this point so as to be understood by everyone.[25]

A brief statement regarding the patriarch's Orthodoxy was then read to the assembled clerics. This written *Declaration,* which Gregory had requested in return for his voluntary withdrawal, was probably read by George Moschabar, the text's original author.[26] The document begins by noting that, even though certain uninitiated had lately suspected the patriarch of heresy, at no time was this the general view. "We [on the contrary] acknowledge him as most Orthodox and most pious; we ask that he withdraw from the patriarchal throne only for men's reconciliation." Even so, the patriarch had agreed to withdraw, subject to a written declaration of his piety; this they willingly would give, provided he gave them, in return, a guarantee of his resignation. Once this was done, they promised, in the name of Christ, to proclaim, both orally and in writing, his piety and Orthodoxy; they, further, agreed to punish severely the foolish and the ignorant who would speak ill of him.[27] This reading was followed by the patriarch's own farewell. He spoke briefly, and then took leave of the emperor and all those present.

It was in this fashion, after weeks of negotiation, that Gregory was finally given the satisfaction of having his Orthodoxy acknowledged publicly. The struggle, though painful, had at least ended as an unambiguous contest for the patriarch. The emperor and the bishops had done as he had asked. It is notable that the assembly did not request from him any personal retraction of the *Tomus* and its doctrine. Indeed, it is remarkable that in all the documents dealing with his resignation, no mention is ever made of the *Tomus.* In plain English, the solemn declaration of Gregory's Orthodoxy in June 1289 cannot be construed as a formal deposition.[28] It is, finally, striking that the assembly permitted Gregory to retain his priesthood. Both of these concessions are made perfectly clear by Gregory's own *Statement of Withdrawal.* This document, which was requested of him by the synod as a guarantee of his resignation, is quoted in its entirety by Pachymeres.[29]

Gregory begins his statement by noting first that God alone was responsible for his accession to the patriarchate, and that neither personal eagerness nor his friends' intrigue had anything to do with his elevation. His six years and more of office, however, were spent uniting and reconciling the Church's different factions. Even so, his lack of success caused a number of his enemies to raise their voices in protest and to declare that peace would never be realized until he withdrew. Thus, it was for the unity of the Church that he agreed to resign his position, his leadership, and his dignity. He refused to give up his priesthood, however, for this he hoped to keep until the end; after all, he had done nothing wrong to be deprived of his priestly rank. "It is solely for the sake of unity, and for their reconciliation with the Church, that I submit this, my act of resignation."[30] The Church could now proceed to the election and designation of a new patriarch who would bring about the reconciliation of all.

> It was not the result of personal effort, or through my friends' assistance, that I was promoted to the patriarchal throne and to this supreme episcopal dignity; I was raised there, as God alone knows. Since then, and for six years and more, I have performed the functions of my office. Everything I did and said had as its purpose the re-establishment of peace, and the union with the Church of those who had been scandalized and separated. But these efforts worked contrary to my intention, so that some individuals charged that this greatly desired peace would never become a reality, unless I removed myself from the scene, and relinquished the patriarchate. Seeing this situation in the Church and being unable to function under such conditions, I chose to see the offended united with the Church, and with one another, rather than remain in office.
>
> I, therefore, resign the patriarchal throne, office, and dignity, for their peace in God and for the cessation of these harmful divisions; I do so, however, without surrendering my priesthood, which, with God's help, I hope to retain to the end. For it is solely for the cause of unity, and for their reconciliation with the Church, that I submit this, my act of resignation, and not because I feel I have done something for which I must relinquish my priesthood. It is, therefore, now possible, with God's approval, to elect a patriarch to the patriarchal throne, and to elevate to this priesthood another who, as canonical and lawful patriarch and bishop, will be able—with God's support and help—to unite and reconcile

the divided elements of the Church. May this be so, through the mercy of our great God and Savior, Jesus Christ, the prayers of our immaculate Lady, Virgin and Mother of God, and the supplications of all the saints.[31]

Gregory would not admit any personal responsibility for the controversy that brought about his resignation. The reason for his withdrawal is simply put—the desire to bring an end to the divisions caused by various factions. These "scandalized and separated" groups presumably include unionists and Arsenites. A fact of utmost importance, too, is Gregory's insistence that his resignation was from the patriarchate and not from the episcopate. The latter was from God; hence, his refusal to give it up. Significantly his successor Athanasius was to make an identical distinction between *ordo* and *jurisdictio* at his resignation in 1293.[32] This was actually in violation of canon law, which states that once a bishop turns to the monastic state he can no longer maintain either the dignity or the function of the episcopate.[33] Even so, the synod did not protest, and Pachymeres makes no mention of the fact.

One further point connected with Gregory's resignation is the absence of a signature. In Pachymeres judgment, this was a device by which the patriarch was preparing in advance to secure the patriarchal office. When all was said and done, he could argue that the reason for his resignation had not materialized. The bishops were still divided, the unionists and the Arsenites had not made their peace, and unity was not yet a reality. This being so, the office was still his. Besides, the patriarch could further argue that "he was, concerning his priesthood, blameless."[34] The absence of Gregory's signature from the *Statement* could ultimately work to his advantage.

Such strategy, however, is by and large expressly denied by Gregory, who concludes his *Statement of Withdrawal* by recommending the immediate election and designation of a new patriarch to fill the vacancy created by his departure.[35] This was his attitude even before his resignation, when he noted that he was ready to ascend, if need be, the pulpit of the Hagia Sophia to declare his resignation, provided his Orthodoxy was first recognized.[36] In addition, there is the fact that the procedure Gregory followed was itself not unusual—in the tenth century Nicholas Mysticus had already set the precedent by omitting his signature from his resignation. What is more, both the emperor and the metropolitan of Philadelphia were not unduly distressed over Gregory's failure to provide a signature.[37] On the contrary, they were grateful for the *Statement* and even managed to convince those who had insisted on a signature to be "satisfied with the letter alone [the *Statement*], since it was an autograph."[38] Still more decisive is the fact that Gregory certainly never attempted to regain his office.

B. *The Aftermath*

As noted above, not all the bishops were reconciled with Gregory. Whereas Theoleptus and his group had made their peace, both John of Ephesus and Daniel of Cyzicus had refused to do so. As a consequence, they found themselves isolated and in disgrace, both with the emperor and with their colleagues and concelebrants, for having treated their patriarch with such hostility.[39] Eventually, they were accused of numerous irregularities by their own diocesan clergy and were deposed. A matter that touched them no less deeply was the loss of their episcopal revenues.[40] That it disturbed John of Ephesus is more than likely, for how else can we interpret his attempt to regain the emperor's and the bishops' favor after his disgrace? Curiously enough, he chose to gain their attention by a discourse on the Arsenite question. To be sure, his canonical position on the issue could not but please his former antagonists. More significantly, this work *On the Arsenite Schism* comes down firmly on the side of Gregory and the *Tomus*.[41] Indeed, the synodal statement of Blachernae, the metropolitan of Ephesus argues, is the very confirmation of piety and Orthodoxy; the wise Gregory must be praised rather than condemned; his alleged theological error was not the result of evil, wickedness, or difference of opinion. On the contrary, he had no other intention than to expose, refute, and vanquish Beccus' falsehood, and to establish permanently the ever-triumphant truth.[42]

Granted this may be questioned for its sincerity and impartial judgment. Obviously, the author was trying to verbalize his change of heart both to the emperor and to those bishops who were all too familiar with his earlier inflexibility toward Gregory and the *Tomus*.[43] He knew how to gain their attention and approval. All the same, this personal apology is both impressive and telling. Simply put, he had abandoned his intransigent position, for which he had failed to win any serious support, and had embraced that of his episcopal colleagues; Gregory was no longer the patriarch who should have been deposed. John's earlier claim—made in his memorandum to the emperor—that Gregory had committed a serious doctrinal error was now being rescinded.

To summarize, within less than a decade, virtually every one of Gregory's most unyielding opponents found himself reconciled to the former patriarch.

By extension, the *Tomus* retained its authority and doctrinal integrity—that is, it continued to be the definitive exposition of the Orthodox case regarding the *Filioque*. All subsequent attempts to discredit or modify the text ultimately foundered and failed. That such attempts were indeed made is well known. This is certainly the case with the commission that was set up shortly after June 1289 to examine the text, to see if it could be changed or modified in any way for the better. The first such meeting, over which the emperor presided was held in the palace, but was quickly dissolved as a result of an earthquake. Subsequent discussions in Blachernae produced no result.[44] Finally, it was agreed to excise altogether from the text, the explanation of the Damascene *testimonium*: "It clearly denotes the manifestation—through the intermediary of the Son—of the Spirit, whose existence is of the Father."[45] This they found preferable to running the risk of still further division in the Church.[46]

This fear of further division should be connected with the Arsenites and their rigidly conservative posture on the development or elaboration of traditional theological formulas. After all, part of their ultimatum to the emperor made shortly after Gregory's resignation was that "the doctrine of the procession 'from the Father through the Son' be suppressed."[47] In sum, the commission set up to examine the *Tomus* after Gregory's resignation may have had in mind the Arsenites' capacity to stir up further controversy; that it decided not to risk another explanation (and possibly further division) may have been due to their pressure or their machinations. Pachymeres' statement that the commission did not want to run the risk of further controversy points to the conservative interests in the Church, and especially to the Arsenites.

It is perhaps within this frame of reference that an appended paragraph, found at the end of a number of manuscripts of the *Tomus*, should be viewed. This paragraph contains a categorical affirmation of procession *a Patre solo*. "Whereas the Son is the living and enhypostatic wisdom of God the Father, the Holy Spirit which proceeds ineffably and eternally from God the Father alone as Scripture affirms, is likewise the light and self-subsistent life of the inaccessible and eternal light. Whosoever is of a different mind...we justly cast out of God's Church."[48] This, to be sure, is not part of Gregory's original text. Its provenance is unknown and we can only assume that it was intended for those readers who would be predisposed to accept the traditional formulation, but would hesitate over the text's notion of an eternal manifestation.[49] The paragraph, however, is not a criticism of the original text. It is chiefly a warning to the reader that the doctrine found in the text is itself not a rejection of the more familiar formulation enunciated by the supplemental paragraph.

But what of the decision to suppress the passage in the *Tomus?* In a genuine sense, it does not seem to have been taken very seriously, and was probably never carried out. Otherwise, we cannot account for the fact that the text of the *Tomus* has been preserved only in its original form—without the suppression. An examination of the numerous extant unpublished manuscripts of the *Tomus* yields no variation in the body of the text.[50] The subscription alone differs, but that is to be expected.[51] Equally, it must be underscored that, even if the commission's decision to suppress the explanation of the Damascene *testimonium* had been carried out, it still would not have affected the *Tomus'* doctrinal integrity. We have had occasion to see that the text did not focus solely on the Damascene passage. Only one of its eleven anathemas actually dealt directly with this proof-text. This being so, the unsuppressed part of the text—an attempt to express the relation between the Son and the Spirit as an "eternal manifestation" of the Spirit by the Son—was not altered. The integrity of Gregory's doctrine would have been maintained even if the agreed suppression had been carried out. The excision constituted no more than a *single sentence* of a text that occupies *twelve columns* in the Migne edition!

More fundamental, perhaps, is the fact that the passage of the *Tomus* which Mark had used in his commentary (and which had caused such controversy) was left untouched. In short, the patriarch's remark which, like the excised sentence, was an explanation of the doctrine of the eternal manifestation, was not the subject of any decision. Obviously, the commission set up to examine the *Tomus* no longer saw anything unusual or ambiguous in the passage. The patriarch's attempt to show that what Mark had written had in no way resembled his own original statement had convinced everyone. We cannot otherwise explain Pachymeres' silence on the matter. What he does mention concerns the Damascene passage only, not that which had stirred up as much, if not more, controversy.

But if Gregory II and the *Tomus* of 1285 were, in fact, solemnly recognized as Orthodox by the episcopate and the emperor, how is it that Gregory's name was ultimately omitted from the list of Orthodox patriarchs contained in the liturgical text of the *Synodicon?*[52] As is well known, this text, which commemorates the suppression of iconoclasm in 843, was read annually in all the churches of the empire on the first Sunday of Lent. Beside listing the defenders of Orthodoxy in the iconoclastic controversy, however, the text also honors the memory of subsequent Orthodox patriarchs. Even so, Gregory's name is nowhere to be found in the catalogue honoring these patriarchs. Is it possible that this exclusion indicates a deliberate repudiation by the Church of both Gregory and his formulation of the "eternal manifestation"?

The listing itself suggests an answer to this question, since it mirrors the way in which the Church often solved its internal problems between the ninth and the thirteenth centuries.[53] By listing, for example, the names of all those patriarchs—Ignatius, Photius, Nicholas, Euthymius—involved in the fierce internal schisms and excommunications of the ninth and tenth centuries, the Church indicated how these conflicts were eventually resolved. That is, all these patriarchs were finally included in the liturgical peace of the Church. The inclusion of their names implied that both the divisions and the excommunications had been resolved. It was as if they had never taken place. Significantly, John of Ephesus was to use this same argument in his defense of the Church against the Arsenites. (The latter, it will be recalled, were unwilling to accept the fact that both Ignatius' and Photius' names were among those listed in the *Synodicon*, and instead preferred to see Photius' and Joseph's case as parallel.)[54]

By analogy, the omission of the names of the late-thirteenth-century patriarchs Nicephorus II, Germanus III, John XI Beccus, John XII Cosmas, and Gregory II of Cyprus reflects the way in which the Church had healed the internal schism caused by the unionist policy of Michael VIII and the Arsenite schism. The omission of Beccus' name, for example, represents the Church's emphatic rejection of the Union of Lyons, while the deletion of the names of the other patriarchs, including Gregory's, reflects the terms by which the Arsenites were reconciled to the Church in 1310. Specifically, these terms included the rehabilitation of Patriarch Arsenius, and the partial condemnation of several of his successors against whom the Arsenites had built up a legacy of hostility. This, as we have seen, was embodied in their view that the consecrations of Arsenius' successors were "uncanonical."[55] Equally important in the settlement of 1310 was the Arsenites' insistence that the Church reaffirm its belief in the traditional faith of the Fathers. The records of the reconciliation, it is true, contain no direct allusion to the passionate theological controversy that had loomed so large in the life of the Church in the seventies and eighties of the thirteenth century.[56] Even so, it is difficult to see what else the Arsenites had in mind with their request. Ultimately, then, the omission of Patriarch

Gregory's name from the *Synodicon* must be seen as part of the Church's conciliatory gesture to the traditionalism of the Arsenites in September 1310. They share responsibility for the omission.

Actually this appears to be corroborated by the fact that the moratorium on Gregory's liturgical acclamation was enforced shortly after his resignation. John of Ephesus, for example, mentions it in his 1296 text *On the Arsenite Schism.*[57] In response to the Arsenites, whom he is addressing, he notes that Gregory was not condemned formally, nor was he declared a heretic; his name was stricken from the "annual acclamation in churches" for reasons of concession or accommodation. That is to say, the bishops worked by reverse procedure. Instead of officially recognizing Gregory's Orthodoxy by means of the *Synodicon*, they satisfied their conscience by their unofficial or private recognition.[58] This course was dictated by their desire to avoid any resistance, either from Gregory's adversaries or from the traditionalist bloc in the Church, which an official recognition would have generated. As John notes, they acted "for the common good." In this connection, the parallel precaution taken on Gregory's death—he was given an Orthodox burial—should be mentioned. The emperor forbade a public funeral, and even asked Raoulaina, Gregory's patron, not to attend, for fear it might cause a disturbance.[59]

And yet, Gregory's memory remained intact despite the deletion of his name from the *Synodicon*. In the fourteenth and fifteenth centuries, there are explicit references to his Orthodoxy, to his struggle for the unity of the Church, and to the catholicity of his teaching. In contrast to the private episcopal recognition by his colleagues in the thirteenth century, numerous writers went out of their way to acknowledge openly his zeal and theology. It is interesting and, perhaps, significant that the Palamite Joseph Calothetus should explicitly call him "God's chosen prelate," knowing well enough that his name was nowhere to be found in the catalogue of the *Synodicon*. In noting how Gregory had labored to heal the internal divisions in the Church, he adds that it was "slander" and "envy" that forced the patriarch to resign his throne. This is the reason why Gregory finally relinquished his office.[60] Nowhere is this author willing to admit that theological issues were the cause of the patriarch's withdrawal. He has, on the contrary, the highest respect for the Council of Blachernae and its achievement.

Another writer, Patriarch Philotheus (one of Palamas' most loyal exponents), defends Gregory for his doctrine of the "divinity, divine energy, holy illumination, and participation." What he says is no less than a *restauratio memoriae*.

> I will refer you to a second authority who...is a patriarch and a teacher; wise in sacred matters—wiser than you and those like you—and, by far, wiser even in secular matters, though he wrote briefly about such things, for he showed himself a lover, and initiate and teacher of the true and highest wisdom. I mean Gregory of Cyprus, who is greatly renowned in the whole Church of the faithful for his beliefs, writings, splendid life, and excellent conduct—and, of course, for his considerable and admirable struggle on behalf of Orthodoxy against those who believed in the Latin doctrine. Let the wise Gregory then, come forward now and teach, in his own words, those matters of divinity, divine energy, holy illumination, and participation, and demonstrate his agreement (as well as ours) with the Fathers and theologians of the past. Rather, I will place before him the writings of those who, at that time, opposed him and the Church, and thus set the writings and theology of Gregory against these.[61]

Patriarch Philotheus, in the fourteenth century, was willing to subscribe to the idea that Gregory's theological posture was in full "agreement" with patristic teaching. Gregory's teaching was not novel, unusual, or heretical. Indeed, his writings could hardly have been "renowned in the whole Church" if this were the case. But this passage of Philotheus' is, likewise, important for the link it provides between Gregory's and Palamas' own ideas. Gregory's notion of the eternal manifestation of God is, for Philotheus, the primitive parallel to Palamas' own distinction between the eternal action or 'energy' of God and the divine nature itself. In simple terms, Philotheus acknowledges the "wise" Gregory as a source of the Palamite synthesis. Gregory's theology—namely, the doctrine of the "divine energy, holy illumination, and participation"—is, in the final analysis, common to both Patriarch Gregory and the Palamites.

The similarity between Palamas' arguments, in his *Apodictic Treatises*, and Gregory of Cyprus' formulations is well known and need not be repeated.[62] Here, another example from Palamas' little-known *Confession*, read to the assembled bishops at the Council of 1351, will suffice to show the bond and identity of thought that unites the two theologians in question.[63] The section dealing with the Holy Spirit is so succinct and precise in expression (Palamas himself noted that the entire text possessed a precision rarely found in his other works) that it deserves to be quoted in full.

On the one hand, the Holy Spirit is, together with the Father and the Son, without beginning, since it is eternal; yet, on the other, it is not without beginning, since it, too—by way of procession, not by way of generation—has the Father as foundation, source, and cause. It also [like the Son] came forth from the Father before all ages, without change, impassibly, not by generation, but by procession; it is inseparable from the Father and the Son, since it proceeds from the Father, and reposes in the Son; it possesses union without losing its identity, and division without involving separation. It, too, is God from God; it is not different since it is God, yet it is different since it is the Comforter; as Spirit, it possesses hypostatic existence, proceeds from the Father, and is sent—that is, manifested—through the Son; it, too, is the cause of all created things, since it is in the Spirit that they are perfected. It is identical and equal with the Father and the Son, with the exception of unbegottenness and generation. It was sent—that is, made known—from the Son to His own disciples. By what other means—the Spirit which is inseparable from the Son—could it have been sent? By what other means could it—which is everywhere—come to me? Wherefore, it is sent not only from the Son, but from the Father and through the Son, and is manifested through himself.[64]

It is within this context—of a direct link between Gregory II and Palamas—that we can best view the attacks leveled against Gregory by Gregoras and Akindynus. As is well known, these theologians carried on a running offensive against the Palamites in the fourteenth century. This famous controversy was occasioned by the refusal of Gregoras and Akindynus to acknowledge Palamas' notion of "energy" and its uncreated or eternal character. Needless to say, in attacking this notion they had to criticize Patriarch Gregory's identical, though differently phrased, concept of a timeless or eternal manifestation. Recent scholarship has shown this to be the case.[65] In point of fact, Akindynus was compelled to declare that Patriarch Gregory had spoken against Orthodoxy by his insistence that what Christ had given to the Apostles, when breathing on them, was an eternal manifestation. If he had said that the most divine Spirit itself was given to the Apostles...or that a grace different from the divine Spirit, neither eternal nor uncreated was in question...he would not have spoken in favor of the Latins, nor contradicted our dogmas."[66] The argument was not new, to be sure. We have seen how it was used against Gregory by his contemporary opponents. But Akindynus also consistently misinterpreted Patriarch Gregory's final year as patriarch in order to buttress his case against Palamas. Gregory's withdrawal from the patriarchate is transformed into a formal deposition. Indeed, the synod in 1289, according to Akindynus, had been much too "lenient" with the patriarch. Not surprisingly, Akindynus even advised Palamas to imitate Patriarch Gregory's example by renouncing his unorthodox beliefs.[67]

But there were others, too, besides the Palamites of the fourteenth century, who harbored a warm affection for Patriarch Gregory II. Gennadius Scholarius, one of the last great representatives of Byzantine learning, would never have treated Gregory *de haut en bas*, as Akindynus had done; it was he who expressed the view that had the *Tomus* been given a hearing at the Council of Florence, it would have convinced even those with "heart of stone"[68] to abandon the union. His rapt admiration of the Council of Blachernae, to which he gave *post factum* ecumenical status, though it was local or regional in externals, is not without interest. He argued that, although the council lacked ecumenicity (in the sense that the West was not represented), it was ecumenical for the truth it enunciated, which is, after all is said and done, what makes a council ecumenical.

> I receive with all my heart the holy and great council that condemned the Latinizer Beccus, and firmly believe it to be ecumenical, since the absence of the West does not remove its ecumenicity.... Note how the Council of Florence [1439] differs from that which met in Constantinople against Beccus [1285]. The latter agrees completely with the faith of the ecumenical councils, both with the eighth [the union Council of Constantinople, 879] and the rest, while Florence disagrees with them all, with both that one and the rest. In Constantinople, the patriarch of Alexandria was present, and the other patriarchs agreed with and approved of the result as a sound and lawful decision.[69]

Characteristically, Gennadius' own personal library contained a copy of the *Tomus*, the copy now in the monastery of Dionysiou on Mount Athos.[70]

Along with Gennadius, mention should also be made of another fifteenth-century ecclesiastic, the metropolitan Anthony of Heracleia. He, too, was convinced that the Council of 1285 possessed universal authority, by virtue of its "agreement" with the received faith. Further, he was prompted to introduce Gregory's *Tomus* into the private behind-the-scenes discussions at Florence. However, the effective lobbying of the unionists, Beccus' fifteenth-century heirs, and particularly the emperor's chaplain, Gregory, were successful in aborting the metropolitan's plan.[71] In the event, the assembly never found out about the *Tomus*. Only later, the narrator of this episode notes, was it learned that the text "was the synodal *Tomus* composed against Beccus and the Union of Lyons," of which—apart from three or four—few knew anything. "Hence, why the malefactor in question [the emperor's chaplain], our adversary, employed all his zeal in preventing us from knowing the work."[72]

The fact that most of the bishops at Florence had not heard of the "synodal *Tomus* against Lyons" should not be exaggerated. It is explained, in part, by the general Byzantine attitude toward Lyons in both the fourteenth and the fifteenth century—it is seldom, if ever, mentioned in the sources. As far as the Byzantines were concerned—one scholar recently advised—the Union of Lyons was nonexistent.[73] Its fraudulent nature was taken for granted. Mention of the union, and of its formal rejection in 1285, would have seemed redundant. And yet, it should also be emphasized that several of the bishops at Florence were aware of the *Tomus* of 1285, even if most of the others were not. Moreover, the thirty-odd extant copies of the text (there is no reason to think that other copies will not be found) are indicative of both substantial interest and readership. Gennadius, when he returned home from Florence, was surprised to find so many copies of the text available.[74]

Such, then, is the evidence for the survival of Gregory's name and theology in the aftermath of his resignation. But what of his own subsequent activity following his withdrawal from office in June 1289?[75] He first resolved to ask forgiveness of all those clergy whom he had displeased during his patriarchate. He even sent word of his desire to be reconciled with Gerasimus of Heracleia (his former spiritual father) and Neophytus of Brusa, both of whom he had previously excommunicated. They responded positively.[76] Gregory then retired to the small monastery of Aristine, in the environs of St Andrew in Crisei, where his friend and patron, the princess Raoulaina, was to shelter him. And, although his stay was brief, it became a major dividend for posterity. It was probably at this monastery that he brought much of his correspondence together, and wrote its long introduction, known today as his *Autobiography*. In addition, he continued to defend his theology by writing *On the Procession of the Holy Spirit*, a remarkably cogent synthesis of his position. The patriarch had never been a very healthy individual as his *Autobiography* and many of his letters clearly indicate.[77] Gregory, the one hundred sixteenth patriarch of Constantinople, died in peace in 1290, a year after his resignation.

NOTES

1. Pachymeres, II, 124.

2. Ibid., 125

3. Ibid 126, J. Verpeaux, *Nicéphore Choumnos, homme d'état et humaniste byzantin* (c. 1250/5-1327) (Paris, 1959), pp. 37-38

4. Cf. Pachymeres, II, 132.

5. Joseph Calothetus, *Vita Athanasii*, ed. A. Pantocratorinus, *Thrakika*, 13 (1940), 87.

6. Ekklesiastikos Pharos, 4 (1909), 103 (letter 152).

7. Ibid., 5 (1910), 217 (letter 171).

8. Pachymeres, II, 127.

9. *PG* 142.128B-C.

10. Pachymeres, II, 128.

11. Ibid. 128-29.

12. Ibid. 119; Troitskij, *Arsenij*, p. 299.

13. πιττάκιον, *PG* 142.269A.

14. V. Laurent, "Les grandes crises relgieuses à Byzance: La fin du schisme arsénite," *Académie Roumaine. Bulletin de la Section Historique,* 26 (1945), 263. Cf. also V. Grumel, "Le IIè concile de Lyon et la réunion de l'église grecque," *DTC,* 9, pt. 1 (Paris, 1926), col. 1408.

15. See V. Laurent, "Un polémiste grec de la fin du XIIIè siècle: La vie et les œuvres de Georges Moschabar," *EO,* 28 (1929), 141.

16. R. Guilland, "Les Logothètes: Etudes sur l'histoire administrative de l'empire byzantin," *REB,* 29 (1971), 106.

17. Ekklesiastikos Pharos, 5 (1910), 224-25 (letter 173).

18. see above, p. 149 n. 55.

19. Codex Chigiana gr. 12, fols. 38v-46r; partially edited in *PG* 142.290B-300B. On the Mouzalon authorship, see M. Jugie, *Theologia dogmatica Christianorum orientalium ab Ecclesia Catholica dissidentium,* II (Paris, 1933), 365n3; and V. Laurent, "Bulletin critique: Catalogues de manuscrits grecs et textes byzantins," *EO,* 27 (1928), 448; idem, "Théodore Mouzalon," *DTC,* 10, pt. 2 (Paris, 1929), col. 2583; H.-G. Beck, *Kirche und theologische Literatur im byzantinischen Reich* (Munich, 1959), p. 680. See also the note in *PG* 142.44C.

20. O. Clément, "Grégoire de Chypre 'De l'ekporèse du Saint Esprit'," *Istina,* 3-4 (1972), 443-56, discusses the text in detail (450-55), but assumes the author to be Gregory.

21. *PG* 142.290C-D; see also 292C-D and 293A-B. Cf. Gregory's praise of this work's "wisdom," in *Ekklesiastikos Pharos,* 4 (1909), 101-102 (letter 145).

22. For his earlier view, see especially Jugie, *Theologia dogmatica,* II, 357-58; idem, *De processione Spiritus Sancti: Ex fontibus revelationis et secundum Orientales dissidentes* (Rome, 1936)

337-38; repeated by M. Candal, "Nueva interpretación del 'per Filium' de los Padres Grie-gos," *OCP,* 31 (1965), 9; and idem, *Oratio dogmatica de unione Bessarionis* (= Concilium Flor-entinum, Documenta et Scriptores, series B. vol. VII, fasc. 1; Rome, 1958), XLVII.

23. Pachymeres, II, 129

24. Ibid., 130; Gregoras, I, 177-78.

25. Pachymeres, II, 130.

26. At least one manuscript (Leiden) preserves the name of the ex-χαρτοφύλαξ as the author of this ἀνακήρυξις. Cf. Laurent, "Un polémiste grec," 157; and Troitskij, *Arsenij,* p. 314*n*1. The document has been published by Migne, *PG* 142.129A-B (with a Latin translation), and by Eustratiades, who included it in his edition of Gregory's letters; see *Ekklesiastikos Pharos,* 5 (1910), 500. See also the earlier edition (from a Vienna manuscript) by A. K. Demetracopou-los, *History of the Schism* (in Greek) (Leipzig, 1867), p.90.

27. Ekklesiastikos Pharos, 5 (1910), 500 (= *PG* 142.129A-B).

28. See John Chilas, *On the Arsenite Schism,* in J. Darrouzès, *Documents inédits d'ecclésiologie byz-antine* (Paris, 1966), p. 401; Cf. J. Meyendorff, *Introduction à l'étude de Grégoire Palamas* (Paris, 1959), p.30.

29. Pachymeres, II, 130-31 (= *PG* 142.129-131A). A Russian translation is provided by Troitskij, *Arsenij,* pp.316-18; an older French version (it is actually more a paraphrase than a transla-tion) will be found in L. Cousin, *Histoire de Constantinople depuis le règne de l'ancien Justin jusqu'à la fin de l'Empire* (Paris, 1673), pp. 565-66; Laurent, *Regestes,* no. 1517.

30. Pachymers, II, 131. For an independent statement of Gregory's conscious championship of ecclesiastical unity, and the role his enemies played in his lack of success, see Joseph Calothe-tus, *Vita Athanasii,* ed. Pantocratorinus, p. 87.

31. Pachymeres, II, 130-31.

32. Ibid., 175-76

33. See Canon 2 of the Council of 879, in G. A. Rhalles and M. Potles, *Constitution of the Divine and Holy Canons* (in Greek), II (Athens, 1852), 707-708; cf. F. Dvornik, *The Photian Schism: History and Legend* (Cambridge, Mass., 1948), p. 193.

34. Pachymeres, II 132.

35. Ibid., 131.

36. *PG* 142.125D.

37. Cf. Troitskij, *Arsenij,* p. 318.

35. Pachymeres, II, 132.

39. Gregoras, I, 180.

40. Ibid., 179; cf. the slightly different picture of their unhappy lot in Constantinople, in Pachymeres, II, 251. Gregory's former friend, the monk Methodius, was appointed bishop of Cyzicus; see Laurent, *Regestes,* no. 1452, p. 242.

41. The text has been edited by Darrouzès, *Documents inédits d'ecclésiologie,* pp. 348-413; he be-lieves that it was composed either in 1296 or—less probably—in 1306 (pp. 93-94).

42. *On the Arsenite Schism,* in Darrouzès, *Documents inédits d'ecclésiologie,* p. 400; cf. also Demetracopoulos, *History of the Schism,* pp. 90-93, for a short quotation from the discourse.

43. Cf. Darrouzès, *Documents inédits d'ecclésiologie,* p. 93.

44. Pachymeres, II, 134.

45. Tomus, *PG* 142-240A

46. Pachymeres, II, 134

47. Ibid., 138.

48. Codex Monacensis gr. 256. fols. 278^v-279^r. This is one of the earliest and best-preserved copies containing the supplemental paragraph.

49. Cf. Laurent, *Regestes,* no. 1490, esp. p. 284.

50. In *Hellenikos Philologikos Syllogos,* 17 (1886), Appendix 42, A. Papadopoulos-Kerameus reported that the Kosinitza 80 manuscript differed from the text published by Banduri. However, Laurent, *Regestes,* no. 1490, excludes the possibility of any difference, and notes that Papadopoulos-Kerameus was probably thinking of the supplemental paragraph and not of the main body of the text, which he may not have examined. My own numerous attempts to procure microfilm of the text from Sophia were frustrating and entirely fruitless.

51. Six examples are given in Laurent, *Regestes,* no. 1490, p. 282.

52. Gouillard, "Le Synodikon de l'Orthodoxie: Edition et commentaire," *Travaux et mémoires,* 2 (1967), 3-316. See also idem, in *BZ,* 60 (1967), 351-53 (a review of Darrouzès' *Documents inédits d'ecclésiologie*), where it is emphasized that a thorough inquiry into the tradition of the *Synodicon* indicates that Gregory's name was never admitted into it. This is also confirmed by a fourteenth-century *Synodicon* of Adrianople; see "The Church of Adrianople in Thrace," *Ekklesiastike Aletheia,* 24 (1904), 372 (Joseph's name is followed immediately by that of Athanasius, without any mention of Gregory).

53. For some of the argument that follows, see especially J. Meyendorff, *Byzantine Theology* (New York, 1979), pp. 87-88.

54. John Chilas, *On the Arsenite Schism,* Darrouzès, *Documents inédits d'ecclésiologie,* p. 382.

55. They were explicit about the removal of Joseph's name, yet, by the sixties of the fourteenth century, his name was again reintroduced into the *Synodicon.* See Gouillard, in *BZ,* 60 (1967), 353. Could this have been as a result of Joseph's canonization under Gregory? The documents for the settlement of 1310 have been edited by Laurent, "Les grandes crises religieuses," 289-313, esp. 290, 298n7, and 301.

56. Even their own early memorandum to the emperor, of 1289, is couched in very general terms, see ibid., 262.

57. For the date of composition, see above, n. 41.

58. *On the Arsenite Schism,* in Darrouzès, *Documents inédits d'ecclésiologie,* p. 401.

59. Pachymeres, II, 152.

60. *Vita Athanasii,* ed. Pantocratorinus, pp. 87-88. For this author, see N. A. Bees, "Joseph Calothetus and a List of his Works" (in Greek), *BZ,* 17 (1908), 86-91.

61. *Against Gregoras, PG* 151.915C-D.

62. Meyendorff, *Introduction à l'étude de Palamas,* p. 26; see also A. Rodovic, *The Mystery of the Holy Trinity According to Gregory Palamas* (in Greek), Analecta Vlatadon, 16 (Thessalonica, 1973) 174-76.

63. see the English translation by A. Papadakis, "Gregory Palamas at the Council of Blachernae, 1351," *Greek, Roman, and Byzantine Studies,* 10, No. 4 (1969), 333-42; Greek text: *PG* 151.763-68.

64. Papadakis, "Gregory Palamas at Blachernae," 338-39

65. Meyendorff, *Introduction à l'étude de Palamas,* p. 29.

66. Ibid.

67. Gregory Akindynos, *Against Palamas,* VII, codex Monacensis gr. 223, fols. 355r-356v.

68. L. Petit et al. (edd.), *Œuvres complètes de Gennade Scholarios,* III (Paris, 1930), 85.

69. Ibid., 173, 89. See also ibid., II (Paris, 1929), 424-26; this is Gennadius' second treatise on the procession of the Holy Spirit, and contains a quotation from the *Tomus.* On councils in the Byzantine Church and Gennadius' views, see M. Jugie, "Le nombre des conciles œcuméniques reconnus par l'Eglise gréco-russe et ses théologiens," *EO,* 18 (1916-1919), 305-20. It has been suggested that John Eugenicus may also be referring to the Council of 1285, when he speaks of the blessing of the "holy patriarchs of the East as from a common synod and canonical decision" in his brief *Doxology for the Restoration of the Church.* More likely, it is a reference to the Council of Jerusalem in 1443, which condemned Florence; see J. Gill, *The Council of Florence* (Cambridge, Mass., 1959), 354n1.

70. Codex Dionysiou, 150, fols. 46^r-53^v.

71. V. Laurent (ed.), *Les "Mémoires" du Grand Ecclésiarque de l'Eglise de Constantinople Sylvestre Syropoulos* (Concilium Florentinum Documenta et Scriptores, series B. vol. IX; Rome, 1971), 342.

72. Ibid., 444. See also Gill, *The Council of Florence,* p. 257.

73. Dossier de Lyon, p. viii.

74. *Œuvres complètes de Gennade,* III, 154.

75. No known text makes any reference to the exact date of the end of his patriarchate.

76. Pachymeres, II, 133.

77. Ekklesiastikos Pharos, 3 (1909), 9-11 (letter 72), 11-12 (letter 73), 24-25 (letter 88); *Autobiography,* in W. Lameere, *La tradition manuscrite de la correspondance de Grégoire de Chypre* (Brussels-Paris, 1937), p. 189, where he complains of bodily ailments and migraine headaches.

9

REFLECTIONS

With the death of Patriarch Gregory II of Cyprus, there passed from the ecclesiastical and intellectual scene one of the more imaginative minds of the late thirteenth century. As it turns out, a "symbolic character" has been attached to his departure. In Byzantine intellectual history it is thought to mark the end of the first phase of the Palaeologan renaissance, and the beginning of the new "rising generation" of scholars represented by Nicephorus Chumnus and Theodore Metochites.[1] It is likewise relevant, however, for the theological sphere, where a new generation of ecclesiastics, such as Theoleptus of Philadelphia, Athanasius of Constantinople, and, later, Gregory Palamas, would take the lead. It is probably an oversimplification, nevertheless, to suggest that Gregory's death marks the abdication of humanism and the triumph of asceticism.[2]

The foregoing examination of Gregory's patriarchate, as noted earlier, has no pretensions to being an exhaustive survey of the subject. In any event, a number of basic conclusions and details were established in the course of the narrative, and these need to be reviewed. One of the general points inherent in this study has been that, for the Byantines, the problem of the *Filioque* was an intentional taking of sides in a matter of faith.[3] We may regret, it is true, the verbosity (not always matched by quality) with which the discussion was often sustained. And yet, the reason for this volume and variety lies in the fact that the problem was ultimately concerned with two different approaches to the Godhead. Above all, the heart of the problem lay in the Cappadocian and Augustinian approaches to the Trinity, for if the Byzantines followed the Cappadocian school, the basis of the Latin tradition was Augustine's writings.

It is not difficult to see why the Byzantines rarely saw the *Filioque* as a mere θεολογούμενον, as some private theological opinion, or as some "liturgical variation." To suggest that the problem was exegetical, liturgical, or even constitutional in nature is to miss the point. The *Filioque* was not just an illegal addition, it was theologically inadmissible. Historically, the most competent theologians—from Photius to Scholarius—placed it at the center of the Byzantine understanding of the Trinity. Seldom did they see the issue as anything other than theological—in the true patristic sense of θεολογία. The length and nature of the debate in Gregory's patriarchate is proof of that, as is, of course, the care and clarity with which the patriarch approached this sensitive issue. Ultimately, for Gregory, the doctrine was the cause for which the schism had occurred.[4]

The discussion in the eighties of the thirteenth century revolved around two poles represented by Gregory and Beccus respectively. Beccus' genuine concern, it is true, was to bridge the division in the Churches. Potentially, this was a step forward. Hence, the affection with which Beccus is usually treated by historians; however, this does not always reflect the reality of the situation. Realistically and theologically, the way in which he attempted to affect unity was misguided. His theological solution, simply put, was not a solution to the above-mentioned fundamental issue of the two distinct approaches to God, but an accommodation of the two; "through the Son" was merely the Greek patristic systematization of the Latin *Filioque*. He had, to be sure, an exaggerated estimate of this famous phrase, which he preferred to take literally. Scant attention was paid to Patriarch Joseph's warning on the matter in 1273, or to Gregory's cautious remarks concerning this approach.

The same persistence of the adequacy of this literal approach was to pervade the discussion of the *Filioque* at Florence.[5] Augustine, who had reduced the divine nature to the categories of unity and simplicity in the West, became the council's guide to the definition of the Trinity, while the two formulations were simply accommodated and declared non-contradictory. Like the Union of Lyons, this Florentine compromise "failed to solve the issue theologically."[6] Neither Beccus nor the theologians of Florence had been able to put their fingers on the solution to the controversial question. Arguably, their inability to grasp the true function of the phrase "through the Son" in Byzantine trinitarian thought (it is not used even once by Gregory of Nazianzus[7]) was part of their problem.

Patriarch Gregory's reading of the question was not only substantially different, but managed to break new ground. Historically speaking, we should first note that he was more concerned with finding, within the patristic context, a genuine solution to the problem of the *Filioque* than with scoring debating points against Beccus and staying the progress of unionism. The characteristic tendency of Byzantinists to lament the treatment meted out to unionists under Gregory's patriarchate by ignoring the fruits of the theological dialogue that took place, is plainly in need of correction; it deplores what, in fact, was peripheral, and ignores what was central. Besides, Gregory—a man of great learning and intellect—was no ogre, tyrant, or reactionary. There is compelling evidence to confirm this. In any event, there is no reason to doubt his good faith or deep religious sense.

As for Gregory's own solution, as we have noted, his faithfulness to doctrinal Orthodoxy and the Cappadocian school is fundamental. Gregory's insistence on the radical incommunicability of the hypostatic attributes or properties of the Trinity was rooted in this tradition; this is equally true of his understanding of the Father's "monarchy," the unique origin or *principium divinitatis* of the Spirit's personal procession. This was ultimately in keeping not only with the Cappadocian settlement of the fourth century, but also with Photius' thesis that the Holy Spirit proceeds from the Father alone.

And yet, Gregory was also willing to acknowledge that not all the different expressions found in the pages of the Fathers could be reduced to Photius' old exclusive schema. One of the more fruitful and creative sides of Gregory's reassessment of the problem was his recognition that the formulation "through the Son" expressed the eternal manifestation or illumination of the Spirit by the Son. The significance of this explanation lies in its open-minded attitude to the *Filioque*, as expressed in the Roman formula *ab utroque*. For, like the *Filioque*, the timeless manifestation of the Spirit was an *eternal* action, and included the Son's participation. Indeed, the Holy Spirit as illumination, or energy, could be said to proceed *ex Patre Filioque*. True, the Son and the Spirit have a unique relation to the Father insofar as one is generated and the other is projected. Even so, they likewise have between them a relation of reciprocity.

In addition to its procession from the Father, the Spirit is also manifested through the Son. Likewise, in addition to the Son's generation from the Father, the Son also manifests the Spirit. In terms of causality, we are dealing with the forward movement of the Spirit—from the Father—toward existence; in terms of the inner trinitarian relation of the Spirit and the Son, we are dealing with the forward progress of the Spirit—from the Son—toward manifestation. The manifestation, however, is not an expression of the consubstantiality—the identity of essence—between the Son and the Spirit. For it would then be possible to have a manifestation of the Spirit from the Father, of the Son from the Spirit and the Father, and of the Father from the Spirit and the Son. Rather, it is an expression of a personal relation, of an indissoluble bond between the Son and the Spirit, in which the Spirit is returned to the

Father by the Son once it is made manifest by Him. The manifestation cannot be denied. To do so would be to deny the Spirit a relation that is personal and, indeed, eternal.

Most of Gregory's contemporaries wished to see the problem primarily from the perspective of the divine economy. Gregory, however, realized that the issue was ultimately concerned with the *abiding* relationship of the Son and the Spirit as divine hypostases, for that is what the patristic and scriptural expressions "through the Son," "Spirit of the Son," or "Spirit of Christ" suggest. Clearly, any solution had to embrace more than the opposition of essence and hypostasis, or the temporal manifestation of the Spirit by the Son, since the common life of the Trinity was also involved. Herein lies Gregory's true contribution. He had the insight and ability to translate the entire patristic tradition to include not only the monarchy of the Father and the relationship of the Spirit and the Son in their economic activity, but the divine movement of reciprocity within the trinitarian life of God as well. Hence, the doctrine of the eternal manifestation, which in no way destroys the personal characteristics of the divine subsistence, any more than it does the economic activity of the Trinity.

That Photius' doctrine was brought to completion and a "new traditional element"[8] was introduced into the debate is indisputable. For although the Cappadocian framework of Byzantine theology was never abandoned, the doctrine did go beyond the Photian formulation and, indeed, complemented it. It was an explanation altogether remarkable for its equilibrium. Besides, the Roman formulation was finally given an Orthodox interpretation. For these reasons alone, the Council of Blachernae and the *Tomus* of 1285 are of the greatest significance. This key *conciliar* decision of the late thirteenth century may well be the most important contribution of the Byzantine Church to the *Filioque* debate. Further, the dogmatic decision of 1285 illustrates Gregory's thought to be far more valuable and significant than the capitulation theology of unionism. Needless to say, Gregory can no longer be viewed only in the shadow of Beccus.

But if Gregory's insight and solution are important, so is his impact on the later Palamite synthesis. Part of that synthesis was actually prepared in the thirteenth century by Patriarch Gregory II of Cyprus. In a very real sense, the fundamental distinction between the essence and the energy is none other than the "working piece"[9] of Palamas' theology. Even so, its formal ratification as dogma by the Palamite councils of 1341, 1347, and 1351, was foreshadowed in the confirmation of the *Tomus* at the Council of 1285. Significantly, all Orthodox scholars who have written on Palamas—Lossky, Krivosheine, Papamichael, Meyendorff, Christou—assume his voice to be a legitimate expression of Orthodox tradition. *Mutatis mutandis* the same is true of Gregory of Cyprus. As one of these scholars has recognized, what is being defended is "one and the same tradition...at different points, by the Orthodox, from St Photius to Gregory of Cyprus and St Gregory Palamas."[10]

Western scholars who have dealt with Gregory II and with Palamas—Jugie, Cayré, Grumel, Laurent, Candal—have seen fit to attack both of them as revolutionary "innovators." Palamas' theology, it is alleged, creates a distinction which destroys the notion of God's simplicity, confuses the idea of God's transcendence, and even introduces a Neoplatonic notion of participation in God.[11] Approval of the *Tomus* of 1285 is as regrettable as the sanction of Palamas' doctrine in the 1340s; both were, unfortunately, never proscribed by any official decision of the Byzantine Church.[12] The Palamite doctrine "might be viewed as a punishment permitted by God, which has managed to be imposed as official dogma."[13] Evidently, the rigid Augustinian-Thomistic position, which is free of such "innovations," is far more consistent with the Church's faith than the strained exegesis of late-Byzantine theology.[14]

Be this as it may, the harsh criticism of Western academic theology remains polemically and theologically unconvincing.[15] Orthodox scholarship argues that late-Byzantine theology is consistent with the theological, liturgical, and mystical tradition of the Church, as well as with the historical evidence; most, if not all, of Patriarch Gregory's and Palamas' contemporaries saw their theology as a genuine development—an ἀνάπτυξις—of the truth of tradition. Few, if any, doubted—once the dust had settled from the tumult attending the controversies in which they were involved—that they spoke for the living tradition of their Church. Indeed, Orthodox scholarship would argue that Gregory II, by anticipation, had refuted Palamas' opponents in the person of Beccus.[16] Finally (to repeat) it must not be forgotten that Palamas and Gregory's thought was sanctioned by conciliar decision.

A main focus of this study had been the near-ceaseless campaign of opposition that Gregory encountered from some of his contemporaries. That a number of theologians and well-placed ecclesiastics actively opposed him is incontestable. Certain, too, is the fact that this opposition was, for the most part, atheological in nature. As Gregory put it: "This was the opportunity for everyone to free himself of all scruples....Each looked out for his own pleasure, his own honor, his own advantage, instead of seeking that which is pleasing to God; and this filled the Church with trouble and disorder."[17] There is irrefutable evidence that this was certainly true in the case of George Moschabar and his circle. John Chilas' eventual approval of Gregory's theology likewise points in the same direction, as does the patriarch's reconciliation with Gerasimus of Heracleia and Neophytus of Brusa.

Additionally, some of these individuals represented the conservative wing of Byzantine medieval theology, and were chiefly motivated by an unenlightened theological conservatism. Hence, their hostile attitude toward Gregory's theological innovation, even if this conformed with or complemented the traditional framework of Byzantine theology. For this group to draw from the past seldom meant adding to that legacy. It was a rigid theology lacking movement, development, or vitality. In sum, it was incapable of breeding new thought or fresh expression. It has been argued recently that what is essential in Palamite teaching had already existed before the arrival of Gregory of Cyprus. Indeed, Gregory's contribution at Blachernae was "an official statement of what had been more or less explicitly taught before him."[18] And yet, this is unlikely, given the substantial militancy against Gregory's formulations.

Gregory categorically denied that he was an innovator, even though the forces of conservatism disagreed with him. Typically, he believed his contribution had a firm basis in the patristic tradition of which he was an heir. His insistence *à outrance* that he would not resign unless his orthodoxy was first publicly acknowledged was a result of this conviction. It is to the credit of the Byzantine episcopate that they accepted Gregory's condition. Indeed, by the end of the decade, few, if any, of Gregory's most obstinate opponents believed that he had put himself irretrievably in the wrong. They no longer saw him as an intruder who had somehow seized control of Byzantine theology, and had forcibly thrown it off its traditional catholic path.

A final observation. Although Gregory had more than a general grasp of theological issues, he was never a systematic theologian. In terms of both volume and organization, his theological output was modest, occasional, and lacked systematic tidiness. Even so, it was a mature and, indeed, homogeneous development of Eastern patristic thought. As Gennadius Scholarius noted, Patriarch Gregory II was in no degree inferior to the most ancient authorities who wrote on the procession of the Holy Spirit.[19] To be sure, the historian, continuity seeker as he is, will not be disappointed by the spirit and insight that informs the theology of Gregory of Cyprus. Gregory was not *sui generis*, without a real theological past, but a true heir of the teaching of the Eastern Fathers.

NOTES

1. Cf. J. Verpeaux, *Nicéphore Choumnos, homme d'État et humaniste Byzantin* (c. 1250/5-1327) (Paris, 1959), pp. 27-28.

2. L. Bréhier, "Le recrutement des patriarches de Constantinople pendant la période byzantine," *Actes du VIè Congrès international des études byzantines* (Paris, 1950), 225.

3. V. Lossky, *The Mystical Theology of the Eastern Church* (London, 1957), p. 13.

4. Tomus, *PG* 142.244D

5. E. Boularand, "L'argument patristique au concile de Florence, dans la question de la procession du Saint-Esprit," *Bulletin de littérature ecclésiastique*, 63 (1962), 161-99.

6. J. Pelikan, *The Christian Tradition: A History of the Development of Doctrine. II: The Spirit of Eastern Christendom 600-1700* (Chicago, 1974), 277.

7. See J. Meyendorff, "La procession du Saint-Esprit chez les Pères orientaux," *Russie et Chrétienté*, 3-4 (1950), 170.

8. J. Meyendorff, *Introduction à l'étude de Grégoire Palamas* (Paris, 1959), p. 27.

9. Cf. G. Barrois' review in *St Vladimir's Theological Quarterly*, 22, Nos. 2-3 (1978), 164, of *Trinitarian Theology: East and West* (Brookline, Mass., 1977).

10. V. Lossky, "The Procession of the Holy Spirit in Orthodox Triadology," *The Eastern Churches Quarterly*, supplementary issue, 7 (1948), 51. The most recent discussion of Gregory's theology (as an expression of Orthodox tradition) is D. Staniloae, *Theology and the Church* (New York, 1980), pp. 16-29. The author, however, finds Gregory's analogy of light and ray as less than felicitous (p. 19). It is the only objection to an otherwise sensitive summary statement of Gregory's position. See also the recent appraisal of the *Filioque* problem in terms of ecumenical relations by T. Stylianopoulos, "The Orthodox Position," *Concilium*, 128 (1979), 23-30.

11. See J. Meyendorff, "The Holy Trinity in Palamite Theology," in *Trinitarian Theology East and West*, p. 28; cf. especially the articles attacking Palamas by several Roman Catholic theologians, in *Istina*, 3 (1974).

12. M. Jugie, *Theologia dogmatica Christianorum orientalism ah Ecclesia Catholica dissidentium*, I (Paris 1926), 431; idem, "Palamite (controverse)," *DTC*, II, pt. 2 (Paris, 1932), col. 1817.

13. Ibid.

14. Cf., for example, J.-P. Houdret, "Palamas et les Cappadociens," *Istina*, 3 (1974), 260-71, who concludes: "Bref, la doctrine du théologien byzantin se découvre ainsi des appuis dès la grande époque des Pères et les Cappadociens apparaissent comme des Palamites avant la lettre! En

fait, comme l'a manifesté cette enquête, les choses sont sans doute différentes." Not all scholars, however, are polemic. Effort to secure an understanding is especially evident in the irenic
and judicious approach of M. Fahey, "Son and Spirit: Divergent Theologies Between Constantinople and the West," *Concilium,* 128 (1979), 15-22.

15. See Meyendorff, "The Holy Trinity in Palamite Theology," 27-30.

16. For the reverse argument, see F. Cayré, "Georges de Chypre," *DTC,* 6, pt. 1 (Paris, 1920), col.
1234.

17. *Autobiography,* in W. Lameere, *La tradition manuscrite de la correspondance de Grégoire de Chypre* (Brussels-Paris, 1937), p. 189.

18. G. Patacsi, "Palamism Before Palamas," *Eastern Churches Review,* 9 (1977), 64.

19. L. Petit et al. (edd.), *Œuvres complètes de Gennade Scholarios,* III (Paris, 1930), 127.

APPENDICES

I

THE *TOMUS* OF 1285

In 1285 the members of the Council of Blachernae formally commissioned Patriarch Gregory II of Cyprus to draw up an official document of its decisions. A text had not been penned during the actual course of the council's discussion from February to August 1285. The result was the *Tomus* of 1285—possibly the single most important conciliar decision of the entire thirteenth century. The document, it is true, is not an objective account of the council's deliberations. Essentially, what the synod requested was a formal statement of its decisions, or a record of its "resolution and judgment," as the eleven anathemas of the text clearly indicate. The document of 1285 is, in fact, a synodal sentence of deposition and a condemnation, not only of Beccus and his lieutenants, George Metochites and Constantine Meliteniotes, but of unionism and the Council of Lyons as well. The text was finally read from the pulpit of the Hagia Sophia at a solemn gathering of the faithful. A signing ceremony followed shortly after.

Besides being a condemnation, however, the *Tomus* is a mature and creative exposition of the Orthodox case—that is, a theological rebuttal of unionism and the foreign and "strange doctrine" of Lyons. The document itself is defined in the body of the text as a στήλη εὐσεβείας—a permanent memorial, or lasting monument, of the Orthodox faith. A large part of the text is thus devoted to the synod's own profession of faith, which—in the form of the traditional creed—also contains a condemnation of the theology of the procession as espoused by Beccus and by Lyons. This theology, the synod argues, is based on a fraudulent exegesis of Scripture and the *testimonia* of the Fathers. Significantly, this creedal section avoids any direct reference to the Photian formula, and simply states that the Spirit proceeds from the Father. The words *a Patre solo* (ἐκ μόνου τοῦ πατρός) are nowhere mentioned. This is followed by another important section, namely, the verbatim text of Beccus' own profession of faith made in 1283.

Eleven anathemas or accusations—with their identical formula-like ex-communications—are then recorded. The theological and trinitarian propositions condemned by the synod in these anathemas are as follows:

a. that the Father is, through the Son, the essential cause of the Spirit.

b. that the Spirit exists through the Son and from the Son.

c. that the preposition "through" is equivalent to "from."

d. that the one unique essence and divinity of the Father and the Son is the cause of the Spirit.

e. that the Father and the Son together constitute a single cause in the procession of the Spirit.

f. that the procession of the Spirit from the Father is an activity of the essence, not of the hypostasis.

g. that the expression "through the Son," when used in reference to the creation of the world, indicates that the Son is the primordial or initial cause.

h. that the Son is the "fountain of life" or the cause of life in the procession of the Spirit, just as the Virgin is said to be the fountain of life in giving birth to Christ.

Each of these accusations likewise contains the synod's rebuttal. Their centering point is the synod's doctrine of the eternal manifestation of the Spirit by the Son (the formula which expressed—in the triadic existence—the lasting or abiding relationship between the Son and the Spirit). Thus, their ultimate focus is the real distinction in God of the essence and the energy—the crucial element or "working piece" of Gregory's (and later of Palamas') theology.

The Council of Blachernae seemingly spent much of its first session discussing the Damascene *testimonium:* "The Father is the projector through the Son of the manifesting Spirit." For all that, of the eleven anathemas, the third alone contains a one-sentence exegesis of this passage: "This, however, can never mean what they say, inasmuch as it clearly denotes the manifestation—through the intermediary of the Son—of the Spirit, whose existence is from the Father." A commission later decided to delete this explanation from the text. The significance of this decision (made shortly after Patriarch Gregory resigned), nevertheless, has been grossly exaggerated and misunderstood. This is equally true of what has been said about the discussions of the council itself. Briefly, because the extant documentation is concerned chiefly with the first session, in which the Damascene proof-text was discussed, scholars have been misled into exaggerating its role in the proceedings and into believing that this was the only topic of discussion.

The removal of the one sentence from the third anathema, dealing with the troublesome proof-text, in no way affected the doctrine of the eternal manifestation enshrined in the synodal *Tomus*. It cannot be stressed enough that the sentence was easily removed without affecting the doctrine itself. The doctrine was allowed to stand. Not only is it mentioned and elaborated more fully elsewhere in several sections of the *Tomus,* but it constitutes, as noted above, the document's very focus. It is, moreover, highly significant that an examination of the manuscripts shows that, in the end, the integrity of the entire text of the *Tomus* was probably retained. The manuscripts yield no variation. The sentence is not omitted in the extant manuscripts. There are no two texts—an original and a purged or emended text! (Cf. Laurent, *Regestes*, no. 1490, esp. p. 284, who notes that his own collation of the majority of the manuscripts did not yield any variation in the body of the text.) In short, the manuscript tradition indicates that the decision was probably never carried out.

There are over thirty known manuscripts of the *Tomus*, most of them dating from the thirteenth to the sixteenth centuries. At least three are from the late-thirteenth century. The translation given below is based on one of these contemporary manucripts, Paris. gr. 1301, fols. 87^r-102^v. This was the manuscript used by Anselm Banduri, a student of Montfaucon's, for his 1711 *editio princeps* of the *Tomus*; it was later reprinted by Migne in the *Patrologia Graeca*. Banduri, however, although cautious and generally reliable, often omits whole sentences or, more frequently, single words; at other times, he substitutes his own readings. And then, too, his readings are not always correct—thus, ἄν for ἕν, or παρεισαγωγαὶ for ἐπεισαγωγαί. These errors, as we should expect, are reprinted in Migne. We have noted the most glaring of these in the apparatus. The manuscript reading (Paris. gr. 1301), where it differs from Banduri, is almost always confirmed by the readings of other manuscripts.

Regrettably, too, both Banduri and Migne reproduce the Greek text without a translation; even a Latin equivalent is not given. An edition of the Greek text, based on the entire manuscript tradition is, of course, also needed. Only the much needed translation into English, however, is offered here. There exists, it is true, Troitskij's translation into Russian—the first into a modern language—but Troltskij's work is both inaccessible and old. It is not mentioned, for example, in Laurent's *Regestes*. Besides, the Russian translation was done directly from Banduri, not from the original manuscript. (Troitskij, however, does include some of the variant readings found in Metochites' and Beccus' refutation of the *Tomus*.)

The style of the *Tomus* is markedly different from the excessive atticizing style of the patriarch's voluminous correspondence. The text is not entirely free, however, of the atticism, the pleonasm, or the luxuriant rhetoric commonly associated with Byzantine ecclesiastical texts. Given the doctrinal nature of the text, our aim above all has been to communicate the meaning of the original. As such, we have tried to promote both clarity and accuracy. This is not to say, however, that we have eliminated all the pleonasm and rhetoric from the text; we have, in fact, tried to remain as faithful as possible to the original. The marginal numbers correspond to the columns in the Migne edition. All biblical quotations are from the Revised Standard Version of the Bible.

Exposition of the Tomus of Faith Against Beccus

By the most holy and ecumenical patriarch, Lord Gregory of Cyprus, who was attacked by certain individuals, and for whom this vigorous reply was given.[1] [233A-B] (fol. 87ʳ) The disturbance and storm, which occurred in the Church a short while ago, had, as it were, for its father and leader, the Adversary himself, who is forever stricken with envy of man's salvation, and who is always seeking to do that which would prevent it. Even so, he also had individuals who, although they were, at first, not the major leaders at fault, but only worked as so many servants and instruments, by preference, did for the disturbance whatever he wanted done. But, since from the beginning, the union [of 1274], the certain harmless accommodation, and the alleged benefit to us were not, in reality, what they claimed, their actual intention was[2] made clear by their actions. And this was proposed as a bait, drawing men's souls[3] to that which was hidden; it was, further, proposed with promises, with the most terrible imprecations, and with solemn oaths, to the effect that they had nothing else in mind other than that which these very things signified—harmlessness, safety, that is, irreproachability. (fol. 87ᵛ) Shortly afterward, however, these imprecations and oaths were forgotten, as if they had been made for some purpose other than[4] that for which they were intended. And the union and accommodation, and their hitherto seemingly important undertaking, are, as it were, cast down, while the words and the deeds of evil are [234A-B] raised up. And someone[5] dares to declare in our midst that the Spirit also proceeds from the Son, just as it does, indeed, from the Father, and that the only-begotten Son—like the Father, who begets the Son—is its cause. This, then, is how the disturbance begins, how the great struggle against the Church is rekindled.

Almost everyone knows (there is no need to explain it again) that this alien doctrine, which disturbed us lately, was not a recent development, but had its genesis with others, not with us. All the same, it was brought here like a foreign plague, and flourished for quite some time. And it was John Beccus who gave it the strength to grow so much (fol. 88[r]) and he accepted it and became the suitable ground, as it were, for its growth; and he nourished it, in my opinion, from the rivers of evil and lawlessness, or, as he falsely said, from Holy Scriptures, interpreting it wrongly, spreading babble from there, and committing sacrilege, while, at the same time robbing the meaning of Scripture, and the sense of those who listened superficially or of those who had an eye on his wealth. Yet, this evil man was almost in his eighth[6] year of office and residence in this city; for this is how long he had been established on the patriarchal throne, the prize for a bad crop. And all this time God allowed the Church to suffer and endure the worst because of the multitude [235A-B] of the sins of everyone, by which we alone provoke the anger of Him who is without passion.

Eventually, however, God pitied us, his servants, and looked upon us with mercy and raised up an emperor—who seems to live only for the purpose of doing his bidding—and the Church, just as, in the past, (fol. 88[v]) He had raised David's fallen and ruined tabernacle through him.[7] And the man who had accepted and nourished the evil and discord was removed from our midst, and the true doctrine concerning the Spirit is expressed with confidence, and those who wish[8] to change the life dearest to God are, in the future, free to build on the foundation of faith. It is, likewise, commendable, and truly[9] salutary, and the work of superior planning to attend to the future safety of the Church and, in every way, to secure its stability so that if someone hateful to God should again attempt to disturb it he will be shown to be acting in vain, because he will be repelled by the unshakable words of our faith. This could be accomplished satisfactorily if we do two things. We should first define our belief dearly, that is, the Orthodox faith, and raise it as a permanent monument to our sublime faith; seen, thus, from a distance—being visible to all—it will attract to itself the spiritual eyes of everyone. Secondly we must make this evil, (fol. 89ʳ) destructive and alien teaching known, so that when this has been exposed we will all turn away from it and despise it and quickly escape from its danger.

Accordingly, the faith which we acknowledge and believe [235C-D] in our heart is as follows. We believe as we have been taught from the beginning and from the Fathers. We have been taught and we believe in one God, the Father almighty, creator of heaven and earth, and of all things visible and invisible, who, being without principle (ἄναρχος), unbegotten, and without cause, is the natural principle and cause of the Son and of the Spirit. We also believe in His only begotten Son, who, being consubstantial with Him, was begotten eternally and without change from Him, through whom all things were made.[10] We believe in the all-Holy Spirit, which proceeds from the same Father, which, with the Father and the Son together, is worshipped as co-eternal, co-equal, co-essential, co-equal in glory, and as joint-creator of the world. We believe that the only-begotten (fol. 89ᵛ) Word of the supersubstantial and life-giving Trinity came down from heaven for us men and for our salvation, was incarnate by the Holy Spirit and the Virgin Mary and became man; that is, He became perfect man while remaining God and in no way altered or transformed the divine nature by His contact with the flesh, but assumed humanity without change. And He, who is passionless according to His divine nature, suffered the passion and the cross and, on the third day, rose from the dead and ascended into heaven and sat at the right hand of God the Father. We believe in accordance with God, holy tradition and teaching [236A-B] in one holy, catholic, and apostolic Church. We acknowledge one baptism for the remission of sins, we look for the resurrection of the dead, and the life of the age to come.

Additionally, we acknowledge a single hypostasis of the incarnate Word, and we believe the same Christ to be one, and we proclaim and know Him after the Incarnation, as redeeming with two natures, (fol. 90ʳ) from which, and in which, and which He is. Consequently, we believe in two energies and two wills of the same Christ, each nature having its own will and its own saving action. We venerate, but not[11] absolutely and without adoration, the holy and sacred images of Christ, of the immaculate Mother of God, and of all the

saints, because the honor we show them passes over to the original. We reject the recently established union [of Lyons] which provoked God's hostility toward us.[12] For this union divided and ravaged the Church, under the pretense of harmless accommodation, persuading it, by their stupidity and deception, to establish their glory, but not God's,[13] and to turn from Orthodoxy and the sound teaching of the Fathers, and to fall down the precipice of heresy and blasphemy.[14] We also render void their dangerous doctrine concerning the procession of the Holy Spirit. (fol. 90ᵛ) We have been taught from God, the Word Himself, that the all-Holy Spirit proceeds from the Father; and we confess that it has its existence from the Father, and that it prides itself—exactly as the [236C-D] Son Himself does—in the fact that the same [Father] is essentially the cause of its being. And we know and believe that the Son is from the Father, being enriched in having the Father as His cause and natural principle, and in being consubstantial and of one nature with the Spirit, which is from the Father. Even so, He is not, either separately or with the Father, the cause of the Spirit; for the all-Holy Spirit's existence is not "through the Son" and "from the Son" as they who hasten toward their destruction and separation from God understand and teach.[15] We shun and cut off from our communion those who do not correctly uphold the sound faith but blaspheme blatantly, and think and speak perversely[16] and perpetuate what is most alarming[17] and unbearable to hear.

They were originally members of our nation and of our doctrine and belonged to the Church, and yet they rebelled against it and put it aside—the Church which had spiritually given them birth and had nourished them. And they placed the Church in ultimate danger (fol. 91ʳ) and showed themselves blameworthy children, estranged sons, who had veered from their paths. You did not repay well—evil and perverse generation[18]—either the Lord God or Mother Church. One should be willing to endure every danger—even death itself should not be rejected—on behalf of the Church and its doctrines. And yet, their behavior toward the Church was worse than that of natural enemies, for they were openly emotionally disturbed and had altogether lost the ability of distinguishing between friend [237A-B] and foe. The first among them, as we said, was John Beccus who (because Christ had visited his own Church, and moved against him and his evil associates, and proceeded clearly forward with the result that he was going to be justly punished for his endless chatter), after appearing to repent for the mischief he had caused when he went raving mad, and, after composing a pious statement and giving it to the synod handling his case, had hardly tasted leniency and escaped condemnation, when he turned back to his own vomit of blasphemy.[19]

This statement[20] should be made known (fol. 91[v]) so that all who hear[21] it may judge if he was justly condemned. The verbatim text was as follows: "Because of my attempt to promote the precarious accommodation of the supposed ecclesiastical union, and to bring everyone around to agree to it, it happened that I spoke and wrote on Church doctrine; certain things which I had said, however, were found to be of a dubious nature and at variance with sacred and holy doctrine and this being so, the synod had them condemned. I said, for example, that the Holy Spirit has, as cause of its personal existence, the Father and the Son, and that this doctrine was in harmony with the formula which declares that the 'Spirit proceeds from the Father through the Son.' In the final analysis, this means that the Spirit has two causes, and that both the direct and the remote principles of causation were implied. That is, the Son is as much the cause of the existence of the Spirit as the meaning of the preposition [237C-D] 'through' allows. And since all these doctrines are found in my own writings and speeches, they are mine, for no one else had thought and written these. Additionally, I said that the Father and the Son [together] constitute a single cause of the Spirit (fol. 92[r]) from whom, as from one principle and source, the Spirit has its being. All this and anything else that may lead to such dogmatic absurdity—before God, his awesome angels, and before the holy and sacred synod—from the bottom of my heart, without deceit, without hiding one thing and saying another, I turn away from, I reject, and I cast out because they lead to the ultimate destruction of the soul. I confess with heart and tongue and I believe as does the holy Catholic Church from the beginning in the Holy Trinity, the one God, thus: that the Father does not have His being either from another or from Himself, but is without beginning and without cause that the only-begotten Son of God has His existence by generation from the Father and has the Father as His cause; I confess and believe that the Holy Spirit has—by procession—its existence from God the Father; and that the Father, according to the voices of the holy teachers, is the cause of the Son and of the Spirit; that the formula 'the Spirit proceeds through the Son' in no way renders the Son, either separately or with the Father, the cause of the Spirit [238A-B] because, according to the dubious and (fol. 92[v]) absurd view of certain individuals, the Son and the Father constitute the one[22] cause and unique principle of the Spirit. These, then, are the doctrines that I confess. I hope it will be these and all the doctrines of the holy catholic Church of God, according to this written confession, that I shall be found confessing unto my last breath. Everyone who, now or in the future, does not confess thus I dissociate myself from, and I cast out far from the Orthodox faith of Christians. This is the statement of my confession and faith, by which I acknowledge and witness to everyone, and by which I indicate clearly that I hold to the faith concerning God, and that I am entirely devoted to the evangelical, apostolic, and patristic doctrine and teaching. Because of my boldness, by which I precariously attempted to delve into certain of the above-mentioned doctrines, I was deposed from the episcopate by the most holy [Joseph], lord and ecumenical patriarch, and by his holy and sacred synod, in which the most holy [Athanasius] pope and patriarch of Alexandria was also present. As such, I approve (fol. 93ʳ) this lawfully and canonically rendered sentence of deposition, and I accept this resolution as justifiable and lawful. I shall never try to regain the priesthood."

Nevertheless, once this confession which he wrote and signed with his own hand was published, he annulled it immediately as soon as the ecclesiastical court had given him a reprieve. And he again composes books and blasphemies, and he again adds spurious doctrines and [238C-D] the opinions of others which our fathers did not know. And he obstinately tries to prove himself superior to these "errors" of this evil, whereas, of course, he should have done this solely by repentance and by the suppression of all that he had written. By ignoring the way,[24] he veered from the straight path and was given to a mind even more reprobate than before.[25] We imagine that the spirit of error left him for a while, but attacked him again with greater force, having brought along not seven, but a whole legion of spirits, and that it took possession of his soul and filled it.[26] Therefore, he is again summoned and asked to account for this change from good to evil. And who summons him (fol. 93ᵛ) but the emperor [Andronicus] who is jealous of God, the God of hosts,[27] and who has become as the hand of the Most High himself in the restoration of the Church and the faith, whom I happily call a new Moses, God's excellent servant,[28] who rescued the present-day people of Israel not from that ancient material bondage of Egypt, but from another one that is far worse. Because of this service, the emperor has been drawn by the hand of God, whose books contain his name.[29] We, therefore, need not write a great deal about him.

And Beccus was asked by the emperor[30] and by the holy [239A-B] synod to state the reasons for which he turned back (after he had obtained the grace of a commendable repentance, and had put—to speak scripturally—his hand to the plow,[31] and had agreed to follow the Church's order), and lost all ability to gain the kingdom of heaven, preferring blasphemy to truth. However, it became clear from his words (he did not say anything that is true), and from his actions (he made no attempt to hide his wickedness), that he is so closely (fol. 94^r) united with heterodoxy that no words would convince him to renounce his position. Accordingly, the entire assembly of the faithful, inspired by the righteous zeal against him and those who share his views, render this[32] decision like the ancient priests pronouncing against their own kin, the sons of Israel, who had broken the law.

1. To John Beccus and to those who follow him, to Constantine Meliteniotes and George Metochites, who were born of us,[33] and who were reared in our customs and doctrines, but who did not abide in them despite the fact that these were their own and of the Fathers, and had been established with the passage of time ever since the Christian faith began to be preached in these parts. But these, against which not even the gates of hell have prevailed nor shall prevail[34]—they have despised, and I do not know why they condemn them, or why they refuse to praise them. But then they introduced instead a belief that was entirely unknown to its authors, for they respect neither the text's antiquity nor those who revealed these truths, namely, the ones who spoke of the things of the Spirit not for any other reason but because they were filled with the Spirit. To these men—because they were so corrupt that they held beliefs both strange and alien (fol. 94^v) to our traditions to the [239C-D] detriment and destruction of the Church; and, sometime later, they renounced this madness and declared by word and in writing before countless eyes and ears that they would be accursed if, in the future, they should not be found in full possession of the traditional faith, but drawn to a belief[35] alien to the Church; and because they did not abide by their own written statement concerning this repentance, but changed their mind and[36] opinion and again turned to their previous apostasy, as if possessed of a rebellious nature and a faithlessness toward ancestral doctrines, to these, because they wickedly turned away and preferred this separation from their own Church, we pronounce[37] the resolution which they have pronounced upon themselves (or[38] in the case of those who, in the future, will dare to do so), we cut them off (since they hold such views) from the membership of the Orthodox, and we banish them from the flock of the Church of God.

2. To the same [John Beccus], and to those who along with him were rash enough to introduce into the apostolic faith matters which the teachers of the

Church did not hand down and which we have not received through them, (fol. 95ʳ) we pronounce the above-recorded resolution and judgment, we cut them off from the membership of the Orthodox, and we banish them from the flock of the Church of God.

3. To the same, who say that the Father is, through the Son, the cause of the Spirit, and who cannot conceive [240A-B] the Father as the cause of the hypostasis of the Spirit—giving it existence and being—except through the Son; thus according to them the Son is united to the Father as joint-cause and contributor to the Spirit's existence. This, they say, is supported by the phrase of Saint John of Damascus, "the Father is the projector through the Son of the manifesting Spirit."[39] This, however, can never mean what they say, inasmuch as it clearly denotes the manifestation—through the intermediary of the Son—of the Spirit, whose existence is from the Father.[40] For the same John of Damascus would not have said—in the exact same chapter—that the only cause in the Trinity is God the Father, thus denying, by the use of the word "only," the causative principle to the remaining two hypostases.[41] Nor would he have, again, said elsewhere, "and we speak, likewise, of the Holy Spirit as the 'Spirit of the Son,' yet we do not speak of the Spirit as from the Son."[42] For both of these views to be true is impossible (fol. 95ᵛ). To those who have not accepted the interpretation given to these *testimonia* by the Fathers, but, on the contrary, perceive them in a manner altogether forbidden by them, we pronounce the above recorded resolution and judgment, we cut them off from the membership of the Orthodox, and we banish them from the flock of the Church of God.

4. To the same, who affirm that the Paraclete, which is from the Frather, has its existence through the Son and from the Son, and who again propose as proof the phrase "the Spirit exists through the Son and from the Son." In certain texts [of the Fathers], the phrase denotes the [240C-D] Spirit's shining forth and manifestation. Indeed, the very Paraclete shines form and is manifest eternally through the Son, in the same way that light shines forth and is manifest through the intermediary of the sun's rays; it further denotes the bestowing, giving, and sending of the Spirit to us. It does not, however, mean that it subsists through the Son and from the Son, and that it receives its being through Him and from Him. For this would[43] mean that the Spirit has the Son as cause and source (exactly as it has the Father), not to say that it has its cause and source more so from the Son than from the Father; for it is said that that from which existence is derived likewise is believed to enrich the source

and to be the cause of being. (fol. 96^r) To those who believe and say such things, we pronounce the above resolution and judgment, we cut them off from the membership of the Orthodox, and we banish them from the flock of the Church of God.

5. To the same, who say that the preposition "through" everywhere in theology is identical to the preposition "from" and, as a result, maintain that there is no difference in saying that the Spirit proceeds "through the Son" from saying that it proceeds "from the Son"—whence, undoubtedly, the origin of their idea that the existence and essence of the Spirit is from the Son. And they either infer a double or a single procession of origin, and join the Son to the Father according to this explanation of "cause," both of which are beyond all blasphemy. For there is no other hypostasis in the Trinity except the Father's, from which the existence and essence of the consubstantial [Son and Holy Spirit] is derived. According [241A-B] to the common mind of the Church and the aforementioned saints, the Father is the foundation and the source of the Son and the Spirit, the only source of divinity, and the only cause. If, in fact, it is also said by some of the saints that the Spirit proceeds "through the Son," (fol. 96^v) what is meant here is the eternal manifestation of the Spirit by the Son, not the purely [personal] emanation into being of the Spirit, which has its existence from the Father.[44] Otherwise, this would deprive the Father from being the only cause and the only source of divinity, and would expose the theologian [Gregory of Nazianzus] who says "everything the Father is said to possess, the Son, likewise, possesses except causality"[45] as a dishonest theologian. To these who speak thus, we pronounce the above-recorded resolution and judgment, we cut them off from the membership of the Orthodox, and we banish them from the flock of the Church of God.

6. To the same, who contend that the unique essence and divinity of the Father and the Son is the cause of the Spirit's existence—an idea which no one who has ever had it in his mind has either expressed or considered making public. For the common essence and nature is not the cause of the hypostasis; nor does this common essence ever generate or project that which is undivided; on the other hand, the essence which is accompanied by individual characteristics does, and this, according to the great Maximus, denotes the hypostasis.[46] But also, according to the great Basil, because he too defines the hypostasis as that (fol. 97^r) which describes and brings to mind what in each thing is common, and which cannot be described by means of individual characteristics which appear in it.[47] Because of this, the indivisible essence al-

ways projects something indivisible (or generates the indivisible [241C-D] that generates),[48] in order that the created may be [simultaneously] the projector as well as the projected; the essence of the Father and the Son, however, is one, and is not, on the whole, indivisible.[49] To these, who absurdly blaspheme thus, we pronounce the above-recorded resolution and judgment, we cut them off from the membership of the Orthodox, and we banish them from the flock of the Church of God.

7. To the same, who teach that the Father and the Son—not as two principles and two causes—share in the causality of the Spirit, and that the Son is as much a participant with the Father as is implied in the preposition "through." According to the distinction and strength of these prepositions, they introduce a distinction in the Spirit's cause, with the result that sometimes they believe and say that the Father is cause, and sometimes the Son. This being so, they introduce a plurality and a multitude of causes in the procession of the Spirit, even though this was prohibited on countless occassions.(fol. 97^v) As such, we pronounce the above-recorded resolution and judgment, we cut them off from the membership of the Orthodox, and we banish them from the flock of the Church of God.

8. To the same, who stoutly maintain that the Father by virtue of the nature—not by virtue of the hypostasis—is the Holy Spirit's cause; the result is that they necessarily proclaim the Son as cause of the Spirit, since the Son has the same nature as the Father. At the same time, they fail to see the absurdity that results from this. [242A-B] For it is necessary first[50] that the Spirit be the cause of someone, for the simple reason that it has the same nature as the Father. Secondly, the number of the cause increases, since as many hypostases as share in nature must, likewise, share in causality. Thirdly, the common essence and nature is transformed into the cause of the hypostasis, which all logic—and, along with this, nature itself—prohibits. (fol. 98^r) To these, who believe in such things strange and alien to truth, we pronounce the above-recorded resolution and judgment, we cut them off from the membership of the Orthodox, and we banish them from the flock of the Church of God.

9. To the same, who state that, in reference to the creation of the world, the phrase "through the Son" denotes the immediate cause,[51] as well as the fact that it denies the Son the right to be creator and cause of things made "through Him." That is to say, in theology proper [the study of the Trinity in itself], even if the Father is called the initial cause of the Son and the Spirit,

He is also, "through the Son," the cause of the Spirit. Accordingly, the Son
cannot be separated from the Father in the procession of the Spirit. By saying
such things, they irrationally join the Son to the Father in the causation of the
Spirit. In reality, even if the Son, like the Father, is creator of all things made
"through Him," it does not follow that He is also the Spirit's cause, because
the Father is the projector of the Spirit through Him; nor, again, does it follow
that, because the Father is the Spirit's projector "through[52] the Son," He is,
through Him, the cause of the Spirit. For the formula "through the Son" here
denotes the manifestation and illumination [of the Spirit by the Son], and not
the emanation [242C-D] of the Spirit into being. If this was not so, it would
be difficult, indeed, even to enumerate the theological absurdities that follow.
To these, who irrationally express such views, and ascribe them to the writings
of the saints, and from these stir up a multitude of blasphemies, we pronounce the above- (fol. 98ᵛ) recorded resolution and judgment, we cut them
off from the membership of the Orthodox, and we banish them from the
flock of the Church of God.

10. To the same, who declare that the Son is said to be the fountain of life
in the same way that the Virgin Mother of God is said to be the fountain of
life.[53] The Virgin is so called because she lent living flesh to the only-begotten
Word with a rational and intellectual soul, and became the cause of mankind
born according to Christ. Similarly, those who understand life to be in the
Holy Spirit will think of the Son as the fountain of life in terms of cause.
Hence, their argument—from conclusions drawn of incongruous comparisons and examples—for the participation of the Son with the Father in the
procession of the Spirit. And yet, it is not because the Virgin is said to be the
fountain of life that the only-begotten Word of God is called the fountain of
life. For she is so called because it is from her that real life came, for the same
Word of God and true God was born according to His humanity, and she became the cause of His holy flesh. As for the Son, He is the fountain of life because He became the cause of life for us who were dead to sin; because he
became as an overflowing river to everyone; [243 A-B] (fol. 99ʳ) and because,
for those who believe in the Son, the Spirit is bestowed as from this fountain
and through Him. This grace of the Spirit is poured forth, and it is neither
novel nor alien to Scripture were it to be called by the same name as Holy
Spirit. For, sometimes, an act (ἐνέργεια) is identified by the name of the one
who acts, since frequently we do not refuse to call "sun" the sun's own luster
and light.[54] To these, whose ambition is to draw such conclusions, and to rec-

oncile what by nature cannot at all be reconciled, we pronounce the above-recorded resolution and judgment, we cut them off from the membership of the Orthodox, and we banish them from the flock of the Church of God.

11. To the same, who do not receive the writings of the saints in the correct manner intended by the Church, nor do they honor what appears to be the closest [interpretation] according to the patristic[55] traditions and the common beliefs about God and things divine, but distort[56] the meaning of these writings so as to set them at variance with the prescribed dogmas, or adhere to the mere word and, from this, bring forth strange doctrine, we pronounce the above-recorded resolution and judgment, we cut them off from the membership of the Orthodox, and we banish them from the flock of the Church of God.

(fol. 99^v) Certainly, the doctrines of the above-listed and already expelled individuals are filled with blasphemy, malice, and fall short of all ecclesiastical prudence. Even if Beccus, the father of these doctrines—or someone among his zealous supporters—confidently affirms that these [243 C-D] teachings are the thoughts of the saints, in reality, we must suppose him a slanderer and blasphemer of the saints. For where have the God-bearing Fathers said that God the Father is, through the Son, the cause of the Spirit? Where do they say that the Paraclete has its existence from the Son and through the Son? Again, where do they say that the same Paraclete has its existence from the Father and from the Son? In what text do they teach that the one essence and divinity of the Father and the Son is the cause of the Holy Spirit's existence? Who, and in which of his works, ever prohibited anyone from saying that the hypostasis of the Father is the unique cause of being of the Son and the Spirit? Who among those who believe that the Father is the cause of the Spirit has taught that this is by virtue of the nature, not by[57] virtue of the hypostasis? And who has failed to maintain this as (fol. 100^r) the characteristic that distinguishes the Father from the other two hypostases? Finally, who says that those other teachings, about which he has lied by insulting the Fathers, belong to the Fathers? He abstains from neither evil. For at some places he alters their own words, and, even when he uses the words without distortion, he does not adhere to their true meaning. Neither does he look at the aim that the author had in mind, but arrogantly passes over the purpose and the desire, and even the express intent of the author's statement, and adheres to the word and, having obtained the shadow instead of the body, composes books. And this is like saying that [244 A-B] he twists ropes of sand and builds houses therefrom to make I do not know what, unless it is a monument and a memorial—the former, an advertisement of his folly the latter, a declaration of the struggle he undertook against his own salvation. This being so, we condemn the doctrines themselves together with their authors, and judge that their memory, like the expelled, be eliminated from the Church with a resounding noise.

They are like thorns and thistles which, by divine (fol. 100ᵛ) permission, have grown within the life-giving precincts of the Church, or like evil weeds which the enemy has sown among the authentic wheat of the gospel.[58] For he found an opportunity for his wickedness in the forebearance of the avenging God. They are a death-bearing brood of vipers[59] (if you prefer something that has a greater resemblance to evil) and, according to Scripture, descendants of serpents bringing death to every soul that approaches them; and they are worth preserving so long as they do not need[60] to be born at all and men do not know of them. They should be destroyed with fire, and with iron, and with every possible means—a task the Church should undertake—and they should be given over to non-being and to ultimate destruction. Indeed, we counsel all the sons of our Church to avoid them with great care, and not even to listen to them in a cursory manner.

But we cannot stop with admonition alone but must supplement this with both threat and fear for[61] the sake of the security of the future. But what does this threat consist of? Is it because the act [of Lyons] which occurred a short while back—I know not why they called it "accommodation" and union,[62] when it deserves a completely different name—confused the Church and finally ravaged it? [244 C-D] (fol. 101ʳ) Indeed, this act introduced precariously and very dangerously the aforementioned and unreasonable doctrines, which had John Beccus as their protector. Thus, we define our position very clearly for everyone, should any individual—living now or in the future—ever dare to revive that act which has been wisely abolished, or attempt to impose doctrines on our Church which have been already profitably condemned, or suggest them either secretly and[63] maliciously, or introduce a proposal in favor of believing or approving these doctrines, or strive for their free acceptance among us, and thus scorn the genuine doctrines of the early Church and its present decrees against the spurious and alien and, indeed, against the accommodation and act by which they crept into the Church to its detriment. This Beccus, and anyone who agrees ever to receive those members of the Roman Church who remain intransigent concerning those doctrines for which they were from the beginning accused by our Church and for which the schism occurred, and who agree to receive them (fol. 101ᵛ) more openly than we were accustomed, that is, prior to this misleading accommodation and worthless union [of Lyons] hostile to the good—this man, besides expelling him from the Church, cutting him off, and removing him from the assembly and society of the faithful, we subject to the terrible penalty of anathema. For he should not even be forgiven [245A-B] by men, he who did not learn not to dare such things (after such an experience of the preceding evil, or after the recent condemnation), and who did not understand not to contrive against the accepted formulations of the Fathers, nor to remain[64] forever a disciple and subject of the Church.

And we proclaim and do these things, as we said, for the sake of remaining spiritually unharmed, for the mutual benefit of everyone, for those who now belong to our devout Church, and for those who after this shall continue to do so.[65] Remain steadfast, true [followers] of God, by avoiding and loathing those other doctrines that are opposed to the truth, and those fabrications (fol. 102ʳ) of Beccus. Avoid not only him, but those individuals mentioned above by name who together with him spew out blasphemies which, till now, they have made their own, and which they accept unrepentantly. By so doing, the Paraclete will abide in you,[66] and will preserve you not only from the plague of such error, but from the greater plague of the passions for the participation in the eternal benefits and the blessedness prepared for the just. And may you be and remain so.

The recorded resolution and decision has now been issued by the Church against those who have rebelled and repudiated the Church. In a short while it will be proclaimed by the supreme Judge, unless, before the arrival of His great and manifest day,[67] they set themselves free by repentance, tears and mourning beyond endurance. [246A-B] For if they repent and look again at the light of Mother Church with the pure eyes of the soul, they will be like those who, in coming to Christ, will not be turned out. To the contrary, Christ will approach the returning one (fol. 102ᵛ) and will embrace him, even if he is a prodigal son who has wasted his inherited portion,[68] or a lost sheep which had abandoned its sheepfold, or an individual who has removed himself from grace. So it is with the Church which in like manner shall gather them together and reckon as its own and forthwith establish them among the ranks and company of its children, provided they lament one day and experience what we experience now. And although we excommunicate them, separate them from the Church of the devout, impose on them the awesome and great judgment of separation and estrangement from the Orthodox, we do not do it because we wish to exult over their misfortune or to rejoice over their rejection. On the contrary, we grieve and bear their isolation with loathing. But why do we need to act in this fashion? Mainly for two reasons: the first being that their unhappiness and bitterness will cause them, after they have realized their folly, to return repentant and save themselves in the Church. Secondly, others will henceforth be chastened and disciplined so as not to attempt anything similar, or attack that which is holy, or behave willfully against that which is sacred; lest, if they show such audacity, they receive the same rewards in accordance with the example that has been set.

NOTES

1. For other longer superscriptions, see Laurent, *Regestes*, no. 1490, p. 282.

2. Paris. gr. 1301, fol. 87^r: εἶναι; omitted by A. Banduri, *Imperium Orientale sive Antiquitates Constantinopolitanae*, II (Paris, 1711), 942 (hereafter Banduri).

3. Paris. gr. 1301, fol. 87^r: ψυχάς; omitted by Banduri (p. 942).

4. Paris. gr. 1301. fol. 87^v: ἥ; Banduri (p. 942): δή.

5. This "someone" is clearly John Beccus. The account here is historically accurate, and refers to the fact that initially the Union of Lyons, as sponsored by Michael VIII, was grounded on the principle of οἰκονομία. However, Beccus' attempt to justify the *Filioque* theologically, shortly after his accession, transferred the issue from the plane of accommodation to that of theology. What was being threatened was the integrity of Byzantine theological tradition and custom, which Michael had promised to retain undisturbed.

6. Beccus' patriarchate: 26 May 1275 to 26 December 1282.

7. Acts 15:16: "After this, I will return, and I will rebuild the dwelling of David, which has fallen, I will rebuild its ruins, and I will set it up."

8. Banduri (p 943) adds "truly (ὄντως) wish"; the word ὄντως is not found in Paris. gr. 1301, fol. 88^v.

9. Paris. gr. 1301, fol. 88^v: ὄντως; omitted by Banduri (p. 943).

10. See John of Damascus, *De fide orthodoxa*, B. Kotter (ed.), *Die Schriften des Johannes von Damaskos*, II (Patristische Texte und Studien, 12; Berlin, 1973), 19-20, 23 (= *PG* 94.809-11, 816C).

11. Paris. gr. 1301, fol. 90^r: ἀλλ' οὐ; Banduri (p. 943): καὶ οὐ.

12. Cf. Rom. 8:7: "For, the mind that is set on the flesh is hostile to God."

13 Rom. 10:3: "For, being ignorant of the righteousness that comes from God, and seeking to establish their own, they did not submit to God's righteousness."

14. The word "blasphemy" is used repeatedly by Gregory to describe Beccus' doctrine concerning the procession of the Spirit. To be sure, the deeply biblical nuance of the word in Scripture and in patristic literature did not escape him. In the New Testament, the word indicates violation of the power and majesty of God (Mark 2:7; Luke 5:21). In the early patristic period, opposing theological views were stigmatized as blasphemy. See especially G. Kittel (ed.), *Theological Dictionary of the New Testament,* I (Grand Rapids-London, 1964), 621-25.

15. Psalm 73:27: "For lo, those who are far from thee shall perish; thou dost put an end to those who are false to thee."

16. Acts 20:30: "And from among your own selves will arise men speaking perverse things, to draw away the disciples after them."

17. Paris. gr. 1301, fol. 90^v: δεινότατον; Banduri (p. 944): δεινοτάτης.

18. Matt. 17:17: "O faithless and perverse generation, how long am I to be with you?" See also Matt. 12:39.

19. 2 Peter 2:22: "It has happened to them according to the true proverb, the dog turns back to his own vomit, and the sow is washed only to wallow in the mire." Cf. Prov. 26:11: "Like a dog that returns to his vomit is a fool that repeats his folly."

20. Marginal note in Paris. gr. 1301, fol. 91^v (reproduced in Banduri, p. 944, and reprinted in Migne): "This is the repentance and rejection of Beccus' blasphemous doctrines, although, shortly afterward, he again changed his mind regarding these things, and, like a dog, turned back to his own vomit."

21. This passage indicates that the text was intended for those who had assembled to "hear" the *Tomus* read from the pulpit of the Hagia Sophia.

22. Paris. gr. 1301, fol. 92^v: ἕν; Banduri (p. 944): ἄν.

23. Paris. gr. 1301, fol. 93^r: ἐπεισαγωγαί; Banduri (p. 945): παρεισαγωγαί.

24. 2 Peter 2:15: "Forsaking the right way, they have gone astray."

25. Rom. 1:28: "And, since they did not see fit to acknowledge God, God gave them up to a base mind and to improper conduct."

26. Cf. Matt. 12:43-45

27. 1 Kings 19:10: "He said, 'I have been very jealous for the Lord, the God of hosts'."

28. Heb. 3:5: "Now Moses was faithful in all God's house as a servant, to testify to the things that were to be spoken later."

29. Cf. Phil. 4:3; Apoc. 17:8.

30. The words παρά τε βασιλέως in Paris. gr. 1301, fol. 93^v are reproduced in Banduri (p. 945), but omitted in the Migne reprint.

31. Luke 9:62: "Jesus said to him, 'No one who puts his hand to the plow and looks back is fit for the kingdom of God'."

32. Paris. gr. 1301, fol. 94^r ταύτην is omitted by Banduri (p. 945).

33. Cf. 1 John 2:19.

34. Matt. 16:18: "And I tell you, you are Peter, and on this rock I will build my church, and the powers of death shall not prevail against it."

35. Paris. gr. 1301, fol. 94^v: φρόνημα; Banduri (p. 945): φρονήσεως.

36. Paris. gr. 1301, fol. 94^v: ὅτι; Banduri (p. 945): ἔτι.

37. Banduri (p. 945) has omitted the words ἐπήγαγον ψῆφον ἐπάγομεν καὶ ἡμεῖς (Paris. gr. 1301, fol. 94^v); without these the text makes little sense.

38. Paris. gr. 1301, fol. 94^v has εἰ, not εἰς (Banduri, p. 945).

39. John of Damascus, De fide orthodoxa, in Kotter, Die Schriften des Johannes von Damaskos II, 36 (= PG 94.849B): "He Himself [the Father], then, is mind, the depth of reason, begetter of the Word, and, through the Word, projector of the manifesting Spirit."

40. This is the sentence which the commission (set up after June 1289) decided to excise from the text. This decision, however, was probably not carried out, for the manuscript tradition has preserved the text in its original form only, without any suppression.

41. John of Damascus, De fide orthodoxa, in Kotter, Die Schriften des Johannes von Damaskos II, 36 (= PG 94-849B)

42. Ibid., 30 (= PG 94-832B).

43 Paris. gr. 1301, fol. 95^v: οὕτω; Banduri (p. 946): ὄντως.

44. The sentence which the monk Mark chose to elaborate upon in his commentary, the synod of bishops later demanded a retraction of his confusing explanation. See above, Chapter 7.

45. Gregory of Nazianzus, Oratio 34, PG 36.252A; cf. also Mouzalon's use and explanation of this proof-text, in PG 142.293A-B.

46. Cf. Maximus the Confessor, Letter 7: To John the Presbyter, PG 91.436A.

47. Basil, locus incognitus.

48. Banduri (p. 946) omits the clause in parentheses: ἢ γεννᾷ καὶ δεῖ τὸ γεννῶν ἄτομον (Paris. gr. 1301, fol. 97r); other manuscripts substitute δὴ for the word δεῖ.

49. On this section, cf. John of Damascus, De fide orthodoxa, in Kotter, Die Schriften des Johannes von Damaskos, II, 27 (= PG 94.825A-B).

50. Paris. gr. 1301, fol. 97^v: πρῶτα; Banduri (p. 947): ἄρα τά.

51. Immediate or primordial cause: προκαταρκτικὴ αἰτία; cf. Basil, On the Holy Spirit, PG 32.136B.

52. Paris. gr. 1301, fol. 98^r: διὰ τοῦ; Banduri (p. 947): δι᾿ αὐτοῦ.

53. For the use of the phrase in patristic literature, see G. W. H. Lampe, A Patristic Greek Lexicon (Oxford, 1961-1968), fasc. 4, 1080.

54. Cf. Patriarch Philotheos' words in Against Gregoras, PG 151.916D: "And this divine splendor and grace, this energy and gift of the all-Holy Spirit, is called Holy Spirit by Scripture...for we call 'sun' not only the solar disk, but the splendor and energy sent forth from there."

55. Paris. gr. 1301, fol. 99^r: πατρικάς; Banduri (p. 947): πνευματικάς.

56. Paris. gr. 1301, fol. 99^r: ἐκβιάζουσι; Banduri (p. 947): ἐκβιβάζουσιν.

57. Banduri (p. 948) adds ἀλλά; the word, which is unnecessary, is not found in Paris. gr. 1301, fol. 99^v.

58. Cf. Matt. 13:24-30.

59. Luke 3:7: "He said therefore to the multitudes that came out to be baptized by him, 'You brood of vipers! Who warned you to flee from the wrath to come?'"

60. Paris. gr. 1301, fol. 100^v: ἐχρῆν; omitted by Banduri (p. 948).

61. Banduri (p. 948) adds καί; the word is not found in Paris. gr. 1301, fol. 100^v. This section, beginning with "But we cannot" and continuing to the end of the *Tomus*, is quoted verbatim by Gennadius Scholarius in his *Second Treatise on the Procession of the Holy Spirit*; see L. Petit et al. (edd.), *Œuvres complètes de Gennade Scholarios*, II (Paris, 1929), 424-26. The patriarch here draws the threads of his argument together, and summarizes the reasons for the rejection of the Union of Lyons. Gennadius was particularly anxious to show that the Church had indeed solemnly and formally rejected the decision of 1274 and the dogmatization of the *Filioque*. Hence his lengthy quotation.

62. Paris. gr. 1301, fol. 101^r: καὶ εἰρήνην; Banduri (p. 948) omits the words.

63. Paris. gr. 1301, fol. 101^r: καί; Banduri (p. 948): ἤ.

64. Paris. gr. 1301, fol. 101^v: μένειν; Banduri (p. 948): μέν.

65. Paris. gr. 1301, fol. 101^v: καὶ ὅσοι τὸ μετὰ ταῦτα τελοῦσιν; Banduri (p. 948) omits the phrase.

66. Paris. gr. 1301, fol. 102^r: ὑμῖν; Banduri (p. 948): ἡμῖν.

67. Acts 2:21: "The sun shall be turned into darkness and the moon into blood, before the day of the Lord comes, the great and manifest day."

68. Luke 15:11-32

II

MARK'S *REPORT* TO THE SYNOD

The original Greek text of Atheniensis 1217, fols. 174^r-176^v, was first published with an introduction in *Greek, Roman, and Byzantine Studies*, 16, No. 2 (1975) 227-39. The English translation given here appeared in *The Greek Orthodox Theological Review*, 21, No. 2 (1976), 147-57. Along with this translation, a number of additions to the apparatus of the edited Greek text were also suggested for greater clarification and understanding. It has already been pointed out in the narrative that the missing folios at the end are not a recent development; J. Sakkelion had noted this fact some ninety years ago in his catalogue of the manuscripts of the National Library of Greece.

Mark's Report to the Synod

1. Your Lordships: On reading a certain passage of the patriarch's *Tomus*, it seemed to me that he had made a distinction in the term procession (ἐκ-πορεύεσθαι) between the eternal manifestation (ἔκφανσις ἀΐδιος) and the procession (πρόοδος) pure and simple of the Holy Spirit as it emerges into being. And I understood him to say that in some of the writings of the saints its eternal manifestation through the Son is indicated by the word "procession," while the procession pure and simple is not so indicated.[1] Because I assumed a double meaning here in the word "procession, I called the term "ambiguous" (ὁμώνυμον), as my own commentary indicates. And if he said, as he is now saying, that the phrase "through the Son" denotes the eternal manifestation apart from the term "procession," why did he add the word "here"? For where else does the phrase "through the Son," alone and without the term "procession," denote the existence of the Holy Spirit, so that one can say that, even if, in others, the phrase "through the Son" denotes the existence of the Holy Spirit, "here" nevertheless it denotes what he called the manifestation?[2] His concern was not (I repeat, not) with the phrase "through the Son" alone, but with the term "procession," which he said means "here's the eternal manifestation through the Son, the word "here" indicating that elsewhere the word "procession" denotes a process by which the Holy Spirit emerges into being, even though "here" it denotes the eternal manifestation. For otherwise what is the meaning of the term "here," put in the middle?

2. Having understood thus the meaning of this phrase, I wrote as on a pious foundation my previously read commentary; and I accepted, or so I thought, the [*Tomus*] of the patriarch and his celebrated literary style as an indisputable witness that I had not strayed from the correct path. Nor was my previously written commentary composed as some kind of novelty, nor as an attempt to lead people astray to an alien doctrine (God forbid !), but as an attempt, supposedly, at agreement with the patriarchal *Tomus*. For this reason, I brought the commentary to the patriarch, who deigned to receive it, and thus, by his permission, it was eventually shown to some others. But since the divine and holy synod has proscribed the commentary, I am first to reject it with all my heart and will give such proof of my rejection as you wish it to have.

3. If the procession of the all-Holy Spirit is susceptible to double interpretation (ὁμώνυμος) [then] this does not mean its [hypostatic] characteristic and mode of existence, but if the procession is the [hypostatic] characteristic and mode of existence of the all-Holy Spirit, which it is, in fact, then its procession is not ambiguous at all. For a characteristic always and uniquely belongs to that thing of which it is a characteristic, whereas the term "ambiguous" is the general name of many and different things, both by definition and by general description; thus, the two are mismatched and incompatible. For the characteristic of something is not ambiguous, while that which is ambiguous in nature is not a characteristic at all.

4. Who of the holy Fathers ever said anywhere that the procession of the all-Holy Spirit denotes wholly the manifesting emanation, the shining forth, and energy, and not the hypostasis and mode of existence of the all-Holy Spirit? If this is so, then Macedonius is again free to speak and deny the all-Holy Spirit's mode of existence; to whom Gregory the Theologian said, "Tell me, what position will you assign to that which proceeds, which has appeared between the two terms of your division, and is introduced by a better theologian than you, our Savior Himself? Or, perhaps, you have taken that word out of your gospels according to your third Testament, 'The Holy Spirit, which proceeds from the Father';' which, inasmuch as it proceeds from that source, is no creature; and, inasmuch as it is not generated, is no Son; and, inasmuch as it is between the unbegotten and the begotten, is God. And. thus, escaping the dangers of your syllogisms, it has manifested itself as God, stronger than your divisions."[4] And again, "The very fact of being unbegotten, and begotten, and proceeding, has given the name of Father to the first, of Son to the second, and, to the third, of which we are speaking, of Holy Spirit, that the distinction of the

three hypostases may be preserved in the one nature and dignity of the god-head."[5] For if the procession of the all-Holy Spirit is ambiguous, and it is identical in meaning to the Son's generation, surely the latter, too, would have an ambiguous meaning, and, hence, Arius would be revived. If on the other hand, the Son's generation is not ambiguous in meaning, neither is the procession of the all-Holy Spirit; for causalities—as a result of their initial and natural cause—are identical, each according to its own hypostatic characteristic and mode of existence, the Son by generation, the Holy Spirit by procession.

5. Who among Orthodox Christians—let alone those who have been bred on ecclesiastical and divine doctrine—have uttered the insane notion that the generation of the Son and the procession of the all-Holy Spirit is not from the Father, or that the Son and the Holy Spirit do not proceed or are generated together? The holy Tarasius, theologizing boldly, confesses thus at the great and holy seventh council, "I believe in one God, the Father almighty, and in one lord Jesus Christ, the Son of God and our God, begotten of His Father timelessly and eternally; and in the Holy Spirit, the Lord and giver of life, who proceeds from the Father through the Son, which, too, is and is acknowledged God, Trinity consubstantial, equal in honor, co-equal, eternal, uncreated, creator of all things created, one principle, one godhead and dominion, one kingdom and power and authority in three hypostases, divided indivisibly and conjoined dividedly; 'not as from three imperfect [principles], one perfect, but as from three perfect [principles], one supremely perfect and beyond perfection,' as the great Dionysius said.[6] So that, from the point of view of the persons' [hypostatic] characteristic, there are three who are worshipped, while, from the point of view of the common essence, it is one God."[7] The holy Maximus exclaims, "Just as the Holy Spirit, in its essence, subsists naturally of God the Father, so, in its essence, it is naturally of the Son, for, in terms of essence, it proceeds ineffably from the Father through the begotten Son."[8]

6. What do you [Gregory] say? Do the holy Fathers here [in the passages just quoted] confess the hypostasis of the all-Holy Spirit when they say that the Holy Spirit proceeds through the Son, or do they denote the Spirit's manifesting emanation, brightness, and energy? Speak on this in the name of truth itself, and do not hide the truth. For if what proceeds is the manifesting emanation and brightness *through* the Son, it also proceeds *from* the Son. It follows that, in your view, procession through the Son is procession from the Son—which is where Beccus' evil falsehood finds its strength. For he obstinately affirms that what proceeds "through the Son" is the equivalent of pro-

ceeding "from the Son," bringing the discussion to a question of existence. Clearly, he accepts procession from the Son, and your statement strongly confirms what we wish to abolish. Who among the holy Fathers known for their piety ever said anywhere that the procession of the Holy Spirit "through the Son" does not denote the personal procession of the all-Holy Spirit as it emerges into being, but its manifesting brightness and energy? If one of the holy Fathers said this, show or prove it and we will accept it. If on the other hand, none of the holy Fathers said this anywhere, then you should abandon such useless explanations. For nowise does it contradict Beccus' most abominable profession; on the contrary, it confirms it.

7. As for a true refutation of Beccus, it is this. If those who contend that the Holy Spirit proceeds "through" the Son, or any one else among the holy Fathers had said that it also proceeds "from" the Son, then, perhaps, you would be justified in saying and professing that "through the Son" is equivalent to "from the Son." But since absolutely no one of the holy Fathers said this, you vainly deceive yourself saying "the phrase 'the Holy Spirit proceeds from the Father through the Son' is the equivalent of 'from the Son'."[9] Also, those who say that "the Father, through the Son, is Projector of the Holy Spirit" is equivalent to the phrase "the Holy Spirit proceeds from the Father through the Son" should know that this is not true.[10] For the phrase "the Holy Spirit proceeds from the Father through the Son" plainly denotes the unity (conjoining) and equality of the Son and the Holy Spirit, the two causalities. But if someone said that the Father's being Projector of the Holy Spirit through the Son is equivalent to procession of the Holy Spirit from the Father through the Son, he would clearly teach that the unity and equality of the Son and Projector amounts to two causes. For if "through the Son" is added to the causality, that is, the Holy Spirit, it clearly represents the unity and equality of the two causalities;[11] if, however, it is added to the cause, that is, the Projector, it teaches clearly the unity and equality of the Son and the Projector as being two causes, which would be absurd. For the phrase "the Holy Spirit proceeds through the Son" denotes that it proceeds in unity and equality with the Son. The phrase "the Father, through the Son, is the Projector..."

NOTES

1.   *Tomus, PG* 142.241A: "If, in fact, it is also said by some of the saints that the Spirit proceeds 'through the Son,' what is meant here is the eternal manifestation of the Spirit by the Son of the purely [personal] emanation into being of the Spirit, which has its existence from the Father."

2. The text here is not clear; the translation is based on the deletion of σημαίνει.

3. John 15:26.

4. *De Spiritu Sancto* (Oratio 5), A. J. Mason (ed.), *The Five Theological Orations of Gregory Nazianzus* (Cambridge, 1899), 154-55 (= *PG* 36.141A-B).

5. Ibid., 156 (= *PG* 36.141D-142A).

6. *Locus incognitus*; but cf. *De Divinis Nominibus* 2.10, in S. Lilla, "Il testo tachigrafico del 'De Divinis Nominibus', *Studi e Testi*, 263 (1970), 65 (= *PG* 3.648C): ἀτελὴς δὲ ἐν τοῖς τελείοις ὡς ὑπερτελὴς καὶ προτέλειος.

7. Tarasius, *Epistola ad Summos Sacerdotes*, in Mansi, XII, 1122 (= *PG* 98.1461C-D).

8. Maximus the Confessor, *Quaestiones ad Thalassium*, *PG* 90.672C.

9. Cf. Pachymeres, I, 481; Beccus' letter to Pope John XXI, in A. Theiner and F. Miklosich (edd.), *Monumenta spectantia ad unionem ecclesiarum graecae et romanae* (Vienna, 1872), p. 24; and Beccus, *On the Union of the Churches of Old and New Rome*, *PG* 141.61D.

10. The passage here is obviously a reference to the Damascene *testimonium* in *De fide orthodoxa*; see B. Kotter (ed.), *Die Schriften des Johannes von Damaskos*, II (Patristische Texte und Studien, 12; Berlin, 1973), 36 (= *PG* 94.849B); Pachymeres, II, 31.

11. Cf. Athanasius, *Quaestiones aliae*, *PG* 28.784c: λοιπὸν γίνωσκε, ὅτι ὁ Πατὴρ μόνος ἐστὶν αἴτιος· ὁ δὲ Υἱὸς οὐκ ἔστιν αἴτιος, ἀλλ᾽ αἰτιατός. ὥστε μὲν αἴτιός ἐστι μόνος ὁ Πατήρ. τὰ δὲ αἰτιατὰ δύο, ὁ Υἱὸς καὶ τὸ Πνεῦμα.

BIBLIOGRAPHY

The following bibliography is a select one, and does not include all general works, basic histories, handbooks, or reference works on the thirteenth century. The list includes primarily those works and articles which have made a significant contribution to the preparation of this book. In short, it is intended to do no more than identify the principal titles cited in the notes. Many works which are not directly connected with the main subject are omitted. Likewise, titles within an author's *Opera omnia* and their various editions are not always cited. Extensive bibliographies can be found in H.-G. Beck, *Kirche und theologische Literatur im byzantinischen Reich* (Munich, 1959).

Collections, Manuals, Registers

Allatius, Leo. *De Ecclesiae occidentales atque orientates perpetua consensione libri tres.* Cologne, 1648.

_____. *Graeciae orthodoxae scriptures,* I-II. Rome, 1652-1659.

Banduri, A. *Imperium Orientale sive Antiquitates Constantinopolitanae,* I-II. Paris, 1711.

Beck, H.-G, et al. *Die mittelalterliche Kirche.* Vol. III, pt. 2 of *Handbuch der Kirchengeschichte,* ed. H. Jedin. Freiburg, 1968.

_____. *Kirche und theolo-ische Literatur im byzantinischen Reich.* Munich, 1959.

Boissonade, J.-F. *Anecdota Graeca e codicibus regiis,* I-V. Paris, 1829-1833.

The Cambridge Medieval History, Vol. IV rev. ea., ed. J. M. Hussey, pt. I: *Byzantium and its Neighbors*; pt. II: *Government, Church and Civilization.* Cambridge, 1966—1967.

Cotelier, J.-B. *Ecclesiae graecae monumenta,* III. Paris, 1686.

Darrouzès, J. *Documents inédits d'ecclésiologie Byzantine.* Archives de l'Orient Chrétien, 9. Paris, 1966.

_____. *Recherches sur les Ὀφφίκια de l'Église Byzantine.* Archives de l'Orient Chrétien, II. Paris, 1970.

Delorme, F. M., and A. L. Tautu. *Acta Romanorum pontificum ab Innocentio V ad Benedictum XI (1276-1304).* Pontificia commissio ad redigendum codicem iuris canonici orientalis, Fontes, series III, vol. V, tom. II. Vatican City, 1954.

Demetracopoulos, A. *History of the Schism.* Leipzig, 1866 (in Greek).

———. *Orthodox Greece.* Leipzig, 1872 (in Greek).

Dölger, F. *Regesten der Kaiserurkunden des oströmischen Reiches 565-1453,* pt. 3: *Regesten von 1204-1282;* pt. 4: *Regesten von 1282-1341.* Corpus der griechischen Urkunden des Mittelalters und der neueren Zeit. Munich-Berlin, 1932, 1960.

Fabricius, J. A. *Bibliotheca Graeca sive notitia scriptorum veterum Graecorum,* VIII. Hamburg, 1802.

Gay, J. *Les Registres de Nicholas III (1277-1280).* Bibliothèque des Écoles Françaises d'Athènes et de Rome. Paris, 1898ff.

Grumel, V. *La chronologie.* Bibliothèque byzantine: Traité d'études byzantines, I. Paris, 1958.

Hefele, C. J., and H. Leclercq. *Histoire les conciles d'après les documents originaux,* VI, pt. 1. Paris, 1914.

Janin, R. *La géographie ecclésiastique de l'empire byzantin,* pt. I: *Le siège de Constantinople et le patriarcat œcuménique,* vol. III: *Les églises et les monastères.* Paris, 1953.

Jugie, M. *Theologia dogmatica Christianorum orientalium ab Ecclesia Catholica dissidentium,* 5 vols. Paris, 1926-1935.

Knowles, D., and D. Obolensky. *The Middle Ages.* Vol. II of *The Christian Centuries: A New History of the Catholic Church,* edd. L. Rogier et al. New York, 1969.

Krumbacher, K. *Geschichte der byzantinischen Literatur (527-1453).* Munich, 1897.

Lampe, G. W. H. *A Patristic Greek Lexicon.* Oxford, 1961-1968.

Laurent, V., and J. Darrouzès, edd. *Dossier Grec de l'Union de Lyon 1273-1277.* Archives de l'Orient Chrétien, 16. Paris, 1976.

Laurent, V., ed. *Les regestes des actes du Patriarcat de Constantinople,* I: *Les actes des patriarches,* fasc. 4: *Les regestes de 1208 à 1309.* Institut français d'études byzantines. Paris, 1971.

Mansi, J. D. *Sacrorum conciliorum nova et amplissima collectio.* Florence-Venice, 1759-1798.

Migne, J.-P. *Patrologiae cursus completus, Series graeca,* 161 vols. Paris, 1857-1866.

———. *Patrologiae cursus completus, Series latina,* 221 vols. Paris, 1844-1855.

Miklosich, F., end d. Müller, edd. *Acta et diplomata Graeca medii aevi sacra et profana,* 6 vols. Vienna, 1860-1890.

Pauly, A. F. von. *Real-Encyclopädie der classischen Altertumswissenschaft.* Vienna, 1837-1852; edd. G. Wissowa, W. Kroll, et al. Stuttgart, 1893ff.

Rhalles, G. A., and Potles, M. *Constitution of the Divine and Holy Canons,* 6 vols. Athens, 1852-1859 (in Greek).

Raynaldus,O. *Annales ecclesiastici,* XXII. Bar-le-Duc, 1870.

Tautu, A. L. *Acta Urbani IV, Clementis IV, Gregorii X (1261-1276).* Pontificia commissio ad redigendum codicem iuris canonici orientalis, Fontes, series III, vol. V, tom. I. Vatican City, 1953.

Theiner, A., and F. Miklosich, edd. *Monumenta spectantia ad unionem ecclesiarum graecae et romanae.* Vienna, 1872.

Trapp, E. *Prosopographisches Lexicon der Palaiologenzeit,* I. Vienna, 1976.

Wolter, H., and H. Holstein. *Lyon I et Lyon II.* Vol. VII of *Histoire des Conciles Œcuméniques,* ed. G. Dumeige. Paris, 1966.

Manuscript Sources

Akindynus, Gregory. *Against Palamas,* V: codex Monacensis gr. 223, fols. 197v-236r; *Against Palamas,* VII: codex Monacensis gr. 223, fols. 313v-363v.

Anonymous. Work against the *Tomus* and Beccus: codex Coislinianus 192, fols. 67r-74v.

Mark, the Monk. *Report* to the synod: codex Atheniensis 1217, fols. 174r-176v.

Meliteniotes, Constantine. Refutation of the *Tomus:* codex Parisinus gr. 1303, fols. 83r-143v.

Mouzalon, Theodore. Antirrhetic against Beccus' blasphemies: codex Chigiana gr. 12, fols. 38v—46r.

Printed Sources

Acropolites, George. *Georgii Acropolitae opera,* I-II, ed. A. Heisenberg. Leipzig, 1903.

Athanasius I, patriarch of Constantinople. *The Correspondence of Athanasius I, Patriarch of Constantinople: Letters to the Emperor Andronicus, Members of the Imperial Family, and Officials.* ed. A.-M. Maffry Talbot. Dumbarton Oaks Texts, 2. Washington, D.C., 1975.

Beccus, John. *PG* 141: this volume (it reproduces most of Allatius' edition) contains all of the unionist patriarch's major works.

Blemmydes, Nicephorus. *Nicephori Blemmydae vitae et carmina,* ed. A. Heisenberg. Leipzig, 1896.

Gennadius, George Scholarius. *Œuvres complètes de Gennade Scholarios,* edd. L. Petit, S. A. Sideridès, M. Jugie, 8 vols. Paris, 1928-1936.

Gregoras, Nicephorus. *Byzantina Historia.* I-III, edd. L. Schopen and I. Bekker (Bonn: Corpus Scriptorum Historiae Byzantinae, 1829-1855).

Gregory II of Cyprus. *PG* 142.1-470: the patriarch's major theological output *(Tomus, Confession, Apology,* etc.) is found in this volume; it also includes his *Eulogies* on Michael VIII and on Andronicus II Palaeologus, and several hagiographic compositions (Ss. George, Marina, John the Baptist, etc.). Also reproduced are the texts of Allatius, M. de Rubeis, and Banduri concerning Gregory.

_____. *Eulogies* on Michael VIII and on Andronicus II: J.-F. Boissonade, *Anecdota Graeca e codicibus regis,* I (Paris, 1829),313-93.

_____. *On the Procession of the Holy Spirit* (Russian translation): I. E. Troitskij, *Khristianskoe Chtenie,* 69, pt. I (1889), 288-352.

_____. *Tomus* (Russian translation): I. E. Troitskij, *Khristianskoe Chtenie,* 69, Pt. I (1889), 344-66.

_____. *Correspondence:* S. Eustratiades, *Ekklesiastikos Pharos,* 1 (1908), 77-108, 409-39; 2 (1908), 195-211; 3 (1909), 5-48, 281-86; 4 (1909), 5-29, 97-128; 5 (1910), 213-26, 339-52, 444-52, 489-500. See also a list of letters in *PG* 142.421-431.

_____. *Autobiography:* with French translation inW. Lameere, *La tradition manuscrite le la correspondance de Grégoire de Chypre* (Brussels-Paris, 1937), 176-91; Russian translation: I. E. Troitskij, *Khristianskoe Chtenie,* 50, pt. I (1870), 164-77.

Joseph Calothetus. *Vita Athanasii,* ed. A. Pantocratorinus, *Thrakika,* 13 (1940), 56-107.

Meliteniotes, Constantine. On *the Procession of the Holy Spirit Through the Son. Oratio I. PG* 141.

Metochites, George. *Historia dogmatica,* ed. A. Mai, *Patrum novae bibliothecae,* VIII, pt. 2 (Books I-II); Rome, 1871. X, pt. 1 (Book III); Rome, 1905.

Pachymeres, George. *De Michaele et Andronico Palaeologis libri tredecim,* I-II, ed. I. Bekker (Bonn: Corpus Scriptorum Historiae Byzantinae, 1835).

_____. *Quadrivium de Georges Pachymère.* Studi e Testi, 94. Vatican City, 1940.

Photius, patriarch of Constantinople. *Mystagogy. PG* 102.280-391.

Syropoulos, Sylvester. *Les "Mémoires" du Grand Ecclésiarque de l'Église de Constantinople Sylvestre Syropoulos,* ed. V. Laurent. Concilium Florentinum Documenta et Scriptores, series B, vol. IX. Rome, 1971.

Secondary Works

Académie Internationale des Sciences Religieuses. *L'Esprit Saint et l'Église.* Actes du symposium organisé par l'Académie Internationale des Sciences Religieuses. Paris, 1969.

Actes du Colloque international du Centre National de la Recherche Scientifique: 1274, Année charnière. Mutations et continuités (Lyon-Paris 30 sept.-5 oct. 1974) Paris, 1977.

Aigrain, R. "Andronic de Sardis," *Dictionnaire d'Histoire et de Géographie ecclésiastiques,* 2 (Paris, 1914), cols. 1774-1776.

Alberigo, G. "L'œcuménisme au moyen âge," *Revue d'histoire ecclésiastique,* 71, nos. 3-4 (1976), 365-91.

Anastasiou, J. E., ed. *The Holy Spirit.* Thessalonika, 1971 (in Greek).

Andersen, C. "Geschichte der abendländischen Konzile des Mittelalters," in *Die ökumenischen Konzile der Christenheit,* ed. H. J. Margull (Stuttgart, 1961), 75-200.

Angold, M. *A Byzantine Government in Exile.* Oxford, 1975.

Barvinok, M. V.-J. *Nicephorus Blemmydes and his Works.* Kiev, 1911 (in Russian).

Bees, N. A. "Joseph Calothetus and a List of His Works," *Byzantinische Zeitschrift,* 17 (1908), 86-91 (in Greek).

Bolides, Th. "Die Schriften des Georgios Moschampar und der Codex Alexandrinus 285," *Bulletin de l'Institut Archéologique Bulgare,* 9 (1935) (= Actes du IVe Congrès international des études byzantines), 259-68.

Boularand, E. "L'argument patristique au concile de Florence, dans la question de la procession du Saint-Esprit," *Bulletin de littérature ecclésiastique,* 63 (1962), 161-99.

Bréhier, L. "Andronic II," *Dictionnaire d'Histoire et de Géographie ecclésiastiques,* 2 (Paris, 1914), cols. 1782-1785.

_____. "Attempts at Reunion of the Greek and Latin Churches," *The Cambridge Medieval History,* IV, edd. J. R. Tanner et al. (New York, 1923), 594-626.

_____. "Notes sur l'histoire de l'enseignement supérieur à Constantinople," *Byzantion,* 3 (1926-1927), 73-94.

_____. "Jean XI Beccos," *Dictionnaire d'Histoire et de Géographie ecclésiastiques,* 7 (Paris, 1934), cols. 354-364.

_____. "L'enseignement classique et l'enseignement religieux à Byzance," *Revue d'histoire et de philosophie religieuses,* 21 (1941), 34-69.

_____. "Le recrutement des patriarches de Constantinople pendant la période byzantine," *Actes du VIe Congrès international des études byzantines* (Paris, 1950), 221-28.

_____. *Le monde byzantin,* I: *Vie et mort de Byzance;* II: *Les institutions de l'empire byzantin,* III: *La civilisation byzantine.* Paris, 1969-1970.

Browning, R. "The Patriarchal School at Constantinople in the Twelfth Century," *Byzantion,* 32 (1962), 167-202; 33 (1963), 11-40.

Bryer, A. "Cultural Relations Between East and West in the Twelfth Century," *Relations Between East and West in the Middle Ages*, ed. D. Baker (Edinburgh, 1973), 77-94.

Camelot, T. "La tradition latine sur la procession du St. Esprit 'a Filio' ou 'ab utroque'," *Russie et Chrétienté*, 3-4 (1950), 179-92.

Candal, E. "Filioque," *Enciclopedia Cattolica*, 5 (Vatican City, 1950), 1298-1299.

_____. "Progresso dogmatico nelle definizioni trinitarie del Concilio II di Lione e del Fiorentino," *Divinitas*, 5, fasc. 2 (1966), 324-44.

Candal, M. "Nueva interpretación del 'per Filium' de los Padres Griegos," *Orientalia Christiana Periodica*, 31 (1965), 5-20.

Cayré, F. "Georges de Chypre," *Dictionnaire de Théologie Catholique*, 6, pt. 1 (Paris, 1920), cols. 1231-1235.

Charitakis, G. "Catalogue of the Dated Codices of the Patriarchal Library of Cairo," *Epeteris Hetaireias Byzantinon Spoudon*, 4 (1927), 109-204 (in Greek).

Chevalier, I. S. *Augustin et la pensée grecque: Les relations trinitaires*. Fribourg, 1940.

Clément, O. "Le schisme entre l'Orient et l'Occident chrétiens et les tentatives d'union au moyen âge," *Messager de l'Exarchat du Patriarche russe en Europe occidentale*, 72-73 (1971), 24-46; 75-76 (1971), 171-90.

_____. "Grégoire de Chypre 'De l'ekporèse du Saint Esprit'," *Istina*, 3-4 (1972), 443-56.

"Concerning the Holy Spirit," *Eastern Churches Quarterly*, 7 (1948). A symposium on the *Filioque*.

Congar, Y. "Quatre siècles de désunion et d'affrontement. Comment Grecs et Latins se sont appréciés réciproquement au point de vue ecclésiologique," *Istina*, 13 (1968), 131-52.

_____. "1274-1974: Structures ecclésiales et conciles dans les relations entre Orient et Occident," *Revue des sciences philosophiques et théologiques*, 58 (1974), 355-90.

Cousin, L. *Histoire de Constantinople depuis le règne de l'ancien Justin jusqu'à la fin de l'Empire*. Paris, 1673.

Darrouzès, J. "Grégoire II (Georges de Chypre)," *Dictionnaire de Spiritualité*, 6 (Paris, 1967), 922-23.

Demetracopoulos, A. K. *History of the Schism*. Leipzig, 1867 (in Greek).

_____. *Orthodox Greece*. Leipzig, 1872 (in Greek).

Dondaine, A. "'Contra Graecos.' Premiers écrits polémiques des dominicains d'Orient," *Archivum Fratrum Praedicatorum*, 21 (1951), 432-46.

Dräseke, J. "Der Kircheneinigungsversuch des Kaisers Michael VIII Paläologos," *Zeitschrift für wissenschaftliche Theologie*, 34 (1891), 325-35.

_____. "Johannes Bekkos und seine theologischen Zeitgenossen," *Neue kirchliche Zeitschrift*, 18 (1907), 877-94.

_____. "Zur Friedensschrift des Patriarchen Johannes Bekkos," *Zeitschrift für wissenschaftliche Theologie*, 50 (1907), 231-53.

Ducellier, A. "Mentalité historique et realités politiques: L' Islam et les Musulmans vus par les byzantins du XIIIe siècle," *Byzantinische Forschungen*, 4 (1972), 31-63.

Dvornik, F. *The Photian Schism: History and Legend.* Cambridge, Mass., 1948.

Eustratiades, S. "The Letters of Gregory of Cyprus: Prolegomena," *Ekilesiastikos Pharos*, 1 (1908), 77-106 (in Greek).

_____. "The Patriarch Arsenius Autorianus (1255-1260 and 1261-1267)," *Hellenika*, 1 (1928), 78-94 (in Greek).

Evdokirnov, P. *L'Esprit Saint dans la tradition Orthodoxe.* Paris, 1969.

_____. "L'Esprit Saint et l'Église d'après la tradition liturgique," *L'Esprit Saint et l Église* (Paris, 1969), 85-111.

Evert-Kappesowa, H. "La société byzantine et l'union de Lyon," *Byzantinoslavica*, 10 (1949), 28-41

_____. "Une page de l'histoire des relations byzantino-latines. Le clergé byzantin et l'union de Lyon (1274-1282)," *Byzantinoslavica*, 13 (1952-1953), 68-92.

_____. "Une page des relations byzantino-latines, I: Byzance et le Saint Siège à l'époque de l'union de Lyon," *Byzantinoslavica*, 16 (1955), 297-317.

_____. "Une page de l'histoire des relations byzantino-latines, II: La fin de l'union de Lyon," *Byzantinoslavica*, 17 (1956), 1-18.

Failler, A. "Le séjour d'Athanase II d'Alexandrie à Constantinople," *Revue des études byzantines*, 35 (1977), 43-71.

Fatouros, F. "Textkritische Beobachtungen zu den Briefen des Gregorios Kyprios," *Rivista di studi bizantini e neoellenici*, N.S. 12-13 (1975-1976), 109-16.

Fliche, A. "Le problème oriental au second concile œcuménique de Lyon (1274)," *Orientalia Christiana Periodica*, 13 (1947) (= *Miscellaneae G. de Jerphanion*), 475-85.

Franchi, A. *Il Concilio II di Lione (1274) secondo la Ordinatio concilii generalis Lugdunensis, Edizione del testo e note.* Rome, 1965.

Fuchs, F. *Die höheren Schulen von Konstantinopel im Mittelalter.* Leipzig, 1926.

Garzya, A. "Observations sur l'Autobiographie Grégoire de Chypre," *Praktika tou Protou Diethnous Kyprologikou Synedriou*, Medieval Section, II (Leukosia, 1972), 33-36.

Geanakoplos, D. J. "Michael VIII Palaeologus and the Union of Lyons," *Harvard Theological Review*, 46 (1953), 79-89.

_____. "On the Schism of the Greek and Roman Churches: A Confidential Papal Directive for the Implementation of Union (1278)," *The Greek Orthodox Theological Review,* 1 (1954), 16-24.

_____. *Emperor Michael Palaeologus and the West, 1258-1282.* Cambridge, Mass., 1959.

_____. "Bonaventura, the Two Mendicant Orders and the Greeks at the Council of Lyons (1274)," *Studies in Church History,* 13, ed. D. Baker (Oxford, 1976), 183-211.

Giannelli, C. "Le récit d'une mission diplomatique de Georges le Métochite et le Vat. Gr. 1716," in M.-H. Laurent, *Le Bienheureux Innocent V (Pierre de Tarentaise) et son temps.* Studi e Testi, 129. Vatican City, 1947.

Gill, J. *The Council of Florence.* Cambridge, Mass., 1959.

_____. "Emperor Andronicus II and Patriarch Athanasius I," *Byzantina,* 2 (1970), 12-19.

_____. "Innocent III and the Greeks: Aggressor or Apostle?" in *Relations Between East and West in the Middle Ages,* ed. D. Baker (Edinburgh, 1973),95-108.

_____. "The Church Union of the Council of Lyons (1274) Portrayed in Greek Documents," *Orientalia Christiana Periodica,* 40 (1974), 5-45.

_____. "John Beccus, Patriarch of Constantinople 1275-1282," *Byzantina,* 7 (1975), 253-66.

_____. "Notes on the De Michaele et Andronico Palaeologis of George Pachymeres," *Byzantinische Zeitschrift,* 68 (1975), 295-303.

_____. *Byzantium and the Papacy 1198-1400.* New Brunswick, N.J., 1979.

Golubovich, P. G. "Disputatio Latinorum et Graecorum seu relatio apocrisariorum Gregorii IX de gestis Nicaeae in Bithynia et Nymphaeae in Lydia," *Archivum Franciscanum Historicum,* 12 (1919), 419-70.

Gouillard, J. "Théolepte, métropolite de Philadelphie," *Dictionnaire de Théologie Catholique,* 15, pt. 1 (Paris, 1946), cols. 339-41.

_____. "Le Synodikon de l'Orthodoxie: édition et cornmentaire," *Travaux et mémoires,* 2 (1967), 1-316.

Grégoire, H. "Le schisme Arséniate et Nicéphore Calliste Xanthopoulos," *Byzantion,* 5 (1929-1930), 758-65.

Grégoire, J. "La relation éternelle de l'Esprit au Fils d'après les écrits de Jean de Damas," *Revue d'histoire ecclésiastique,* 64 (1969), 713-55.

Grumel, V. "Les ambassades pontificales à Byzance après le IIe concile de Lyon (1274-1280), *Échos d'Orient,* 23 (1924), 437-47.

_____. "En Orient après le IIe concile de Lyon, brèves notes d'histoire et de chronologie," *Échos d'Orient,* 24 (1925), 321-25.

_____. "Un ouvrage récent sur Jean Beccos, patriarche de Constantinople," *Échos d'Orient,* 24 (1925), 26-32.

_____. "Le IIe concile de Lyon et la réunion de l'église grecque," *Dictionnaire de Théologie Catholique,* 9, pt. 1 (Paris, 1926), cols. 1391-1410.

_____. "Saint Thomas et la doctrine des Grecs sur la procession du Saint-Esprit," *Échos d'Orient,* 25 (1926), 257-80.

_____. "Nicéphore Blemmidès et la procession du Saint-Esprit," *Revue des sciences philosophques et théologiques,* 18 (1931), 344-66.

_____. "Les aspects généraux de la théologie byzantine," *Échos d'Orient,* 30 (1931), 385-96.

_____. "Le patriarcat byzantin: De Michel Cérulaire à la conquête latine. Aspects généraux," *Revue des études byzantines,* 4 (1946), 257-63.

_____. "Photius et l'addition du 'Filioque' au symbole de Nicée-Constantinople," *Revue des études byzantines,* 5 (1947); 218-34.

Guilland, R. "Les Logothètes. Études sur l'histoire administrative de l'empire byzantin," *Revue des études byzantines,* 29 (1971), 5-115.

Guillou, M.-J. Le. "Filioque," *Catholicisme,* 4 (Paris, 1956), 1279-86.

_____. "Réflexions sur la théologie des Pères grecs en rapport avec le Filioque," *L'Esprit Saint et l'Église* (Paris, 1969), 195-219.

Harnack, A. *Lehrbuch derDogmengeschichte,* II. Tübingen, 1931.

Haugh, R. *Photius and the Carolingians: The Trinitarian Controversy.* Belmont, Mass., 1975.

Heath, R. G. "The Western Schism of the Franks and the 'Filioque'," *Journal of Ecclesiastical History,* 23, no. 2 (1972), 97-113.

Heisenberg, A. *Aus der Geschichte und Literatur der Palaiologenzeit.* Munich, 1920.

Hill, G. *A History of Cyprus,* III. Cambridge, 1948.

Hoffman, G. "Patriarch Johann Bekkos und die lateinische Kultur," *Orientalia Christiana Periodica,* 11 (1945), 141-64.

_____. "Johannes Damaskenos, Rom und Byzanz (1054-1500)," *Orientalia Christiana Periodica,* 16 (1950), 177-90.

Hunger, H. "Von Wissenschaft und Kunst der frühen Palaiologenzeit," *Jahrbuch der Österreichischen byzantinischen Gesellschaft,* 8 (1959), 123-55.

Irmscher, J. "Autobiographien in der byzantinischen Literatur," *Studia Byzantina,* II (Berlin, 1973) (= Berliner byzantinistische Arbeiten, 44), 3-11.

Joussard, G. "De quelques conséquences et particularités qu'a entrainées en patristique grecque l'adoption du genre florilège pour traiter l'argument de tradition," *Analecta Gregoriana,* 58 (1954), 17-25.

Jugie, M. "Bulletin de littérature byzantine: Nicéphore Blemmidès et ses écrits," *Échos d'Orient,* 17 (1914), 153-56.

_____. "Le nombre des conciles œcuméniques reconnus par l'Église gréco-russe et ses théologiens," *Échos d'Orient,* 18 (1916-1919), 305-20.

_____. *De processione Spiritus Sancti: Ex fontibus revelationis et secundum Orientales dissidentes.* Rome, 1936.

_____. "Les actes du Synode photien de Sainte-Sophie (879-880)," *Échos d'Orient,* 37 (1938), 89-99.

_____. "Origine de la controverse sur l'addition du 'Filioque' au Symbole," *Revue des sciences philosophiques et théologiques,* 28 (1939), 369-85.

_____. *Le Schisme byzantin. Aperçu historique et doctrinal.* Paris, 1941.

Karmiris, I. N. "The Latin Confession of Faith of 1274 Attributed to Michael VIII Palaeologus," *Archeion Ekklesiastikou kai Kanonikou Dikaiou,* 2 (1947), 127-47 (in Greek).

Kelly, J. N. D. *Early Christian Creeds.* London, 1960.

Kerr, R. "George Moschampar: New Light on the Transmission of One of His Chapters," *Résumés des communications, XVe Congrès international d'études byzantines* (Athens, 1976), no pagination.

Kugeas, S. "Zur Geschichte der Münchener Thukydides-Handschrift Augustanus F," *Byzantinische Zeitschrift,* 16 (1907), 588-609.

Laiou, A. E. *Constantinople and the Latins: The Foreign Policy of Andronicus II, 1282-1328.* Cambridge, Mass., 1972.

Lameere, W. *La tradition manuscrite de la correspondance de Grégoire de Chypre.* Brussels-Paris, 1937.

"La procession du Saint-Esprit," *Istina,* 3-4 (1972). A volume devoted to the procession of the Holy Spirit.

Laurent, M.-H. "Georges le Métochite ambassadeur de Michel VIII Paléologue auprès d'Innocent V," *Studi e Testi,* 123 (Vatican City, 1946) (= *Miscellanea Giovanni Mercati,* III), 136-56.

Laurent, V. "La date de la mort de Jean Bekkos," *Échos d'Orient,* 25 (1926), 316-19.

_____. "Le serment anti-Latin du patriarche Joseph Ier (juin 1273)," *Échos d'Orient*, 26 (1927), 396-407.

_____. "Les signataires du second synode des Blakhernes (été 1285)," *Échos d'Orient*, 26 (1927), 129-49.

_____. "Un polémiste grec de la fin du XIIIe siècle: La vie et les œuvres de Georges Moschabar," *Échos d'Orient*, 28 (1929), 129-58.

_____. "Théodore Mouzalon," *Dictionnaire de Théologie Catholique*, 10, pt. 2 (Paris, 1929), cols. 2582-84.

_____. "L'excommunication du patriarche Joseph Ier par son prédécesseur Arsène," *Byzantinische Zeitschrift*, 30 (1929-1930), 489-96.

_____. "Les manuscrits de l'histoire byzantine de Georges Pachymeres," *Byzantion*, 5 (1929-1930), 129-205.

_____. "La question des Arsénites," *Hellenika*, 3 (1930), 463-70.

_____. "Le cas de Photius dans l'apologétique du patriarche Jean XI Beccos (1275-1282) au lendernain du deuxième concile de Lyon," *Échos d'Orient*, 29 (1930), 396-415.

_____. "À propos de Georges Moschabar, polémiste antilatin. Notes et rectifications," *Échos d'Orient*, 35 (1936), 336-47.

_____. "Grégoire X et son projet de ligue antiturque," *Échos d'Orient*, 37 (1938), 257-73.

_____. "Les Actes du Synode photien et Georges le Métochite," *Échos d'Orient*, 37 (1938), 100-106.

_____. "La croisade et la question d'Orient sous le pontificlt de Grégoire X (1272-1276)," *Revue historique du sud-est européen*, 22 (1945), 105-37.

_____. "Les grandes crises religieuses à Byzance: La fin du schisme arsénite," *Bulletin de la Section Historique, Académie Roumaine*, 26, pt. 2 (1945), 225-313.

_____. "Le patriarche d'Antioche Cyrille II (29 juin 1287-c. 1308)," *Analecta Bollandiana*, 68 (1950), 310-17.

_____. "Un théologien unioniste de la fin du XXIIIe siècle: Le métropolite d'Adrianople Théoctiste," *Revue des études byzantines*, II (1953) (= *Mélanges Martin Jugie*), 187-96.

_____. "Les crises religieuses à Byzance: Le Schisme anti-arsénite du métropolite Théolepte de Philadelphie († c. 1324)," *Revue des études byzantines*, 18 (1960), 45-54.

_____. "Melanges: I. Les dates du second patriarcat de Joseph Ier (3I XII 1282-av. 26 IV 1283)," *Revue des études byzantines*, 18 (1960), 205-208.

_____. "La chronologie des patriarches de Constantinople au XIIIe siècle (1208-1309)," *Revue des études byzantines*, 27 (1969), 129-50.

_____. "Notes de chronologie et d'histoire byzantine de la fin du XIIIe siècle," *Revue des études byzantines*, 27 (1969), 209-28.

Loenertz, R.-J. "Théodore Métochite et son père," *Archivum Fratrum Praedicatorum*, 23 (1953), 184-94.

_____. "Mémoire d'Ogier, protonotaire, pour Marco et Marcheto nonces de Michel VIII Paléologue auprès du Pape Nicholas III. 1278 printemps-été," *Orientalia Christiana Periodica*, 31 (1965), 374-408.

Lossky, V. "The Procession of the Holy Spirit in the Orthodox Triadology," *The Eastern Churches Quarterly*, supplementary issue, 7 (1948), 31-53.

_____. *The Mystical Theology of the Eastern Church*. London, 1957.

_____. "On the Question of the Procession of the Holy Spirit," *Messager de l'Exarchat du Patriarche russe en Europe occidentale*, 25 (1957), 54-62 (in Russian).

_____. *À l'image et à la ressemblance de Dieu*. Paris, 1967.

_____. *Orthodox Theology: An Introduction*. New York, 1978.

Maffry Talbot, A.-M. "The Patriarch Athanasius (1289-1293; 1303-1309) and the Church," *Dumbarton Oaks Papers*, 27 (1973), 13-38.

Margerie, B. de. *La Trinité Chrétienne dans l'histoire*. Paris, 1975.

Martland, T. R. "A Study of Cappadocian and Augustinian Trinitarian Methodology," *Anglican Theological Review*, 47 (1965), 252-63.

Menidès, R. "Saint Bonaventure, les Frères mineurs et l'unité de l'Église au concile de Lyon de 1274," *La France franciscaine*, 18 (1935), 363-92.

Meyendorff, J. "La procession du Saint-Esprit chez les Pères orientaux," *Russie et Chrétienté*, 3-4 (1950), 158-78.

_____. "At the Sources of the *Filioque* Quarrel," *Pravoslavnaia Mysl'*, 9 (1953), 114-37 (in Russian).

_____. *Introduction à l'étude de Grégoire Palamas*. Paris, 1959.

_____. "Projets de concile œcuménique en 1367: Un dialogue inédit entre Jean Cantacuzène et le légat Paul," *Dumbarton Oaks Papers*, 14 (1960), 147-77.

_____. "Society and Culture in the Fourteenth Century. Religious Problems," *Rapports du XIVe Congrès international des études byzantines*, I (Bucharest, 1971), 51-65.

_____. *Byzantine Theology*. New York, 1979.

_____. "Spiritual Trends in Byzantium in the Late Thirteenth and Early Fourteenth Centuries," *The Kariye Djami,* IV, ed. P. A. Underwood (Princeton, 1975), 93-106. Reprinted from *Art et société à Byzance sous les Paléologues.* Venice, 1971.

_____. "The Holy Trinity in Palamite Theology," *Trinitarian Theology, East and West* (Brookline, Mass., 1977), 25-43.

Misch, G. "Die Schriftsteller-Autobiographie und Bildungsgeschichte eines Patriarchen von Konstantinopel aus dem XIII. Jahrhundert," *Zeitschrift für Geschichte der Erziehung und des Unterrichts,* 21 (1931), 1-16.

_____. *Geschichte der Autobiographie,* III, pt. 2. Frankfurt am Main, 1962.

Mpalanos, D. S. *The Byzantine Ecclesiastical Authors.* Athens, 1951 (in Greek).

Mpilales, S. S. *The Heresy of the Filioque,* I: *Historical and Critical Review of the Filioque.* Athens, 1972 (in Greek).

Müller, B. A. "Gregorios von Kypern," A. Pauly and G. Wissowa, *Real-Encyclopädie der classischen Altertumswissenschaft,* 7 (Stuttgart, 1912), 1852-57.

Nicol, D. M. "The Greeks and the Union of the Churches: The Preliminaries to the Second Council of Lyons, 1261-1274," *Medieval Studies Presented to A. Gwynn, S. J.,* edd. J. A. Watt et al. (Dublin, 1961), 454-80.

_____. "The Greeks and the Union of the Churches. The Report of Ogerius, Protonotarius of Michael VIII Palaiologos, in 1280," *Proceedings of the Royal Irish Academy,* 63, sect. C, I (1962), 1-10.

_____. "Constantine Akropolites. A Prosopographical Note," *Dumbarton Oaks Papers,* 19 (1965), 249-56.

_____. "The Byzantine Church and Hellenic Learning in the Fourteenth Century," *Studies in Church History,* 5, ed. G. J. Cuming (Leiden, 1969), 23-57.

_____. "Byzantine Requests for an Œcumenical Council in the Fourteenth Century," *Annuarium Historiae Conciliorum,* 1 (1969), 69-95.

_____. "The Byzantine Reaction to the Second Council of Lyons, 1274," *Studies in Church History,* 7, edd. G. J. Cuming and D. Baker (Cambridge, 1971), 113-46.

_____. *Byzantium: Its Ecclesiastical History and Relations with the Western World.* London, 1972.

_____. *The Last Centuries of Byzantium, 1261-1453.* London, 1972.

_____. "The Papal Scandal," *Studies in Church History,* 13, ed. D. Baker (Oxford, 1976), 141-68.

Nikolsky, V. "The Union of Lyons: An Episode from Medieval Church History, 1261-1293," *Pravoslavnoe Obozrenie,* 23 (1867), 5-33, 116-44, 352-78; 24 (1867), 11-33 (in Russian).

Norden,W. *Das Papsttum undByzanz.* Berlin, 1903.

Ostrogorsky, G. *History of the Byzantine State,* trans. J. Hussey. Oxford, 1968.

Palmieri, A. "Filioque," *Dictionnaire de Théologie Catholique,* 5, pt. 2 (Paris, 1913), cols. 2309-43.

Papadakis, A. "Gregory II of Cyprus and an Unpublished Report to the Synod," *Greek, Roman, and Byzantine Studies,* 16, no. 2 (1975), 227-39.

_____. "Gregory II of Cyprus and Mark's Report Again," *The Greek Orthodox Theological Review,* 21, no. 2 (1976), 147-57.

Papadopoulos-Kerameus, A. "The Unpublished Synodal Definition Enacted by the Synod Held at Nymphaeum in the Year 1234," *Ekklesiastike Aletheia,* 3 (1882), 72-74 (in Greek).

Papadopoulos, Ch. "Attempts at Union of the Churches During the Frankish Occupation in Constantinople (1204-1261)," *Theologia,* 14 (1936), 5-23 (in Greek).

_____. *History of the Church of Antioch.* Alexandria, 1951 (in Greek).

Papadopoulos, S. G. "Gregory of Cyprus," *Threskeutike kai Ethike Enkyklopaideia,* 4 (Athens, 1964), 731-34 (in Greek).

Pelikan, J. *Development of Doctrine: Some Historical Prolegomena.* New Haven, 1969. *The Christian Tradition: A History of the Development of Doctrine,* I: *The Emergence of the Catholic Tradition, 100-600;* II: *The Spirit of Eastern Christendom, 600 - 1700.* Chicago, 1971-1974.

_____. "The Doctrine of *Filioque* in Thomas Aquinas and its Patristic Antecedents," *St. Thomas Aquinas Commemorative Studies,* I. Pontifical Institute of Mediaeval Studies (Toronto, 1974), 315-36.

Petit, L. "Mélanges II: La profession de foi de l'impératrice Théodora (1283)," *Échos d'Orient,* 18 (1916-1918), 284-88.

_____. "Mélèce le Galésiote ou le confesseur," *Dictionnaire de Théologie Catholique,* 10, pt. 1 (Paris, 1929). cols. 536-38.

Pétridès, S. "Sentence synodique contre le clergé unioniste (1283)," *Échos d'Orient,* 14 (1911), 133-36.

_____. "Chrysobulle de l'impératrice Théodora (1283)," *Échos d'Orient,* 14 (1911), 25-28.

_____. "Le moine Job," *Échos d'Orient,* 15 (1912), 40-48.

Pichler, A. *Geschichte der kirchlichen Trennung zwischen dem Orient und Occident,* I. Munich, 1865.

Popov, I. V. *Personality and Doctrine of the Blessed Augustine,* I. Sergiev Posad, 1917 (in Russian).

Prestige, G. L. *God in Patristic Thought.* London, 1952.

Radovic, A. *The Mystery of the Holy Trinity According to Gregory Palamas.* Analecta Vlatadon, 16. Thessalonika, 1973 (in Greek).

Régnon, T. de. *Études de théologie positive sur la Sainte Trinité.* 4 vols. Paris, 1892-1898.

Roberg, B. *Die Union zwischen der griechischen und der lateinischen Kirche auf dem II. Konzil von Lyon (1274).* Bonner historische Forschungen, 24. Bonn, 1964.

Rodzianko, V. "Filioque in Patristic Thought," *Studia Patristica,* 2, Papers presented to the second International Conference on Patristic Studies, Oxford, 1955. *Texte und Untersuchungen,* 64 (1957), 295-308.

Romanides, J. S. "H. A. Wolfson's Philosophy of the Church Fathers," *The Greek Orthodox Theological Review,* 5 (1959), 55-82.

_____. "Filioque," *Messager de l'Exarchat du Patriarche russe en Europe occidentale,* 89-90 (1975), 89-115.

Rubeis, B. M. de. *Gregorii Cyprii patriarchae Constantinopolitani vita,* PG 142.17-220.

Runciman, S. *The Sicilian Vespers. A History of the Mediterranean World in the Late Thirteenth Century.* Cambridge, 1958.

_____. *The Eastern Schism.* Oxford, 1963.

_____. *The Great Church in Captivity.* Cambridge, 1968.

_____. *The Last Byzantine Renaissance.* Cambridge, 1970.

Salaville, S. "Georges le Métochite," *Dictionnaire de Théologie Catholique,* 6, pt. 1 (Paris, 1920), cols. 1238-39.

_____. "Une lettre et un discours inédits de Théolepte de Philadelphie," *Revue des études byzantines,* 5 (1947), 101-15.

_____. "Deux documents inédits sur les dissensions religieuses byzantines entre 1275 et 1310," *Revue des études byzantines,* 5 (1947), 116-36.

_____. "Un directeur spirituel à Byzance au début du XIVe siècle: Théolepte de Philadelphie. Homélie inédite sur Noël et la vie religieuse," *Mélanges Joseph de Ghellinck,* II (Gembloux, 1951) 877-87.

Schemrnel, F. "Die Schulen von Konstantinopel von 12.-15. Jahrhundert," *Berliner philologische Wochenschrift,* XXV, 237, no. 8 (1925), 236-39.

Schiemenz, G. P. "Zur politischen Zugehörigkeit des Gebiets um Sobesos und Zoropassos in den Jahren um 1220," *Jahrbuch der Österreichischen byzantinischen Gesellschaft,* 14 (1965), 207-38.

Schmemann, A. "St. Mark of Ephesus and the Theological Conflicts in Byzantium," *St. Vladimir's Seminary Quarterly*, N.S. 1 (1957), 11-24.

_____. *The Historical Road of Eastern Orthodoxy*. Chicago, 1966.

Schmitt, W. O. "Lateinische Literatur in Byzanz. Die Übersetzungen des Maximos Planudes und die moderne Forschung," *Jahrbuch der Österreichischen byzantinischen Gesellschaft*, 17 (1968), 127-47.

Segovia, A. "Equivalencia de fórmulas en las sistematizaciones trinitarias griega y latina," *Estudios ecclesiásticos*, 21 (1947), 435-78.

Setton, K. M. "The Byzantine Background to the Italian Renaissance," *Proceedings of the American Philosophical Society*, 100, no. 1 (1956), 1-76.

_____. *The Papacy and the Levant (1204-1571)*, I: *The Thirteenth and Fourteenth Centuries*. Philadelphia, 1976.

Ševcenko, I. "The Imprisonment of Manuel Moschopoulos in the Year 1305 or 1306, *Speculum*, 27, no. 2 (1952), 133-57.

_____. "The Anti-iconoclastic Poem of the Pantocrator Psalter," *Cahiers archéologiques*, 15 (1965), 39-60.

. Theodore Metochites, the Chora, and the Intellectual Trends of His Time," *The Kariye Djami*, IV, ed. P. A. Underwood (Princeton, 1975), 19-91.

Skrutén, J. "Apologia des Mönchpriesters Job gegen die Argumente zugunsten der Lateiner," *Bulletin de l'Institut Archéologique Bulgare*, 9 (1935), 326-30.

Sotomayor, M. "El patriarca Becos, según Jorge Paquimeres (semblanza histórica)," *Estudios ecclesiásticos*, 31 (1957), 327-58.

Souarn, R. "Tentatives d'union avec Rome: un patriarche grec catholique au XIIIe siècle, *Échos d'Orient*, 3 (1899-1900), 229-337, 351-61.

Southern, R. W. *Western Society and the Church in the Middle Ages*. Vol. II of *The Pelican History of the Church*, ed. O. Chadwick. London, 1970.

Swete, H. B. *On the History of the Doctrine of the Procession of the Holy Spirit from the apostolic Age to the Death of Charlemagne*. Cambridge, 1876.

_____. *The Holy Spirit in the Ancient Church: A Study of Christian Teaching in the Age of the Fathers*. London, 1912.

Sykoutres, I. "Methodius the Monk and Gregory of Cyprus," *Hellenika*, 5 (1932), 117-26 (in Greek).

_____. "Concerning the Schism of the Arsenites," *Hellenika*, 2 (1929), 257-332; 3 (1930), 15-44; 5 (1932), 107-17 (in Greek).

Treu, M. "Manuel Holobolos, *Byzantinische Zeitschrift*, 5 (1896), 538-59.

Troitskij, I. E. "Toward a History of the Dispute on the Question of the Procession of the Holy Spirit," *Khristianskoe Chtenie,* 69, pt. I (1889), 338-77, 581-605; 69, pt. II (1889), 280-352, 520-70 (in Russian).

_____. *Arsenij i Arsenity,* ed. J. Meyendorff. London, 1973.

Tuiller, A. "Recherches sur les origines de la Renaissance byzantine au XIIIe siècle," *Bulletin de l'Association Guillaume Budé,* 3 (1955), 71-76.

Vernet, J. "IIe Concile œcuménique de Lyon," *Dictionnaire de Théologie Catholique,* 9, pt. 1 (Paris, 1926), cols. 1374-91.

Verpeaux, J. *Nicéphore Choumnos, homme d'État et humaniste byzantin (c. 1250/5-1327).* Paris, 1959.

_____. "Notes chronologiques sur les livres II et III de De Andronico Palaeologo de Pachymère," *Revue des études byzantines,* 17 (1959), 168-73.

Viller, M. "La question de l'union des Églises entre Grecs et Latins depuis le concile de Lyon Jusqu'à celui de Florence (1274-1438)," *Revue d'histoire ecclésiastique,* 17 (1921), 260-305. 515-33; 18 (1922), 20-60.

Voigtländer, T. "Gregor von Cypren Aus der Kirchën- und Schulgeschichte des 13. Jahrhunderts," *Zeitschrift für die historische Theologie,* 43 (1873), 449-62.

Vryonis, S. *The Decline of Medieval Hellenism in Asia Minor and the Process of Islamization from the Eleventh Through the Fifteenth Century.* Berkeley, 1971.

Wendel, C. "Planudea," *Byzantinische Zeitschrift,* 40 (1940), 406-45.

Wilson, N. G. "The Church and Classical Studies in Byzantium," *Antike und Abendland,* 16 (1970), 68-77.

Wolff, R. L. "The Organization of the Latin Patriarchate of Constantinople, 1204-1261; Social and Administrative Consequences of the Latin Conquest," *Traditio,* 6 (1948), 33-60.

_____. "Politics in the Latin Patriarchate of Constantinople, 1204-1261," *Dumbarton Oaks Papers,* 8 (1954), 225-303.

Zotos, A. D. *John Beccus, Patriarch of Constantinople, New Rome, the Latinizer.* Munich, 1920 (in Greek).

INDEX